THE SCHOOLS HISTORY PROJECT

S·H·P

OFFICIAL TEXT

ENGLAND 1625–1660

CHARLES I, THE CIVIL WAR AND CROMWELL

Dale Scarboro
Series Editor: Ian Dawson
Academic Consultant: Colin Davis

HODDER
EDUCATION
AN HACHETTE UK COMPANY

In the same series

Britain 1783–1851: *From Disaster to Triumph?*	Charlotte Evers and Dave Welbourne	ISBN-13: 978 0 7195 7482 5
Britain 1851–1918: *A Leap in the Dark?*	Michael Willis	ISBN-13: 978 0 7195 7489 4
Communist Russia under Lenin and Stalin	Chris Corin and Terry Fiehn	ISBN-13: 978 0 7195 7488 7
The Early Tudors: *England 1485–1558*	David Rogerson, Samantha Ellsmore and David Hudson	ISBN-13: 978 0 7195 7484 9
Fascist Italy	John Hite and Chris Hinton	ISBN-13: 978 0 7195 7341 5
Modern America: *The USA 1865 to the Present*	Joanne de Pennington	ISBN-13: 978 0 7195 7744 4
The Reign of Elizabeth: *England 1558–1603*	Barbara Mervyn	ISBN-13: 978 0 7195 7486 3
Weimar and Nazi Germany	John Hite and Chris Hinton	ISBN-13: 978 0 7195 7343 9

The Schools History Project

Set up in 1972 to bring new life to history for students aged 13–16, the Schools History Project continues to play an innovatory role in secondary history education. From the start, SHP aimed to show how good history has an important contribution to make to the education of a young person. It does this by creating courses and materials which both respect the importance of up-to-date, well-researched history and provide enjoyable learning experiences for students.

Since 1978 the Project has been based at Trinity and All Saints University College Leeds. It continues to support, inspire and challenge teachers through the annual conference, regional courses and website: http://www.schoolshistoryproject.org.uk. The Project is also closely involved with government bodies and awarding bodies in the planning of courses for Key Stage 3, GCSE and A level.

Although every effort has been made to ensure that website addresses are correct at time of going to press, Hodder Education cannot be held responsible for the content of any website mentioned in this book. It is sometimes possible to find a relocated web page by typing in the address of the home page for a website in the URL window of your browser.

Papers used in this book are natural, renewable and recyclable products. They are made from wood grown in sustainable forests. The logging and manufacturing processes conform to the environmental regulations of the country of origin.

Orders: please contact Bookpoint Ltd, 130 Milton Park, Abingdon, Oxon OX14 4SB. Telephone: (44) 01235 827720. Fax: (44) 01235 400454. Lines are open from 9.00 to 5.00, Monday to Saturday, with a 24-hour message answering service. Visit our website at www.hoddereducation.co.uk.

© Dale Scarboro, 2005
First published in 2005 by Hodder Education, an Hachette UK Company, Carmelite House, 50 Victoria Embankment, London EC4Y 0DZ

Impression number   10 9
Year   2015

Layouts by Stephen Rowling/Springworks
Artwork by Oxford Designers and Illustrators Ltd
Typeset in 10/12pt Berthold Walbaum by Fakenham Phototypsetting Ltd, Fakenham, Norfolk
Printed and bound by CPI Group (UK) Ltd, Croydon, CR0 4YY

A catalogue record for this title is available from the British Library

978 0 7195 7747 5

Contents

Acknowledgements

Dedication
For Alison, Emma and Jonathan, who gave their time so generously.

And for my parents: my father Dewey, who first inspired my interest in the seventeenth century during a trip to Jamestown Virginia; and my mother Andrea, who died while the book was being written. Chapter 8 is dedicated to her memory.

With thanks to...
I would like to thank several people for their help in the preparation of this book. Ian Dawson for his encouragement, his patience, and his help in keeping me focused on the educational purpose of the project. Professor Colin Davis for his enthusiasm, his close scrutiny of the text, and for trying to bring me up to date with the rapidly changing seventeenth-century historiography. Their professionalism has saved me from many errors and oversights. Those that remain are mine alone. Jock Dykes of King Edwards Five Ways, who laid the foundations. James Turtle of the Gloucestershire County Record Office for permission to use his collection of source material, which forms the basis of Chapter 6. Philippa Tomlinson, my copy editor, for knocking a complicated text into shape. Finally, my thanks to Jenny Francis for turning ideas into reality, and to Jim Belben for inviting me to write about my favourite subject.

Photo credits
Cover *background* Private Collection/Bridgeman Art Library, *l* The Cromwell Museum, Huntingdon, *r* Louvre, Paris/Lauros/Giraudon/Bridgeman Art Library; **p.2** *l* Time Life Pictures/Getty Images, *r* National Portrait Gallery, London (NPG 536); **p.6** Private Collection/Bridgeman Art Library; **p.12** PA/Empics; **p.16** Private Collection/Christie's Images/Bridgeman Art Library; **p.17** City of Westminster Archive Centre, London/Bridgeman Art Library; **p.21** Private Collection/Ken Welsh/Bridgeman Art Library; **p.25** Paul Brown/Rex Features; **p.26** Christie's Images/Bridgeman Art Library; **p.28** Dale Scarboro; **p.30** The Royal Collection © 2005, Her Majesty Queen Elizabeth II; **p.32** Private Collection/The Stapleton Collection/Bridgeman Art Library; **p.35** Private Collection/The Stapleton Collection/Bridgeman Art Library; **p.41** *l* National Portrait Gallery, London (NPG 1246), *r* Louvre, Paris/Lauros/Giraudon/Bridgeman Art Library; **p.42** By courtesy of the Rector and Fellows of Lincoln College, Oxford; **p.43** Private Collection/The Stapleton Collection/Bridgeman Art Library; **p.44** National Portrait Gallery, London (NPG 2692); **p.47** Gloucestershire Record Office (MA19/3); **p.50** Private Collection/Peter Willi/Bridgeman Art Library; **p.54** Fitzwilliam Museum, University of Cambridge/Bridgeman Art Library; **p.60** *t* © David McGill/Collections, *b* Private Collection/Bridgeman Art Library; **p.62** © Peter Hoare; **p.64** *both* Dale Scarboro; **p.65** The Royal Collection © 2005, Her Majesty Queen Elizabeth II; **p.68** British Library, London/Bridgeman Art Library; **p.69** The Royal Collection © 2005, Her Majesty Queen Elizabeth II; **p.76** Fotomas/Topfoto; **p.80** Private Collection/Bridgeman Art Library; **p.81** Bibliothèque des Arts Décoratifs, Paris/Archives Charmet/Bridgeman Art Library; **p.82** Bibliothèque des Arts Décoratifs, Paris/Archives Charmet/Bridgeman Art Library; **p.85** Private Collection/Bridgeman Art Library; **p.90** Fotomas/Topfoto; **p.92** Columbia/Irving Allen/The Kobal Collection; **p.95** Topfoto; **p.98** *t* courtesy Althorp, *b* Private Collection; on loan to the National Portrait Gallery, London (NPG L202); **p.99** *l* National Portrait Gallery, London (NPG 2108), *r* National Portrait Gallery, London (NPG 494); **p.107** Getty Images; **p.110** *tl* British Library, London/Bridgeman Art Library, *tr* Fotomas/Topfoto, *bl* Private Collection/Bridgeman Art Library, *br* The National Archives (SP28/264 no. 311); **p.116** Dale Scarboro; **p.125** © Bingham Library Trust, Cirencester, reproduced courtesy of the Trustees of the Bingham Library Trust; **p.138** Private Collection/Bridgeman Art Library; **p.139** By permission of the British Library (E.99.(14)); **p.148** Fotomas/Topfoto;

p.149 Trustees of Leeds Castle Foundation, Maidstone, Kent/Bridgeman Art Library; **pp.160–61** Private Collection/Bridgeman Art Library; **p.163** National Portrait Gallery, London (NPG 4519); **p.165** Private Collection/Bridgeman Art Library; **p.167** Ashmolean Museum, University of Oxford/Bridgeman Art Library; **p.168** Ashmolean Museum, University of Oxford/Bridgeman Art Library; **p.180** Private Collection/Bridgeman Art Library; **p.182** Fotomas/Topfoto; **p.185** *t* Getty Images, *b* Fotomas/Topfoto; **p.189** Private Collection/Bridgeman Art Library; **p.190** Corporation of London/HIP/Topfoto; **p.191** The Royal Collection © 2005, Her Majesty Queen Elizabeth II; **p.192** Private Collection/Bridgeman Art Library; **p.197** National Portrait Gallery, London (NPG 5589); **p.202** *l* Phil Mynott/The Cromwell Museum, Huntingdon, *r* © John D Beldom/Collections; **p.206** The Cromwell Museum, Huntingdon; **p.215** Corporation of London/HIP/Topfoto; **p.219** *t* Private Collection/Bridgeman Art Library, *b* © Tom Thistlethwaite/Edifice; **pp.222–23** Private Collection/Bridgeman Art Library; **p.229** Topfoto; **p.261** Private Collection/Ken Welsh/Bridgeman Art Library; **p.263** *l* National Portrait Gallery, London (NPG 536, detail), *c* Private Collection/Bridgeman Art Library, *r* The Cromwell Museum, Huntingdon; **p.264** Fotomas/TopFoto; **p.267** *tl* © Birmingham Museums and Art Gallery/Bridgeman Art Library, *tr* Private Collection/Bridgeman Art Library, *bl* The Cromwell Museum, Huntingdon, *br* National Portrait Gallery, London (NPG 536); **p.268** Private Collection/Bridgeman Art Library; **p.269** *tl* The Royal Collection © 2005, Her Majesty Queen Elizabeth II, *tr* Private Collection, Philip Mould, Historical Portraits Ltd, London/Bridgeman Art Library, *bl & br* Fitzwilliam Museum, University of Cambridge/Bridgeman Art Library; **p.270** Private Collection/The Stapleton Collection/Bridgeman Art Library; **p.271** *t* British Library, London/Bridgeman Art Library, *b* Fotomas/TopFoto; **p.272** Time Life Pictures/Getty Images; **p.280** *t* The Royal Collection © 2005, Her Majesty Queen Elizabeth II, *b* © Edwin Smith (photo: Sidney Sussex College, Cambridge); **pp.282–83** Museum of London/Bridgeman Art Library; **p.286** Houses of Parliament, Westminster, London/Bridgeman Art Library; **p.287** Private Collection/Bridgeman Art Library.

t = top, *b* = bottom, *l* = left, *r* = right

Using this book

This is an in-depth study of the English Civil War. It contains everything you need for examination success and more. It provides all the content you would expect, as well as many features to help both independent and class-based learners. So, before you wade in, make sure you understand the purpose of each of the features.

Focus routes

On every topic throughout the book, this feature guides you to produce the written material essential for understanding what you read and, later, for revising the topic (e.g. pages 13, 36, 39). These focus routes are particularly useful for you if you are an independent learner working through this material on your own, but they can also be used for class-based learning.

Activities and Discussion

The activities and discussion boxes offer a range of exercises to enhance your understanding of what you read to prepare you for examinations. They vary in style and purpose. There are:

- a variety of essays (e.g. pages 36, 166, 274)
- source investigations (e.g. pages 34, 89, 109, 181–83)
- examination of historical interpretations, which is now central to A level history (e.g. pages 40, 196, 277)
- decision-making exercises which help you to see events from the viewpoint of people at the time (e.g. pages 18, 129)
- exercises to develop Key Skills such as communication (e.g. pages 48, 240).

These activities help you to analyse and understand what you are reading. They address the content through the key questions that the examiner will be expecting you to have investigated.

Overviews, summaries and key points

In such a large book on such a massive topic, you need to keep referring to the big picture. Each chapter begins with an overview and each chapter ends with a key-points summary of the most important content of the chapter.

Learning trouble spots

Experience shows that time and again some topics cause confusion for students. This feature identifies such topics and helps students to avoid common misunderstandings (e.g. pages 54, 235). In particular, this feature addresses some of the general problems encountered when studying history, such as explaining contemporary ideas (e.g. pages 15, 208).

Charts

The charts are our attempts to summarise important information in note or diagrammatic form (e.g. pages 25, 224). There are also several grid charts that present a lot of information in a structured way (e.g. page 173). However, everyone learns differently and the best charts are the ones you draw yourself! Drawing your own charts in your own way to summarise important content can really help understanding (e.g. pages 143, 169), as can completing assessment grids (e.g. page 248).

Glossary

This book has been written in an accessible way but occasionally it has been necessary to use advanced or specialist vocabulary. Some of this may be new to you. These words are often explained in glossary boxes close to the text in which they appear. The first time a glossary word appears in the text it is in SMALL CAPITALS like this.

Talking points

These are asides from the normal pattern of written exercises. They are discussion questions that invite you to be more reflective and to consider the relevance of this history to your own life. They might ask you to voice your personal judgement (e.g. pages 22, 72); to make links between the past and present (e.g. pages 48, 104); or to highlight aspects of the process of studying history (e.g. pages 91, 172).

The English Civil War was one of the most important events in English history. It is a popular and fascinating topic for AS and A2 study. Throughout this book you will be problem solving, working with others, and trying to improve your own performance as you engage with deep and complex historical issues. Our hope is that by using this book you will become actively involved in your study of history and that you will see history as a challenging set of skills and ideas to be mastered, rather than as an inert body of factual material to be learned.

Introduction
England 1625–1660:
Charles I, the Civil War
and Cromwell

A tale of two Englishmen

SOURCE 1 King Charles I. 'A subject and a sovereign are clean different things.'

SOURCE 2 Oliver Cromwell. 'What if a man should take upon him to be king?'

ACTIVITY

1 What do you already know about Charles I and Oliver Cromwell? Note down your thoughts about them.
2 Now read the stories on page 3. Reconsider your initial thoughts. Have your views been changed by reading these stories?

These images (Sources 1 and 2) are familiar to all students of the English Civil War: Charles I as the austere, arrogant King, a man who believed that he ruled by Divine Right, who made war on his own people, and eventually was beheaded by Oliver Cromwell and the Puritans. Cromwell is seen as the brilliant commander, whose 'Ironsides' smashed the King's armies. After the King's execution, Cromwell took it upon himself to steer England through the chaos of revolution, bringing stability and freedom to the English people in spite of themselves.

How true are these images? As historians, we must question the common view and look beneath the popular image. The following stories may help you to think differently about these two famous men who fought against each other in the seventeenth century.

The English Civil War
Many names have been used to describe the conflicts of the 1640s and 1650s. There were three main wars:

1 the First Civil War, 1642–46: also known as the Civil War or the English Civil War
2 the Second Civil War, 1648
3 the Scottish War, 1650–51: also sometimes called the Third Civil War.

These three wars are sometimes known collectively as the English Civil War.

A 'gap' year in Madrid?

In 1623 Prince Charles and the Duke of Buckingham made a secret trip to Spain. The journey was dangerous; if their identity were discovered before they arrived, the King of England's only son and heir might be robbed, kidnapped or murdered.

Why did Charles take this enormous risk? Because he was in love. For several years England and Spain had been negotiating a marriage between Charles and the King of Spain's daughter, the infanta. The negotiations had stalled, so Charles took matters into his own hands. He would turn up in Spain unannounced to claim his bride!

James I, Charles's father, wasn't happy about the visit. His intuition turned out to be sound. When Charles arrived unexpectedly in Madrid, the Spanish government was embarrassed. The young English prince was treated courteously, but the bemused Spaniards were not going to be bounced into marriage. Charles found their formality frustrating; at one point he scaled the wall of the infanta's residence, climbing up the ivy like Romeo to catch a glimpse of his beloved.

It was to no avail. Charles realised that his mission had failed, and returned to England, where King James was relieved to have 'Baby Charles' home safe and sound.

On 26 November 1630 Oliver Cromwell was remanded in custody for six days by the PRIVY COUNCIL for making a 'disgraceful and unseemly speech' against the mayor of Huntingdon. Two weeks later he was ordered to make a full public apology. Cromwell apologised, but the humiliation was unbearable. A year later he moved his family to nearby St Ives.

The week that Cromwell spent in prison was the result of a misjudged venture into local politics. His family fortunes were already in trouble; their ancestral home had recently been sold, and he was affected by the decline of the Cromwells' local status. In 1630 a new charter for Huntingdon named a group of aldermen (councillors) for the town – and passed over Oliver Cromwell. In his disappointment, Cromwell became involved in a bitter argument with those who had got the better of him. To the people of Huntingdon, Oliver Cromwell looked like a bad loser, a man of failing fortune whose temper made him look ridiculous.

For the next five years Cromwell's income was so low that he slipped from the rank of a gentleman to that of a yeoman farmer. Suffering from severe depression, he had a nervous breakdown. Without medical help he was forced to confront his inner demons: around 1636 he experienced a religious conversion, becoming what would now be called a 'born-again Christian'.

Humiliation in Huntingdon

PRIVY COUNCIL
The Privy Council was the King's secret council, chosen by him to give advice and help with the tasks of government.

The extraordinary events that unfolded in England in the period covered by this book threw the destinies of these two men into the melting pot, linking them forever in the public mind (see Chart A over the page). The Great Rebellion and Civil War turned Charles I and Oliver Cromwell into the historical figures they appear today.

■ A Parallel lives

CHARLES I

OLIVER CROMWELL

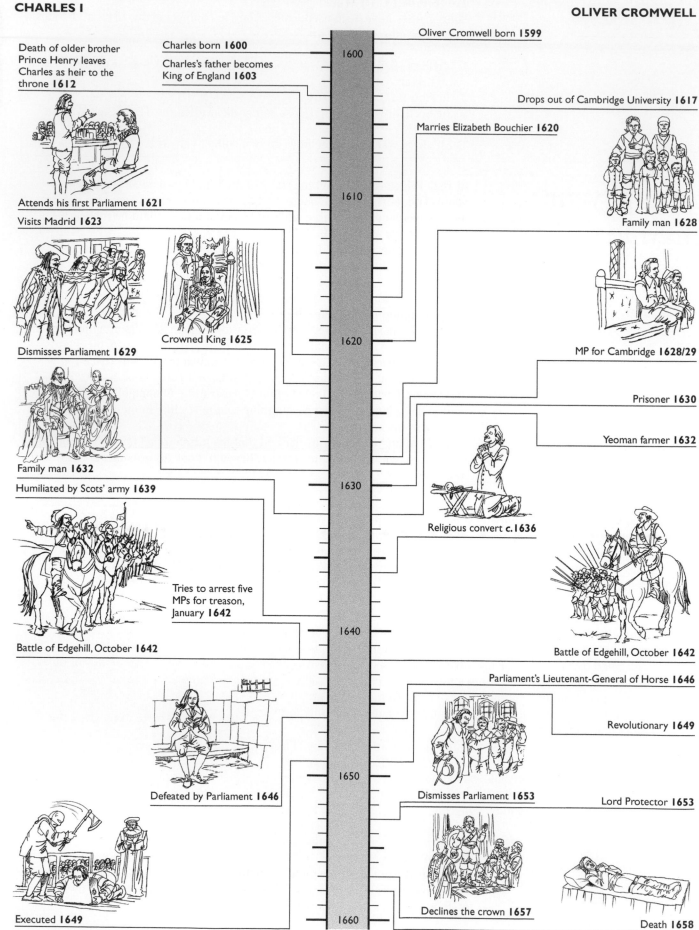

Death of older brother
Prince Henry leaves
Charles as heir to the
throne **1612**

Charles born **1600**

Charles's father becomes
King of England **1603**

Oliver Cromwell born **1599**

Drops out of Cambridge University **1617**

Marries Elizabeth Bouchier **1620**

Attends his first Parliament **1621**

Visits Madrid **1623**

Crowned King **1625**

Dismisses Parliament **1629**

Family man **1628**

MP for Cambridge **1628/29**

Prisoner **1630**

Yeoman farmer **1632**

Family man **1632**

Religious convert *c.***1636**

Humiliated by Scots' army **1639**

Tries to arrest five
MPs for treason,
January **1642**

Battle of Edgehill, October **1642**

Battle of Edgehill, October **1642**

Parliament's Lieutenant-General of Horse **1646**

Revolutionary **1649**

Defeated by Parliament **1646**

Dismisses Parliament **1653**

Lord Protector **1653**

Executed **1649**

Declines the crown **1657**

Death **1658**

1600
1610
1620
1630
1640
1650
1660

1625 ↓ 1629 ↓		Charles I gets off to a bad start with Parliament. Wars with Spain and France are costly failures. Arguments develop over religion, taxation, foreign policy and the king's friendship with the Duke of Buckingham. The King becomes convinced that England and its government have to change.
1629 ↓ 1640 ↓	**The Personal Rule of Charles I**	Charles I sets out to rule without Parliament. He makes peace with Spain and France, while beginning a series of reforms aimed at increasing central control over county government. Specific measures include the following: • imposing uniformity of worship on the Church of England • increasing revenue to decrease the Crown's dependence on Parliament's taxes • strengthening the king's government in Scotland and Ireland. These policies provoke opposition, culminating in war with Scotland. Failure in this war forces Charles to call a new Parliament, ending the Personal Rule.
1640 1642 ↓	**The Long Parliament**	Parliament attacks many aspects of the King's rule. A Royalist party begins to form around the king. A series of crises leads to the outbreak of civil war.
1642 ↓ 1646 ↓	**The First Civil War**	Individuals and communities are drawn reluctantly into war. At first the Royalists seem to be winning, but during 1644 the Roundheads start to gain the upper hand. Unable to finish off the King's forces, Parliament introduces sweeping changes to county government. Parliament's New Model Army wins in 1646.
1646 ↓ 1649 ↓	**The English Revolution**	Parliament splits into two main groups, known as Independents and Presbyterians. Negotiations with the King get nowhere, while religious and social radicalism emerge as powerful forces. A Second Civil War breaks out in 1648, which Parliament also wins. King Charles is put on trial for treason and executed. The monarchy is abolished.
1649 ↓ 1653 ↓	**The Commonwealth**	England is a republic, governed by the House of Commons. Oliver Cromwell wins military campaigns in Ireland and Scotland. Continuing arguments over Parliament's failure to reform provoke Cromwell and the Army to forcibly expel Parliament.
1653 ↓ 1658 ↓	**The Protectorate of Oliver Cromwell**	Cromwell governs the country as Lord Protector. His main aims are: • to provide security for the new government against Royalist plots and foreign threats • to promote 'godly' reformation of English life • to persuade the nation to put the civil wars behind it through healing and settling. He meets with partial success, but fails to establish the new regime on a firm constitutional footing.
1658 ↓ 1660 ↓	**The Restoration**	Cromwell's death plunges the nation into a new crisis. The threat of a new civil war is ended with the restoration of the monarchy when Charles II returns to England from exile.

Study Chart A, Parallel lives.

1 Which of these events are Charles I and Oliver Cromwell best known for?
2 Cromwell and Charles didn't meet each other until 1647. Did they have anything in common?

Did the English Civil War matter?

In the short term, the English Civil War obviously mattered to the people who fought it; by one estimate it killed ten per cent of the male population. In 1649 the King was executed and both the monarchy and the House of Lords were abolished. For the next eleven years England was a republic, the only time in its history this has happened.

What of the long term? In 1660, two years after Oliver Cromwell's death, the monarchy was restored. Englishmen wanted to forget the Civil War and get back to normal. But 'normality' was no longer the same. The experience of civil war and revolution cut deeply into the collective consciousness of the English people, giving them an aversion to rebellion and military rule that has affected their behaviour ever since. Consider the following facts:

• In 1688 King James II was overthrown in a bloodless coup known as the 'Glorious Revolution'.
• In the Act of Settlement of 1707, Parliament took it upon itself to determine who would be the next king.
• During the French Revolution (1789–1815) the English monarchy survived the most serious threat to its existence in modern times.
• During the nineteenth century the English constitution came to be regarded as a model of stability and prosperity throughout the world.

In many ways the Great Rebellion or Civil War laid the foundations for the way the English people responded to the many crises and challenges through which the nation subsequently passed. There is a bit of Oliver Cromwell, and perhaps a bit of Charles I, in all of us.

Why was the Crown quarrelling with Parliament?

By 1603 a number of issues had begun to sour relations between the Crown and Parliament. During the reign of James I (1603–25) these issues developed into a running argument between the King and the House of Commons. In 1625 Charles I succeeded to the throne at a difficult time.

■ C Crown vs Parliament

Charles I opening Parliament, 1625

THE DIVINE RIGHT OF KINGS

Both James and Charles believed in the 'Divine Right of Kings'. A king was God's REGENT on Earth, answerable only to divine judgement after death. In 1610 James claimed that kings were 'not only God's lieutenants upon Earth, and sit upon God's throne, but even by God himself they are called gods'. Charles believed this even more strongly.

BUT Parliament believed the King had to act within the law.

ROYAL PREROGATIVE

James and Charles believed the King had the power to make decisions that were beyond the competence of Parliament:

- Foreign policy: the King was free to make and break alliances, arrange royal marriages and take England to war.
- The army was the King's army, and took its orders only from him.
- Parliament was called and dissolved at the King's pleasure. The king could 'prorogue' Parliament: interrupting its sitting for as long as he liked.
- The King appointed all judges and ministers. Ministers did not have to be chosen from Parliament, nor were members of the Privy Council answerable to Parliament.
- The King was the Supreme Governor of the Church of England. The King appointed the bishops and decided doctrine.

BUT Parliament had the privilege of freedom of speech.

REGENT
Someone who rules on behalf of another.

SUBSIDIES
Tax money approved by Parliament to help the king cover the costs of government.

COMMONWEALTH
Those aspects of the kingdom of England that affected everyone or in which everyone had an interest.

ACTIVITY

Study Chart C. Then copy and complete the following table. This should help to focus your attention on the issues that were dividing King and Parliament by 1625.

ISSUES	THE KING'S VIEW	PARLIAMENT'S VIEW
The Divine Right of Kings		
Royal prerogative		
Royal Finance		
Parliament's privileges		
Impeachment		
The Church of England		

ROYAL FINANCE

Parliament expected the King to pay the costs of his household, court and government from the Crown's private income – his 'ordinary revenue'. The growing costs of government, inflation, and James I's extravagance made this more difficult without 'extraordinary revenue' – SUBSIDIES voted by Parliament.

- Therefore, the King called Parliament more frequently to ask for money.
- Parliament expected the King to explain why he needed more money.
- Parliament was learning to withhold subsidies until the King had addressed its grievances.
- Parliament's grievances were encroaching on issues that the King thought were part of his royal prerogative – for example foreign policy, the Church of England.

BUT the King believed that he had the right to raise money without Parliament's consent if he judged it necessary.

PARLIAMENT'S PRIVILEGES

By 1603 Parliament had a strong sense of its own rights.

- The King had no right to enter the chamber of the House of Commons.
- Members of Parliament enjoyed freedom from arrest during the existence of a Parliament, after which they might be called to account for what they had said or done outside the chamber. What passed between them within the House was theoretically sacrosanct, yet still there were grey areas, notably the legal standing of MPs accused of treason.
- Freedom of speech: the Crown accepted that MPs had the right to discuss matters which affected the COMMONWEALTH: things such as taxation, the Poor Law, the state of the highways, crime.

BUT the Crown defended its right to formulate policy. In 1621 James I clashed with Parliament over this. When the Commons passed a PROTESTATION criticising him for failing to respect Parliament's privileges, James was so angry that he ripped it from the Commons' Journal with his own hands. The problem was that no clear distinction could be made between the King's prerogative and Parliament's legitimate interests.

IMPEACHMENT

By the early 1620s Parliament was turning itself into a court of law by reviving the medieval process of impeachment. The House of Commons impeached the accused person, who then stood trial before the House of Lords. It was clear that Parliament would use impeachment as a way of bringing the King's ministers to account.

BUT the King said his choice of ministers was a matter of royal prerogative.

THE COMMONS' PROTESTATION, 18 DECEMBER 1621
The liberties of Parliament are the ancient and undoubted birthright and inheritance of the subject of England; and affairs concerning the King, State, and defence of the realm and of the Church of England, and the maintenance and making of laws, and redress of grievances are proper subjects and matters of counsel and debate in Parliament.

FOCUS ROUTE

Who's who in the English Civil War? As you work through this book, you will encounter many people who had a major impact on events. At various places in the margin you will find a 'Who's who?' box, drawing your attention to a significant individual. Use the indexes of history books and search on the internet to find out more about these people. You could also try looking them up in the *Oxford Dictionary of National Biography* (2004). Make notes on each person to create your own 'Who's who in the English Civil War?' reference list or database.

ACTIVITY

Study Chart D, The Elizabethan Settlement.

1 Which aspects of the Church of England were taken from Catholicism and which from Protestantism?

2 Why was the settlement unlikely to win over the extremists on both sides?

Why were the English quarrelling about religion?

Alongside the constitutional quarrels (see Chart C), a problem of special importance was religion. Protestants and Catholics had been fighting each other in Europe for nearly 100 years. The Church of England, dating from the Elizabethan Settlement of 1559, tried to create a national church in which all but the most extreme Catholics and Protestants could worship side by side (see Chart D). By isolating the extremists, Elizabeth I had hoped to defuse dangerous religious tensions.

■ D The Elizabethan Settlement

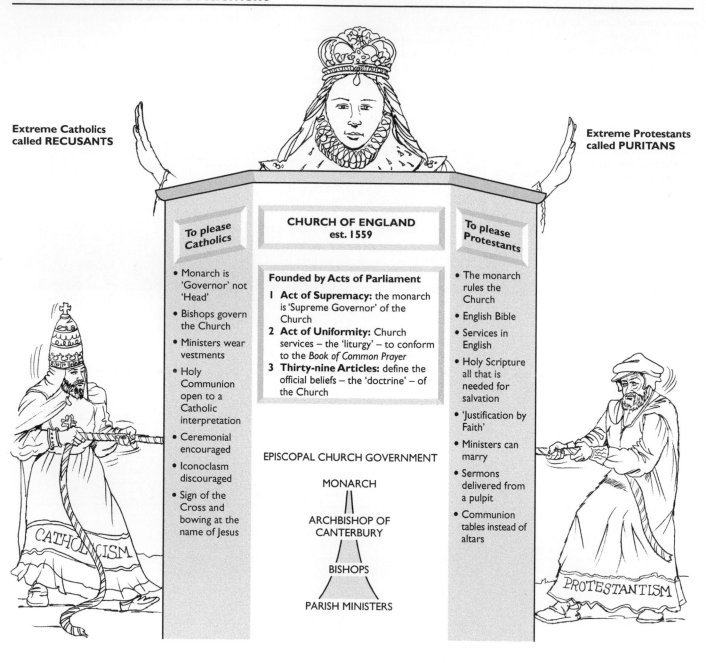

Extreme Catholics called RECUSANTS

Extreme Protestants called PURITANS

To please Catholics

CHURCH OF ENGLAND est. 1559

To please Protestants

Founded by Acts of Parliament

1 **Act of Supremacy:** the monarch is 'Supreme Governor' of the Church

2 **Act of Uniformity:** Church services – the 'liturgy' – to conform to the *Book of Common Prayer*

3 **Thirty-nine Articles:** define the official beliefs – the 'doctrine' – of the Church

- Monarch is 'Governor' not 'Head'
- Bishops govern the Church
- Ministers wear vestments
- Holy Communion open to a Catholic interpretation
- Ceremonial encouraged
- Iconoclasm discouraged
- Sign of the Cross and bowing at the name of Jesus

- The monarch rules the Church
- English Bible
- Services in English
- Holy Scripture all that is needed for salvation
- 'Justification by Faith'
- Ministers can marry
- Sermons delivered from a pulpit
- Communion tables instead of altars

EPISCOPAL CHURCH GOVERNMENT

MONARCH

ARCHBISHOP OF CANTERBURY

BISHOPS

PARISH MINISTERS

CATHOLICISM

PROTESTANTISM

PENAL LAWS
A series of laws aimed at Catholics, which imposed penalties on those who refused to attend Church of England services.

England was now a Protestant country, but some Catholics still hoped to convert England to the Catholic faith. By the time James I ascended the throne in 1603, the Crown was coming under pressure from Puritans to enforce the anti-Catholic PENAL LAWS more strictly.

The Crown's view of the religious problem was different from that of the Puritans. Elizabeth and James believed the real threat to stability came from the Puritans themselves, who threatened to drive loyal Catholics into the arms of the extremists. The Puritans saw all Catholics as potential traitors whose loyalty was already suspect. They therefore saw no risk in persecution, believing that the Crown's 'softly softly' approach was misguided and dangerous.

The Catholics themselves were divided. Most were loyal subjects. Their position was compromised by the extremists; incidents such as the Gunpowder Plot in 1605 seemed to confirm the Puritan view of the seriousness of the Catholic threat. At the heart of the Protestant nightmare (see Chart E) lay the belief that the Catholics would stop at nothing to destroy England and the Protestant faith.

■ E The Protestant nightmare

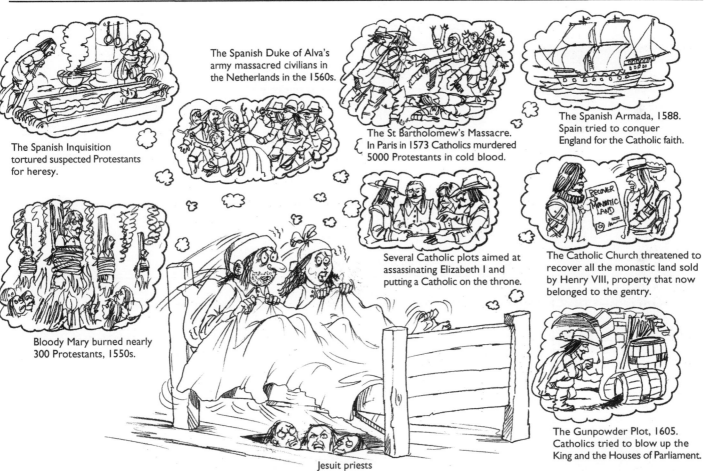

The Spanish Inquisition tortured suspected Protestants for heresy.

The Spanish Duke of Alva's army massacred civilians in the Netherlands in the 1560s.

The St Bartholomew's Massacre. In Paris in 1573 Catholics murdered 5000 Protestants in cold blood.

The Spanish Armada, 1588. Spain tried to conquer England for the Catholic faith.

Bloody Mary burned nearly 300 Protestants, 1550s.

Several Catholic plots aimed at assassinating Elizabeth I and putting a Catholic on the throne.

The Catholic Church threatened to recover all the monastic land sold by Henry VIII, property that now belonged to the gentry.

The Gunpowder Plot, 1605. Catholics tried to blow up the King and the Houses of Parliament.

Jesuit priests

Unless these religious quarrels were handled very skilfully, the Elizabethan Settlement might fail in its aim of defusing religious tensions.

Was it possible to govern England successfully despite these quarrels?
At the heart of the debate about the origins of the English Civil War lie two questions.

1 Was the Civil War inevitable? Was England bound to pass through a period of extraordinary violence before the problems it faced in 1603 could be resolved?
2 What was the Civil War about? What does it tell us about the strengths and weaknesses of English government and society at that time?

These issues underpin the main lines of enquiry of this book.

DISCUSS

Look back over pages 6–9. Do you think that the problems that existed could have been resolved peacefully?

section

Why did England have
a civil war?

Starting points

How far back in time should we look for the origins of the English Civil War? Various answers have been given to this question, which puzzled contemporaries as much as it puzzles us.

DISCUSS

Why might historians disagree about a starting point for explaining why the Civil War began?

1640	The Long Parliament?
1625	The accession of Charles I?
1603	The beginning of the Stuart monarchy?
1559	The Elizabethan religious settlement?
1532	The Henrician Reformation?
1066	The Norman Conquest?

There is a sense in which any historical event is dependent on all the events which preceded it. This is true, and it is also a truism: it gets us no further towards understanding why the Civil War happened.

The question of starting points is bound up with the question of interpretations. Interpretations of the causes of the Civil War belong in one of three categories shown in Chart A. The further to the right your interpretation on Chart A, the closer to the Civil War you should place its origins.

■ A Interpretations of the causes of the Civil War

Long-term causes: The Civil War was inevitable.	The Civil War was probable, but not inevitable.	Short-term causes: The Civil War was an accident.
• Charles I inherited an uncontrollable situation, which had been developing since the mid-sixteenth century. • England faced a crisis that could not be resolved peacefully. • If Charles himself hadn't faced a civil war, sooner or later someone else would have.	• Charles I inherited a dangerous situation, which he made worse by his mistakes. • Europe was having a 'general crisis'. It wasn't just England that was having trouble. • The 'little ice age' was making matters worse. The weather was significantly colder, resulting in frequent harvest failures that made politics unstable.	• Charles I inherited a difficult situation, but one that was perfectly manageable. • Charles's personality, along with other short-term factors, led to the political crisis of 1640. • The fact that the crisis of 1640 led on to civil war was largely accidental, a question of poor judgement and bad timing.

Why the English Civil War began is one of the most controversial questions in English history. Many interpretations have focused on long-term issues and these can be explored in several excellent books readily available to students. A level questions, however, tend to focus on the short term, from 1637 to 1642. A sound knowledge of the events of these years is essential to answer these questions well. We will return to the question of inevitability in the section Review on pages 104–06.

A working hypothesis

Section 1 of this book offers an interpretation that will help you to make sense of the events of the period 1637–42. The views offered here are intended as a guide, in the hope that in due course your curiosity will lead you deeper into the arguments about the causes of the Civil War. If you feel confident enough eventually to challenge this interpretation, then this section will have served its purpose. It can be summarised briefly as follows:

- In the 1620s Charles I was alarmed at England's weakness. The King was unable to influence events on the continent at a time when religious and dynastic conflict was reaching a climax in the THIRTY YEARS' WAR.
- In the 1630s the King embarked on a programme of reform. This meant strengthening royal control, leading to accusations that he was trying to impose absolutism (see Chapter 2). Charles's main concern was to impose uniformity and accountability on the state and its office-holders. He equated diversity with weakness. He did this without Parliament because he felt that Parliament would obstruct his aims.
- The King's reforms aroused opposition from many people from all social ranks, who saw in them an attack on the ancient liberties of the subject. The King's ideal of uniformity threatened the freedom of local office-holders to use their discretion in law enforcement. Religion played a particularly important role in focusing opposition to the King's reforms. By 1640 the King had been forced to abandon his reforms and seek Parliament's help.
- A deepening crisis after 1640 polarised opinion and led to the creation of opposing armies. In 1640 the King had almost no support, but from the summer of 1641 a resurgence of support for the King led to the formation of a Royalist army. It was this that made the Civil War possible.

The four chapters in Section 1 focus on these four stages of explanation.

THIRTY YEARS' WAR

A European war that broke out in Germany in 1618. It was widely seen as a decisive war between Catholic and Protestant states. Like the Spanish Civil War in the 1930s, many English and Scottish soldiers went to Germany to fight for the Protestants.

DISCUSS

Which of the three interpretations in Chart A is this hypothesis closest to?

LOCAL GOVERNMENT

Counties were divided into hundreds and parishes, which were largely self-governing.

At county level the main officers were the Lord Lieutenant, his Deputy (sometimes more than one), and the sheriff. Some county gentlemen served as Justices of the Peace to maintain law and order.

At parish level the churchwardens, overseers of the poor and constables were elected to serve for a limited time before handing over their offices to someone else.

The Lord Lieutenant and the sheriff were appointed by the King, but all the others were local men who volunteered their time to help regulate their communities. They knew their neighbours well and used their common sense in enforcing the law.

Why did Charles I resort to Personal Rule in 1629?

CHAPTER OVERVIEW

The Commons defies the King

On 2 March 1629 an extraordinary scene was played out in Parliament, in the House of Commons. King Charles I had decided to close the Parliament. He had sent his messenger, 'Black Rod', to Westminster to inform the Commons that they were to end their session. When Black Rod arrived, the doors of the House of Commons were slammed shut in his face. This had never happened before. Anxious to carry out his instructions, Black Rod began hammering on the doors of the House.

Inside the House of Commons an even more extraordinary scene was taking place. The Speaker of the House knew that the King wanted Parliament to close. He stood up to announce that all debates were ended – and was immediately assaulted by several MPs, who grabbed him by the arms and forced him back into his chair. On seeing this, the PRIVY COUNCILLORS, who sat in on Commons debates, tried to intervene. A scuffle broke out, with the Privy Councillors trying to free the Speaker, while the MPs, just as determined, held him back in his chair long enough to allow one of the Members, Denzil Holles, to shout out three resolutions condemning the King's government (see Source 1.14 on page 34). When he had finished, the MPs shouted 'Aye, aye!', thereby adopting what became known as the Commons' Protestation of 1629. Then the Speaker was released and the doors opened to Black Rod.

> **PRIVY COUNCILLORS**
> Members of the Privy Council (see page 45). They were the King's advisers, chosen by him.

FOCUS ROUTE: WHO'S WHO?

Make brief notes on Denzil Holles to include in your Who's who? list.

SOURCE 1.1   Nothing like this had ever happened before. It was the first time the House of Commons challenged the King's right to close Parliament. Today the event is commemorated at the State Opening of Parliament: when the Queen sends Black Rod to invite the Commons to attend her in the House of Lords, the doors are politely but firmly slammed in his face and opened again when he hammers on the door with his staff

When Charles I heard what had happened, he was not pleased. A riot in the House of Commons was an affront to his dignity, and an assault on his Speaker was like an assault on the King himself. But in fact King Charles had already had his bellyful of parliaments. He had already decided to do without them.

Between 1625 and 1629 King Charles I had called three successive parliaments. Now, just four years after his succession, Charles decided to rule without Parliament. In a royal proclamation he made it clear that his decision might be permanent (see Source 1.2).

SOURCE 1.2   King Charles I's declaration that he intended to rule without Parliament

We shall account it presumption for any to prescribe any time unto us for parliaments, the calling, continuing and dissolving of which is always in our own power; and we shall be more inclinable to meet in parliament again when our people shall see more clearly into our intentions and actions, when such as have bred this interruption shall have received their condign [well-deserved] punishment, and those who are misled by them and by such ill reports as are raised upon this occasion shall come to a better understanding of themselves and us.

The purpose of this chapter is to investigate the reasons for the dramatic and swift collapse of trust between Parliament and Charles I. Chart IA gives four explanations for the breakdown in relations. Each explanation is given as a **theory**. None of these theories is the <u>correct answer</u> – in History there is usually no such thing as a correct explanation, only correct facts. Some theories, however, are more valid than others, depending on how well informed they are.

■ IA Four theories for the breakdown in relations between Parliament and Charles I

THEORY 1: IT WAS THE DUKE OF BUCKINGHAM'S FAULT.
Charles fell under the influence of a wicked advisor – the Duke of Buckingham – who led him into a disastrous foreign policy. This propelled him into confrontation with Parliament. Buckingham was unpopular because he had too much influence over the King.

THEORY 2: IT WAS PARLIAMENT'S FAULT.
Parliament decided to take advantage of the King's youth and inexperience. The House of Commons, in particular, decided to take away some of the King's royal power – his prerogative.

THEORY 3: IT WAS THE KING'S FAULT.
When Charles I came to the throne in 1625 he was young and inexperienced, so he was bound to make mistakes. But he also believed that his subjects were obliged to obey him.

THEORY 4: IT WAS NOBODY'S FAULT.
Charles I came to the throne at a moment when a confrontation between the King and Parliament was inevitable. Whoever became King in the 1620s would have found himself on a collision course with Parliament.

FOCUS ROUTE

As you work through this chapter, collect evidence to support the theories in Chart IA. You could do this on paper or, ideally, on a computer spreadsheet, as this will enable you to add material as you find it, expanding the spreadsheet cells as necessary.

Theory	Supporting evidence
I It was the Duke of Buckingham's fault.	
2 It was Parliament's fault.	
3 It was the King's fault.	
4 It was nobody's fault – an inevitable crisis.	

A The Duke of Buckingham – did he poison relations between the King and Parliament? (pp. 15–19)

B Why did Charles's relationship with Parliament begin so badly? (pp. 20–21)

C Did Charles I threaten the ancient liberties of English people? (pp. 22–23)

D Why was Parliament suspicious of the King's religion? (pp. 24–30)

E Why didn't Buckingham's assassination save the relationship between King and Parliament? (pp. 31–35)

F Review: why did Charles I resort to Personal Rule in 1629? (pp. 36–37)

■ 1B Key events of the 1620s

Charles I's relationship with Parliament began in 1621, when his father James I instructed him to sit in on the House of Lords to prepare him for the day when he would succeed to the throne. That day came in March 1625.

1621 **January** **November** **December**	**James I's third Parliament**, the first since 1614 House of Commons revives impeachment Second session of Parliament Commons' Protestation (see Chart C on pages 6–7) James I dissolves Parliament and tears the Protestation out of the Commons' Journal
1623 **March–October**	Prince Charles and Duke of Buckingham visit Madrid
1624 **February**	**James I's fourth Parliament** War against Spain begins
1625 **January** **March** **May** **June** **August** **September**	Mansfeld's expedition fails **James I's death. Accession of Charles I** Marriage of Charles I and Henrietta Maria **Charles I's first Parliament** Commons attacks Arminian clergy promoted by Charles Tonnage and Poundage granted for one year only Commons grants two subsidies Commons attacks Buckingham Cadiz expedition fails
1626 **June** **September**	**Charles I's second Parliament** Buckingham tries to remove leading opponents in the Commons by having them appointed sheriff Commons discusses four subsidies Impeachment of Buckingham **Charles dissolves Parliament** Forced Loan
1627 **February** **October** **November**	York House Conference on religion War against France begins Charles I resorts to extraordinary measures to fight the war without enough money: • Billeting of troops around ports • Martial law declared around troop concentrations • Ship Money raised Ile de Ré expedition fails Five Knights' case
1628 **March** **June** **July** **August** **December**	**Charles I's third Parliament** Petition of Right William Laud promoted to Bishop of London Buckingham assassinated Richard Montague promoted to Bishop of Chichester Thomas Wentworth appointed Lord President of the Council of the North
1629 **January** **March**	Second session of Parliament Commons' Protestation Charles I dissolves Parliament in scenes of turmoil **Beginning of the PERSONAL RULE**

PERSONAL RULE
The eleven years from 1629 to 1640 when the king ruled without calling Parliament. Also once known as the Eleven Years' Tyranny. See Chapter 2.

As you work through this section,
collect evidence that could be used to
support Theory 1 (see Chart 1A).

FOCUS ROUTE

Remember also to collect any evidence
that might be used to support the
other theories.

IMPEACHMENT

The process by which Parliament
acted as a court of law. The accused
person was impeached (accused) by
the House of Commons and then tried
by the House of Lords, which acted as
a jury.

A The Duke of Buckingham – did he poison relations between the King and Parliament?

'The cause of all our miseries'?

In the summer of 1628 Sir Edward Coke, one of Parliament's leaders in the
House of Commons, declared that the Duke of Buckingham was 'the cause of
all our miseries', 'the cause of all the evils the kingdom suffered, and an enemy
to the public'. When Charles I heard this he sent a message to Parliament
warning it not to attack the Duke. The result, according to one witness, was a
near riot in the Commons, with 'such a spectacle of passions as the like had
seldom been seen in such an assembly – some weeping, some expostulating,
some prophesying of the fatal ruin of our kingdom'.

This attack on the Duke of Buckingham was the latest of a long line of
attacks. Ever since 1625, Parliament had been demanding Buckingham's
downfall, believing that he was responsible for all the bad decisions the King
had made. The King had resolutely defended his friend. In 1626 Charles
dissolved Parliament rather than allow the Commons to IMPEACH the Duke.
Source 1.6 (page 17) shows how the King refused to accept Parliament's view
that Buckingham was to blame.

The Duke of Buckingham (1592–1628)
George Villiers, Duke of Buckingham, was King James I's favourite from 1615
until James's death in 1625. Buckingham's rise to power was extraordinary.
Promoted by his friends at court, he had quickly achieved an unusual amount of
influence over the King. His influence was personal as well as political: the King,
who had lost his favoured eldest son, Prince Henry, to typhoid in 1612, formed an
emotional attachment to the man he called 'Steenie' and showered him with
favours. Soon Buckingham had become the King's closest friend and favourite,
his bedfellow, Privy Councillor and confidant.

■ Learning trouble spot

Favourites and factions

A favourite was a courtier who was particularly close to the King, and trusted
by him. In the days before Prime Ministers, the favourite often made
important decisions for the King. Usually the promotion of a favourite
showed the success of one court faction over the others.

A faction was a group of courtiers who formed a political grouping opposed
to others. In the days before political parties, factions dominated court
politics. In King James I's reign, these factions were aligned around foreign
policy issues – for instance, a pro-Spanish faction and an anti-Spanish faction.

■ 1C The Duke of Buckingham's career

1615	George Villiers comes to James I's notice
1616	Viscount Villiers
1617	Earl of Buckingham
1618	Marquess of Buckingham
1623	Duke of Buckingham Visit to Madrid with Prince Charles
1624	Persuaded King James and Parliament to make war on Spain
1625	Cadiz expedition
1626	Impeachment proceedings by the House of Commons
1627	Persuaded King Charles to make war on France Ile de Ré expedition
1628	Assassinated in Portsmouth

FOCUS ROUTE: WHO'S WHO?

Make brief notes on the Duke of Buckingham to include in your Who's who? list.

PATRONAGE

A patron is someone who uses their wealth or influence to help another person, or to promote a cause. Patronage is therefore the support of a patron.

SOURCE 1.3 The Duke of Buckingham, 1626, by Daniel Mytens. The self-assurance of the older man helped to establish his hold over the impressionable young King Charles

Why was Buckingham so unpopular at court?

As James's favourite, Buckingham made many enemies. A common complaint was that he monopolised PATRONAGE at court. No one could gain office or advance their career without Buckingham's support. Patronage was very important: finding a patron was the only way to find promotion. But Buckingham's influence went beyond this. He controlled access to the King, so James was unlikely to hear any opinion that Buckingham did not approve of. If Buckingham did not like you, or if you would not pay him a big enough bribe, you and your opinions got filtered out.

The fact that Buckingham exploited King James's homosexuality brought himself, the court and the King into disrepute. Excluded courtiers could only wait for James to die, knowing that nothing but the King's death would break Buckingham's grip on power. Buckingham held so many titles and offices (see Source 1.4) that a backlog of frustration and envy waited for his downfall.

Why did Buckingham's influence survive into Charles's reign?

When James I died in 1625, the excluded courtiers thought their moment had finally come. But they were disappointed. Buckingham cultivated a close friendship with Prince Charles, an insecure young man who was susceptible to Buckingham's air of worldly confidence and his knowledge of court life and government. Charles was flattered by the attentions of his father's favourite, who took him into his confidence. Their friendship was sealed by their visit to Madrid in 1623: the shared experience of gatecrashing the Spanish court ensured that, when James died, Buckingham's position at court continued unchanged. Buckingham enjoyed a seamless transition of power that confounded his enemies, a tribute to his political skill. It soured relations between the King, the disappointed courtiers, and Parliament.

SOURCE 1.4 George Villiers's titles, quoted from the Commons' impeachment of the Duke of Buckingham, 1626

George, Duke, Marquis and Earl of Buckingham, Earl of Coventry, Viscount Villiers, Baron of Whaddon, Great Admiral of the kingdoms of England and Ireland, and of the principality of Wales and of the dominions and islands of the same, of the town of Calais and of the marches of the same, and of Normandy, Gascony, and Guienne, General Governor of the seas and ships of the said Kingdoms, Lieutenant General, Admiral, Captain General and Governor of His Majesty's Royal Fleet and Army, lately set forth, Master of the Horse of our Sovereign Lord the King, Lord Warden, Chancellor, and Admiral of the Cinque Ports and of the members thereof, Constable of Dover Castle, Justice in Eyre of all the forests and chases on this side of the river of Trent, Constable of the Castle of Windsor, Gentleman of His Majesty's Bedchamber, one of His Majesty's most Honourable Privy Council in his realms both in England, Scotland and Ireland, and Knight of the most Honourable Order of the Garter . . .

ACTIVITY

1 How could Source 1.4 be used to explain why Buckingham was unpopular at court?
2 Why would Buckingham's power become even greater if England went to war?
3 How does Source 1.4 suggest that Buckingham's influence over Charles I was personal as well as political?
4 Summarise the reasons why Buckingham was unpopular at court.

What did Parliament think of Buckingham?

In 1626 the House of Commons tried to get rid of Buckingham by impeaching him. The King stopped the impeachment by dissolving Parliament. By doing this he prevented Parliament from passing a bill that would have given him four subsidies – money which he desperately needed to fight the war with Spain.

Edward Earl of CLARENDON, Lord High CHANCELLOR of England and Chancellor of the University of Oxford. An.º Dom.1663.

Edward Hyde, Earl of Clarendon (1609–74)

Edward Hyde wrote one of the most important primary sources for the Civil War. *The History of the Rebellion and Civil Wars in England* was first published in 1702, but was mostly written during the 1640s and 1650s. He wrote it at the request of Charles I, who wanted someone he trusted to explain how the war had started and to tell his side of it.

Hyde was an interesting choice. As MP for Saltash, Devon, at first he was a critic of the King and his policies. During 1641 he came to believe that Charles's opponents were going too far, and began supporting the King. When civil war broke out in 1642 he became a Royalist, but one who continued to work for a peaceful resolution of the King's problems with Parliament. At times he was very critical of Charles I, a fact which gave him more credibility as the author of the King's official history of the war.

When the Royalists lost the war in 1646 Hyde went into exile, where he continued to work for the King. When Charles I was executed in 1649, Hyde supported his son's claim to the thrones of England, Scotland and Ireland as King Charles II. For his loyalty he was given the title Earl of Clarendon. When Charles II ascended the throne in 1660, Hyde became Lord High Chancellor of England. He served as the King's Chief Minister for seven years until his political downfall in 1667.

Hyde's history of the Civil War was the first and, for nearly 150 years, the most important version of the story. When you read extracts from it, you need to remember who Hyde was – a constitutional Royalist who thought the King had made mistakes, but who worked constantly for the restoration of the monarchy.

SOURCE 1.5   Edward Hyde, Earl of Clarendon, *History of the Rebellion and Civil Wars in England*, 1702

There is a protection very gracious and just which princes owe to their servants, when, in obedience to their just commands, they swerve from the strict rule of the law. But for the supreme power to interpose, and shelter an accused servant from answering, does not only seem an obstruction of justice, but leaves so great a scandal upon the party himself that he is generally concluded guilty of whatsoever he is charged. Without question, it had been of sovereign use to the King if parliaments had been taught to know their own bounds by being allowed to proceed as far as they could go. But the course of exempting men from prosecution by dissolving of parliaments made the power of parliaments much more formidable, since the sovereign power seemed to be compelled . . . to that rough cure . . .

ACTIVITY

Read Source 1.5.

1 Summarise the main points of this passage in modern English.
2 What mistake did Hyde think Charles I had made in 1626?
3 Do you agree with Hyde? Or do you think that Charles I did the right thing?
4 If Charles I had sacrificed the Duke of Buckingham, do you think his relations with Parliament would have improved?

ACTIVITY

Study Source 1.6.

1 What was the point that Charles I was making in this speech?
2 Do you think that what Charles was doing in this speech was wise or foolish? Explain your answer.
3 Why was the King determined to defend his right to choose his own servants?

SOURCE 1.6   Charles I's speech to Parliament, 29 March 1626

Concerning the Duke of Buckingham, His Majesty hath commanded me to tell you, That himself doth know better than any man living the sincerity of the Duke's proceedings; with what caution of weight and discretion he hath been guided in his public employments from His Majesty and his blessed father; what enemies he hath procured at home and abroad; what peril of his person and hazard of his estate he ran into for the service of His Majesty . . . and therefore His Majesty cannot believe that the aim is at the Duke of Buckingham, but findeth that these proceedings do directly wound the honour and judgement of himself and of his father.

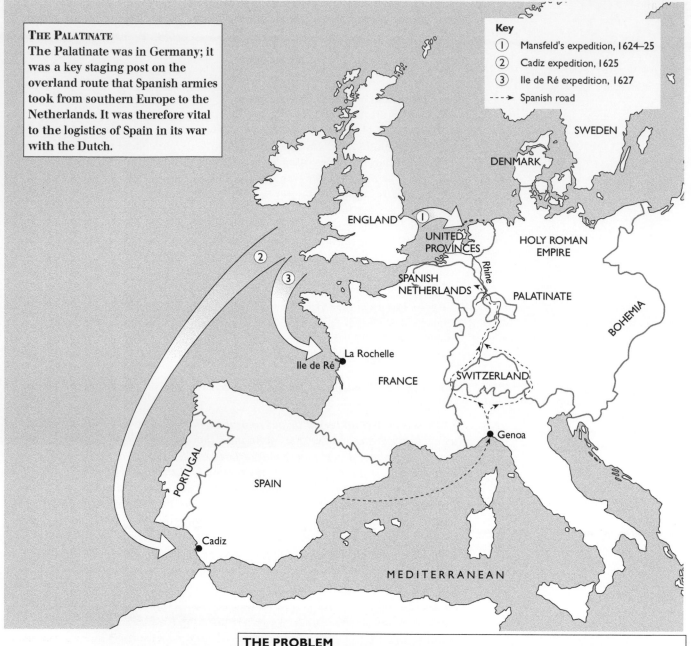

THE PALATINATE
The Palatinate was in Germany; it was a key staging post on the overland route that Spanish armies took from southern Europe to the Netherlands. It was therefore vital to the logistics of Spain in its war with the Dutch.

Key
① Mansfeld's expedition, 1624–25
② Cadiz expedition, 1625
③ Ile de Ré expedition, 1627
- - -> Spanish road

ACTIVITY

Did Buckingham lead Charles into a disastrous foreign policy?
You are going to take the role of the King's Privy Council. Your task is to advise the King on foreign policy. Begin by studying Chart 1D, which outlines the situation facing England in 1623. Then discuss the options on page 19 and choose which one you would advise the King to follow.

THE PROBLEM

Charles's sister and her husband have lost their lands in Germany, and have been forced to flee into exile. The aim is to recover THE PALATINATE (see map) for them.

How has the problem arisen?
• England has been at peace since 1604.
• Prince Charles's sister, Princess Elizabeth, is married to Frederick V. Frederick, the Elector Palatine, is one of seven electoral princes who choose the Holy Roman Emperor. He is also a Protestant.
• In 1618 Frederick was offered the throne of Bohemia (see map). King James warned him not to accept it, but he did. His decision provoked a European crisis.
• In 1619 a new Holy Roman Emperor, Ferdinand, took the German throne. Ferdinand is a Catholic, and a Habsburg, related to the King of Spain, Philip III.
• In 1620 Frederick's army was defeated by the Emperor's army at the Battle of the White Mountain. Frederick lost not only Bohemia, but also his hereditary lands in the Palatinate, which have been occupied by two Catholic armies – one Imperial, the other Spanish.
• Elizabeth and Frederick are very popular in England. Spain's decision to occupy the Palatinate has inflamed English public opinion. Parliament has offered money if the King should end up going to war. King James, on the other hand, blames Frederick for accepting the Bohemian throne against his advice.
• To complicate matters further, in 1621 the truce between Spain and the Netherlands expired. The Dutch are Protestants. Many English people think that England should be helping them to fight Spain.

OPTION 1

Send an army to invade the Palatinate and throw out the Catholics.

Advantages
• Do-it-yourself action gets to the heart of the matter.

Disadvantages
• England hasn't got an army. You will have to hire one from Germany.
• You have no direct access to the Palatinate. You will have to go through some other country to get there.
• Expensive. In 1621 Parliament rejected the idea of paying for such a war.

OPTION 2

Try to persuade Spain to use its influence with the Emperor to return the Palatinate to Frederick.

Advantages
• Avoids war.
• Cheap.

Disadvantages
• The King of Spain does not actually have that much influence on his German cousin, the Emperor.
• This could take a long time.
• What could England offer Spain in return?

OPTION 3

Declare war on Spain. The aim would be to force Spain to evacuate the Palatinate, and to persuade the Emperor to do the same.

Advantage
• Popular with English Protestants.

Disadvantages
• England hasn't got an army. The English navy is in poor condition.
• How is attacking Spain going to encourage the Spanish army to leave the Palatinate?

OPTION 4

Try to persuade France to declare war on Spain and invade the Palatinate.

Advantage
• Gets a major European power on your side.

Disadvantage
• You may be sacrificing the French Protestants.

OPTION 5

Accept the loss of the Palatinate. Cut your losses and move on.

Advantages
• Allows England to think again about its foreign policy.
• Cheap.
• The King will have less need of Parliament.

Disadvantages
• Loss of honour.
• Unpopular with some Protestants.

■ IE What Buckingham actually did

1623	Option 2 – Encouraged Prince Charles to visit Spain unannounced in an attempt to marry the Spanish infanta. Charles and Buckingham returned empty-handed.
1624	Option 3 – Encouraged King James and Parliament to declare war on Spain.
1624	Encouraged King James to send a hired army to invade the Palatinate. Mansfeld's Expedition was a fiasco, and achieved nothing.
1625	Led the Cadiz expedition to attack Spain. The army landed on the coast, got drunk, and had to be evacuated. On the way home many of the ships ran out of food and water, and many soldiers died. Option 4 – Arranged the marriage between Charles I and Henrietta Maria, the sister of the French King. France did not join England's war against Spain.
1627	An option nobody had thought of – Encouraged Charles I to declare war on France, while the war with Spain was still going on. Led the Ile de Ré expedition to try to relieve the Protestants of La Rochelle. Forced to retreat after heavy losses.

MANSFELD'S EXPEDITION

Mansfeld was a mercenary officer who led a small army to Europe to try to fight its way through to the Palatinate. It ground to a halt in the Netherlands, destroyed by disease and desertion.

ACTIVITY

Study Chart IE. What were the strengths and weaknesses of Buckingham's advice?

1 How good was Buckingham's advice to King Charles?
2 How far was English foreign policy in the 1620s driven by personal considerations – for example honour, ambition, humiliation, pride?
3 Why did England's foreign policy weaken the King's position in his struggle with Parliament?

TONNAGE AND POUNDAGE
Taxes on imports and exports. Since 1347 most of this money had been allocated to the navy.

FOCUS ROUTE

The succession of Charles I in 1625 appears to have focused many of the long-term issues that had been developing between Parliament and the Crown. Select evidence from this section that could be used to support Theory 2 or Theory 3 (page 13).

B Why did Charles's relationship with Parliament begin so badly?

When a new king took the throne, Parliament usually went out of its way to give him an easy time. Every new king expected a 'honeymoon' period with his subjects. Every king since Henry VII had been granted TONNAGE AND POUNDAGE for life. Charles I expected his reign to begin the same way.

SOURCE 1.7 Conrad Russell, *The Causes of the English Civil War*, 1990, p. 185

'You cannot believe the alteration in the opinion of the World touching His Majesty.' This comment, by the Earl of Kellie to the Earl of Mar, marks the end of the 'honeymoon period' at the beginning of Charles's reign, and it is dated 26 July 1625, when Charles had only been four months on the throne. It marks a remarkably swift general recognition, during Charles's first year, that as a king he was not a success, and that judgement is one which has never been reversed.

It seems unlikely that the sudden change referred to in Source 1.7 could lie in events that happened in the short period between March and June 1625, yet there had been important changes in that time:

- Charles had married Henrietta Maria.
- Plague had broken out in London. The MPs were anxious to leave the city as quickly as possible, and did not want long, drawn out arguments.
- The failure of Mansfeld's expedition to recover the Palatinate had become common knowledge. English troops had been dumped at Ostend without adequate provisions, and had fallen apart in chaos.
- Charles I had already begun collecting Tonnage and Poundage without Parliament's consent.

What were the issues over which the King and Parliament quarrelled?

Foreign policy
Charles's first Parliament in 1625 was bracketed by two military failures – the Mansfeld and Cadiz expeditions. Parliament blamed Buckingham for these and expected the King to remove him. The subsidies that Parliament had voted in 1624 for a war against Spain appeared to have been misappropriated and wasted on a foolhardy enterprise, but no proper accounting was being offered.

Finance
Parliament agreed to vote the new King Tonnage and Poundage for only one year, to make the point that it was a gift from the people to their King. Charles needed the money, and believed it was his right to collect it – so he went ahead and collected it both *before* Parliament approved it and *after* the first year had run out.

The royal marriage
Charles had married Henrietta Maria, the Catholic sister of the King of France. The terms of the marriage contract said that she was free to continue as a practising Catholic, so she brought with her priests to the court at Whitehall. Parliament saw these priests as a threat to the English Church.

Divine Right
Charles I did not explain himself adequately to his first Parliament. He may have seen Parliament's willingness, or not, to trust his judgement as a test of its loyalty.

Royal interference in the choice of MPs
Before the Parliament of 1626 met, Buckingham and the King tried to remove the main opposition leaders from the Commons by selecting them to be sheriffs. Once appointed, it was the sheriffs' duty to remain in their counties, away from London. MPs such as Sir Robert Phellips, Sir Thomas Wentworth

(later the Earl of Strafford) and Sir Edward Coke were all removed in this way, but new Commons' leaders simply came to the fore, including John Pym and Sir John Eliot (whose former patron was Buckingham).

Parliamentary privileges

- The King antagonised the Lords by sending the Earl of Arundel to the Tower. When the Lords protested, the King released him.
- When Sir John Eliot and Sir Dudley Digges brought Buckingham's impeachment charges before the House of Lords, the King sent them to the Tower. The Commons refused to consider any further business until they were released, and the King was forced to back down.
- These episodes left the impression that Charles I did not believe in Parliament's privileges.

Impeachment

The Parliament of 1626 began impeaching Buckingham. Before doing this, it introduced a bill to give the King four subsidies. Parliament would pass the bill only if Buckingham's impeachment were allowed to run its course. The King dissolved Parliament to protect Buckingham, and so lost the subsidies.

ACTIVITY

Read Source 1.8.

1 What was Charles I accusing Parliament of doing?
2 What threat was the King making?
3 Do you think this threat would have made Parliament more compliant or more obstinate? Give reasons for your answer.

SOURCE 1.8 Charles I to Parliament, 1626

Now that you have all things according to your wishes and that I am so far engaged that you think there is no retreat [from the war], now you begin to set the dice and make your own game. But I pray you be not deceived. It is not a parliamentary way, nor is it a way to deal with a King. Remember that parliaments are altogether in my power for their calling, sitting and dissolution. Therefore, as I find the fruits of them good or evil, they are to continue or not to be.

Sir Edward Coke (1552–1634): a thorn in the side of the early Stuarts

Sir Edward Coke was a lawyer and MP with a vast amount of experience, having served as Speaker of the House of Commons, Attorney General (the Crown's chief legal officer), and Chief Justice of two of the Crown Courts. Coke raised objections to the prerogative trend of the Stuart monarchy, upholding the authority of the common law against the prerogative courts. When James I claimed that kings ruled by Divine Right, Coke replied that in England the common law was superior to the King himself.

In 1621 Coke led the charge against the royal prerogative (see page 6). In a heated argument over foreign policy, James told Parliament that it owed its privileges to the Crown's generosity. Coke helped to write the Protestation, asserting that their privileges were 'the ancient . . . birthright and inheritance of the subjects of England'. He spent eight months in the Tower for his defiance.

The succession of Charles I led to the showdown between Coke, the common-law champion, and the Stuart monarchy. In 1625 Coke supported the decision to grant the new king Tonnage and Poundage for one year only, which Charles took as a personal insult. The King chose him as a county sheriff to keep him out of the Parliament of 1626. In 1627 Charles I dispensed with Parliament and put the royal prerogative into practice by imposing SHIP MONEY, imprisoning five knights without trial, billeting troops and raising the Forced Loan (see page 22). No lawyer of Coke's stature could allow this to go unchallenged. In 1628 Coke drafted the Petition of Right. He retired before the session of 1629.

SHIP MONEY
Money raised from ports and coastal counties as a tax to pay for warships to defend trade against piracy.

FOCUS ROUTE: WHO'S WHO?

Make notes on Sir Edward Coke to include in your Who's who? list.

FOCUS ROUTE

Was the King to blame for the collapse of trust between himself and Parliament? In this section you will examine some of the evidence that might be used to support Theory 3 (page 13).

MARTIAL LAW
A situation where normal civilian law is replaced by military discipline; where punishments are more severe; and where the normal rights of the accused are suspended.

JUSTICES OF THE PEACE
Magistrates who worked alongside parish churchwardens, constables and other unpaid officials to perform many of the functions of local government.

DISCUSS

Why were many people alarmed by the King's instructions to the JPs to keep a list of everyone who refused to pay the Forced Loan?

TALKING POINT

Would you agree that there are times when the chief executive of any country, be it a King, President or Prime Minister, might have to take extraordinary measures that are not strictly within the legal limits placed on the power of his or her office?

TALKING POINT

In 2005 the British government announced that it would place a small number of suspected terrorists under indefinite house arrest, without making formal charges.
   Why did it do this? Did it have the right to do it?

C Did Charles I threaten the ancient liberties of English people?

The Petition of Right

In 1628 several MPs drew up the Petition of Right. The Petition asked the King to acknowledge four simple points that Parliament claimed were basic precepts of English law, dating back hundreds of years:

1 It was illegal to raise taxes without Parliament's consent.
2 It was illegal to imprison people without showing the cause of their imprisonment.
3 It was illegal to impose the forced billeting of troops on civilians.
4 It was illegal to impose MARTIAL LAW on civilians.

The King accepted the Petition. Many people hoped that Charles now understood that there were limits to his powers as King, and that the laws and customs of the realm would be observed. But the Petition of Right solved nothing. Within a year the King had dissolved Parliament and embarked on the Personal Rule.
   Was Charles I a tyrant in the making? Or did he have the right, in certain circumstances, to set the law aside? To answer this question we need to look more closely at the events of 1626–27.

Why did Charles I raise the Forced Loan?

After dissolving the Parliament of 1626, Charles found himself at war without enough money to pay for it. He responded by taking emergency measures. The most lucrative was the Forced Loan, by which the King insisted that his subjects should make a gift of money to the Crown, equivalent to the amount they would have paid if Parliament had voted the anticipated subsidies. It followed an unsuccessful attempt by the Crown to persuade the gentry of the counties to make a 'Free Gift' to the King, with instructions to the JUSTICES OF THE PEACE (JPs) to record the names of everyone who refused to pay.
   When the Free Gift failed to raise enough money, the King resorted to the more insistent expedient of the Forced Loan. The Forced Loan maintained the fiction that the tax was voluntary, but it was not. Any who refused to pay were to be imprisoned. It raised serious questions about Parliament's role in voting taxation.
   Within two years of ascending the throne, Charles I had presented the kingdom with a dilemma it had never faced under either Elizabeth or James. If the King could set the law to one side during an emergency, and if only the King could declare an emergency, what safeguards did his subjects have against the abuse of this authority?
   The Forced Loan raised more money for the King than the four parliamentary subsidies would have done. Charles concluded that finance could be raised more efficiently without the uncertainty, delay and expense of calling Parliament.

The Five Knights' case

The Forced Loan led to a famous trial in 1627 known as the Five Knights' case. Five gentlemen were imprisoned for refusing to pay the Forced Loan. They challenged their imprisonment by issuing writs of HABEAS CORPUS, demanding to know why they had been imprisoned.

HABEAS CORPUS
Literally translated this means 'You have the body'. Habeas corpus prevented the king or any official from imprisoning someone without producing the person in court and making formal charges. It formed the basis of the assumption that a person is innocent until proven guilty.

The trial focused on the main constitutional issue: did the King have the right to remand prisoners without showing 'just cause' or not? It came down to an argument over MAGNA CARTA itself.

The Five Knights' case in the end was a victory for the King. It seemed to vindicate his belief that he ruled by 'Divine Right'. But the opposition it provoked showed that Charles's rule was pushing his sovereign rights to their limits – and possibly beyond.

MAGNA CARTA
In 1215 King John was forced to agree to the 'Great Charter', a statement of the liberties of freeborn Englishmen. Magna Carta was one of the most important legal documents in England, frequently reissued by kings who wanted to impress upon their people the fact that they intended to rule within the existing law of the land. The Petition of Right of 1628 was supposedly in this tradition.

■ 1F Opposition to the Forced Loan

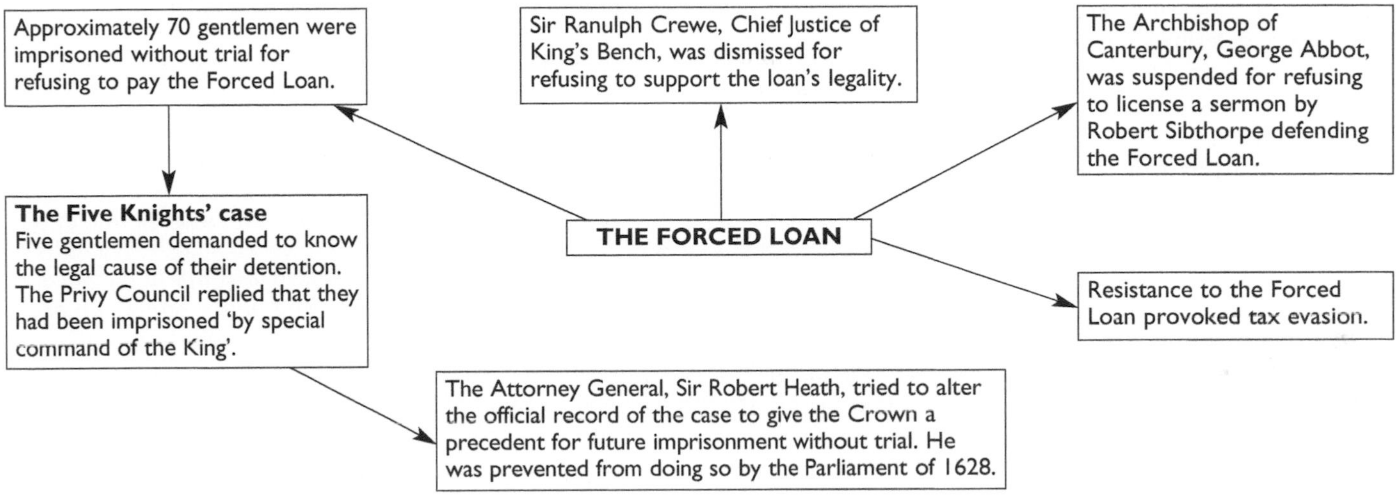
THE FORCED LOAN
Approximately 70 gentlemen were imprisoned without trial for refusing to pay the Forced Loan.
Sir Ranulph Crewe, Chief Justice of King's Bench, was dismissed for refusing to support the loan's legality.
The Archbishop of Canterbury, George Abbot, was suspended for refusing to license a sermon by Robert Sibthorpe defending the Forced Loan.
The Five Knights' case
Five gentlemen demanded to know the legal cause of their detention. The Privy Council replied that they had been imprisoned 'by special command of the King'.
Resistance to the Forced Loan provoked tax evasion.
The Attorney General, Sir Robert Heath, tried to alter the official record of the case to give the Crown a precedent for future imprisonment without trial. He was prevented from doing so by the Parliament of 1628.

ACTIVITY

Consider the whole episode of the Forced Loan and the Five Knights' case. What conclusions might the following people have drawn from this experience:

a) the King
b) the opponents of his methods?

What other measures did the King take which appeared to threaten ancient liberties?

The Petition of Right mentioned three other issues that were causing grave concern in Parliament.

- **Billeting of soldiers** As troops were concentrated in preparation for war, mostly around major ports, the King demanded that civilian households should put them up and feed them at their own expense.
- **Martial law** Soldiers and civilians don't mix. England had never had a permanent army, so the presence of troops in towns and villages was bound to cause trouble. The Crown's response was to declare martial law in these areas. This meant that the normal legal process was suspended. In its place came military law, trial by court martial, and summary sentences carried out without the right of appeal. Local civilians resented being made to feel that they were living in a state of siege.
- **Ship Money** Drawing on an old tradition, the Crown levied a one-off tax on coastal counties and ports to pay for ships to protect trade. The King claimed sovereignty over the English Channel, and foreign ships encountering an English warship were expected to dip their flags in salute.

FOCUS ROUTE

Did Charles's government threaten the ancient rights and liberties of the English people? Consider your answer to this question and add your findings to the Focus Route begun on page 13.

Why was Parliament suspicious of the King's religion?

Religion – the fire of division?

In the dying moments of Parliament in 1629, the Commons threatened the death penalty for anyone who tried to change the Church of England (see Source 1.9).

SOURCE 1.9 Resolution of the Protestation of the House of Commons, 2 March 1629

Whosoever shall bring in innovation of religion, or by favour or countenance seek to extend or introduce POPERY or Arminianism, or other opinion disagreeing from the true and orthodox Church, shall be reputed a CAPITAL ENEMY to this Kingdom and Commonwealth.

Just two weeks before, a House of Commons sub-committee had warned the King that Catholicism was threatening the kingdom (see Source 1.10).

SOURCE 1.10 Extract from the Heads of Articles, House of Commons, 24 February 1629

Here in England we observe an extraordinary growth of Popery, insomuch that in some counties, where in Queen Elizabeth's time there were few or none known RECUSANTS, now there are above 2,000, and all the rest generally apt to revolt. A bold and open allowance of their religion, by frequent and public resort to mass, in multitudes, without control, and that even to the Queen's Court, to the great scandal of his Majesty's government. The subtle and pernicious spreading of the Arminian faction; whereby they have kindled such a fire of division in the very bowels of the state, as if not speedily extinguished, it is of itself sufficient to ruin our religion.

Catholics and Protestants

If the growing fear of Catholicism was one of the contributing causes of the English Civil War, we need to understand what Catholicism was (Chart 1G), and what it meant to English Protestants. Similarly, if the King mistrusted Puritanism and the extreme form of Calvinism it represented, then we need to know what the Calvinists believed (Chart 1H).

POPERY
Catholicism. The term 'Popery' was used in a pejorative sense to describe Catholicism as a dangerous, foreign, superstitious, misguided religion. Catholics were termed 'Papists'.

CAPITAL ENEMY
A capital crime is one that deserves the death penalty.

RECUSANT
A Catholic who refused to accept the Act of Supremacy acknowledging the King as 'Supreme Governor' of the Church.

FOCUS ROUTE

Was religion the main cause of the breakdown in relations between King and Parliament? If so, was it the King or Parliament who was most to blame? As you work through this section, collect evidence that could be used to answer the following questions.

1 Why did most English people fear Catholicism so deeply?
2 Who were the Puritans? Why did the King oppose them?
3 Who were the Arminians? Why did the King support them?
4 Why did Parliament accuse the Arminians of being Catholics?
5 Why could the Elizabethan Settlement be interpreted in different ways?

CHURCH GOVERNMENT
- The Pope is the Supreme Head of the Church.
- The Church is governed by a system of archbishops and bishops.

THE CLERGY
- Priests work the miracle of the Mass.
- Priests may not marry. They must remain celibate.

DOCTRINE
- Seven sacraments – baptism, confirmation, marriage, the last rites, ordination, penance, the Eucharist (Mass or Holy Communion).
- The Mass is performed before the high altar by the priest. The Mass is a highly theatrical re-enactment of Christ's sacrifice.
- Transubstantiation – in the Eucharist the wine and bread are transformed into the body and blood of Christ. This miracle is worked by the priest.
- Salvation is achieved through faith, good works, prayer, and the cycle of confession – penance – absolution.

RELIGIOUS PRACTICES
- The liturgy (rites of worship) is in Latin.
- The Bible is in Latin.
- Services are highly ceremonial. Churches are lavishly decorated.
- Priests wear elaborate vestments.
- The high altar is at the east end of the church, in a space separated from the congregation.
- The priest conducts the Mass with his back to the congregation, facing the altar.
- Making the sign of the cross. Bowing at the name of Jesus.
- Veneration of saints. Saints' days are holidays.
- Veneration of holy relics – saints' bones, pieces of the true cross, etc.
- Intercession between generations of the communion of the faithful – the living could help the dead.

Salvation Road (Catholic)

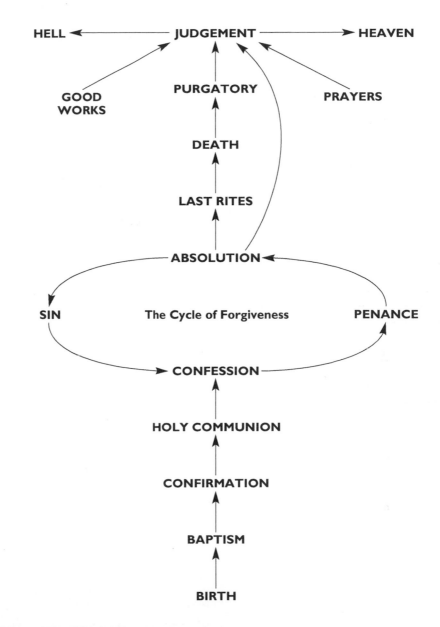

Interior of the Church of St Chapelle, Paris. The richly decorated interior of this Catholic church in France shows what English cathedrals and churches may have looked like before the Reformation. The overall effect is overwhelming

CHURCH GOVERNMENT
- The Pope is at best merely the vicar of Rome – at worst, the Anti-Christ.
- The Church is governed by a General Synod consisting of members drawn from synods (church councils) elected by local congregations.

THE CLERGY
- Ministers are preachers, not miracle-workers.
- Ministers may marry.

DOCTRINE
- Two sacraments – baptism and the Eucharist.
- The Eucharist is a commemorative act in which the believer is fed with a real but spiritual substance. The bread and wine are not physically transformed.
- Salvation can only be achieved through faith – the doctrine known as 'Justification by Faith'.
- Predestination. God already knows which people will be saved, known as the Elect.

RELIGIOUS PRACTICES
- The Bible is in English.
- The liturgy is in English.
- Services are simple, built around the preaching of a sermon.
- Churches are plain, to focus attention on the sermon.
- Ministers are plainly dressed.
- The altar is replaced with a Communion table, which is placed near the centre of the church, among the congregation.
- The minister conducts the service facing the congregation. He delivers the sermon from the pulpit.
- Catholic rituals, such as making the sign of the cross and bowing at the name of Jesus, are banned.
- No veneration of saints and relics.

Salvation Road (Calvinist)

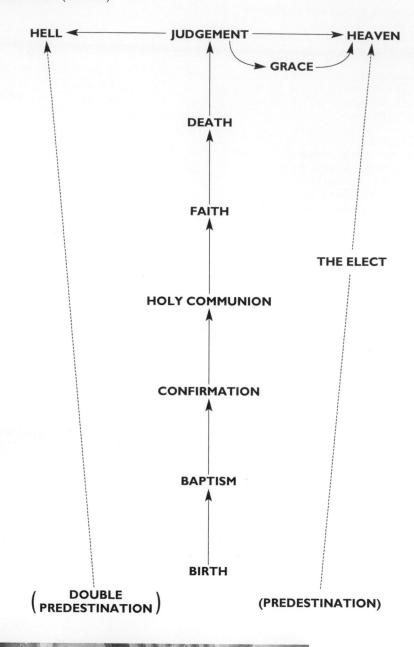

The Church of St Bavo, Haarlem, the Netherlands, by Isaac van Nickele (1633–1703). Cleansed of its medieval colour and décor during the Reformation, the interior of this Calvinist church shows what English Puritans wanted English cathedrals and churches to be like. The effect is stark but not austere, focusing attention on sermons preached from the pulpit

The Church of England – the 'true and orthodox church'?

The Church of England dates from the Elizabethan Settlement of 1559, which consisted of two Acts of Parliament.

- The Act of Supremacy established royal control over the Church by making the monarch its 'Supreme Governor'.
- The Act of Uniformity laid down in detail, through an official *Book of Common Prayer*, the form that church services were to take. The Church of England was therefore an established church, an official state church, forming a part of the English constitution.

The English church was a Protestant church, but it kept some of the traditions and appearance of Catholicism. The theology of the church was Protestant, based on justification by faith and predestination. The *Book of Common Prayer* was based on the Prayer Book of 1552, the second and more Protestant prayer book of Edward VI's reign. Church services were said in English, not Latin. The Bible was translated into English and people were encouraged to read it. The approved doctrine of the English church was set out in the Thirty-nine Articles of the Faith, one of which stated that 'Holy Scripture containeth all things necessary to salvation'. So the complex rituals of Catholic salvation theology – confession, absolution, penance and the like – were completely rejected. It would be difficult for Catholics to worship in the Church of England.

Elizabeth tried to encourage Catholics (in 1558 they probably still formed the vast majority of her subjects) to worship in the Anglican Church. The Act of Supremacy designated the monarch as the Supreme *Governor* of the English Church, implying that the *Head* of the church might lie somewhere else – for example Rome. The new *Book of Common Prayer* offered a fudged version of the Eucharistic prayer, which might be interpreted in a Catholic way. Elizabeth wanted her subjects to feel a sense of continuity with the past when they entered their parish churches, the burial chambers of their ancestors. So the clergy wore surplices, the people bowed at the name of Jesus, and Elizabeth herself kept two candlesticks, and possibly a crucifix, on her own altar. The Church of England was intended to marry the intellectual certainties of Calvinism with the psychological comforts of the Catholic world.

Attendance at church services was not voluntary. The church played too important a role in the ordering of life and the communication of information for its influence to be left to chance. Non-attendance was punishable by a fine. The government reserved the right to force compliance, and non-attendance could be used as a means of identifying Catholic recusants if the need arose.

The government of the Church of England was episcopal, meaning that the church was governed by bishops. The country was divided into the two Arch-Episcopal Sees of Canterbury and York, with another 26 Episcopal Sees. This episcopal structure was something the Anglican Church inherited from its Catholic past, a fact which laid it open to criticism from Puritans.

What made England's episcopal structure very different from its Catholic origins was the fact that it was established by an Act of Parliament. The royal supremacy over the church was acknowledged by the Submission of the Clergy (May 1552) and confirmed by Parliament in 1534. This was the 'King in Parliament' in action, a royal supremacy established not by royal decree but by the Crown working with Parliament to declare independence from the Catholic Church.

SOURCE 1.11 The Eucharistic prayer, from the *Book of Common Prayer*, 1559

The Body of Our Lord Jesus Christ, which was given for thee ... Take and eat this in remembrance that Christ died for thee ...

DISCUSS

Read Source 1.11.

1 Why might this be acceptable to both Protestants and Catholics?
2 Why might it be acceptable to neither?

■ II THE CHURCH OF ENGLAND

CHURCH GOVERNMENT
• The monarch is the Supreme Governor of the Church.
• The Church is governed by an episcopal system, but administered at parish level by clergy working with locally elected, unpaid churchwardens.

THE CLERGY
• Ministers combine the reading of a sermon with the liturgy of the *Book of Common Prayer*. They do not perform miracles.
• Ministers may marry.

DOCTRINE
• Defined in the Thirty-nine Articles.
• 'Holy scripture containeth all things necessary to salvation.'
• Predestination (the idea that some people are the Elect, destined for heaven).
• Double predestination (the idea that the rest of mankind, by definition, is destined for hell).
• Two sacraments – baptism and the Eucharist.
• The Eucharist is open to different interpretations.
• Salvation can only be achieved through faith – 'Justification by Faith'.

RELIGIOUS PRACTICES
• The Bible is in English.
• The liturgy is in English.
• Services combine preaching and ceremonial. Churches have been stripped of most of their Catholic decoration, statues and images.
• Ministers wear vestments.
• Communion tables normally stand at the east end of the church, where the altar had stood.
• The minister conducts the service facing the congregation. He delivers the sermon from the pulpit.
• Making the sign of the cross and bowing at the name of Jesus are encouraged.
• No veneration of saints or holy relics.
Note: There was great diversity of practice in different parishes, a fact that worried both Puritans and Arminians. In the 1630s Charles I and Archbishop Laud set out to turn the theoretical uniformity envisaged by the Act of Uniformity of 1559 into reality.

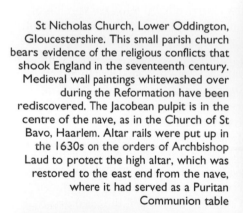

St Nicholas Church, Lower Oddington, Gloucestershire. This small parish church bears evidence of the religious conflicts that shook England in the seventeenth century. Medieval wall paintings whitewashed over during the Reformation have been rediscovered. The Jacobean pulpit is in the centre of the nave, as in the Church of St Bavo, Haarlem. Altar rails were put up in the 1630s on the orders of Archbishop Laud to protect the high altar, which was restored to the east end from the nave, where it had served as a Puritan Communion table

ACTIVITY

The Church of England was a compromise, intended to create a national church in which all English people could worship. It was criticised by both Puritans and Catholics, each group wanting to pull the Church of England more in their direction.

THE CHURCH OF ENGLAND	
PROTESTANT ASPECTS	CATHOLIC ASPECTS

1 Using Charts 1G, 1H and 1I and the sources in this section, compare the Church of England with the Catholic and Calvinist churches. Complete your own copy of the above table, marking on it which aspects of the Anglican Church were Protestant and which were Catholic in origin.
2 What conclusions can you make about
  a) the doctrine
  b) the government
  c) the atmosphere
  of the Church?
3 Prepare a criticism of the Church of England from either the Puritan or the Catholic point of view. Which aspects of the Church would you:
  a) have disliked, but could have lived with
  b) have felt unable to accept?

Arminians and Puritans

By the 1620s two groups within the Anglican Church were locked in a fierce power struggle. Both the Arminians (or High Church party) and the Puritans claimed to represent the original intentions of the Elizabethan Settlement of 1559. Each group accused the other of wishing to make illegal 'innovations' or changes to that settlement.

During James I's reign, both Arminian and Puritan clergy had been frustrated by the King's refusal to promote their members. The succession of Charles I upset the delicate balance maintained by his father, as the new King made clear his preference for the Arminian party.

■ 1J The growing importance of Arminianism under Charles I

1624	William Laud preaches sermon to the opening session of Charles I's first Parliament
1625	Laud promoted to Bishop of Bath and Wells, Dean of Chapel Royal
1626	Laud and Richard Neile appointed to the Privy Council
1627	Charles pardons Robert Sibthorpe and Roger Manwaring for preaching sermons that support royal prerogative and Divine Right, after Parliament threatens to discipline them Richard Montagu promoted to Bishop of Chichester
1629	Laud promoted to Bishop of London
1633	Laud promoted to Archbishop of Canterbury

The Arminians ◄ ··· ► **The Puritans**
(more 'Catholic')   (more 'Protestant')

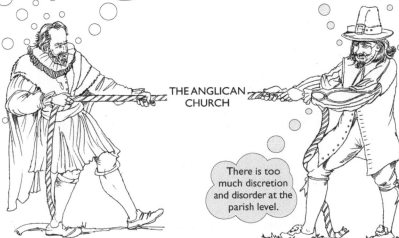

Bishops are an essential support for the monarchy. The pulpit should be used to preach sermons supporting the Divine Right of Kings.

Is a man never to be called to account for the choices he has made in life? People are moral beings with the free will to choose.

The Act of Uniformity was forced on Elizabeth I by political considerations, a staging post on the road to an English Calvinist Church.

The Word is the only thing of any real importance. Preaching must become a much more important aspect of Anglican worship. To achieve this we need a well-educated clergy.

The history and traditions of the medieval (Catholic) Church are important. During the Reformation the 'church-wreckers' went too far. The 'beauty of holiness' should be restored to encourage a sense of mystery, the timeless unity between the congregation, the monarchy and God.

Double predestination is too harsh. It means that many people are destined to eternal damnation without any hope of salvation. Christ died for all mankind, not just for the Elect.

The English Reformation is unfinished business. We must now 'purify' the Church by sweeping away all surviving signs of Catholic influence – vestments, bowing at the name of Jesus, incense, and so on.

All the existing altars should be taken from the east end of the church and repositioned as Communion tables among the congregation.

Ritual and ceremonial is needed to maintain an unchanging and confident social order based on rank and privilege.

THE ANGLICAN CHURCH

Government by bishops is dangerous. They have no scriptural authority, as they are not mentioned in the Bible. They have too much power over parish ministers, especially through the church courts.

There is too much discretion and disorder at the parish level.

There is too much discretion and disorder at the parish level.

The Church is full of abuses such as pluralism (the practice of holding more than one benefice, or church position, at a time) and non-residence. This must be put right.

The anti-Catholic penal laws must be strictly enforced.

RECUSANCY LAWS
Recusancy (or penal) laws dated back to the reign of Elizabeth I. They imposed fines on people who failed to attend Church of England services. Puritans believed they should be more strictly enforced.

ACTIVITY

The Arminians and the Puritans both claimed to represent the original intentions of the Elizabethan Settlement of 1559 (see Chart D on page 8).

a) Why was it so difficult to say with any certainty what the original intentions of the 1559 settlement were?
b) Both the Arminians and the Puritans accused each other of trying to introduce 'innovations' (changes) into the Anglican Church. Why was the charge of 'innovating' such a serious one?

Queen Henrietta Maria (1609–69)

In 1625 Charles I married Henrietta Maria, the daughter of King Henry IV of France. The marriage aimed at strengthening England in its war with Spain. The terms of the marriage treaty had important consequences in England. Henrietta Maria was Catholic, and was allowed to hear Mass in the court at Whitehall. She was permitted a personal confessor and a number of priests to say Mass. The treaty required the King to suspend the RECUSANCY LAWS, and England agreed to provide the French king with help in his campaign to defeat the Protestant rebels in La Rochelle.

At first Charles did not love his new bride, whose first years in England were miserably unhappy. She found her husband cold and distant, and her rooms at the palace dingy and unattractive. Henrietta Maria was so ashamed of her royal apartments that she received visitors in the dark, with the curtains drawn. In 1626 she smashed a window with her fist during a quarrel. The King made no secret of the fact that he preferred the Duke of Buckingham's company to hers. In 1626 the Queen's personal household servants were dismissed and sent back to France.

After England went to war with France in 1627, she found herself unpopular. Nevertheless, she was England's Queen. Assuming that she and Charles had children, she would be responsible for raising them and preparing them to rule.

DISCUSS

Why did Charles's marriage raise Protestant fears of Catholic influence at court?

SOURCE 1.12 Extract taken from King Charles I's Declaration prefixed to the Articles of Religion, November 1628

That the Articles of the Church of England do contain the true doctrine of the Church of England agreeable to God's Word: which we do therefore ratify and confirm, requiring all our loving subjects to continue in the uniform profession thereof, and prohibiting the least difference from the said Articles ...

That therefore in these both curious and unhappy differences, which have so many hundred years, in different times and places, exercised the Church of Christ, we will, that all further curious search be laid aside, and these disputes shut up in God's promises ... And that no man hereafter shall either print, or preach, to draw the Article aside any way, but shall submit to it in the plain and full meaning thereof: and shall not put his own sense or comment to be the meaning of the Article, but shall take it in the literal and grammatical sense.

That if any public Reader in either of our Universities, or any Head or Master of a College shall affix any new sense to any Article, or shall publicly read, determine, or hold any public disputation, or suffer any such to be held either way or if any divine in the Universities shall preach or print any thing either way, other than is already established in Convocation with our royal assent; he shall be liable to our displeasure, and the Church's censure ...

ACTIVITY

1 Study Source 1.12. Explain why the King's Declaration was seen by the Puritans as an attack on them and their religious practices.
2 What defence could Charles have made of his decision to issue this Declaration as a prefix to the Articles of Religion?

E **Why didn't Buckingham's assassination save the relationship between King and Parliament?**

In August 1628 the Duke of Buckingham was assassinated. News of the assassination was whispered into the King's ear while he was at prayer. Charles showed no emotion on hearing the news. When prayers were finished, he retired to the privacy of his chamber and wept.

John Felton was apprehended at the scene of the murder. Felton, a lieutenant in the army who had been present at the Ile de Ré expedition in 1627, blamed Buckingham for England's military failures. He was tried and executed. How did the country react to news of Buckingham's assassination?

■ **1K Reactions to the assassination of the Duke of Buckingham**

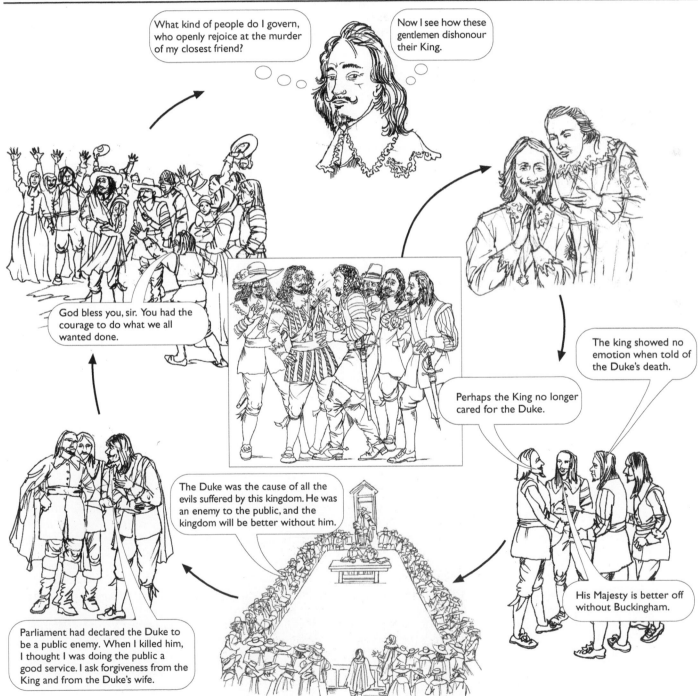

Consequences of Buckingham's assassination

Reshuffling the deck

Buckingham's assassination was a turning point in the politics of Charles I's court. His death gave the King the opportunity to reallocate all the titles and offices Buckingham had held since the early 1620s. Men who had been excluded from court by the Duke's monopoly of power could once again hope to influence the King's decisions. Some of these men had been involved in defending parliamentary privileges in the 1620s. There was a general belief that Charles would now find his feet and become his own man. In the months after Buckingham's death, Charles I assembled the team with which he governed the country during the Personal Rule.

■ **Learning trouble spot**

The Earl of Strafford was known simply as Thomas Wentworth until 1639 when the King gave him his title in recognition of his service.

Earl of Suffolk

Appointed
Warden of the Cinque Ports

Earl of Arundel

Returned to the Privy Council

Sir Thomas Wentworth
(later Earl of Strafford)

Appointed
Lord President of the
Council of the North

Francis, Baron Cottington

Appointed
Chancellor of the Exchequer

Sir Richard Weston, Earl of
Portland, Lord Treasurer

Became more influential

William Laud

Appointed
Bishop of London

Falling in love with the Queen

SOURCE 1.13 This portrait of Charles I and Henrietta Maria was engraved in 1642 by George Vertue, after the painting in 1634 by Anthony Van Dyck, Charles I's 'Principall Paynter'. It shows Henrietta Maria handing Charles an evergreen wreath, a symbol of conjugal fidelity. The Queen is receiving from her husband's hand an olive branch, representing peace between England and France

DISCUSS

Why was the improvement in Charles's relationship with Henrietta Maria controversial?

ACTIVITY

As the French Ambassador to England, write a short diplomatic despatch to King Louis XIII to report on how the government of King Charles I is changing in the aftermath of Buckingham's death.

FOCUS ROUTE: WHO'S WHO?

Make notes on Sir John Eliot to include in your Who's who? list.

FOCUS ROUTE

Return to the central question of Section E – why didn't the assassination of Buckingham mark a decisive turning point in the King's relationship with Parliament? Whose fault was it that this opportunity was lost?

Van Dyck's painting (Source 1.13) is exceptionally skilful in showing the love that had developed between Charles and the Queen. This is revealed through the delicacy of the King's pose, leaning slightly towards his Queen yet restrained, full of respectful tenderness.

The marriage between Charles I and Henrietta Maria had not started well. As soon as Buckingham was dead, it improved. As Charles I was forced to come into his own as a King and a man, he and Henrietta Maria fell deeply and passionately in love. This was something of a novelty at the English court, where no monarch had enjoyed a settled, faithful family life since the death of King Henry VII in 1509. In 1629 Henrietta Maria suffered a miscarriage, followed by the births of their eldest son Charles in 1630, of Mary (1631), James (1633), Elizabeth (1635), Ann (1637), a stillborn girl (1638) and Henry (1640).

Changes in the House of Commons

By the time Parliament met again in January 1629, the leadership of the Commons had changed significantly. Coke had retired. Sir Thomas Wentworth (later the Earl of Strafford), who had insisted on forcing the King to do things in a 'parliamentary way', had now gone over to the King's service, becoming Lord President of the Council of the North. Wentworth saw the Petition of Right as proof of Charles's intention to rule within the law. Some of his former parliamentary colleagues regarded him as a turncoat who placed personal advancement over principle.

This left the House of Commons under the leadership of Sir John Eliot, John Pym (see page 80), Sir Robert Phellips, Sir Nathaniel Rich, John Selden and Denzil Holles. The new Commons leaders understood that the King expected this session to be more harmonious; with the Petition of Right, Buckingham's death and Coke's retirement behind him, Charles was hoping that Tonnage and Poundage might now be formally granted.

Why didn't King and Commons now reach agreement?

Three issues were to prevent agreement from happening:

- **The Petition of Right** The King reluctantly gave in and agreed to a version which made no mention of royal prerogative. However, in the printed version that was issued to the public, he insisted on laying claim to prerogative powers.
- **Tonnage and Poundage** Charles still insisted that this belonged to him, with or without Parliament's consent. He considered that established practice had made Parliament's act of voting this tax a mere formality.
- **Religion** The continued advancement of Arminian clergy was now becoming a major source of conflict. In July and August, William Laud and Richard Montagu had been promoted Bishops of London and Chichester respectively. For Pym, Arminianism was linked to the trend towards absolutism (see Chapter 2).

When the Commons criticised the Customs officers who had seized merchants' goods in lieu of tax, the King intervened to make clear that 'what those men have done they have done by his [the King's] command'. It was no longer possible to maintain the fiction that only the King's servants were at fault – the quarrel was now clearly and openly with the King himself.

In these circumstances it was unlikely that Parliament was going to vote for Tonnage and Poundage for life, in favour of Charles. Since this was the whole point of the parliamentary session, the King decided to end it.

The manner of its ending confirmed Charles's opinion that Parliament had outlived its usefulness. The scenes described at the beginning of this chapter now took place, with the Speaker being forcibly held in his chair to prevent him from closing the Parliament, while Black Rod hammered on the door. In its dying moments the House of Commons passed a Protestation – it was to echo down the next decade as a warning to those who would co-operate with the Personal Rule.

SOURCE 1.14 The Protestation of the House of Commons, 2 March 1629

1 Whosoever shall bring in innovation of religion, or by favour or countenance seek to extend or introduce Popery or Arminianism, or other opinion disagreeing from the true and orthodox Church, shall be reputed a capital enemy to this Kingdom and Commonwealth.

2 Whosoever shall counsel or advise the taking and levying of the subsidies of Tonnage and Poundage, not being granted by Parliament, or shall be an actor or instrument therein, shall be likewise reputed an innovator in the Government, and a capital enemy to the Kingdom and Commonwealth.

3 If any merchant or person whatsoever shall voluntarily yield, or pay the said subsidies of Tonnage and Poundage, not being granted by Parliament, he shall likewise be reputed a betrayer of the liberties of England, and an enemy to the same.

SOURCE 1.15 Extract from King Charles I's declaration explaining his intention to rule without Parliament for an indefinite period

1 We are not ignorant how much that House [the Commons] hath of late years endeavoured to extend their privileges ... In these innovations (which we will never permit again) they pretended indeed our service, but their drift was to break ... through all respects and ligaments of government, and to erect an universal over-swaying power to themselves, which belongs only to us, and not to them.

7 We have thus declared the manifold causes we had to dissolve this Parliament, whereby all the world may see how much they have forgotten their former engagements at the entry into the war, themselves being persuaders to it; promising to make us feared by our enemies and esteemed by our friends, and how they turned the necessities grown by that war to enforce us to yield to conditions incompatible with monarchy.

ACTIVITY

1 Study Source 1.14. A 'capital' crime is one that received the death penalty.
   a) Who was being threatened with death in the Protestation, and why?
   b) Resolution 2 of the Protestation threatens not only those who advised the King to collect Tonnage and Poundage, but also anyone who was 'instrumental' in collecting it. Why might this have been an effective way of preventing the King from collecting this money?
2 Study Source 1.15.
   How convincing is the King's argument that the failure of his relations with Parliament was Parliament's fault?

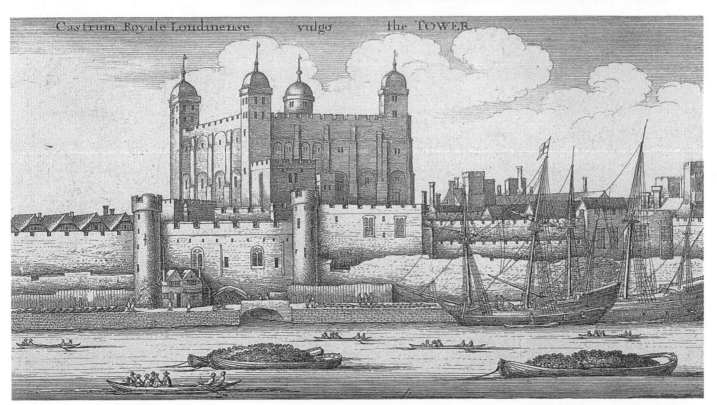

SOURCE 1.16 The Tower of London

As soon as the Parliament of 1628–29 had been dissolved, the King ordered the arrest of Sir John Eliot, Denzil Holles, Benjamin Valentine and five other MPs on a charge of treason. The King intended to try them in the Court of Star Chamber, but that court, consisting mostly of Privy Councillors, advised him against making them rule in a case that would clash with Parliament's privilege of freedom from arrest. When the MPs issued writs of habeas corpus, demanding to know the reason for their detention, Charles replied that parliamentary privileges did not extend to political subversion.

Five of the arrested MPs submitted by admitting their guilt, and were released. Holles was fined and lived in exile for 7–8 years. Eliot and Valentine were tried in 1630, found guilty, and imprisoned in the Tower of London. Eliot refused to ask pardon from the King, and died in the Tower in 1632. The King refused to release his body to his family for burial in his native Cornwall. Valentine also refused to ask for pardon. He remained in the Tower until 1640.

F Review: why did Charles I resort to Personal Rule in 1629?

FOCUS ROUTE

So what were the reasons for the dramatic collapse of trust between Parliament and Charles I? Return to the four theories you began to consider at the start of this chapter (see Chart 1A on page 13).

• It was the Duke of Buckingham's fault.
• It was Parliament's fault.
• It was the King's fault.
• It was nobody's fault.

You should have found evidence to support all four theories. You must decide how much importance to give each of them, and come up with your own view.

■ Learning trouble spot

Writing a history essay

A sixth form essay is longer than an essay written for GCSE. It needs to be planned more carefully. It is also more rewarding; at AS level more importance is attached to your opinions. To make your point of view as convincingly as possible is the ultimate goal of a sixth form essay.

A history essay is similar in many ways to the essays you might write for other arts subjects, for example English. Most English and history teachers will teach you to write your essay in three main sections:

• an introduction
• the main body of the essay
• a conclusion.

The introduction

Use the opening paragraph to summarise what you have to do to answer the question. Focus on the key words and explain their significance. Any dates in the title need to be explained. Summarise your answer to the question.

Paragraphs in the main body

Use each paragraph to focus on one part of the answer. Begin with an assertion – a sentence that makes a statement. Now support this statement with the best evidence you have. Normally two or three good facts will do. Finish the paragraph with some discussion of what these facts mean and try to link in to the next paragraph. By the time you have done all of this, each paragraph should be at least six or seven lines long.

The conclusion

End the essay with a final paragraph that summarises your answer. Explain how the paragraphs link together to support your basic answer to the question.

You need to give careful thought to all three parts of the essay. Here is some general advice about how to write a good history essay.

1 Write out the entire question at the top of the page. The question is the title of the essay.
2 Identify the key words in the title. Make sure that you fully understand what is meant by the title. If any dates are mentioned, make sure you understand their significance.
3 Brainstorm before you start writing. Brainstorming means noting down ideas as they come into your head. Then make sure that you have not missed any key issues.
4 Organise what you have to say into paragraphs, gathering all the information about one point in one place. Your essay should form a logical sequence of paragraphs.
5 You should have a clear idea of what each paragraph will be about and how it will fit into your argument. If you don't, then you aren't ready to start writing.
6 If the essay is well planned, you should be free to concentrate on each paragraph without worrying about the rest of the essay. Make each paragraph as effective as possible.
7 Support all statements with facts. Use the best evidence available.
8 Write clearly, especially in exams. Try to develop a fairly formal style.
9 Spelling, punctuation and grammar matter. History is a subject that is communicated through language. Your use of English is crucial to your ability to argue persuasively.

1 England's foreign policy in the 1620s was disastrous. Every English military expedition failed.

2 The Duke of Buckingham was blamed for these disasters. He was unpopular for having too much influence over the King. Parliament demanded his downfall, but Charles I defended him from impeachment by dissolving Parliament.

3 The King needed Parliament's financial help because of the wars with Spain and France. Parliament used this power to claim the right to discuss issues that had traditionally been part of the King's royal prerogative. These issues included foreign policy and religion.

4 Frustrated by Parliament's refusal to grant tax unconditionally, Charles I resorted to 'prerogative' taxation, for example the Forced Loan. He also collected Tonnage and Poundage without Parliament's permission.

5 Charles I was apparently ill-suited to the task of persuading Parliament to co-operate with him. His belief in the Divine Right of Kings led him to insist that Parliament should show its trust in him by voting subsidies without demanding the redress of grievances.

6 War with Europe's two greatest powers applied pressure to England's financial and military institutions. If the King were to pursue a long war effectively, he needed long-term, regular finance – not the irregular supplies of Parliament's subsidies. This encouraged Charles I to claim prerogative powers which, according to his opponents, undermined the traditional liberties of English subjects.

7 Both the King and his parliamentary critics therefore accused each other of trying to introduce 'innovations' in government. Both sides looked to English history for examples to support their claims.

8 Nowhere was this charge of 'innovation' more dangerous than in religion. Charles I's promotion of Arminian clergy was seen by Puritans as an attempt to introduce Catholicism under a different name. Religious quarrels introduced an ideological element into the political and constitutional struggle.

9 In 1628 it appeared that England might be emerging from political crisis. These hopes were soon dashed in renewed conflict over taxation and religion.

10 In 1629 Parliament closed in scenes of outright violence and defiance, which helped to convince the King that he was better off trying to rule without Parliament.

Was Charles I trying to establish royal absolutism?

CHAPTER OVERVIEW

In January 1649 Parliament put the King on trial for his life on a charge of high treason. The trial was an indictment of the King's entire reign. Parliament accused Charles of having a

wicked design to erect and uphold in himself an unlimited and tyrannical power to rule according to his will, and to overthrow the rights and liberties of the people

Is this what Charles I was trying to do? From 1629 until 1640 the King ruled without Parliament, but did he intend to do away with Parliament forever?

> **PREROGATIVE COURTS**
> Special courts that could remove cases from common law and hear them in secret.

■ 2A Two views of the 1630s

View 1: The Eleven Years' Tyranny

Charles decided to rule without Parliament permanently. He forbade anyone in his presence to even suggest the recall of Parliament.	Charles's government raised taxes without Parliament's consent. This was an attempt to make the Crown financially independent, in order to avoid ever having to call Parliament. This was also a clear violation of Magna Carta.	The Earl of Strafford showed how absolutism could be imposed through the rigorous use of the PREROGATIVE COURTS and other government agencies. He used Ireland as a model to show how England could be governed.	Archbishop Laud sympathised with the King's authoritarian tendencies. Using the prerogative courts, he launched an attack on Puritanism that drove many Puritans into exile.

PARLIAMENT	TAXATION	'THOROUGH'	THE CHURCH OF ENGLAND

Charles decided to rule without Parliament temporarily, until wiser counsels prevailed among MPs. He was perfectly within his rights to do so.	Charles's government did what its critics had always demanded, trying to enable the Crown to 'live of its own' income. By discovering sources of income neglected by his father or forgotten by the more affluent Tudors, the King was not breaking the law.	Strafford believed in 'Thorough' government (see page 50) – something which early seventeenth-century England sorely needed. The 1620s had revealed how inefficient and corrupt government had become. Strafford may have been authoritarian, but he was no absolutist, as is shown by his continued use of the Irish Parliament.	Archbishop Laud took the Elizabethan Act of Uniformity seriously, trying to ensure that religious worship was indeed uniform throughout the kingdom. He was trying to preserve some of the artistic heritage of the medieval church – but this did not make him a Catholic.

View 2: The Personal Rule

(ROYAL) ABSOLUTISM

A method of government in which the king has unlimited power over his subjects. In much of Europe during the seventeenth century, absolutism was becoming the dominant political theory. Parliaments had little or no place in an absolutist state; either they would be made powerless or be abolished altogether.

DISCUSS

Nobody in 1640 would have put Charles on trial for treason. The King was protected from direct criticism by the principle that 'the King could do no wrong'. People blamed the King's 'evil advisers' for his mistakes. Why were people so careful to avoid insulting the majesty of kingship?

FOCUS ROUTE

What if Charles I had been put on trial for treason in 1640? Is there enough evidence in the 1630s to convict him of trying to set up an unlimited monarchy that would overthrow his people's rights?

At the end of this chapter you will hold a trial in which you review the evidence for and against Charles I, and reach a verdict. Collect evidence as you work through the chapter.

Aspects of the Personal Rule	Evidence that the King *was* trying to build 'an unlimited and tyrannical power'	Evidence that the King *was not* trying to build 'an unlimited and tyrannical power'
The King's image		
The court		
The government of the realm		
Finance		
The Earl of Strafford and 'Thorough'		
Archbishop Laud and the Church of England		

Charles's government censored the press to silence its critics. It imposed cruel punishments on Puritans such as William Prynne who were accused of sedition.

Charles used propaganda in the form of paintings, masques and sermons to create an image of Divine Right monarchy by reminding his subjects of their duty of obedience.

The court reinforced the image of Divine Right by distancing the King from his subjects.

Charles was forced to call Parliament by his defeat in the war with Scotland. The Earl of Strafford advised him to do so in the belief that he could manage the Parliament in England as he had managed the Irish Parliament.

Therefore, Charles I was guilty of attempting to create an absolute monarchy in violation of the ancient laws of England. Had he succeeded, Parliament would have become nothing more than a 'rubber stamp', summoned occasionally not to debate, but merely to approve, royal commands.

| SILENCING OPPOSITION | PROPAGANDA | THE COURT | STRAFFORD'S ADVICE | ABSOLUTISM? |

Censorship of the press was only to be expected in the seventeenth century. The punishments imposed on William Prynne and others were cruel, but they were not unusual.

Charles was a great patron of the arts, but that does not make him a tyrant. Charles's mistake was in failing to use the arts effectively for propaganda purposes.

This propaganda failure led to a country-wide perception that the court was decadent, corrupt and immoral, when in fact Charles I's court was a model of decency and order.

Charles called Parliament in 1640 on the advice of Strafford. If Charles had forbidden anyone from ever suggesting that Parliament should be recalled, then why did Strafford feel able to suggest it?

Therefore, Charles was innocent of attempting to create an absolute monarchy in England. He believed Parliament had failed to fulfil its duties during the 1620s, when England was at war. The Personal Rule was a temporary measure aimed at strengthening central government to enable England to compete with the powerful states on the continent.

DISCUSS

What reasons can you suggest to explain why historians have produced different interpretations of the 1630s, such as Views 1 and 2 on pages 38–39?

■ 2B Timeline of the Personal Rule, 1629–37

The Personal Rule of Charles I lasted from 1629 to 1640. Chapter 2 focuses on the period when things seemed to be going well for the King, so it only goes up to 1637. The period from 1637 to 1640 is covered in Chapter 3.

1629 **March** **April**	Charles dissolves Parliament England makes peace with France
1630 **November**	England makes peace with Spain
1632 **January**	Sir Thomas Wentworth (made Earl of Strafford in 1639) appointed Lord Deputy of Ireland
1633 **August**	Charles visits Scotland Feoffees for Impropriations abolished (see page 54) William Laud appointed Archbishop of Canterbury
1634 **February** **September** **October**	William Prynne imprisoned and mutilated for writing *Histriomastix* condemning court masques Chief Justice of the Common Pleas dismissed for opposing Laud's Church reforms First Ship Money writs
1635 **June**	Ship Money extended to the whole kingdom
1637 **June** **November**	Prynne, Bastwick and Burton branded, mutilated and imprisoned for publishing pamphlets attacking bishops Trial of John Hampden begins for refusing to pay Ship Money

A Did the image of the King create a sense of absolutism? (pp. 41–42)

B Was the King out of touch with his people? (pp. 42–44)

C Did the King govern tyranically? (pp. 44–48)

D Finance – absolutism, or just good housekeeping? (pp. 48–49)

E The Earl of Strafford – 'Black Tom Tyrant'? (pp. 50–53)

F Did Archbishop Laud use the Church of England to develop absolutism? (pp. 53–55)

G Review: was Charles I trying to establish royal absolutism? (pp. 55–56)

SOURCE 2.1   A portrait of Charles I by Daniel Mytens, 1631. Myten's portrait is probably a good likeness of Charles. It shows him at the age of 31, honest and approachable, a man whose awkward stance invites familiarity

SOURCE 2.2   Charles I at the hunt by Anthony Van Dyck, 1635. Here is a king who ruled by Divine Right. Like the altars in his churches, this king is not to be approached without permission

DISCUSS

1 Study Sources 2.1 and 2.2. How does Van Dyck's portrait differ from Mytens'? Look closely at:

 • Charles's face
 • his clothes
 • his stance
 • the horse and figure behind him. What could this be intended to represent?

2 Study Source 2.2.
 a) Why is Charles dressed so casually and attended only by a groom? Why does he look like a gentleman rather than a monarch?
 b) Would Elizabeth I ever have allowed herself to be represented so casually?

In recent years we have grown used to the activities of 'spin doctors', people employed by governments to create a certain image of national leaders or to present their policies in a favourable light. These portraits of Charles were painted within four years of each other. They illustrate the transformation of Charles's public image that took place during the Personal Rule.

Van Dyck was a greater artist than Mytens. His skill was employed by Charles to glorify the monarchy, lending majesty to the diminutive figures of Charles I and his Queen. Charles was 5 foot 4 inches tall (about 1 metre 62), Henrietta Maria considerably shorter.

Charles's interest in painting went beyond portraits of himself and his family. Through his patronage of the arts, Charles planned to create a legacy of artistic triumphs to glorify the Stuart dynasty.

The keystone in this policy of 'art for art's sake' was the creation of the Royal Collection. Charles became the most ambitious collector of paintings in Europe. He cultivated artistic and diplomatic links with the Catholic courts of the greater continental monarchies. His love of Catholic European civilisation clashed with the prevailing political culture of English Protestantism.

There is, however, a serious problem with the view that Charles used art as propaganda to project a more majestic image of himself. Most of the portraits of the King remained in royal palaces, or in the great aristocratic houses. Charles seems to have been indifferent to his public image, as if the existence of the image were enough to confirm Charles's image of himself. If Charles intended his portraits to be used as propaganda, perhaps this was ineffective because the court failed to concern itself with public relations.

FOCUS ROUTE

Return to the main Focus Route on page 39. Do you think the King's image was being deliberately changed to create the impression that he ruled by Divine Right? If so, how effectively was this image transmitted beyond the court?

B Was the King out of touch with his people?

After Buckingham's death, Charles began to reorder the morals, manners and etiquette of life at court. Under James I, the court had become disorganised and unwholesome, marked by sexual scandal, intrigue, favouritism and even murder. Under Charles, this riot of disorder was replaced by a formal regime more suited to the dignity of a royal household. The court was to be a model of moral restraint, establishing an ideal of royal virtue at the heart of the kingdom.

Access to the King was severely restricted. Under James, the royal household had become a free-for-all, with court jesters, dwarves and American Indians providing entertainment for the many people who wandered freely through the court. Charles I's sense of dignity led to greater formality. The King was to be a remote figure, his semi-divine status safeguarded by a strict formal hierarchy and proper etiquette.

THE PULPIT

In the seventeenth century, the pulpit was the principal means of mass communication. Everyone was required by law to attend church. The pulpit was the most important means by which the official image of monarchy could be spread through the country.

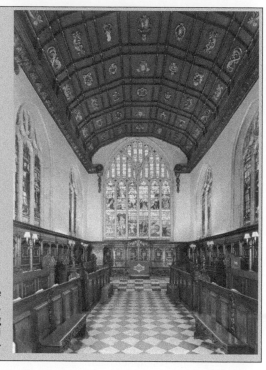

SOURCE 2.3 Lincoln College Chapel, Oxford. Built in 1629–31, this chapel dates from the beginning of the Personal Rule. The Chapel Royal at Whitehall was very similar

ECCLESIASTICAL CANONS
Church laws.

ACTIVITY

Why did the image of the King matter:

a) to the King and Court
b) to foreign ambassadors
c) to the kingdom as a whole?

In 1640 the Crown issued a new set of ECCLESIASTICAL CANONS. They included an explicit endorsement of the doctrine of the Divine Right of Kings, which every parish priest was to read four times a year at morning prayer.

SOURCE 2.4 Sir Philip Warwick describes King Charles I. Warwick was one of the Lord Treasurer's secretaries, an official in the King's government

His deportment was very majestick; for he would not let fall his dignity, no not to the greatest Forraigners that came to visit him and his Court; for tho' he was farr from pride, yet he was carefull of majestie, and would be approacht with respect and reverence. His conversation was free, and the subject matter of it was most commonly rational; or if facetious, not light . . . His way of arguing was very civil and patient; for he seldom contradicted another by his authority, but by his reason: nor did he by any petulant dislike quash another's arguments; and he offered his exception by this civill introduction, 'By your favour, Sir, I think otherwise on this or that ground' yet he would discountenance any bold or forward address to him.

SOURCE 2.5 William Murray, a Gentleman of the Bedchamber, to Sir Henry Vane, 1631

The court is like the earth, naturally cold, and reflects no more affection than the sunshine of their master's favour beats upon it.

SOURCE 2.6 Extract from 'Orders set down by his Majesty for civility in sittings in the Chapel', 1630

1. *That in our going & coming from the Chapel all men keep their rank orderly & distinctly, & not break them with pretence of speaking one with an other . . . that being one of the most eminent & frequent occasions wherby men's rank in precedence are distinguished & discerned.*
2. *That no man whatsoever presume to wait upon us to the Chapel in boots & spurs . . .*
3. *That all the stalls beyond [the Dean's] seat be kept only for ladies whether there be many or few women.*
4. *That when we are present, no man presume to put on his hat at the sermon . . .*
5. *That our Chapell be all the year thoroughly kept, both morning and Evening with solemn music like a Collegiate church unless it be at such time in the summer when we are pleased to spare it . . .*
6. *That in all their places, both noblemen & others use great distance & respect to our person, as also civility one to an other, & those that are young offer not to fill up the seats from those which are either elder or more infirm or Councillors, though perhaps below them in rank.*

ACTIVITY

Study Sources 2.4, 2.5 and 2.6.

1 In what ways do Sources 2.4 and 2.5 agree about Charles's personality?
2 What did William Murray mean by his comment in Source 2.5 about the court?
3 Why, according to Source 2.6, was it so important to maintain standards of behaviour during attendance at the Chapel Royal?

■ 2C The progression of rooms at court from the entrance gate to the royal bedchamber

Access to the King was strictly regulated by the sequence of chambers at court, becoming progressively more exclusive. Only the princes of the blood or King's personal body servants attended the King in the royal bedchamber. The Presence Chamber contained the throne, which was treated with reverence even when the King was not there

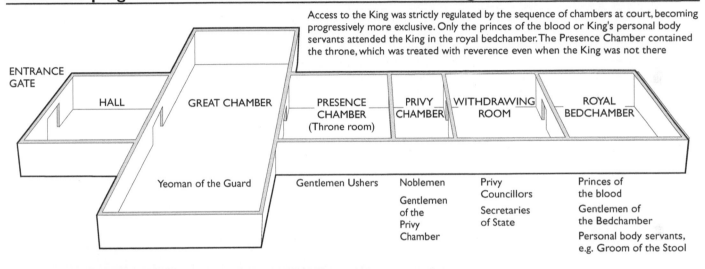

ENTRANCE GATE

| HALL | GREAT CHAMBER | PRESENCE CHAMBER (Throne room) | PRIVY CHAMBER | WITHDRAWING ROOM | ROYAL BEDCHAMBER |

Yeoman of the Guard

Gentlemen Ushers

Noblemen

Gentlemen of the Privy Chamber

Privy Councillors

Secretaries of State

Princes of the blood

Gentlemen of the Bedchamber

Personal body servants, e.g. Groom of the Stool

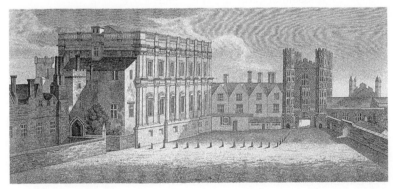

SOURCE 2.7 The Banqueting House, built by Inigo Jones in 1626, is all that is left of the palace of Whitehall, destroyed by fire in the 1690s. Charles I stepped onto the scaffold from this building in 1649

'Court versus Country'

One theory about the causes of the Civil War is that Charles's reordering of the court failed to make any impression on public opinion. According to this theory, the Personal Rule alienated the 'Country' as the 'Court' came to be seen as Catholic, exclusive, corrupt and un-English. When Charles's reign reached its crisis in 1642, the King failed to find support from many of the country gentry. Did Charles allow his court to dismiss national feeling when the absence of parliaments made it especially important to maintain this link with public opinion?

DISCUSS

1 Why might Charles's court have alienated 'country' opinion?
2 Why would the King have been unable to understand such criticism of his court?

William Prynne and *Histriomastix*

Prynne was a Puritan pamphleteer, an opponent of Arminianism and critic of stage plays. In 1632 he published a book called *Histriomastix* in which he attacked the court for its plays and masques. He referred to actresses as 'notorious whores'.

His timing was unfortunate, if deliberate. Queen Henrietta Maria was taking part in a masque at court. His reference to whores was taken as a deliberate insult to the Queen, and Prynne was hauled before the Court of Star Chamber. He was fined £5000, deprived of his Oxford degree, expelled from Lincoln's Inn, pilloried, had the tops of his ears cut off, and was sentenced to life imprisonment. In spite of these punishments, he continued to publish pamphlets from his prison cell.

FOCUS ROUTE: WHO'S WHO?

Make notes on William Prynne to include in your Who's who? list.

Court masques

One aspect of court life which drew particular criticism from Puritans was the performance of masques. A masque was a spectacular stage performance that combined elements of theatre, opera, royal pageantry, ballet and tableaux. Their subject matter was allegorical, drawn from classical mythology or ancient history. Their theme was the mystique of authority: the right to govern other people comes from self-control. England's aristocracy had power, but its authority must come from a natural quality of nobility born of self-restraint.

The stage sets for these dramatic extravaganzas stretched the technology of the day to its limits. The sets included mechanical engines which made it possible to achieve spectacular special effects. The King would cross the sky like Apollo in a fiery chariot. The Queen, supported by invisible wires, would float above the stage like an angel. At the sound of trumpets the clouds rolled back to allow the King and Queen to descend to earth, bringing peace and order to a tempestuous world.

Masques were not just lavish entertainment: they had a serious purpose, underlining royal authority and reminding courtiers of the ageless nature of authority and responsibility.

DISCUSS

1 Why did Puritans such as Prynne oppose the performance of court masques? Was it simply the fact that women were appearing on the English stage for the first time?
2 What do the punishments imposed on William Prynne for *Histriomastix* suggest about the importance of masques to the court?

ACTIVITY

If the court were supposed to communicate the ideals of order and virtue to the kingdom as a whole, then why did a gulf open up between 'Court' and 'Country' during the 1630s? How might each of the following questions help to explain this gulf?

• Did the court provoke exactly the opposite reaction to the one it was supposed to?
• Did the King care whether his people got his message or not? Was he a victim of his own propaganda?
• Was the court an effective communicator of royal values?
• Did the kingdom want the kind of order the King was offering?

FOCUS ROUTE

Return to the Focus Route on page 39. Does Charles's court provide evidence of an intention to rule the kingdom through an absolutist system? What kind of court would exist in an absolutist state?

C Did the King govern tyranically?

When Charles I decided to rule without Parliament, he thought it would be possible to rule the kingdom without the legislature to pass new laws. Several early seventeenth-century Parliaments had failed to pass any new legislation. The Crown would have to find a way of bending the existing laws to meet its needs.

■ 2D The Government of England under the Personal Rule: a blueprint for absolutism?

45

Charles's decision to rule without Parliament forced the King to fall back on his own power and that of the judges

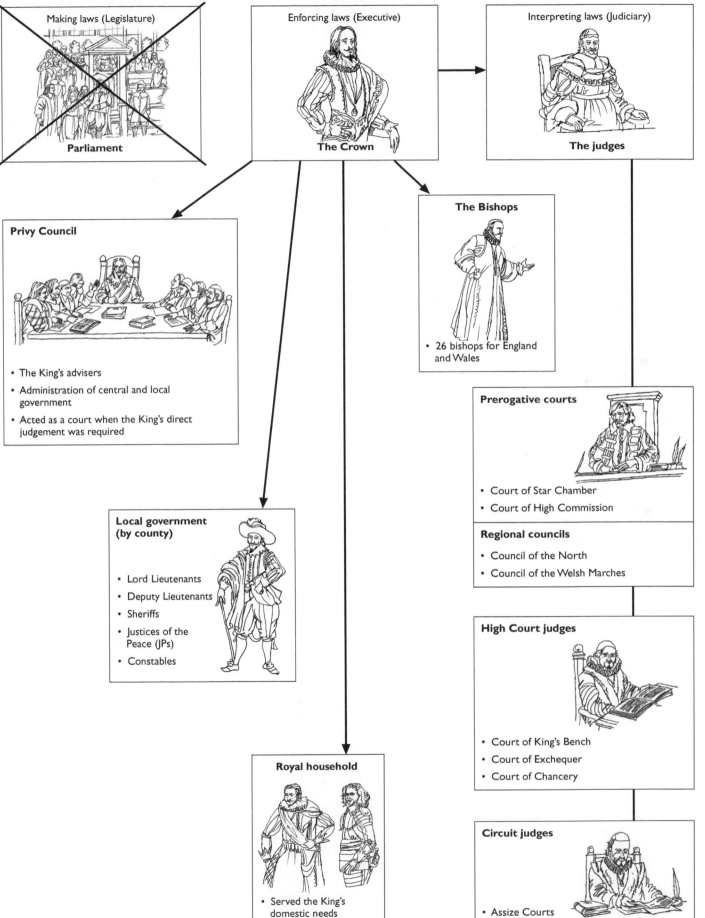

Making laws (Legislature)

Parliament

Enforcing laws (Executive)

The Crown

Interpreting laws (Judiciary)

The judges

Privy Council

- The King's advisers
- Administration of central and local government
- Acted as a court when the King's direct judgement was required

The Bishops

- 26 bishops for England and Wales

Prerogative courts

- Court of Star Chamber
- Court of High Commission

Regional councils

- Council of the North
- Council of the Welsh Marches

Local government (by county)

- Lord Lieutenants
- Deputy Lieutenants
- Sheriffs
- Justices of the Peace (JPs)
- Constables

High Court judges

- Court of King's Bench
- Court of Exchequer
- Court of Chancery

Royal household

- Served the King's domestic needs

Circuit judges

- Assize Courts

WAS CHARLES I TRYING TO ESTABLISH ROYAL ABSOLUTISM?

The King's law enforcement powers were formidable. He appointed all the judges, and could expect favourable verdicts in high-profile political cases. The Privy Council had the authority to investigate any aspect of government business, and to punish offenders. The Crown stood at the head of the local government structure, appointing in each county the Lord Lieutenants and the sheriffs. The King was the Supreme Head of the Church of England, whose courts were responsible for the enforcement of family law and for punishing offences such as adultery and non-attendance.

But there were also severe limits on royal power. JPs, juries, constables, sheriffs and churchwardens were all unpaid officials. A culture of local discretion and mediation permeated the administration of justice and government.

In the absence of Parliament the only way the Crown could 'legislate' was to ensure that the existing laws of the realm were reinterpreted to achieve, in effect, new laws. In the struggle to achieve this, two institutions stand out for having played a vital role in the Personal Rule:

1 **The prerogative courts**
   a) **The Court of Star Chamber** Consisted of members of the Privy Council hand-picked by the King. The Crown could remove cases such as conspiracy, riot or perjury from the common-law courts and have them heard in secret before the Court of Star Chamber. Unlike in the common-law courts, defendants could be questioned in private. Star Chamber could not sentence a man to death, but could inflict fines, imprisonment and corporal punishment.
   b) **The Court of High Commission** The highest ecclesiastical court in the land, which could be used for enforcing religious uniformity. Cases where the defendant was found guilty were passed to Star Chamber for sentencing. After 1633 Archbishop Laud sat on both courts, and was said to have made a point of always passing the most extreme sentence possible.

2 **The regional councils**
   a) **The Council of the North** Based in York, it was used as a prerogative court for enforcing royal policy against powerful northern families.
   b) **The Council of the Welsh Marches** Based in Ludlow, its original purpose was to protect England's border with Wales. By the seventeenth century it was less important than the Council of the North because the local English magnates were less powerful than their northern cousins.

Local government – an instrument of absolutism, or a safeguard against it?

Today, 'the government' consists of two parts: the elected politicians, who pass legislation through Parliament; and the Civil Service, which translates Parliament's decisions into action, uniformly, throughout the country. When Parliament passes a new law, the Civil Service enforces it.

England did not possess a modern civil service in the 1630s. The government relied for the implementation of royal policy on local unpaid officials to maintain the King's Peace. Keeping law and order was the main concern of such officials. Persuasion was far more effective than coercion. It had to be, when the class most affected by government initiatives was the very landowning class responsible for their enforcement. Local government was precisely that – government 'of the county, by the county, for the county' – not, as we would now understand it, the imposition of central government policy on local communities. During the 1630s, Charles I placed local government officials in a quandary by calling upon them to assist his efforts to raise money through non-parliamentary methods. Their lethargic, inefficient reaction frustrated the King.

DISCUSS

Consider the case of William Prynne (page 44). Were the prerogative courts effective in silencing opposition?

FOCUS ROUTE

Return to the main Focus Route on page 39. Use the following questions to help you complete the third section of the table.

• Why might Charles I have found the system of government he inherited from his father frustrating and inefficient?
• What measures did the King take to remedy this situation?
• Why did some people find these measures alarming?

BLAEU'S MAP OF GLOUCESTERSHIRE, 1648

Counties were divided into 'hundreds', the basic administrative unit of English local government. Within each hundred, several parish churches brought local government down to a personal level.

SHERIFFS

The King chose the sheriff, who worked with local communities to select the constables, and supervised their work. A sheriff's main task was the administration of justice, holding alleged criminals in gaol and presenting them for trial at the county assizes. The sheriff received JUDICIAL WRITS and enforced the judgements of the courts. In the 1630s sheriffs were responsible for collecting unpopular taxes such as Ship Money. Being a sheriff was a highly unpopular office.

CONSTABLES

The job of policing the hundreds fell to the constables, men with local knowledge who were answerable to the county sheriff. Constables were drawn from the local community, serving unpaid for one year at a time. They were ideally suited to upholding the common law, but poor instruments for imposing central government orders. Their loyalty was to the community they served and – in an abstract form – to the King.

JUSTICES OF THE PEACE (JPs)

The JPs formed the bedrock of the judicial system. They depended on the constables for the presentation of cases and offenders. Their main responsibility was to judge lesser criminal cases and send more serious cases for trial by jury under the supervision of the circuit judges. The Privy Council expected JPs to enforce an ever-growing list of regulations and statutes, such as supervising poor relief, regulating alehouses and maintaining roads.

JPs did not form a reliable army of royal officials in the provinces. They were local men, appointed on the advice of sheriffs and Lord Lieutenants. They served for the honour of the office and the opportunity to enhance their social standing.

JPs had the chance to belong to a wider political world, held together by the circuit judges during the half-yearly county assizes. All JPs had to attend the assize courts, where the importance of major national trials such as the Five Knights' case (1627) or the Ship Money case (1637) would have been explained to them. Charles I may have ruled without Parliament, but this did not stifle national political debate.

LORD LIEUTENANTS

The Lord-Lieutenant of the county organised local defence and, in times of national emergency, mobilised the county militias into a national army. The Deputy Lieutenants actually did the work, but were ill-equipped to train amateur militias. The Crown appointed one Lord Lieutenant for each county, choosing what the Earl of Clarendon called 'the prime gentlemen of quality' from local aristocratic families.

| JUDICIAL WRITS | Legal instructions |

FOCUS ROUTE

Was the King's financial policy intended to do away permanently with the need to call Parliament? Or was the King simply making the most of his resources? Return to the main Focus Route on page 39 as you work through this section and collect evidence in the two columns of the table.

TALKING POINT

There is in law a concept called the 'statute of limitations'. It refers to the idea that if something – usually money – is not claimed within a reasonable amount of time, the person who could claim it loses the right to do so.

• What relevance could this idea have to the search for the 'King's mines'?
• Can you think of any examples where this concept applies in modern life?

DISCUSS

1 The Venetian Ambassador clearly thought that Charles I was trying to establish absolutism in England. Why might he have regarded the King's financial policies as proof that this was what Charles intended?
2 Venice was one of the first countries to send permanent embassies to other countries. Their ambassadors regularly sent detailed reports home to their government. Venice was a Catholic republic with trading interests throughout Europe. How reliable is the Venetian Ambassador's report likely to be?

D Finance – absolutism or just good housekeeping?

SOURCE 2.8   Article 12 from Magna Carta, 1215

No scutage or aid [taxes] shall be imposed in our kingdom unless by common counsel of our kingdom ...

Magna Carta was a fundamental part of English law. Article 12 was taken to mean that the King could not raise taxes without the consent of Parliament. Tax money was classified as 'extraordinary' revenue – money collected over and above the 'ordinary' sources of the Crown's private income.

Charles needed to find a way of governing England without calling on Parliament for taxes. The Crown had to exploit its 'ordinary' revenue as efficiently as possible.

The charge against the King is that he went further than this by introducing new taxes without Parliament's consent to make the Crown permanently independent of parliamentary subsidies.

Searching for the 'King's mines'

During the Personal Rule, William Noy, the Attorney General, was given the task of searching through English history to find forgotten laws, lapsed practices and medieval precedents that could be exploited to raise income. Many of the measures used to raise money in the 1630s resulted from these efforts to search for the 'King's mines', money that had rightfully belonged to the Crown in the distant past.

SOURCE 2.9   The Venetian Ambassador's report to his government on the Ship Money case, 1637

Your Excellencies can easily understand the great consequences involved in this decision [that of the judges in favour of Ship Money], as at one stroke it roots out for ever the meeting of Parliament and renders the King absolute and sovereign. It has created such consternation and disorder that one cannot judge what the outcome will be. If the people submit to this present prejudice, they are submitting to an eternal yoke ... thus finally the goal will be reached for which the King has been labouring so long.

ACTIVITY

Study Chart 2F.

1 Which sources of income were undeniably parts of the Crown's 'ordinary' revenue?
2 Were any of these sources of income clearly illegal?
3 Overall, do you see in the King's policy an intention to do away permanently with the need to call Parliament?

Sources of income	Definition	Problems
Rents from Crown lands	Income received from rented Crown land, usually over a term of 99 years.	Inflation had eaten away at the real value of rents at fixed rates. The Crown had sold a lot of land since the 1550s.
Purveyance	The Crown's right to purchase food and other necessities at below market value. Could be paid either in kind (livestock, wheat and other produce) or by 'composition' in cash by countles.	Met with widespread resistance in the counties.
Wardship	When a landowner died leaving a child heir, the Crown had the right to administer the estate until the heir came of age.	The Crown was frequently accused of exploiting vulnerable estates.
Tonnage and Poundage	Customs duties on imports and exports. As trade revived after the wars with France and Spain, the value of customs duties rose quickly.	Had not been approved by Parliament. This issue had been a running sore with Parliament ever since 1625.
Credit	Borrowing money from the City of London and other financiers. The crown jewels were pawned in the Netherlands in the 1620s.	Lord Treasurer Sir Richard Weston and William Juxon, Bishop of London, worked hard to wean the Crown off borrowed money. Their aim was to reduce the crippling interest payments on outstanding loans.
Monopolies	Selling corporations the sole right to produce, import or sell products. Monopolies held by individuals had been illegal since 1624, but were still granted to corporations.	Led to charges of corruption at court. When the Lord Treasurer (Sir Richard Weston) procured a monopoly of soap for his friends, the product was derided as 'Popish soap'.
Distraint of Knighthood	Men owning estates worth £40 per year were, in theory, supposed to present themselves to be knighted at a new King's coronation. Charles fined people for not doing so, even though the practice had not been used for many years.	Not employed since the early Tudors. Gentlemen fined for failing to present themselves felt caught out by an outdated law. Oliver Cromwell was among the many victims.
Revival of Forest Laws	The government researched the extent of medieval royal forests for the purpose of fining landowners whose estates now encroached on the ancient boundaries.	Many landowners could not produce title deeds for land held by their families for centuries. This was a tax on population growth and land improvement that fell on the rich and powerful. The Earl of Salisbury was fined £20,000.
Fines for breaching building regulations	Ancient laws to prevent chartered towns spilling out beyond the city walls were rediscovered and used to fine property developers.	Widely seen as a way of exploiting the growth of London. Since 1603, 60,000 houses had been built outside the wall of the capital.
Enclosure fines	Fines imposed on landowners for fencing off open fields and common land for conversion from arable to pasture.	Seen by landowners as a penalty for trying to improve their estates.
Ship Money	An ancient tax levied on coastal counties and ports to build ships to protect trade from piracy. Traditionally levied on an *ad hoc* basis as needed. In 1634 the Crown made a traditional levy. In 1635 the levy was extended to the inland counties as well, on the grounds that the whole kingdom benefited from a strong navy. Further levies were imposed annually from 1636 onwards.	Ship Money provoked hostility for two reasons: • The only precedent for raising the levy from inland counties was during the Armada crisis of 1588. • There was no precedent for raising the levy as an annual, permanent tax.

FOCUS ROUTE

Does Strafford's career suggest that he was experimenting with absolutist methods that could be used in England? Return to the Focus Route on page 39 and collect evidence for and against this idea as you work through this section.

FOCUS ROUTE: WHO'S WHO?

Make notes on Sir Thomas Wentworth, later Earl of Strafford, to include in your Who's who? list.

MUSTERS

Men whose names appeared on the muster rolls were required to give up some of their time each year for military training.

E The Earl of Strafford – 'Black Tom Tyrant'?

When Parliament attacked the Personal Rule in 1641, its first target was the Earl of Strafford. Of all the King's men, he was the one they feared the most. What had Strafford done to earn Parliament's hatred?

The Earl of Strafford (1593–1641)

The picture, by Van Dyck, shows the Earl of Strafford with Sir Philip Mainwaring in 1639/40.

Strafford sat as an MP in the parliaments of 1614, 1621, 1624 and 1625, where he was a critic of the Crown. In 1626 Charles I kept him out of Parliament by appointing him Sheriff of Yorkshire. He was imprisoned in 1627 for refusing to pay the Forced Loan. In 1628 he helped to draft the Petition of Right.

In 1628 he became a loyal supporter of Charles, earning himself the nickname 'the Grand Apostate'. He was quickly rewarded: in 1629 Charles made him Lord President of the Council of the North, where he earned a reputation for strict and impartial efficiency. In 1631 he was appointed Lord Deputy of Ireland, where he carried into practice his vision of effective, authoritarian government. His enemies called him 'Black Tom Tyrant'.

'Thorough'

In their letters, Strafford and Archbishop Laud wrote about something they called 'Thorough'. The essence of Thorough was accountability, a government that looked closely at the actions of officials and held them responsible for their oversights and mistakes. They thought that Charles's problems sprang from the fact that he was not well served. If the existing structures of church and government could be made to do their jobs properly, the result would be a King in harmony with his subjects.

Thorough struck a chord with Charles. Many of his problems in the 1620s originated in the inefficiency of a local government system that relied on unpaid local officials to enforce unpopular policies. The King needed a way of making local officials fear the Crown more than they feared the disapproval of their neighbours.

The first step was the publication in 1631 of the *Book of Orders*. This was a book of instructions for sheriffs and JPs, clarifying their responsibilities and laying out a system for making all officials accountable to higher authority through regular written reports, overseen by the Privy Council. Local government was to be reformed to place it firmly under the gaze of centralised authority.

The King also set about improving the militia. The wars of the 1620s had revealed many deficiencies in the weapons and training of the county militias, and widespread resistance to the MUSTERS. Counties were ordered to maintain stores of powder and shot, improve their weapons and provide proper drill. Commissioners were appointed by the Privy Council to find out whether or not the reforms were being put into place.

The best examples of Thorough in action come from Strafford's activities, first as Lord President of the Council of the North, then as Lord Deputy of Ireland.

Strafford in the North of England

As Lord President of the Council of the North, Strafford was an efficient, ruthless servant of the Crown. He used the Council as a prerogative court to demand accountability from local officials. Strafford tried to enforce the King's Peace, impartially and strictly. It was this aspect of his government that made him so many enemies: English local government 'worked' through a kind of benign inefficiency, relying on local officials and their knowledge of individual circumstances. Accountability hardly entered into it. Strafford's administration threatened the ancient balance between central and local government, as Protestants, Catholics, knights, JPs, sheriffs and noblemen found themselves called before the Council.

Strafford frequently showed his exasperation with Charles's subjects. He thought authoritarian rule was good for the people: only through strong government could they enjoy their rights and property. The kingdom had to be coerced into order and obedience, for its own sake.

■ 2G Black Tom Tyrant?

> The authority of a king is the keystone which closeth up the arch of order and government, which contains each part in due relation to the whole and which, once shaken and informed, all the frame fall together into a confused heap.

> The welfare of the realm is the supreme law.

> If Parliament refuses to supply the King with funds in the usual way, the King must provide for the safety of the kingdom however he sees fit.

DISCUSS

Refer to Chart 2G. What did Strafford mean by these words?

PLANTATIONS

The settlement of Ireland by English and Scottish families, occupying land confiscated from Irish Catholics. This began in earnest in 1607.

Strafford in Ireland: a blueprint for absolutism in England?

Strafford had misgivings about his promotion to Lord Deputy of Ireland. Ireland was the graveyard of political reputations, a posting from which ambitious men rarely recovered. Strafford had enemies at court, and his distance from London would make it difficult to counteract them. The only way he could secure his future was to impose some sort of order on the volatile situation in Ireland.

■ 2H The three main ethnic groups of Ireland

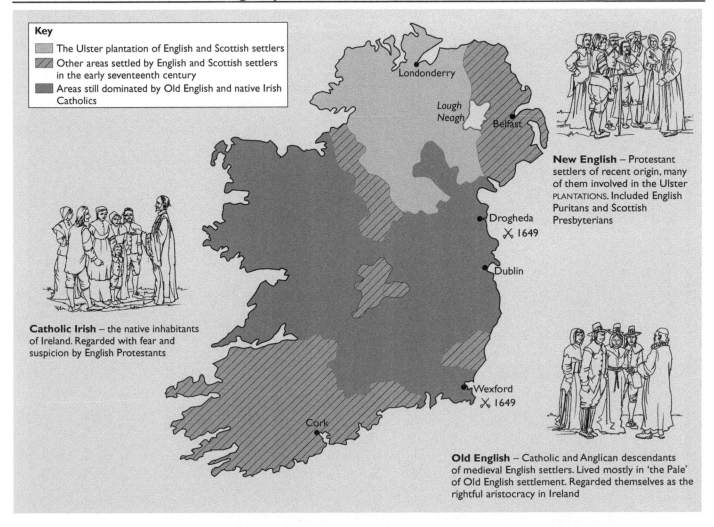

Key

- The Ulster plantation of English and Scottish settlers
- Other areas settled by English and Scottish settlers in the early seventeenth century
- Areas still dominated by Old English and native Irish Catholics

Londonderry

Lough Neagh

Belfast

Drogheda ✕ 1649

Dublin

Wexford ✕ 1649

Cork

New English – Protestant settlers of recent origin, many of them involved in the Ulster PLANTATIONS. Included English Puritans and Scottish Presbyterians

Catholic Irish – the native inhabitants of Ireland. Regarded with fear and suspicion by English Protestants

Old English – Catholic and Anglican descendants of medieval English settlers. Lived mostly in 'the Pale' of Old English settlement. Regarded themselves as the rightful aristocracy in Ireland

The situation in Ireland was dangerously complicated. Three ethnic groups existed there, with very different interests and perceptions. Because of the complexities of Irish politics, English policy in Ireland was traditionally based on 'divide and rule', allying with one ethnic group in order to govern the others.

The New English had the strongest hand in English politics. These Protestant settlers used their religion as a weapon with which to outmanoeuvre the Old English, who urged restraint in England's colonial policy. By playing the 'religion card', the New English kept English eyes focused on the Catholic threat. This enabled them to treat the Catholic Irish in the same way that English settlers in America treated the Indians – as people who had given up their rights to the land by failing to make good use of it.

Strafford refused to play the old game. He refused to be manipulated by the New English, demanding that all three ethnic groups be subservient to the Crown. Above all, he refused to allow the New English and their Puritan backers to make a profit at the Crown's expense. If Ireland were to be a worthwhile colonial venture, it was the Crown that should benefit.

■ 21 Strafford in Ireland

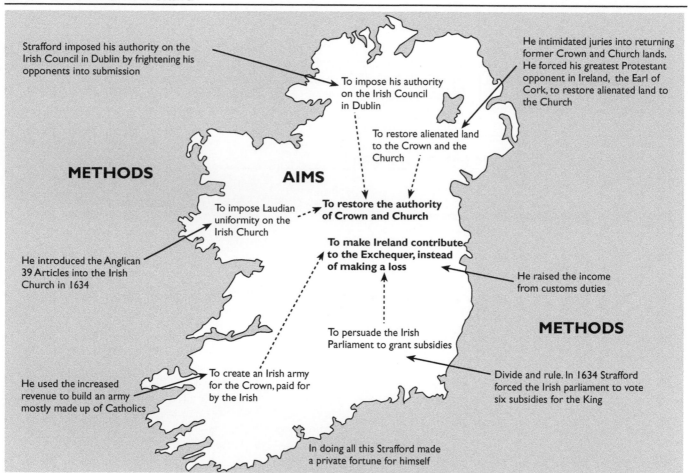

METHODS

Strafford imposed his authority on the Irish Council in Dublin by frightening his opponents into submission

He intimidated juries into returning former Crown and Church lands. He forced his greatest Protestant opponent in Ireland, the Earl of Cork, to restore alienated land to the Church

To impose his authority on the Irish Council in Dublin

To restore alienated land to the Crown and the Church

AIMS

To impose Laudian uniformity on the Irish Church

To restore the authority of Crown and Church

He introduced the Anglican 39 Articles into the Irish Church in 1634

To make Ireland contribute to the Exchequer, instead of making a loss

He raised the income from customs duties

METHODS

To persuade the Irish Parliament to grant subsidies

He used the increased revenue to build an army mostly made up of Catholics

To create an Irish army for the Crown, paid for by the Irish

Divide and rule. In 1634 Strafford forced the Irish parliament to vote six subsidies for the King

In doing all this Strafford made a private fortune for himself

SOURCE 2.10 Sir Thomas Roe to Elizabeth, Queen of Bohemia (Charles I's sister), 1634

The Lord Deputy of Ireland does great wonders, and governs like a king. He has taught that kingdom to show us an example of envy, by having parliaments, and knowing wisely how to use them, for they have given the King six subsidies. This is a great service, and to give a character of the man: he is severe abroad and in business, and sweet in private conversation; retired in his friendships, but very firm; a terrible judge, and a strong enemy; a servant violently zealous in his master's ends and not negligent of his own; one that will have what he will, and though of great reason, he can make his will greater when it may serve him, affecting glory by a seeming contempt; one that cannot stay long in the middle region of fortune, being entreprenant, but will either be the greatest man in England or much less than he is . . .

ACTIVITY

Write a letter similar to the one in Source 2.10, but as a New English settler in Londonderry writing to a Puritan friend in London. Explain your opinion of Strafford and his policies, and explain whether you think this has implications for the likely future development of government in England.

ACTIVITY

Strafford believed that all four ethnic groups in Ireland would come to recognise the inherent justice of life under an authoritarian, even-handed regime. Instead, all four groups resented his rule and were alienated by different aspects of his policies.

1 a) Make a copy of the diagram 'Wheels within wheels'.
   b) Which group(s) had England traditionally allied with to impose order on Ireland? Indicate this on your copy of the diagram.
2 a) How did Strafford's policy differ from the traditional methods used?
   b) Working outwards from the centre of the diagram, indicate which aspects of Strafford's Irish policy alienated each group.
3 Why did Strafford's short-term success in Ireland appear so dangerous to the opponents in England of Charles's Personal Rule?

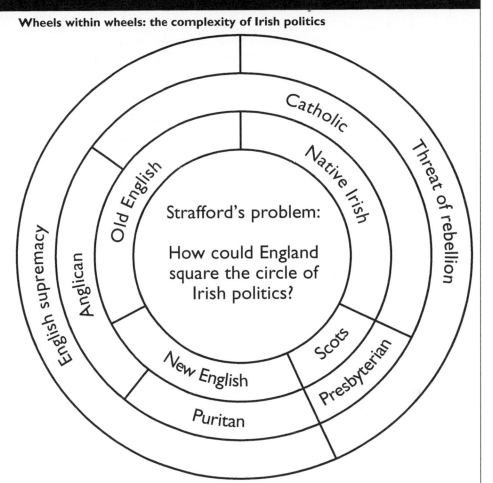

Wheels within wheels: the complexity of Irish politics

Strafford's problem:

How could England square the circle of Irish politics?

Catholic · Native Irish · Threat of rebellion · Scots · Presbyterian · Puritan · New English · English supremacy · Anglican · Old English

FOCUS ROUTE

Return to the main Focus Route on page 39. Collect evidence from this section to place in the last two columns of your table.

FOCUS ROUTE: WHO'S WHO?

Make notes on William Laud, Archbishop of Canterbury, to include in your Who's who? list.

F Did Archbishop Laud use the Church of England to develop absolutism?

The other person Parliament was determined to destroy in 1641 was the Archbishop of Canterbury, William Laud. Hatred of Laud united opposition to Charles's government even more than fear of Strafford. Even some of the King's supporters found Laud spiteful and arrogant. Laud was accused of introducing 'innovations' in the Church of England that would have restored Catholicism in all but name, and of using the Church as an instrument of absolutism.

■ 2J Promotions of William Laud

Laud enjoyed rapid promotion under Charles I:

• Dean of Gloucester (1616)
• Bishop of St David's (1621)
• Bishop of Bath and Wells (1625)
• Bishop of London (1629)
• Archbishop of Canterbury (1633)
• In the 1630s he was a Privy Councillor, sitting on both the Court of High Commission and the Court of Star Chamber.

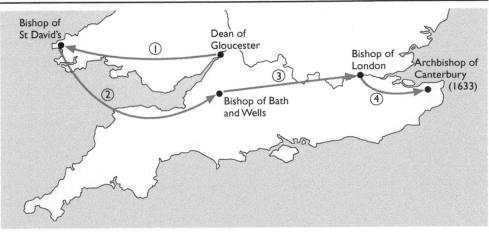

■ 2K Archbishop Laud's application of Thorough to the Church of England

IMPOSING UNIFORMITY
- Strict conformity to the *Book of Common Prayer* as required by law.
- Strict adherence to the Thirty-nine Articles and to existing ecclesiastical canons.
- 'Metropolitical Visitations' introduced; Laud or his commissioners visited every diocese to see whether the bishop was enforcing uniformity.
- Priests to wear vestments, to bow at the name of Jesus, and to light candles on the altar.
- Clergy who refused to conform were disciplined, suspended or deprived of their livings.
- Altars to be placed at the east end of the chancel, not used as Communion tables in the nave.
- Altar rails to separate the altar from the rest of the church, creating a sacred area in which only the priest was allowed.
- Church services to be performed at the east end, with greater emphasis on ceremonial and ritual.

DESTROYING PURITANISM
- Laud used the Courts of High Commission and Star Chamber to prosecute Puritan critics of the Church. In 1630 Alexander Leighton was fined, pilloried, lashed, had his ears cut off, his nose slit and his cheeks branded for attacking the bishops in 'Sion's Plea Against the Prelacy'. The punishment of William Prynne in 1634 was part of this campaign.
- In 1637 Prynne, Bastwick and Burton were punished for further attacks on the Church. (See Chapter 3.)
- In 1633 the Court of Exchequer ordered the dissolution of the Feoffees for Impropriations, an organisation of wealthy Puritans which tried to bestow benefices on Puritan preachers. Its assets were confiscated by the Crown.
- Hostile books and pamphlets were censored.
- Town corporations and individuals who appointed Puritan lecturers to give street sermons were prosecuted.

SOURCE 2.11 Archbishop Laud, by Van Dyck, 1635

RESTORING THE FABRIC OF THE CHURCH
- Many churches were dilapidated after years of neglect. Common problems included lead stolen from roofs; animals wandering freely into churches; churches used as markets, pigsties and stables.
- St Paul's Cathedral was of particular concern. One man caught going to the toilet in St Paul's argued that he did not realise he was in a church. In 1633 the King launched a special levy for the restoration of St Paul's. Records were kept of those who did not pay.
- Laud tried to address the fundamental economic reasons for the impoverishment of the Church and the clergy: since the Reformation, tithes were paid to the gentry instead of the clergy in many parishes. This provoked hostility from some landowners who accused Laud of threatening their property.
- Bishops and priests were instructed to live in their sees and benefices.

USING THE CHURCH'S AUTHORITY TO REINFORCE THE DIVINE RIGHT OF KINGS
- Laud encouraged the clergy to preach sermons supporting the divine nature of royal authority.
- Bishops were given prominent places in Charles's government. In 1635 Bishop Juxon of London became Lord Treasurer.

■ Learning trouble spot

Tithes, lay impropriations and advowsons

Students are often confused by tithes and the related problem of how ministers were appointed to parish churches. Until the Reformation, tithes were paid to the Catholic Church. Tithes were a tax of one-tenth of a person's income, collected for the purpose of paying the parish priest. In some parishes the tithes had been appropriated by a monastery, which appointed a vicar to perform the duties of the parish priest in return for a proportion of the tithe.

During the Reformation, tithes that had been in monastic hands were impropriated or transferred to laymen – perhaps as much as two-thirds of all tithe revenue. As local gentry purchased land confiscated from the monasteries, these lay impropriations brought with them advowsons, the right to present a nominee to be the vicar of the parish.

The sudden expansion of lay patronage over the clergy gave the gentry considerable power over the Church. This was one of the biggest obstacles to Laud's attempts to enforce uniformity of worship: however much the bishops might try to enforce the ecclesiastical canons, they were not responsible for the appointment of many of the ministers in their dioceses. The fact that tithes were now a form of property payable to the gentry made for one of the greatest problems facing the English church in the seventeenth century.

DISCUSS

The Parliament of 1628 attempted to impeach Manwaring for his sermon (Source 2.12). Why did the MPs take exception to what he said?

SOURCE 2.12 Extract taken from Roger Manwaring's sermon preached before the King at Oatlands, 4 July 1627. Manwaring was an Arminian clergyman who was promoted to a bishopric by Laud

Among all the powers that be ordained of God the regal is most high, strong and large: kings [are] above all, inferior to none, to no multitudes of men, to no Angels, to no order of Angels. All the significations of a royal pleasure are, and ought to be, to all loyal subjects in the nature and force of a command.

Nay, though any king in the world should command flatly against the law of God, yet were his power no otherwise at all to be resisted but for the not doing of his will, in that which is clearly unlawful, [and] to endure with patience, whatsoever penalty his pleasure should inflict upon them. By which patient and meek suffering of their sovereign's pleasure they should become glorious martyrs, whereas by resisting of his will they should for ever endure the pain and stain of odious traitors and impious malefactors.

ACTIVITY

More than any other issue, religion played a vital role in arousing opposition to Charles's Personal Rule in the 1630s.

1 Some Puritans found Laud's government of the Church so unacceptable that they emigrated to New England. Why?
2 Both Laud and his critics accused each other of trying to introduce 'innovations' into the Church of England. Both sides were claiming to defend the Elizabethan Settlement from such innovations. Why was it possible for both sides to make a plausible claim to be doing this?

Review: was Charles I trying to establish royal absolutism?

ACTIVITY

What if Charles I had been put on trial in 1640? In 1641 Parliament stated in the 'Grand Remonstrance' (see Chapter 4):

The root of all this mischief we find to be a malignant and pernicious design of subverting the fundamental laws and principles of government.

Was this a fair accusation? Work in two groups to prepare the cases for and against the King, under the following headings:

• The King's image
• The court
• The government of the realm
• Finance
• Thomas Strafford, Ireland and Thorough
• Archbishop Laud and the Church of England.

Discuss your findings.

ACTIVITY

Choose from one of the following essay titles:

a) To what extent does Charles's Personal Rule reveal a plan to 'uphold in himself an unlimited and tyrannical power to rule according to his will'?
b) Discuss the view that many of the reforms Charles implemented in the 1630s were necessary if England were to remain a powerful and competitive state.

Was Charles I trying to establish royal absolutism?

1 Controversy surrounds Charles I's decision to introduce Personal Rule in 1629. It is not clear from what he said whether he ever intended to call another Parliament or not. We therefore have to base our conclusions on what he actually did during the 1630s.

2 Charles used painting, architecture, music, theatre and the Church to create an image of the monarchy that would support belief in the Divine Right of Kings. However, most of the paintings of himself and his family were never publicised, being kept in royal palaces, and the masques were performed only in front of a limited audience at court.

3 In order to govern without Parliament, Charles fell back on the judiciary to reinterpret the law to his advantage. He was aided in this by his use of prerogative courts, which could appropriate cases from the common-law courts.

4 In order to finance his government without Parliament, Charles employed ministers to search back through ancient records for sources of income that had fallen into disuse. Some of these sources were of doubtful legality.

5 The most important of these, and the most controversial, was Ship Money.

6 Strafford demonstrated how effective the King's government could be, first in the North of England and then in Ireland. He believed in Thorough government.

7 William Laud, whom Charles appointed Archbishop of Canterbury in 1633, agreed with Strafford's approach to government, and tried to apply Thorough to the Church of England. His critics accused him of being a crypto-Catholic. During the 1630s many Puritans sold up and moved to New England to escape religious persecution.

8 Charles's government appears to have lost the support of many people who ought to have been the Crown's natural allies, particularly among the gentry and great landowners. Charles felt the loss of their support keenly when his government reached a crisis in the early 1640s.

Why did the King abandon the Personal Rule in 1640?

CHAPTER OVERVIEW

SOURCE 3.1   Edward Hyde, Earl of Clarendon, *The History of the Rebellion and Civil Wars in England*, written during the Civil Wars and published in 1702

[Between 1629 and 1641] this kingdom, and all his Majesty's dominions enjoyed the greatest calm and the fullest measure of felicity that any people in any age for so long a time together have been blessed with; to the wonder and envy of all the parts of Christendom.

In 1637 England was still a 'country in working order'. And so it appeared to Clarendon, looking back from the mid-1640s when he began writing his history of the Great Rebellion. His passage describing England under the Personal Rule gives no hint that the country was on the brink of disaster.

By 1640 the situation was very different. England had lost a war with Scotland. The King's policies were in ruins. In April the King called Parliament to help him out of his predicament. Parliament launched a blistering attack on his government, and Charles dissolved the so-called Short Parliament after only three weeks. Six months later he was forced to accept that the kingdom could no longer be governed without Parliament's help, and the LONG PARLIAMENT began.

> **LONG PARLIAMENT**
> The Parliament which sat from November 1640 until 1653. After Pride's Purge in 1648 it was known as the Rump. Expelled by Oliver Cromwell in 1653, it returned briefly in 1659 and again in 1660 to help in the restoration of the king.

Did he fall or was he pushed?

This chapter focuses on the many possible explanations for the sudden failure of the Personal Rule. Your task is to weigh the importance of the various factors that contributed to this collapse. At the end of the chapter you will write an essay on the collapse of the Personal Rule. To help you to answer it, here are two theories (see Focus Route), around which to build your evidence.

FOCUS ROUTE

Find evidence to support each of the following theories.

Theory 1 The Personal Rule collapsed from within. Charles's government was opposed by so many people in England that it was doomed to fail.	**Theory 2** The Personal Rule was destroyed from without. Only some external agency could have forced Charles to end it. This was provided by the war with Scotland.
1 Why was there opposition to the Personal Rule? 2 How widespread was this opposition? 3 Could the Personal Rule have been sustained indefinitely had England not got involved in a war?	1 Why did war break out between England and Scotland in 1638? 2 Why did the English army perform so badly against the Scots? 3 How important was the war with Scotland in bringing the Personal Rule in England to an end?

■ 3A Timeline of the ending of the Personal Rule, 1637–40

1637	
June	Prynne, Bastwick and Burton branded, mutilated and imprisoned for publishing pamphlets attacking bishops
July	Riots in Edinburgh against the introduction of the English Prayer Book
November	Trial of John Hampden for refusing to pay Ship Money
	Elections to a Scottish National Assembly

1638	
February	Scottish National Covenant
November	Scottish Assembly abolishes episcopal church government in Scotland
	Charles decides to send an English army to Scotland

1639	
	First Anglo-Scottish Bishops' War
	Lord Saye and Sele and Lord Brooke briefly imprisoned for refusing to take an oath of loyalty to the King
June	First Bishops' War ended by the Pacification of Berwick
September	Strafford returns from Ireland and advises Charles to recall Parliament

1640	
April–May	The Short Parliament
	New ecclesiastical canons issued by a Convocation of the Church of England
August	Second Anglo-Scottish Bishops' War
	Battle of Newburn
	Scottish army captures Newcastle, cutting off London's coal supplies
	Assembly of Peers advises the King to recall Parliament
October	Second Bishops' War ended by the Treaty of Ripon
November	Long Parliament begins

Chapter 3 sets out to investigate the two theories introduced in the Focus Route on page 57. Section A explores opposition to the Personal Rule in England. Sections B–F explore the impact of events in Scotland.

A How strong was opposition to the Personal Rule in England? (pp. 58–64)

B The British problem (pp. 64–66)

C The Prayer Book Rebellion in Scotland (pp. 67–68)

D Why did Charles I lose the First Bishops' War? (pp. 69–72)

E The Short Parliament – why did the King dissolve it within three weeks? (pp. 73–74)

F The Long Parliament – why did the King call another Parliament in November 1640? (pp. 74–77)

G Review: why did the King abandon the Personal Rule in 1640? (p. 77)

A How strong was opposition to the Personal Rule in England?

When Parliament met in 1640 it launched an all-out attack on the Personal Rule. The strength of this opposition suggests that the Personal Rule was very unpopular in England. It is more difficult to find evidence of this unpopularity from the 1630s, but there is evidence to show that the King's government was encountering opposition, some of which was well organised.

The Puritan network

By 1641 Charles I believed he faced a conspiracy. Leading Puritans linked by family connections and business partnerships had formed a network of potential opposition as early as 1630. Membership of this network reads like a roll-call of the 'GODLY PARTY', made up of merchant adventurers, lords, gentry and lawyers. In the absence of Parliament this group formed the core of political opposition to Charles, using meetings of two colonial ventures – the Providence Island Company and the Saybrooke Venture (companies formed to encourage colonisation and trade in the New World) – as a forum for secret political discussions. No written records of their meetings were kept.

'GODLY PARTY'
Politically active Puritans.

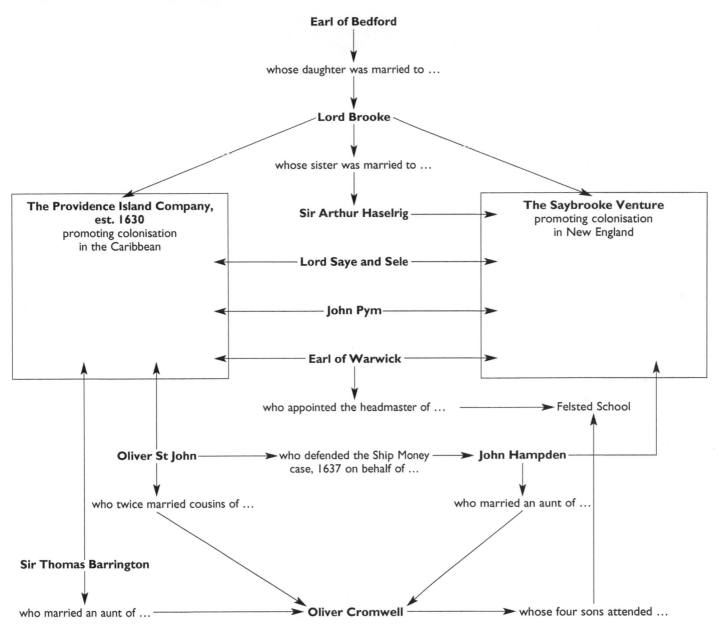

Nowhere else in England does opposition to the Personal Rule appear to have been as well organised. Other potential centres of opposition – the universities of Oxford and Cambridge, or the Inns of Court – depended on royal patronage, and were too large and too public to have openly criticised the King. Many individuals from these institutions, however, opposed aspects of Charles's government.

FOCUS ROUTE

As you work through the rest of Sections 1 and 2, make notes on the following members of the Puritan network. Build up a Royalist police file on the 'godly' party and their role in the events of 1637–49.

- Lord Saye and Sele
- John Pym (died 1643)
- Oliver St John
- John Hampden (died 1643)
- Sir Arthur Haselrig
- Oliver Cromwell

SOURCE 3.2 Broughton Castle, near Banbury, Oxfordshire, the home of William Fiennes, Viscount Saye and Sele, 1582–1662. Lord Saye and Sele was a leading member of the Puritan network. His home was used for gatherings of the Providence Island Company. The meetings were held in a small room at the top of the left-hand tower

The trial of Prynne, Bastwick and Burton, 1637

In 1637 William Prynne found himself again before the Court of Star Chamber, along with other leading Puritans John Bastwick and Henry Burton, accused of attacking the bishops. From prison Prynne had continued to publish anti-episcopal pamphlets such as *Newes from Ipswich*. What remained of Prynne's ears was cut off and his cheeks were branded with the letters SL for 'seditious libeller'. Bastwick and Burton received similar treatment, being mutilated, pilloried and imprisoned.

Their sentences aroused widespread horror that punishments usually given to common criminals should be inflicted on gentlemen, and they quickly assumed the status of martyrs in the anti-Laudian cause. Prynne claimed the letters SL stood for 'stigmata Laudis' (the stigmata were the wounds of Christ). The King ordered that the three men should be dispersed to distant prisons to avoid public disturbances.

SOURCE 3.3 A Puritan woodcut circulated after the second trial of William Prynne, 1637

On a large sheet of paper, copy the following source interrogation matrix, placing a photocopy of Source 3.3 in the central rectangle. Working in pairs, answer the questions as fully as possible, working outwards from the centre.

What other questions do I need to ask?

What does this source not tell me?

What can I infer from this source?

What information does this source give me?

A copy of the source you are interrogating goes here. Working out from the centre, answer the questions in as much detail as possible.

The Ship Money trial, 1637

Opposition to Ship Money had been building since 1635 as opponents of Charles's financial measures searched for a case with which to test its legality in the courts. They found one in John Hampden, a highly respected gentleman, whose resistance was encouraged by Lord Saye and Sele. Hampden's trial focused attention on the issue of non-parliamentary taxation.

Hampden's case was heard before the Exchequer Court, consisting of twelve judges. The trial aroused enormous public interest. Before the case came to trial, county sheriffs reported a much slower response to the tax as people awaited the verdict, though it picked up again once the trial was over. Since Hampden did not deny refusing to pay the tax, the Crown's case rested on two assertions:

1 that the King had the right to command his subjects to pay Ship Money when the kingdom was in danger
2 that the King was 'the sole judge both of the danger, and when and how the same is to be prevented and avoided'.

The King's argument was the same one that he had used for the Forced Loan in 1626; the kingdom faced a national emergency (the threat of invasion), and it was the King's right and duty to provide for its security, with or without Parliament's consent. In 1626, though, the country had been at war. In 1637 it wasn't, so the King had to argue that national security was threatened by the Navy's unpreparedness. Building ships, the Crown argued, takes a long time. If war were to break out, it would be too late to start a shipbuilding programme; the ships had to be built before the crisis became serious.

John Hampden, 1594–1643

John Hampden was born into a wealthy Buckinghamshire family with a long history of royal service as courtiers, Members of Parliament and sheriffs. In 1609 he entered Magdalen College, Oxford, and in 1613 he went to the Inner Temple to study law. He was an MP in the Parliament of 1621 where he became a close friend of Sir John Eliot (see page 35). In 1626 he was imprisoned briefly for refusing to pay the Forced Loan. He was therefore closely connected with some of the leading parliamentary opponents of Charles I's government.

In 1635 he came to prominence as the leading opponent of Ship Money, refusing to pay his assessment of 20 shillings. The Ship Money trial in 1637 was an event of national importance. Although he narrowly lost the case, the trial turned him into a leading public figure. He played a major role in both the Short and Long Parliaments. In January 1642 he was one of the Five Members that Charles I tried to arrest for treason.

When war broke out in 1642, Hampden raised his own regiment of foot soldiers for Parliament. He served on Parliament's Committee of Safety where he advocated an aggressive military strategy. In June 1643 he was mortally wounded in the Battle of Chalgrove Field. His death was a great blow to the Parliamentary cause.

Hampden's defence lawyer was Oliver St John. St John did not deny the King's right to levy taxes without Parliament in an emergency. He argued instead that England was not at war, and that the Ship Money writs gave the King's subjects seven months in which to pay the tax – plenty of time to call Parliament. He also used the trial as an opportunity to explain the role played in English government by Parliament and the law courts.

SOURCE 3.4 Extract from Oliver St John's defence of John Hampden in the Ship Money trial, 1637

His Majesty is the fountain of justice; and though all justice which is done within the realm flows from this fountain, yet it must run in certain and known channels. And as without the assistance of his Judges, who are his settled counsel at law, His Majesty applies not the law and justice in many cases unto his subjects; so likewise in other cases: neither is this sufficient to do it without the assistance of his great Council in Parliament neither can he out of Parliament alter the old laws, nor make new . . . and yet is the Parliament His Majesty's Court too. It is His Majesty that gives life and being to [Parliament], for he alone summons, continues, and dissolves it and after the dissolution of it, by supporting his Courts of Justice, he keeps them still alive . . .

The verdict of the court was sensational. The Crown won, but five of the judges ruled in favour of Hampden. Dozens of petitions against Ship Money were presented to the Privy Council, leading in 1639/40 to a 'tax revolt'. This was not a violent uprising, but took the form of non-cooperation and foot-dragging both by those who had to pay it and, more worryingly, by many of the county officials who had to collect it.

SOURCE 3.5 The Venetian Ambassador's report on resistance to Ship Money, 1637

The Earl of Warwick made no bones of telling the King frankly that his tenants were all old and accustomed to the mild rule of Queen Elizabeth and King James. They would consider their fault too grave if they died under the stigma of having, at the end of their lives, signed away the liberties of the realm, and of their free will deprived their posterity of those benefits which had been left to them uncontaminated as a sacred treasure by their ancestors. For his own part he was as ready as anyone to sacrifice his blood as well as his goods for his Majesty, but he did not know how he could use force against his people.

■ 3C The collection of Ship Money, 1635–39

Year tax collected	Amount of tax imposed	Amount of tax collected	% of tax imposed that was collected	Speed with which tax was paid
1635	£218,500	£213,964	98	Very quickly
1636	£196,400	£189,493	96	More slowly
1637*	£196,413	£178,599	91	Very slowly
1638	£69,750**	£55,690	80	Slowly
1639	£210,400	£53,000	25	Slowly

* Year of the Ship Money trial
** Low figure probably caused by the outbreak of war with Scotland, and the King's expectation that other charges (for example Coat and Conduct Money) would be payable

ACTIVITY

Study Source 3.4.

1 According to Oliver St John, what was the main purpose of a court of law such as the Exchequer Court in which John Hampden was being tried?

Study Source 3.5.

2 What reasons did the Earl of Warwick's tenants give for refusing to pay Ship Money?
3 How useful is this source as evidence of widespread resistance to Ship Money?

Study Chart 3C.

4 How would you explain the apparent willingness of the country to pay Ship Money in 1635?
5 Do these statistics suggest that the late 1630s witnessed a collapse of the government's credibility? Or do they suggest that much of the country complied with Ship Money?

Other causes of opposition

An important theme of the Personal Rule is the way it alienated people who ought to have been the King's natural supporters. How and why did the Personal Rule drive moderate Englishmen from all walks of life into opposition to the King's government?

ACTIVITY

How did the Personal Rule alienate the King's natural supporters?
Match the groups of people and the reasons with the policies that alienated people from the King's government.

Policies
• Revival of Forest Laws
• Distraint of Knighthood
• Monopolies
• Abolition of Feoffees for Impropriations
• Use of prerogative courts
• Ship Money

People antagonised
• Puritans
• University-trained teachers
• Sheriffs and JPs
• County gentry
• Common lawyers
• County gentry
• Common people
• Aristocracy
• Merchants and common people

Reasons
• Led to higher prices for necessities such as soap and salt
• Undermined attempts to improve the quality of parish clergy and to bring God's Word to all people
• Placed in an awkward position, being expected to force their friends and neighbours to pay an unpopular – and arguably illegal – tax
• Insisted that the King had to rule within the existing law of the land
• The greatest landowners were most likely to have unwittingly encroached on medieval forests and to be liable for fines
• Gentlemen with enough income to qualify were specifically targeted
• Stifled competition and removed opportunities for profit

DISCUSS

Compare Sources 3.6 and 3.7. What do these two churches tell us about the different religious attitudes and beliefs of Archbishop Laud and the Puritans?

FOCUS ROUTE

Return to Theory 1 in the Focus Route on page 57. What evidence can you find in pages 58–64 that can be used to support this theory?

The altar controversies

One form of evidence about opposition to the Personal Rule comes from reactions to Laud's instructions that, in churches, the Communion table should be railed off at the east end of the chancel like an altar (see Chapter 1). In the reigns of Elizabeth I and James I, parishes had been left to decide how their Communion table should be used. In many parishes it had been placed among the worshippers in front of the pulpit.

The King wanted the table placed in the 'highest' part of the church and Holy Communion to be given at the altar rails. To the Puritan mind this was unacceptable, as it encouraged the congregation to worship the altar itself, a graven image forbidden by the Ten Commandments. The process of breaking Puritan resistance began at St Gregory's Church, near St Paul's Cathedral, in 1634.

Victory for the King at St Gregory's did not put an end to the altar controversies. At many churches, for example at Beckington, Somerset, resistance continued until the full weight of episcopal power forced compliance. William Pierce, the Bishop of Bath and Wells, ordered churches throughout his diocese to follow the example of St Gregory's. The churchwardens at Beckington refused to comply, and were excommunicated by the Bishop's court. After an unsuccessful appeal to the COURT OF ARCHES, they naively petitioned Archbishop Laud, who threw them in jail. They finally gave in, and Beckington submitted to uniformity.

SOURCE 3.6 King Charles and Archbishop Laud wanted an altar like this one, at Blisland, Devon, placed at the east end of every church. This was the 'beauty of holiness'

SOURCE 3.7 Puritans wanted the church organised around a Communion table, like this one at Hailes Church, Gloucestershire

B   The British problem

The alternative theory says that the Personal Rule was brought down by events *outside* England. Charles ruled three kingdoms with different religions, institutions, cultures and interests. The origin of the crisis of 1640 is therefore to be found in the English colonisation of Ireland, the succession of the Stuarts to the English throne, and in Charles's religious policy towards Scotland.

The year 1603 is significant, as it marks the Stuart succession and the beginning of the colonisation of Ulster by English and Scottish Protestants. The situation that Charles I inherited in 1625 was unstable. How could the King persecute subjects in one of his kingdoms for religious practices that were legal in one of the other two? Between 1637 and 1642 there was a billiard-ball effect (see Chart 3E), with crises in the outlying kingdoms having a profound, and eventually disastrous, effect in England itself.

SOURCE 3.8 'Charles I in three positions', by Van Dyck

IRELAND

Mainly Catholic. In Ireland the English were trying to impose order on the Catholic native Irish, Catholic Old English and Calvinist New English (including many Presbyterian Scots). The Irish Privy Council and Parliament were answerable to the English Privy Council. The Lord Deputy of Ireland ruled like a viceroy in the name of the King of England.

ENGLAND

Mainly Anglican, with large numbers of Catholics in the North and Midlands. Many Puritans within the established church, particularly in East Anglia, Somerset and Lincolnshire. England was the dominant power in the British Isles, but was weak compared to Spain and France. The Stuarts wanted to unite their kingdoms and impose Anglican unity on them.

SCOTLAND

Lowland Scotland fiercely PRESBYTERIAN. Highlands and islands mainly Catholic. Scotland was an independent country, with its own Privy Council and Parliament. Since the late sixteenth century the lowland Scottish lords had become used to running their own affairs, a result of the fall of Mary Queen of Scots and the Stuart succession to the English throne. Strongly Calvinist, many Scots hoped to convert England to Presbyterianism.

PRESBYTERIAN
The form of Calvinist church government based on a series of representative councils called presbyteries or synods.

ACTIVITY

You are members of the English Privy Council in 1633. You have been asked by the King for advice about how to govern his Majesty's three kingdoms. He wants to know whether government policy should be:

   a) to continue to govern his three kingdoms separately, with different religions and institutions; or

   b) to bring all three kingdoms into uniformity, thereby ending the diversity of religions and institutions.

1 After discussing the possible risks inherent in both policies, write a memo to the King outlining these risks and recommending a policy.
2 If you find it difficult to proceed, draw up a list of questions you would like answered before you reach your conclusions.
3 Having found the answers to these questions, proceed with your recommendations.

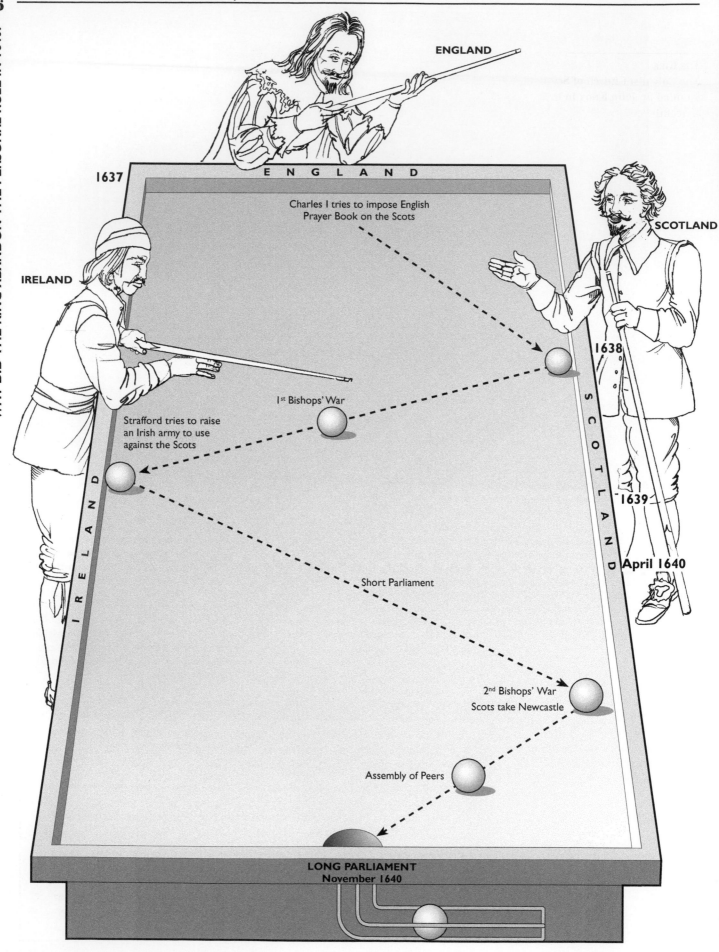

ENGLAND

1637

E N G L A N D

IRELAND

SCOTLAND

Charles I tries to impose English
Prayer Book on the Scots

1638

S C O T L A N D

1st Bishops' War

Strafford tries to raise
an Irish army to use
against the Scots

1639

I R E L A N D

April 1640

Short Parliament

2nd Bishops' War
Scots take Newcastle

Assembly of Peers

LONG PARLIAMENT
November 1640

C The Prayer Book Rebellion in Scotland

THE KIRK
The Calvinist Church of Scotland founded by John Knox in the sixteenth century.

Charles upset the Scottish nobles in 1625 by announcing his intention to revoke all gifts of land by the Crown and the KIRK made since 1540. This was simply a device to enable him to acquire their tithes in exchange for confirming their possession of the land, but the way it was done – without reference even to the Scottish Privy Council – provoked resentment.

In 1633 Charles made his first visit to Scotland, and was crowned King in Edinburgh. The visit highlighted the differences between Charles's religious practices and those of most of his Scottish subjects. Charles was appalled by the Presbyterians' lack of ceremony and unscripted prayers. The Scots were shocked by the mitres and surplices worn by the bishops during the coronation, and ridiculed the Anglican liturgy's 'praying-by-numbers' approach. As a result, Charles decided to bring Scotland's religious practice into line with England's. A new Prayer Book was to be used throughout Scotland from July 1637.

Charles's decision was taken without the advice of the Scottish Privy Council, the Scottish Parliament, or the General Assembly of the Kirk. By imposing the Prayer Book by proclamation, the King aroused Scottish nationalism at the very moment he needed support for a deeply unpopular religious policy. As in England, he alienated many of the people who should have been his natural supporters.

Some of Scotland's bishops tried to prevent catastrophe by persuading Charles to modify the Prayer Book. The King undermined their efforts. In 1635 a new set of ecclesiastical canons (church laws) required the Scottish clergy to swear to enforce the new liturgy before it was even published. Their credibility with the public had already been damaged when the King appointed several bishops to the Scottish Privy Council, for which there was no precedent. Yet even now the King refused to accept that he was asking the Scots to accept 'innovations'.

On 23 July 1637 a riot broke out in St Giles' Cathedral, Edinburgh, when Dean Hannah tried to read the service from the new liturgy. A woman named Jenny Geddes threw her stool at the Dean, who was pelted with 'cricketts, stooles, stickes and stones' in a carefully planned demonstration of popular outrage. The new Prayer Book provoked so much violence that the Bishop of Brechin threatened his congregation with two loaded pistols while he read the new service.

The political reaction in Scotland was swift and effective. An emergency body known as 'The Tables' was formed to organise opposition. In February 1638 they drew up the NATIONAL COVENANT. More was to follow. In November 1638 the General Assembly of the Kirk abolished Scotland's bishops completely. Charles had provoked a national rebellion that swept away in sixteen months the years of painstaking work that James I had put into securing a role for bishops in Scotland.

Some time in 1638 Charles decided to use force. Concessions announced in September 1638 were little more than a ploy to buy time in which to prepare his English army for an expedition to Scotland. Any hope that he could intimidate the Scots was dashed by the news that they, too, were preparing for war.

THE NATIONAL COVENANT
A declaration of allegiance that bound together Scottish nationalism and the Calvinist faith. Those who took it, the Covenanters, were taking a sacred religious and patriotic pledge to defend the true religion and Scotland's political rights. It contained the Confession of Faith of 1580 (an affirmation of Calvinist doctrine) and the 'Negative Confession' of 1581 (a condemnation of Catholicism and the Papacy that had become a test for public office). It also condemned the ecclesiastical canons of 1635 and the Prayer Book.

THE WIDER PICTURE

The drive towards uniformity in Scotland was not an isolated event. Since 1626 there had been a campaign to put an end to religious diversity among Charles's subjects. English communities abroad, for example the Merchant Adventurers in the Netherlands, English and Scottish regiments in the service of the Dutch, and English communities in the Channel Islands and New England, had already been ordered to conform to Anglican practice. In 1634 Strafford introduced the Thirty-nine Articles into Ireland. The Scottish Prayer Book was part of a wider policy aimed at tidying up the chaotic legacy of the Reformation in the British Isles.

The Arch-Prelate of St Andrewes in Scotland reading the new Service-booke in his pontificalibus asaulted by men & women, with Crickets stooles Stickes and Stones.

SOURCE 3.9   The tumult in St Giles's Cathedral, Edinburgh, 23 July 1637

■ 3F Timeline of events in Scotland, 1633–39

1633	Charles's first visit to Scotland. Coronation in Edinburgh Charles decides to introduce an English-style Prayer Book for Scotland
1635	Archbishop Spottiswoode appointed Chancellor of Scotland – evidence of the growing importance of bishops in the civil administration of Scotland New canon laws introduced which threaten to excommunicate anyone who objects to the new Prayer Book (this had not yet been written)
1637 **July** **23 July** **November**	New Prayer Book introduced throughout Scotland Riot in St Giles' Cathedral, Edinburgh Formation of The Tables, an emergency government chosen from the Scottish Parliament
1638 **February** **September** **November**	Scottish National Covenant Charles suspended the new Prayer Book and the 1635 canons General Assembly of the Kirk General Assembly bans the Prayer Book and 1635 canons Bishops excommunicated
1639 **March** **June**	Scottish General David Leslie seizes Edinburgh Castle English army invades Scotland First Bishops' War

D Why did Charles I lose the First Bishops' War?

What happened?

In 1639 the King believed that his English army would quickly overcome Scottish resistance. The Scots had not won a war with England since 1314. Nothing in the recent history of relations between the two countries suggested that the Scots could win a war with England.

The King did not expect to have to fight a real war. The Duke of Hamilton would take the English fleet into the Firth of Forth, cutting off Edinburgh from the Highlands. The English army would assemble at York before invading Scotland. The Scots were expected to desert rather than face their King in battle, paving the way for a negotiated settlement and the arrest of the leading Covenanters. To prepare for the campaign, Charles appointed the Earl of Arundel Captain-General of the army, supported by the Earl of Essex. He then angered them both by giving Lord Holland independent command of the cavalry.

SOURCE 3.10 'The Portraiture of the Mighty Monarch Charles', by Wenceslaus Hollar, 1639. This picture was made when Charles was preparing to march north against the Scots

DISCUSS

How does this picture (Source 3.10) express the confidence felt at court that the King had overwhelming force on his side?

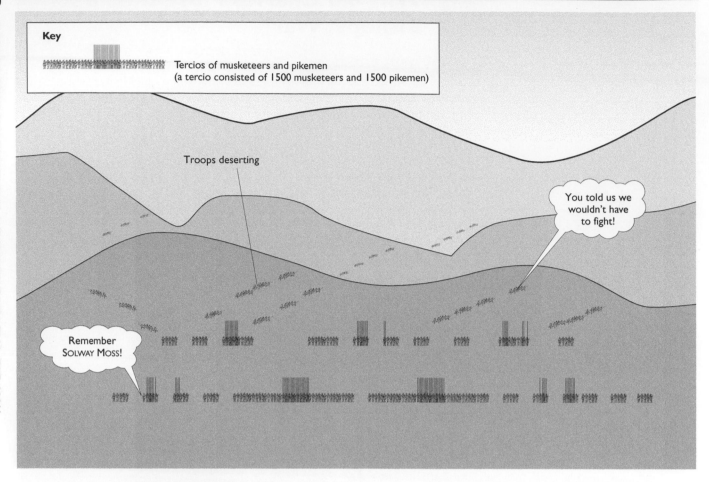

SOLWAY MOSS
The battle in 1542 in which an invading English army soundly defeated the Scots.

DISCUSS

'Rebel' is a derogatory word. How might the Scots have described themselves?

This was not a straight fight between England and Scotland. Charles I was King of both, and had Scottish advisers with him in London. The King was counting on support from within Scotland, a party that would come into the open when he arrived in force and to which he could hand over power once the war was over. Charles expected victory to strengthen his position in England, driving home the futility of resistance to his programme of reform. The English opponents of the Personal Rule watched the approach of war with alarm. Some went further than this; leading members of the Puritan network began secret negotiations with the Scottish rebels.

Charles used the war to embarrass his opponents amongst the English peerage. From York he called upon all the English lords to join his army with money and weapons, and demanded that they take an oath of allegiance. This provoked open defiance from Lord Saye and Sele and Lord Brooke, who refused in the King's presence to take the oath. They were briefly imprisoned.

Charles was deluded if he thought that the Scottish army would melt away on his approach. The commander of the Scots, Alexander Leslie, was a veteran of the Thirty Years' War in Germany. Many Scots had served in the Swedish army, fighting for the Protestant cause. Across Scotland veterans of these wars prepared for conflict and began seizing places of strategic importance.

The King's delusion lasted until his army crossed the border into Scotland. His decision to give Lord Holland an independent command now backfired, when the cavalry, far in front of the infantry, ran unsupported into the Scottish army at Kelso. Leslie had drawn up his army on the forward slope of a hill, expertly dispersed to give the impression that it was much larger than it actually was. The English cavalry turned and fell back to join the infantry, bringing with them exaggerated reports of the Scots' strength. Only now did the

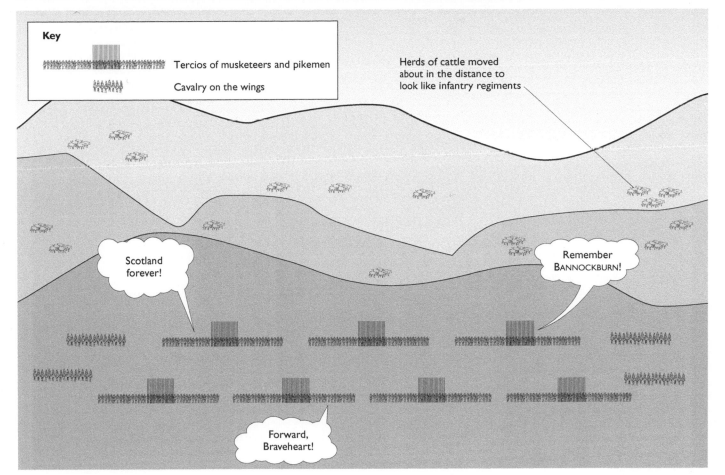

Key

Tercios of musketeers and pikemen

Cavalry on the wings

Herds of cattle moved about in the distance to look like infantry regiments

Scotland forever!

Remember BANNOCKBURN!

Forward, Braveheart!

BANNOCKBURN
The battle in 1314 in which Robert the Bruce defeated a much larger English army, thus establishing Scotland's independence.

King realise that the Scots were prepared to fight, and that his own army was in no state to take them on. The whole premise on which the campaign had been launched was exposed as false.

Charles had little choice but to open negotiations with the Scots at Berwick-upon-Tweed. In the Pacification of Berwick, both sides agreed to disband their armies and the King agreed to a Scottish General Assembly and Parliament. The treaty solved nothing. The Scots refused to disband and the King began preparing for another war.

SOURCE 3.11 Thomas Windebank, son of Sir Francis Windebank, Charles's Catholic Secretary, in a private letter written after the Pacification of Berwick (quoted in Conrad Russell, *The Fall of the British Monarchies*, 1991, p. 83)

We have had a most cold, wet and long time of living in the field, but kept ourselves warm with the hopes of rubbing, fubbing and scrubbing those scurvy, filthy, dirty, nasty, lousy, itchy, scabby, shitten, stinking, slovenly, snotty-nosed, logger-headed, foolish, insolent, proud, beggarly, impertinent, absurd, grout-headed, villainous, barbarous, bestial, false, lying, roguish, devilish, long-eared, short-haired, damnable, atheistical, puritanical crew of the Scottish Covenant. But now there is peace in Israel.

SOURCE 3.12 Brilliana Harley, writing to her son at Oxford. She was the Puritan wife of an MP who fought for Parliament in the Civil War. She defended their castle in Herefordshire against a long siege by Royalists

But if we fight with Scotland, and are engaged in that war, then a foreign enemy may take his time of advantage. The cause is the Lord's; and He will work for his own glory. Dear Ned, you may remember I have often spoken to you about these times; and my dear Ned, would I were with you one day, to open my mind more largely than I can by writing.

ACTIVITY

1 Read Source 3.11. What effect does this source suggest the First Bishops' War had on Charles's loyal supporters?
2 Read Source 3.12. Analyse this source using a source interrogation matrix (see page 61).

DISCUSS

Study Sources 3.11 and 3.12.
  What do these sources suggest about the effects of the Scottish war on English opinion?

■ 31 Why did the King lose the First Bishops' War?

The deficiencies of the English military system
Early seventeenth-century England was caught in the transition from medieval private armies to modern public armies. The old feudal system no longer existed, but it had not yet been replaced with a professional standing army paid for by taxation. The 'English army' was put together from the county militias, poorly trained and equipped and uncommitted to any national cause. There was also the usual problem of desertion, made worse by lack of pay.

The discretionary nature of English local government
Government 'of the county, by the county, for the county' was not a system likely to produce an efficient, well-trained national army during an unpopular war. Unpaid local officials trying to raise troops and money faced the wrath of friends and neighbours, many of whom would rather have made war on the Spanish than on the Scots. Counties were reluctant to part with their weapons, which were owned privately and intended for local defence.

WHY DID THE KING LOSE THE FIRST BISHOPS' WAR?

The unpopularity of the war
Leading Puritans such and Lord Saye and Sele and Lord Brooke were not the only people who thought that the Scottish cause was just. Throughout the country there were people who had no desire to fight Scotland, which they saw as a godly country courageously defending itself against policies that were deeply unpopular in England itself.

The absence of Parliament
No English king in recent times had fought a war without parliamentary support. Charles had to try to finance the conflict from his non-parliamentary taxes, supplemented with personal loans and private gifts. Ship Money receipts were dwindling away. Charles faced a creeping paralysis of local government brought on by his failure to communicate with the kingdom through regular parliaments.

The King's political blunders
Charles I miscalculated badly during the First Bishops' War. He tried to frighten the Scots into submission by leaking his intentions of raising foreign, Catholic troops from Ireland and Spain to fight on his side. If anything could provoke the Scots into open rebellion, it was the prospect of an invasion by Catholic armies. He reinforced this threat in 1639 when he allowed a Spanish army to march from port to port across southern England to avoid the Dutch fleet. His belief that a Royalist party in Scotland would assert itself when he approached proved unfounded.

TALKING POINT

King James was wise and learned, but King Charles wants a good headpiece [brain].

(quoted in C. Russell, *The Fall of the British Monarchies*, p. 86)

Would you have agreed with this sentiment?
   Can you think of any other major historical events that might be explained by the poor judgement of some important individual?

FOCUS ROUTE

Make notes on the reasons why Charles I lost the First Bishops' War. Pay particular attention to:

• institutional weaknesses in England
• political mistakes made by the King
• the consequences of the war.

E The Short Parliament – why did the King dissolve it within three weeks?

Why did the King decide to call Parliament?

In September 1639 the King brought Strafford back from Ireland to advise him on how to deal with the Scottish crisis. Strafford advised him to call Parliament. He believed the MPs could be won over by a combination of bribes, threats and skilful speeches. Strafford also counted on anti-Scottish patriotism to persuade MPs to vote subsidies for the war.

Charles consulted a secret committee of the Privy Council, which unanimously recommended that he call a new Parliament, advising the King that such a gesture would bring him a lot of public support. A letter had been intercepted from the Scots to the King of France, asking for help against England. When its contents were shown to the House of Commons, then surely the threat of war with France would focus the MPs' minds and all loyal men would rally to the King's cause? But the new Parliament lasted only three weeks.

Why did the King then decide to dissolve Parliament?

Could the Short Parliament have succeeded? The King demanded that Parliament vote taxes before he would consider its grievances. The Commons was led by John Pym and John Hampden, who were determined to call the government to account for the Personal Rule. Strafford was unexpectedly delayed in Ireland by illness. When Parliament turned its attention to religion, the King quickly dissolved Parliament.

SOURCE 3.13 Edward Hyde, Earl of Clarendon, *The History of the Rebellion and Civil Wars in England*, 1702

There could not a greater damp have seized upon the spirits of the whole nation than this dissolution caused, and men had much of the misery in view which shortly after fell out. It could never be hoped that more sober and dispassioned men would ever meet together in that place nor could any man imagine what offence they had given which put the King to that resolution. . . .

Within an hour after the dissolving, Mr. Hyde [Clarendon himself] met Mr. St. John, who had naturally a great cloud in his face and very seldom was known to smile, but then had a most cheerful aspect, and seeing the other melancholic, as in truth he was from his heart, asked him, 'What troubled him?' who answered, 'That the same which troubled him, he believed troubled most good men; that in such a time of confusion, so wise a Parliament, which could only have found remedy for it, was so unseasonably dismissed.' The other answered with a little warmth, 'That all was well: and that it must be worse before it could be better; and that this parliament would never have done what was necessary to be done;' as indeed it would not what he and his friends thought necessary.

With hindsight, it is easy for us to see that the Short Parliament was always likely to be short! Several aspects of this episode should alert us to the possibility that, behind the scenes, a number of people wanted it to fail.

WHY DID THE KING ABANDON THE PERSONAL RULE IN 1640?

ACTIVITY

Study Source 3.13.

1 Why was Oliver St John smiling when he spoke to Edward Hyde?
2 What was Hyde's personal view of Charles I's decision to dissolve the Short Parliament?
3 Having read Hyde's account of his encounter with St John, to which group – the godly or the moderate MPs – do you think he belonged?

THE KING

It is hard to believe that Charles I expected the Short Parliament to succeed. None of his previous parliaments had been a success. By April 1640 the country had gone eleven years without a parliament, so he must have realised that the House of Commons would want its grievances addressed before voting taxes. If Parliament failed yet again to co-operate, the King would feel justified in resorting to prerogative taxation, as in 1627.

THE MODERATE MPS

Most MPs wanted Parliament to succeed. They believed passionately in the ideal of King and Parliament working harmoniously together to 'heal the nation's wounds'. However, the war with Scotland was very unpopular. Could King and Parliament be reconciled?

THE GODLY MPS

It is hard to believe that the 'godly party' (see page 58) wanted Parliament to succeed. 'Success' would involve granting the King subsidies with which to fight another war with the Scots. Even if the King made some concessions, it is hard to see how the 'godly party' would benefit from the defeat of the Covenanters. The godly MPs wanted this Parliament to fail without taking the blame for its failure.

THE SCOTS

It is hard to believe that the Scots wanted the English Parliament to succeed, since 'success' would result in the King raising money for another war. On the other hand, the Covenanters must have known that only an English Parliament could limit the King's power enough to protect Scotland from Charles's religious policy. The Scots did not want this Parliament to reach agreement with the King.

DISCUSS

1 What does the Short Parliament suggest about the relationship between events in England and in Scotland?
2 Is it correct to argue that, by calling the Short Parliament, Charles I had finally abandoned his Personal Rule?

F The Long Parliament – why did the King call another Parliament in November 1640?

The decision to renew the war

The King was determined to fight another war with the Scots. The day after the Short Parliament was dissolved, the Privy Council met to discuss the King's options. As in 1627, Parliament's failure to provide the King with money for a war could be used to justify raising taxes on the King's own authority. Offers of loans totalling £360,000 came in from private individuals and corporations, but this figure fell far short of the amount needed. The King needed the support of the City of London, but the City refused to lend the King money unless he recalled Parliament.

SOURCE 3.14 Strafford, speaking in the Privy Council, offers the King the use of the Irish army, as noted by Sir Henry Vane. Vane was the King's Secretary of State on the eve of the Civil War, and a member of the Privy Council

You have an army in Ireland you may employ to reduce this kingdom.

SOURCE 3.15 The Earl of Northumberland, Lord General of Charles's army, writing two days after the Short Parliament was dissolved

Notwithstanding this dissolution, the King intends vigorously to pursue his former designs, and to levy the same army of 30,000 foot and 3,000 horse. About 3 weeks hence, they are to be drawn together, but as yet I can not learn by what means we are certain to get one shilling, towards the defraying this great expense. What will the world judge of us abroad, to see us enter into such an action as this is, not knowing how to maintain it for one month? It grieves my soul to be involved in these counsels; and the sense I have of the miseries that are like to ensue, is held by some a disaffection in me.

The Canons of 1640

At this moment, Laud issued a new set of ecclesiastical canons to assert the King's authority. The new canons were an attempt to wrong-foot religious opposition by placing the blame for 'innovations' squarely on the shoulders of the King's Puritan critics. The clergy were required to swear an oath asserting their support for the Thirty-nine Articles, the Prayer Book and the *'discipline, or government established in the Church of England, as containing all things necessary to salvation'*. This shifted the ideology of salvation, as defined in the Thirty-nine Articles, away from Holy Scripture towards the bishops.

SOURCE 3.16 Explicit endorsement of the doctrine of Divine Right as included in the canons of 1640. Every clergyman was to read this declaration four times a year at morning prayer

The most high and sacred order of kings is of divine right, being the ordinance of God himself, founded in the prime laws of nature, and clearly established by express texts both of the Old and New Testaments. A supreme power is given to this most excellent order by God himself in the Scriptures, which is, that kings should rule and command in their several dominions all persons of what rank or estate soever. . . .

This marked a significant shift from the canons of 1604, which asserted that the Prayer Book was, at worst, unobjectionable. The canons of 1640 were one more piece in the great game of chess that would determine the boundaries of the royal prerogative.

SOURCE 3.17 The Great Game of Chess. A drawing that suggests some people were bemused by the growing hostility between the King and his subjects

This Canons feal'd, well forg'd, not made of lead,
Give fire, O noe, 't will breake and strike vs dead,

That I.A.B. doe fweare that I doe approve the Doctrine and Difcipline or Government eftablifhed in the Church of England, as containing all things neceffary to Salvation; And that I will not endeavour by my felf or any other, directly or indirectly to bring in any Popifh Doctrine, contrary to that which is fo eftablifhed: Nor will I ever give my confent to alter the Government of this Church, by Archbifhops, Bifhops, Deanes, and Arch-Deacons, &c as it ftands now eftablifhed, and as by right it ought to ftand: Nor yet ever to fubject it to the ufurpations and fuperftitions of the Sea of Rome, And all thefe things I doe plainly and fincerely ac-knowledge and fweare, according to the plain and common fence, and underftanding of the fame words, without any equivocation or mentall evafion, or fecret refervation whatfoever. And this I doe heartily, willingly and truly, upon the faith of a Chriftian: So help me God in Iefus Chrift.

Prime, lay the Trayne, thus you must mount, and levell,
        then fhall we gett the day, but freind the Devill,
Turne, wheele about, take tyme, and stand your ground,
        this Canon cannot faile, but 'tis not found,
Feare not, weel cast it, 'tis a defperate cafe,
        weel fweare it, and enjoyne it, but 'tis bafe,
The Mettalls brittle, and 'tis ram'd fo hard,
        with an Oath &c: that hath fowly marr'd
All our defignes, that now we have no hope,
        but in the fervice of our Lord the Pope,
Diffolve the Rout, each man vnto his calling
        which had we kept, we had not now beene falling

SOURCE 3.18 'A Satire against Archbishop Laud', by Wenceslaus Hollar, 1640. Hollar's cartoon is a pun on the ecclesiastical canons of 1640. At the top of the page is the oath that all clergy had to take. Laud's 'canons' have exploded in his face, and the oath is falling short of its mark

ACTIVITY

Study Source 3.18.

1 Read the oath above the picture. Why would Puritans have objected to this?

2 Explain the meaning of the statement below the picture.

3 In the mid-1630s a cartoon like this would have landed the author and publisher before the Court of High Commission. What does the appearance of this cartoon in 1640 tell you about the way the political situation in England had changed?

The Second Bishops' War

Once again an English army moved northwards against the Scots, although Charles had great difficulty finding a commander for it: the Earl of Northumberland, pleading illness, had excused himself, and Strafford, who was given the job, was struck down by gout. The King remained in London. This time the English did not expect the Scots to be overawed by the panoply of war. The Scots, too, meant business: they would not wait for the English to invade Scotland. While the bulk of the King's army was still at York, the Scots brushed aside opposition at the Battle of Newburn and captured Newcastle, the source of London's coal supplies. With Strafford incapacitated through illness, the English army was paralysed by indecision. Once again desertion began to decimate the ranks, while the Covenanters were in correspondence with English opponents of the Personal Rule.

In desperation, Charles called a meeting of the lords of the realm. On 24 September the Council of Peers met at York, and their advice was clear and to the point. The King had to recall Parliament. The immediate task was to prevent the Scots from marching on York, so on 21 October 1640 the King signed the Treaty of Ripon, agreeing to the following terms:

- The Scots would continue to occupy Newcastle until a settlement was reached.
- The King would pay the Scots £850 a day until this was done.
- The English Parliament would be recalled.

In November 1640 the King issued the writs to the county sheriffs to hold another parliamentary election. The Personal Rule was over.

G Review: why did the King abandon the Personal Rule in 1640?

FOCUS ROUTE

Return now to the Focus Route on page 57. Consider the strengths and weaknesses of the two theories. Do you find either theory on its own convincing?

- If so, make notes to explain why you find one theory convincing but not the other. Any essay you are likely to write on this topic will require you to consider both theories.
- If not, then it is time to devise a third option. Is the distinction between 'domestic' and 'foreign' opposition to Charles I unhelpful? What should we replace it with?

ACTIVITY

Choose from one of the following essay titles:

a) Why was Charles I forced to abandon the Personal Rule in 1640?
b) How far were events in Scotland responsible for the failure of Charles I's Personal Rule in England?
c) 'Charles I's Personal Rule failed because he lost the active co-operation of the county magistrates in executing his orders.' How far do you agree with this judgement?

KEY POINTS FROM CHAPTER 3

Why did the King abandon the Personal Rule in 1640?

1 The Personal Rule aroused opposition within England for many different reasons.

2 Religion played a crucial role in focusing opposition to the Personal Rule. This helped to motivate people who might not otherwise have actively resisted it.

3 The critical year was 1637. Charles had to face the trial of Prynne, Bastwick and Burton; the Ship Money trial; and the Scottish Rebellion. From this moment on, the Personal Rule was in serious trouble.

4 The Bishops' Wars played a vital role in forcing Charles to recall Parliament.

5 Charles's defeat in the Bishops' Wars was largely caused by domestic factors – the unpopularity of the wars; the inefficiency of local government; the financial weakness of the Crown.

When did the Civil War become inevitable?

CHAPTER OVERVIEW

When the Long Parliament opened in November 1640, there was no immediate prospect of civil war. It takes two sides to fight a civil war, but for the first year the King had almost no supporters. Of the 493 MPs elected to the Long Parliament, at least 399 considered themselves 'Country' MPs opposed to the King's policies. There was general agreement that the King had overstepped the mark, and had to be prevented from returning to Personal Rule. The first session of the Long Parliament concentrated on curbing the King's power.

By the summer of 1642, the country was at war. All over England people had to choose between Parliament and the King. The King had raised an army of loyal subjects and many MPs who had attacked the Personal Rule were now coming over to his side.

FOCUS ROUTE

When did the Civil War become inevitable? There were several key events after which, one could argue, armed conflict in England could not be avoided. As you come to each of the following events, explain in your notes whether or not you think this was the moment when the point was reached at which conflict could not be avoided.

1 The Earl of Strafford's execution, May 1641
2 The Irish Rebellion, October 1641
3 The Grand Remonstrance, November 1641
4 The Attempt on the Five Members, January 1642
5 The Militia Ordinance, March 1642

■ 4A Timeline of the coming of civil war, 1640–42

THE LONG PARLIAMENT'S FIRST SESSION, NOVEMBER 1640–AUGUST 1641

Characteristics
General agreement in Parliament. Concerned mainly with curbing the King's power. Many Acts of Parliament to destroy the Personal Rule.

1640 November	Long Parliament begins Impeachment of Strafford and Laud Parliament attacks the Personal Rule
1641 February	Triennial Act
March	Trial of the Earl of Strafford begins
April	Prosecution of Strafford fails to prove its case Army Plot
May	Bishops' Exclusion Bill Strafford executed Riots in London Act preventing the dissolution of this Parliament without its own consent
June	Tonnage and Poundage Act House of Lords rejects the Bishops' Exclusion Bill
July	Acts abolishing the Court of Star Chamber and the Court of High Commission
August	Act abolishing Ship Money Limitation of Forests Act Act prohibiting the Distraint of Knighthood

Characteristics

Opposition programme becomes more radical, aiming at more fundamental constitutional changes. Formation of a Royalist party.

August	Charles visits Scotland
October	Irish Rebellion
November	The Grand Remonstrance
December	Militia Bill
	Mobs control London
	Rumours that the Queen is to be impeached
1642	
4 January	Charles attempts to arrest the Five Members
	Charles I abandons London for the north of England
February	King signs Act excluding bishops from the House of Lords
	Queen leaves England to seek foreign assistance
March	Militia Ordinance issued by Parliament without the King's consent
April	Sir John Hotham refuses to surrender the royal arsenal at Hull to the King
June	Commissions of Array issued by the King
	Nineteen Propositions
	Fighting breaks out nationwide between rival militia captains
July	Parliament appoints a Committee of Safety to conduct military operations
	Parliament votes to raise an army
August	Charles I's standard raised at Nottingham
	War begins

WHEN DID THE CIVIL WAR BECOME INEVITABLE?

FOCUS ROUTE

How far did Parliament encroach on the King's royal prerogative between November 1640 and August 1642? Focusing on this question will help you to answer several key issues:

1 Why did the anti-royal consensus that existed in November 1640 break down?
2 Why did a Royalist party form around the King in late 1641/early 1642?
3 How much of his prerogative was Charles prepared to give up to reach settlement with his subjects?
4 Why, in spite of this revival of Royalist support, was Parliament able to mount a sustained challenge to the King's power?

A The beginning of the Long Parliament (p. 80)

B Why did the trial of the Earl of Strafford push England towards civil war? (pp. 81–87)

C The Irish Rebellion, October 1641 – what effect did it have on England? (pp. 88–91)

D The Attempt on the Five Members (pp. 92–94)

E The coming of civil war (pp. 95–97)

F For King or Parliament? (pp. 97–99)

G Review: when did the Civil War become inevitable? (pp. 99–103)

A # The beginning of the Long Parliament

The Long Parliament opened on 3 November 1640, in an atmosphere of great excitement and optimism. Parliament had the King over a barrel, raising expectations of political reform and religious reformation. Some Puritans hoped that the Reformation could now be completed, ending the compromises of the Elizabethan Settlement. For a moment it was possible to believe that King and Parliament could achieve the sort of harmony that had eluded them since 1625.

John Pym warned Parliament that the country faced a Catholic conspiracy. Pym drew a frightening picture of a plot that had spread into every corner of the country, aimed at altering the kingdom 'both in religion and government'. Alongside religion, taxation and the use of the prerogative courts, Pym accused the government of stirring up war between England and Scotland; of trying out absolutism in Ireland; and of planning to use the Irish army to reduce England to order.

The King's ministers were accused of high treason. Strafford and Laud were impeached and imprisoned awaiting trial. To destroy any remaining morale in the King's government, Parliament threatened to impeach any sheriff or customs officer who had collected Ship Money or Tonnage and Poundage. The King's Catholic secretary, Francis Windebank, fled for safety across the English Channel, and many lesser courtiers slipped quietly away from London to their country estates, in fear for their lives.

The opening months of the Long Parliament focused on the impeachment of Strafford, collecting evidence for his trial before the House of Lords. The presence in the Lords of the bishops, however, was problematical, as they could not be relied on to find their former masters guilty. The existence of bishops was called into question by the 'Root and Branch Petition', which called for the abolition of episcopal government. Petitions for and against 'root and branch' reform poured into Parliament, showing that religion was already a divisive issue.

In February 1641 the King signed the Triennial Act. A new Parliament would have to be held every three years, whether the King called it or not. This was a radical change from the old constitution, beginning the process that would make Parliament a permanent feature of English political life.

DISCUSS

Sheriffs and customs officers were not responsible for making policy, so why did Parliament threaten to impeach them if they had, in the past, collected Ship Money or Tonnage and Poundage?

Reade in this Image him, whose dearest blood
Is thought noe price to buy his Countryes good,
Whose name shall flourish, till the blast of fame
Shall want a Trumpet, or true worth, a name.
Edw: Bower pinxit   G: Glover fecit

John Pym (1584–1643)
Pym, a Somerset MP, was the most important parliamentary leader after the deaths of Sir Edward Coke and Sir John Eliot. During the 1620s he became a prominent government critic, defending parliamentary privileges and common law against arbitrary rule while recognising that the Crown was dangerously underfunded. He was a prominent member of the Puritan network. In 1640 he quickly established his leadership of the Commons in both the Short and Long Parliaments, working alongside other prominent parliamentarians such as Oliver St John and John Hampden.

A highly skilled politician, Pym's revelation of the Army Plot in May 1641 persuaded a reluctant House of Lords to approve the Bill of Attainder that sent Strafford to his death (see page 84). In the autumn of 1641 Pym managed to steel Parliament's nerve in the face of the growth of a Royalist party, just securing the passage of the Grand Remonstrance (see page 91) through the Commons. His connections with the City of London enabled him to mobilise mob support at critical moments.

When war broke out in 1642, Pym held together a fragile coalition of the 'middle group' and the 'war party' in Parliament to outvote the 'peace party'. Under his guidance Parliament passed many of the resolutions which paved the way for eventual military victory, leading to charges of 'parliamentary absolutism'. His final contribution to the war effort was to bring the Scots into the war as Parliament's allies. He died in December 1643.

FOCUS ROUTE

1 Strafford's trial was a power struggle between the King and the Commons. Look back over Strafford's career. Why did Pym choose to make an example of him?

2 As you work through this section, consider whether civil war could have broken out during Strafford's trial. Did the trial push England closer to civil war?

B Why did the trial of the Earl of Strafford push England towards civil war?

On the morning of 12 May 1641, Strafford was executed on Tower Hill. King Charles had promised Strafford he would come to no harm. From his prison cell Strafford had written to the King releasing him from this obligation, expressing the hope that his death would help to restore order to the kingdom. In private, his thoughts were not so charitable: 'Put not your trust in princes,' he advised.

The King consulted the Privy Council, and listened in tears to its advice that he had to sign Strafford's death warrant. Right up until his own death in 1649, Charles believed that abandoning Strafford was the one true sin of his life, for which he and the kingdom were punished by God through civil war.

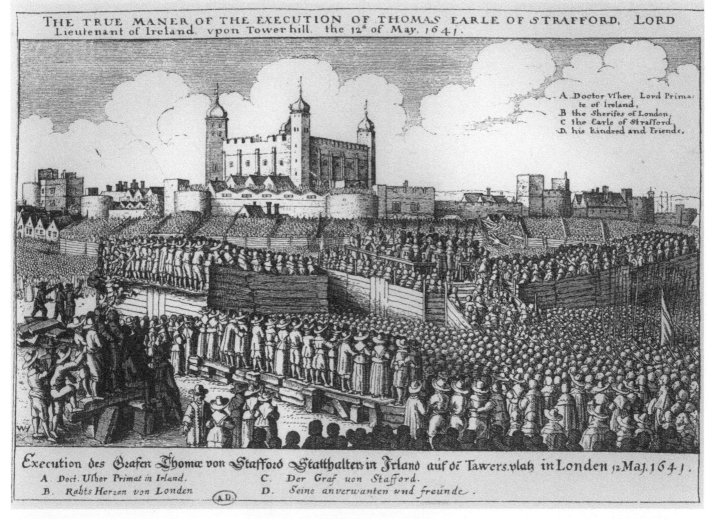

SOURCE 4.1 The execution of Thomas Wentworth, Earl of Strafford. Ussher was the Archbishop of Armagh, the Calvinist primate of the Church of Ireland. Strafford had tried to replace Ussher's policies in Ireland with those of William Laud

The impeachment trial

Strafford's impeachment led to the most important state trial since the reign of Elizabeth I. It was essential to the success of Parliament's programme of reform, but it carried an enormous risk. If Strafford survived he could turn the tables on Parliament's leaders. He knew that Pym, Lord Saye and Sele, Lord Brooke, the Earl of Warwick and others had been in communication with the Scots during the Bishops' Wars.

The trial began before the House of Lords on 22 March 1641. The King assured him that no harm would come to him, regardless of the verdict. Strafford was accused of trying to establish 'arbitrary government'. The underlying theme was that he had committed treason by sowing division between the King and his subjects. The prosecution argued that, taken together, Strafford's actions added up to an attempt to rule the kingdoms by force – a charge known as 'constructive treason'. Strafford's defence was that each charge had to be taken on its own merits; he might have lacked political wisdom, but the charges did not amount to high treason.

Strafford defended himself with considerable skill. The Lords were reluctant to find him guilty of treason, for which he would be hanged, drawn and quartered. Some of them had sat in on the very Privy Council meetings from which evidence was being thrown at him. If Strafford could be found guilty, no one was safe. It looked as if the trial might collapse.

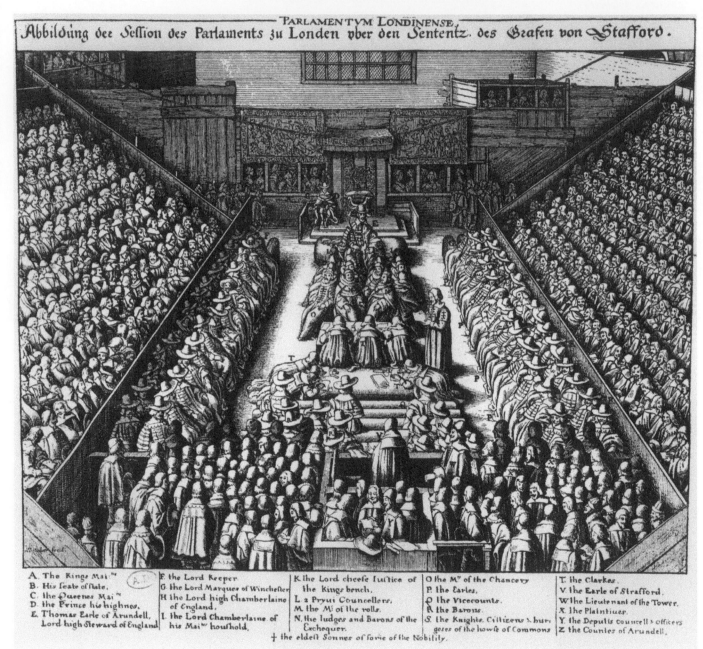

SOURCE 4.2   A contemporary picture of the trial of the Earl of Strafford before the House of Lords. The King is shown watching the trial from the royal box at the far end of the chamber

1 Why did the impeachment trial of Strafford go badly for his accusers? Match the accusations made against Strafford with some of the comments he made in his defence.
2 Which of these accusations was the most serious one made against Strafford, and why?
3 Why was the House of Lords unlikely to find Strafford guilty of treason?
4 What were the likely consequences for Pym and Parliament if Strafford's trial collapsed?

Accusations made against the Earl of Strafford

1 Making excessive profits from the customs in Ireland.
2 'My Lord of Strafford did say in discourse, "Your Majesty . . . you have an army in Ireland, which you may employ here to reduce this kingdom," or some words to this effect.' (Testimony given by Sir Harry Vane on Strafford's comments at a Privy Council meeting)
3 'If this treason had taken effect our souls had been enthralled to the spiritual tyranny of Satan, our consciences to the ecclesiastical tyranny of the Pope.'
4 Strafford was accused, by a man who was nearly deaf, of saying, 'The little finger of the King was heavier than the loins of the law.'
5 'It is the law that unites the king and his people, and the author of this treason hath endeavoured to dissolve that union even to break the mutual, irreversible, indissoluble bond of protection and allegiance whereby they are, and I hope ever will be, bound together.'

Comments made by the Earl of Strafford in his own defence

A The witness 'appears to have such an infirmity of hearing that he must now be whoopt to at the bar, before he can hear.'
B 'The happiness of a kingdom consists in the just balance of the King's prerogative and the subject's liberty, and that things should never be well till these went hand in hand together. I have and shall ever aim at a fair and bounded liberty, remembering always that I am a freeman, but a subject; that I have a right, but under a monarch.'
C 'I never knew the making of a good bargain turned on a man as treason.'
D 'Never a servant in authority beneath the king my master who was more hated and maligned, and am still, by these men than myself, and that for a strict and impartial execution of the laws against them. Hence your Lordships may observe that the greater number of the witnesses used against me are men of that religion.'
E 'If words spoken to friends, in familiar discourse, spoken in one's chamber, spoken at one's table, spoken in one's sick-bed shall be brought against a man as treason, this takes away the comfort of all human society. If these things be strained to take away life and honour it will be a silent world.'

The Bill of Attainder

On 10 April Pym dramatically changed tactics. The Commons abandoned the impeachment trial, bringing instead a Bill of Attainder declaring the Earl a traitor. But the King would have to sign the bill.

Pym's problem was still the House of Lords, which, except for the Earl of Essex who insisted on his death, was reluctant to condemn one of their own members. Something more was needed to focus the minds of the Lords.

1 In 2004 a cross-party group of MPs suggested that the Prime Minister, Tony Blair, should be impeached over the Iraq war. Why did they resort to this idea, and why was it not likely to work?

2 The President of the USA, Bill Clinton, was impeached by the House of Representatives (the American equivalent of the Commons) over his relationship with Monica Lewinski. He was tried in the Senate, which threw out the case. Since the House, like the Commons in the seventeenth century, doesn't hold the trial, why did its members feel they could impeach the President without taking responsibility for the outcome?

3 What other recent American President was threatened with impeachment, and why?

■ **Learning trouble spot**

The Long Parliament

Up until the Triennial Act of February 1641, it was the King's undoubted right to dissolve Parliament whenever he wanted. The Triennial Act changed the law by forcing the King to call a new Parliament at least every three years, which the King could dissolve after 50 days. On this occasion, and for this Parliament only, he gave away this right. The consequences were disastrous, not only for him but eventually for Parliament too. Faced with civil war and its aftermath, the Long Parliament refused to dissolve itself, leading in 1648 to a military coup called Pride's Purge. In 1653 Oliver Cromwell expelled the remainder of the Long Parliament (called the Rump) by force. This led to accusations that nothing Cromwell and his government did after 1653 was legal. In 1660 the Long Parliament reconvened in order to dissolve itself, paving the way for the restoration of the monarchy.

■ **Learning trouble spot**

The impeachment of Strafford and the Bill of Attainder

Students sometimes fail to understand the precise difference between the impeachment of Strafford and the Bill of Attainder that followed. Since 1621 Parliament had been acting as a court of law by impeaching individuals, for example the Duke of Buckingham. During an impeachment, the House of Commons 'impeached' the accused by voting to put them on trial. The trial was held in the House of Lords. So, to be successful, both Houses of Parliament had to agree to remove the accused person from office, and the Lords had to find the accused guilty. The King was not directly involved.

By contrast, a Bill of Attainder was an Act of Parliament, not a trial. Both Houses of Parliament had to pass the bill but, crucially, the Lords did not have to find the person guilty. In Strafford's case they simply passed a bill saying that Strafford was a traitor. For the bill to become an Act, however, the King had to sign it. By switching from an impeachment to a Bill of Attainder, Pym accomplished two things:

1 He avoided a verdict in the House of Lords that might have found Strafford not guilty.

2 He forced the King to take personal responsibility for Strafford's death.

The Army Plot

With Strafford's fate hanging in the balance, Pym revealed that a group of army officers, with the King's support, had been plotting a *coup d'état*.

Angered by Parliament's treatment of their King, the officers planned to bring the army south from York to London, free Strafford from the Tower, and forcibly dissolve Parliament. The King went along with the plan. On 3 May he sent a hundred soldiers to seize the Tower of London, but the Tower was well defended and the plot collapsed.

It was enough to persuade the Lords to pass the Bill of Attainder. Strafford's life was now in the hands of the King.

The Army Plot seemed to confirm Protestant fears of a Catholic conspiracy (which this diagram from page 9 summarised)

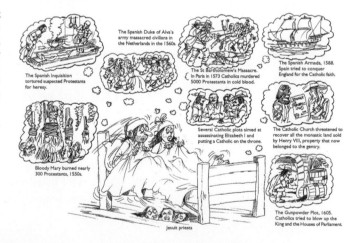

Why did the King sign Strafford's death warrant?

Until his dying day, Charles believed that signing Strafford's death warrant was the greatest sin of his life. So why did he do it?

On the day he signed the warrant, Charles also signed an Act which prevented him from dissolving the Long Parliament without its own consent. For the King this was disastrous. With one stroke of the pen he had given away his prerogative right to dissolve this Parliament. This was so uncharacteristic of Charles that it suggests he was under great emotional pressure. What was going on?

The Army Plot had brought the country to the brink of civil war. Crowds had gathered outside Whitehall Palace, which was poorly defended. The King probably feared for the safety of the Queen and his children. He was under intense pressure from both Lords and bishops to sacrifice Strafford in the interests of peace.

The Lords are telling me I have no choice.

Parliament will refuse to pay off the Scots if I don't sign.

If I refuse to sign, there could be civil war.

The bishops have urged me to sign.

The House of Commons is demanding Strafford's death.

My wife and family are in danger. I cannot protect them from the mob.

SOURCE 4.3 Edward Hyde, Earl of Clarendon describes a conversation he had with the Earl of Bedford in early April 1641

The Earl said, 'This business concerning the Earl of Strafford was a rock upon which we should all split. The passion of the parliament would destroy the kingdom. The King was ready to do all they could desire, if the life of the Earl of Strafford might be spared. The King was satisfied, that the Earl had proceeded with more passion in many things, than he ought to have done. If they would take the Earl's life upon them by their own powers of jurisdiction, the King would not interpose any act of his own conscience: but since they had declined that way and meant to proceed by an act of parliament, to which he himself must be party, it could not consist with his conscience, ever to give his royal assent to that act. The King had heard nothing proved by which he could believe that the Earl was a traitor, either in fact or in intention. Therefore his majesty did most earnestly desire that the two houses would not bring him a bill to pass, which in conscience he could not, and therefore would not consent.'

ACTIVITY

Read Source 4.3. How does this source help to explain:

a) why many men believed that Strafford had to die, whether he was guilty or not

b) how Pym placed the King in an impossible position by switching to a Bill of Attainder?

FOCUS ROUTE

1 Why did Strafford's trial push the kingdom towards civil war? Consider in your answer:
  • the effect the trial had on relations between the Lords and the Commons
  • the effect on the King of being forced to take ultimate responsibility for Strafford's death
  • what would happen to Pym and his supporters if the King should ever regain the political initiative.
2 Does the switch from a trial (due process of law) to a statute (a political act) suggest some reason why moderates might become concerned about the lengths to which Parliament's leaders were prepared to go?

FOCUS ROUTE

Return to the Focus Route on page 78. Do you think civil war was inevitable after Strafford's execution?

The end of prerogative government

Strafford's execution left the King isolated and demoralised. He had no choice but to concede to Parliament's demands. Parliament was free to destroy the instruments of the Personal Rule. During the next three months, a collection of laws was passed by Parliament and signed by the King, each Act another nail in the coffin of prerogative rule.

■ 4C The effects of Strafford's death

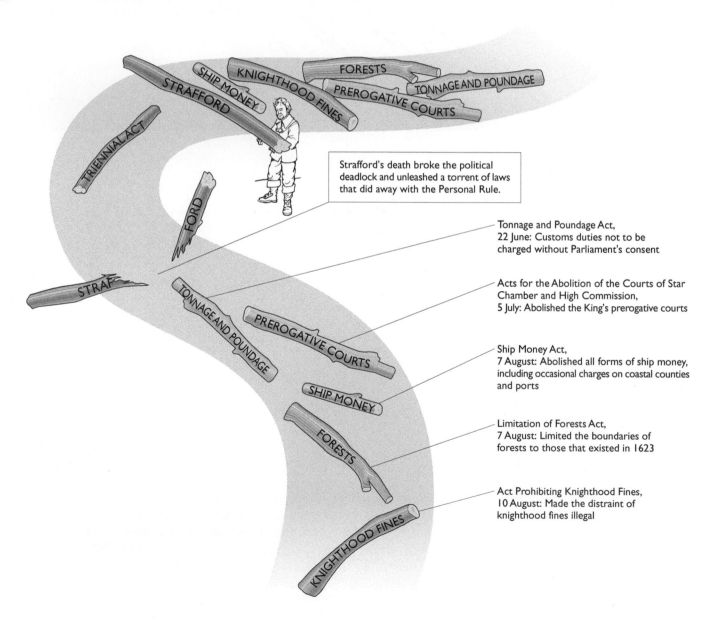

Strafford's death broke the political deadlock and unleashed a torrent of laws that did away with the Personal Rule.

Tonnage and Poundage Act,
22 June: Customs duties not to be charged without Parliament's consent

Acts for the Abolition of the Courts of Star Chamber and High Commission,
5 July: Abolished the King's prerogative courts

Ship Money Act,
7 August: Abolished all forms of ship money, including occasional charges on coastal counties and ports

Limitation of Forests Act,
7 August: Limited the boundaries of forests to those that existed in 1623

Act Prohibiting Knighthood Fines,
10 August: Made the distraint of knighthood fines illegal

Charles I trustworthiness survey

By the end of August 1641, the Personal Rule had been destroyed. But Pym and his supporters were not satisfied. They feared the King would take the first opportunity to undo everything they had done. Pym did not believe that Charles I could be trusted.

The time has come for you to reach some conclusions about Charles I's character. Answer the following questions without discussing them with your class. For each question, record an answer from a) to e).

After completing the exercise, you may wish to discuss your answers and the weighting given to them in the results grid on page 291.

1 If Charles I had another army at his disposal, where would he most likely order it to go?
   a) Wales
   b) Scotland
   c) Yorkshire
   d) London
   e) Ireland

2 Does Charles still believe in the Divine Right of Kings?
   a) very likely
   b) likely
   c) possibly
   d) unlikely
   e) very unlikely

3 Which of the following statements most accurately summarises Charles's attitude towards Ireland?
   a) Ireland has been pacified by the Earl of Strafford.
   b) Ireland is ripe for settlement.
   c) Ireland is the great unknown factor in the resolution of my troubles.
   d) Ireland has destroyed the Earl of Strafford.
   e) Ireland is the least easily governed of my three kingdoms.

4 If Charles had the opportunity, would he seek revenge for the death of the Earl of Strafford?
   a) very likely
   b) likely
   c) possible
   d) unlikely
   e) very unlikely

5 If Charles could order the arrest of one man, who would it be?
   a) Earl of Warwick
   b) Lord Brooke
   c) John Hampden
   d) Lord Saye and Sele
   e) John Pym

6 If Charles could undo any one of the Acts of the Long Parliament, which one would it be?
   a) Ship Money Act
   b) Triennial Act
   c) Limitation of Forests Act
   d) Act against dissolving the current Parliament
   e) Act prohibiting knighthood fines

7 If Charles could go back to the 1620s, knowing what he knows now, which of the following of his decisions would he most likely avoid making again?
   a) to promote William Laud to be Bishop of London
   b) to collect the Forced Loan
   c) to dissolve Parliament in 1626
   d) to collect Tonnage and Poundage
   e) to accept the Petition of Right

8 Which of the following statements best describes Charles's attitude towards Scotland?
   a) Making peace with Scotland is the most important thing I can do.
   b) Making war on Scotland is the most important thing I can do.
   c) For the time being I should ignore the Scots.
   d) Given enough time, the Scottish problem will melt away.
   e) I was wrong to try to force the Prayer Book on the Scots.

9 Which English monarch does Charles I most admire?
   a) Henry V (for winning the Battle of Agincourt against the French)
   b) James I (his father)
   c) Henry VIII (for making the King of England stronger)
   d) Elizabeth I (for defeating the Spanish Armada)
   e) Queen Mary (for trying to make England Catholic again)

10 Where does Charles believe he is most likely to find loyal subjects who would support him in the event of a civil war?
   a) Scotland
   b) Yorkshire
   c) Ireland
   d) Wales
   e) London

Check your answers and find out your score on page 291.

WHEN DID THE CIVIL WAR BECOME INEVITABLE?

FOCUS ROUTE

As you work through this section, make notes on the following:

1 Why was the parliamentary opposition running out of steam by autumn 1641?
2 In what ways were English Protestants already primed to expect something like the Irish Rebellion? What had John Pym done to promote such expectations?
3 Why did the Irish Rebellion of October 1641 drive England forward into political crisis?

Return to the Focus Route on page 78. Was the Civil War inevitable after the Irish Rebellion?

C The Irish Rebellion, October 1641 – what effect did it have on England?

The situation in the autumn of 1641

By September the political situation in England appeared to have reached stalemate. Parliament had been wrong-footed by its own success. Many leading members of the Puritan opposition had been promoted into the King's government. It was therefore more difficult to maintain the argument that the King was surrounded by evil advisers. Pym did not trust Charles, but each further concession made by the King undermined the argument for further change.

Reshuffling the deck. Charles's concessions brought several leading parliamentarians into his government

Charles was now in Scotland, trying to regain control of the political initiative. His priority was to persuade the Scots to remove their army from England. To achieve this he pursued a dual strategy: he made concessions to the Covenanters, meeting with the Scottish Parliament and General Leslie, and he promoted the Earls of Montrose and Rothes. At the same time he was preparing to strike at the Covenanters, exploiting divisions between the Scottish clans and also the jealousy between Montrose, who was increasingly alienated from the Covenanting cause, and the Marquess of Argyll, who was deeply committed to it. The King's intrigue came to a head in an abortive plot, known as the 'Incident', to arrest Argyll and Hamilton. Like the Army Plot in England, the Incident confirmed the impression that Charles could not be trusted.

When the Long Parliament resumed in mid-October, the dominant issue was the growing rift between the Commons and the Lords. Pym was determined to secure cast-iron guarantees against the King's duplicity. For Pym and his friends, gaining office was the key to power and security, but the King was bypassing them to promote others who had opposed the Personal Rule. If they couldn't persuade the King to give them office, they could only protect themselves by making further inroads into the royal prerogative. But the Lords were unlikely to go along with deep-rooted constitutional change.

Pym's solution was a bill to exclude the bishops and the Catholic peers from the House of Lords. This would remove around a third of the Lords, and allow the Commons to regain control of Parliament. To do this, Pym needed to raise again the spectre of a Catholic plot, but where was the evidence that England was in the grip of a Catholic conspiracy?

The Irish Rebellion

On 1 November 1641 the Privy Council asked permission to speak to the Commons urgently on a matter of great importance. The House listened in stunned silence as the Earl of Leicester read out letters he had received the previous day from the Irish Council in Dublin, telling him that a rebellion had broken out in Ireland. Thousands of English Protestants were being massacred, and many castles and strongholds had fallen to the rebels.

London was soon filled with stories of atrocities committed by Irish Catholics on English and Scottish Protestants. Accounts of Irish atrocities were printed and widely circulated, illustrated with lurid scenes of rape and torture.

News of the Irish Rebellion arrived while the King was still in Scotland. An army would have to be raised and sent to Ulster to save the Protestants and crush the rebellion – but who would command such an army? The Catholic rebels in Ireland claimed to be acting for the King – could the King be trusted with another army, in the light of the Army Plot and the Incident?

SOURCE 4.4 Extract from Thomas Partington's letter to a friend in England describing some of the events in Ireland. Partington was an English settler in Ireland. The letter was read out in the House of Commons

All I can tell you is the miserable estate we continue under, for the Rebels daily increase in men and munitions in all parts except the Province of Munster, exercising all manner of cruelties, and striving who can be most barbarously exquisite in tormenting the poor Protestants wheresoever they come, cutting off their privy members, ears, fingers and hands, plucking out their eyes, boiling the heads of little children before their Mothers' faces, and then ripping up their Mothers' bowels; stripping women naked . . . killing the children as soon as they are born, and ripping up their Mothers' bellies as soon as they are delivered; driving men, women and children by hundreds upon Bridges and from thence cast them down into Rivers, such as drowned not they knocked their brains out with poles or shoot them with Muskets . . . Ravishing wives before their Husbands' faces and Virgins before their Parents' faces. . . .

SOURCE 4.5 John Milton comments on the Irish Rebellion

The poor afflicted remnant of our martyred countrymen that sit there on the Sea-shore, counting the hours of our delay with their sighs, and the minutes with their falling tears, perhaps with the distilling of their bloody wounds . . . can best judge how speedy we are to their relief.

The Irish Rebellion confirmed Protestant fears of a Catholic conspiracy (which this diagram from page 9 summarised)

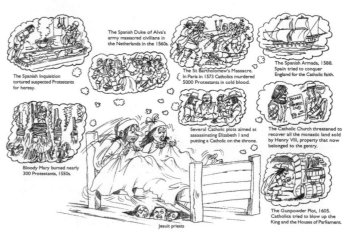

ACTIVITY

Study Sources 4.4 above and 4.6 on page 90.

1 In what ways does the evidence of Source 4.6 support the evidence of Thomas Partington in Source 4.4?
2 Why is it hard to decide how much of these sources was true and how much was Protestant propaganda?
3 Why did the native Irish Catholics rebel against the English and Scottish Protestants in Ulster?
4 Why would the publication of material such as Sources 4.4 and 4.5 have put both the King and Parliament under pressure to react forcefully to the Irish Rebellion?

Driuinge Men Women & children by hund: reds vpon Briges & casting them into Riuers, who drowned not were killed with poles & shot with muskets.

The Lord Blany force, to ride 14 miles with: out Bridle or Sadell to saue his life, his Lady lodged in Strawe beeing allowed 2 a day to releue her & her Children, slew a kinsman of hers and hanged him vp before her face. 2 dayes telling her she must expect the same to terrifie the moore.

M Dauenant and his Wife bound in their Chaires Striped the 2 Eldest Children of 7 yeares old rosted vpon Spittes before their Parents faces Cutt their throte and after murdred him.

Arthur Robinsons daughter 14 yeares old the Rebbels bound her armes a broad, deflowered her one after an other, tell they spoyled her then pulled the haire from her head and cut out her tongue that she might not tell of their Cruelty, but she declared it by writing.

A Minister and his wife came to Dublin Ian. 30 1641 left behinde him some goods with a sup: posed frend, sent for them but could not be de: liuered vnlesse he or his Wife came for them she came and presently they hanged her vp.

M ffordes house rifled, and to make her Confesse where her mony lay, they tooke hot tonges clapping them to the Soules of her feete & to the Palmes of her handes so tormented her that with the paine thereof shee died.

They haue set men & women on hot Grideorns to make them Confesse Where there money was.

Hauing rauished Virgens & Wifes they take there Children & dase there braines against the walls in sight of there weepinge Parents & after destroyed them likewise.

M Ierome Minister of Brides his Body mangled & his members cut of

The Grand Remonstrance

The Irish Rebellion gave Pym an opportunity to further weaken the King. Money for an Irish expeditionary army would only be granted if Charles agreed to further concessions. Pym's aim was to strengthen Parliament's resolve and halt the slow but steady growth in royal support among MPs who felt that the King had proven his willingness to co-operate with Parliament.

To achieve this he turned to a document he had prepared earlier in the year. The 'Grand Remonstrance' was a review of Charles I's entire reign, stating point by point the evidence for a conspiracy lying at the heart of the King's government. The Grand Remonstrance therefore amounts to the first full 'history' of Charles's reign, albeit one with a deliberate bias against the King. Embedded in the Remonstrance was a list of demands for radical constitutional changes:

- Parliament to control the King's ministers
- Bishops and Catholic peers to be excluded from the House of Lords
- Root and branch reform of the Church.

Pym's aim was to force reluctant MPs to support further attacks on the royal prerogative. The clauses of the Grand Remonstrance could not be voted on individually: the document stood or fell as a single item. Wavering MPs could not reject the more radical clauses without rejecting the critique of the entire reign, which commanded widespread acceptance. To vote against the Remonstrance might also be dangerous in the prevailing climate.

Pym's strategy very nearly failed. The Remonstrance was passed by only eleven votes, 159 to 148. Nearly 200 MPs either abstained or did not attend the debate. For many MPs it was the turning point, the moment when a Royalist party began to form visibly around the King.

Realising that the Remonstrance had no chance of success in the Lords, Pym avoided humiliation by not sending it to them. The Commons published the Remonstrance anyway.

SOURCE 4.7 Extract from the Grand Remonstrance

The root of all this mischief we find to be a malignant and pernicious design of subverting the fundamental laws and principles of government, upon which the religion and justice of this kingdom are firmly established. The actors and promotors hereof have been:

1. *The Jesuited Papists, who hate the laws, as the obstacles of that change and subversion of religion which they so much long for*
2. *The Bishops, and the corrupt part of the Clergy, who cherish formality and superstition as the natural effects and more probable supports of their own ecclesiastical tyranny and usurpation*
3. *Such Councillors and Courtiers as for private ends have engaged themselves to further the interests of some foreign princes or states to the prejudice of His Majesty and the State at home.*

DISCUSS

Was the Grand Remonstrance a political triumph for Pym or a serious miscalculation?

TALKING POINT

Why do we need to think carefully about the reliability of websites?

THE GRAND REMONSTRANCE

The full text of the Grand Remonstrance can be found on the internet at the following address: www.constitution.org/eng/conpur043.htm

ACTIVITY

1 Access the full text of the Grand Remonstrance and read it. This will give you an overview of how the parliamentary opposition viewed Charles I's reign.
2 Draw up a short document from the King's perspective, outlining how Charles would have viewed Parliament dating back to 1625.

■ **Learning trouble spot**

The Five Members

The 'Attempt on the Five Members' was actually an attempt to arrest six people – five MPs and a peer:

- John Pym
- John Hampden
- Denzil Holles
- Sir Arthur Haselrig
- William Strode
- Edward Montagu

Edward Montagu was also known as Baron Kimbolton and Viscount Mandeville before becoming Earl of Manchester in early 1642. This can be a source of some confusion when reading various textbooks. The King granted him the earldom in a failed attempt to bring him over to the Royalist cause.

SOURCE 4.8 A still from the film *Cromwell*, 1973, showing Charles I's attempt to arrest the Five Members. This scene illustrates both the benefits and the dangers of using films to illustrate historical events. The portrayal of this famous incident is realistic visually, but Oliver Cromwell was not one of the Five Members, nor did civil war break out as soon as the King left the chamber

APPRENTICE BOYS
Young men serving an apprenticeship to learn a skill. The London apprentices were politically radical – like students in the 1960s.

TRAINED BANDS
Companies of locally trained militia.

D The Attempt on the Five Members

On 4 January 1642 the King attempted a *coup d'état* against Parliament's leaders. Supported by his armed guard, and accompanied by his dispossessed nephew Frederick, the Elector Palatine, Charles made his way to Westminster from Whitehall and approached the House of Commons. Leaving his soldiers at the door, he entered the Commons chamber, to the amazement of the MPs. Apologising to the Speaker for having to 'make bold' with his chair, the King then ordered him to point out the MPs whose impeachment he had demanded on the previous day. The Speaker famously replied: 'May it please Your Majesty, I have neither eyes to see nor tongue to speak, except as the House shall direct me.'

The Five Members were not there. They had slipped out of the chamber into a boat, which had taken them down the Thames to a safe house in the City. With the comment, 'I see that the birds have all flown', the King returned empty-handed to Whitehall.

In the days that followed it became clear that Charles had made a disastrous mistake. In this one move he had undone the growing impression that he was a king who could be trusted, destroying months of work by moderate Royalists such as Edward Hyde and Viscount Falkland. By trying to resort to force, Charles had halted – at least temporarily – the growth of a Royalist party, and given credibility to rumours of a Catholic plot. Support for the King was in ruins even in the Lords, which accepted the bill excluding bishops from Parliament. Charles had made it impossible for himself and his court to remain in London, where Whitehall offered no adequate security against the angry mobs of APPRENTICE BOYS and the London TRAINED BANDS. On 10 January the King left London for Hampton Court and the Five Members returned to Parliament in triumph.

SOURCE 4.9 Captain Robert Slyngesbie to Sir John Pennington, 6 January 1642. Captain Slyngesbie was an eyewitness to the attempt on the Five Members, being one of the soldiers who accompanied the King to Westminster on 4 January

Since my last [letter] we have been a little quieter from the tumults of the citizens, they partly being terrified by the multitude of gentry and soldiers who flock to the court, which I never saw so thronged as now it is, and the royal entertainment that was like to be given them if they came again; and partly being satisfied with the impeachment of the 12 Bishops of high treason for their protesting.

But since that another thing has bred a greater expectation of troubles than all those tumults did: on Monday last the King's Attorney did impeach Lord

Mandeville and the five members of high treason in the Upper House. The next day, notwithstanding their impeachment, some of them came and sat in the House. All parts of the Court being thronged with gentlemen and officers of the army, in the afternoon the King went with them all, his own Guard, and the PENSIONERS, most of the gentlemen armed with swords and pistols.

When we came into Westminster Hall, which was thronged with the number, the King commanded us all to stay there, and himself with a very small TRAIN went into the House of Commons, where never king was (as they say) but once – King Henry VIII. He came very unexpectedly, and at his first coming in he commanded the Speaker to come out of his chair, and sat down in it himself, asking divers times whether these traitors were there, but had no answer; but at last an excuse that, by the Orders of the House, they might not speak when their Speaker was out of his chair. The King then asked the Speaker, who excused himself that he might not speak but what the House gave order to him to say. Whereupon the King replied that it was no matter, for he knew them all if he saw them; and after he had viewed them all, he made a speech to them very majestically, declaring his resolution to have them, though they were then absent; promising not to infringe any of their liberties of Parliament, but commanding them to send the traitors to him if they came there again, and, after his coming out, gave order to the Serjeant-at-Arms to find them out and attach them. Before the King's coming the House was very high, and, as I am informed, sent to the City for 4,000 men to be presently sent down to them for their guard; but none came, all the City being terribly amazed with that unexpected charge of those persons, shops all shut, many of which do still continue so. They likewise sent to the trained bands in the CORPS-DE-GARDE before Whitehall to command them to disband, but they stayed still.

After the King had been in the House there was no more spoken, but only to adjourn till the next day. Yesterday it was my fortune, being in a coach, to meet the King with a small train going in to the City; whereupon I followed him to the Guildhall, where the Mayor and all the Aldermen and Common Council were met. The King made a speech to them, declaring his intentions to join with the Parliament in extirpation of Popery and all schisms and sectaries, and of redressing of all grievances of the subject, and his case to preserve the privileges of Parliament, but to question these traitors; [then gave] the reason of his Guards for securing himself, the Parliament, and them, from those late tumults, and [said] something of the Irish [business], and at last had some familiar discourse with the Aldermen, and invited himself to dinner to the Sheriff's. After a little pause a cry was set up amongst the Common Council, 'Parliament! Privileges of Parliament!' and presently another, 'God bless the King.' These two continued both at once a good while. I know not which was loudest.

After some knocking for silence the King commanded one to speak, if they had anything to say. One said, 'It is the vote of this Court that your Majesty hear the advice of your Parliament;' but presently another answered, 'It is not the vote of this Court; it is your own vote.' The King replied, 'Who is it that says I do not take the advice of my Parliament? I do take their advice, and will; but I must distinguish between the Parliament and some traitors in it, and these he would bring to legal trial.' Another bold fellow in the lowest rank stood upon a FORM, and cried, 'The privileges of Parliament!' Another cried out, 'Observe the man; apprehend him!' The King mildly replied, 'I have and will observe all privileges of Parliament, but no privilege can protect a traitor from a legal trial,' and so departed. In the outer hall were a multitude of the ruder people, who, as the King went out, set up a great cry, 'The privileges of Parliament!'

The House is yet very thin, as I am told, about 200 of them are in the country who cannot come up according to the Proclamation, by reason of the great floods, and many in town forbearing to come there. There is no other discourse but of open arms if these men be not brought to trial. The ill-affected party, which are those that follow the Court, do now speak very favourably of the Irish as those whose grievances were great, their demands moderate, and may stand the King in much stead.

PENSIONERS
The Gentlemen Pensioners, who formed the royal bodyguard. Otherwise known as Beefeaters, or Yeomen of the Guard.

TRAIN
A group of followers.

CORPS-DE-GARDE
The soldiers who guarded the King's palace at Whitehall.

FORM
A wooden bench.

ACTIVITY

Study Source 4.9 and answer the following questions.

1 What evidence can you find in this source of military power available both to the King and to Parliament in London?
2 What do the events at the London Guildhall tell us about the political effects of the attempt on the Five Members?
3 Why was the King surprised at the suggestion (paragraph 5) that he did not take Parliament's advice?
4 What evidence can be found in this source to suggest that many MPs were deliberately staying away from London at this time? Why might they do this?
5 What does this source tell us about Charles I's character?
6 Why did the attempt on the Five Members bring the kingdom closer towards civil war?

■ 4D Why did the King make such an enormous mistake?

With hindsight it is easy to see that the attempt on the Five Members was disastrous for the King. If he had been successful, we might look upon his decision to arrest the MPs differently. Why did Charles judge that the time was right to try to turn the tables on his opponents?

Don't do anything rash! Support for your Majesty has been growing since the summer. Less than a third of MPs voted for the 'Grand Remonstrance'. Time is on your side – your support will continue to grow as long as your Majesty does nothing rash.

Edward Hyde, MP (Earl of Clarendon) – a voice in the wilderness

'Grand Remonstrance', November 1641

Impeachment of twelve Bishops

Exclusion Bill

John Pym

Growth of a Royalist party

Attempt on the Five Members, 4 January 1642

Rumours that the Queen was to be impeached, December 1641

Growing rift between the House of Commons and the House of Lords

Tumults in London

Support for your Majesty has been growing since the summer. Less than a third of MPs voted for the 'Grand Remonstrance'. Now is the time to strike back at Pym and the other traitors.

Lord Digby

In France the King can go in person to the *Parlement* and order it to obey his commands. You have a duty to protect your Queen, your children and your Crown.

Queen Henrietta Maria

FOCUS ROUTE

Return to the Focus Route on page 78. Was the Civil War inevitable after the attempt to arrest the Five Members?

TALKING POINTS

1 Can you think of any other moments in history when some individual has taken a decision which appears rash or foolhardy in hindsight, but which, had it worked, would have enappeared very differently?
2 Is it possible that John Pym deliberately provoked Charles in order to strengthen Parliament's resolve after the Grand Remonstrance?

E The coming of civil war

The King's attempted *coup d'état* may have brought England to the brink of civil war, but there was another six months of manoeuvre and negotiation before the armies took to the field. Charles had lost London, and went north in search of arms and support. The Queen left England to seek foreign help. In Parliament Pym now reigned supreme, and began preparing for war. Yet there was still the hope that war could be avoided.

SOURCE 4.10 Movements of the King and Queen, January–August 1642

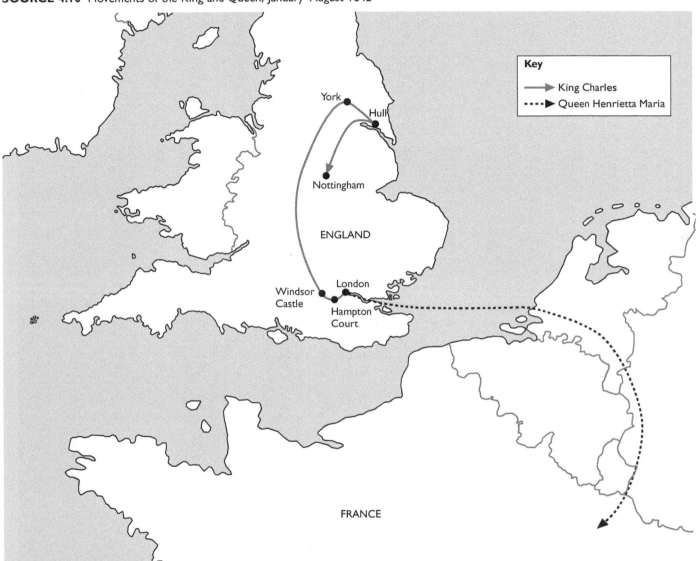

SOURCE 4.11 In April the King tried to seize the arms and ammunition that had been stored in Hull since the Bishops' Wars. He was refused entry to Hull by the Governor, Sir John Hotham. Hotham later regretted what he had done and tried unsuccessfully to go over to the Royalists. He was executed on Parliament's orders

COMMISSIONS OF ARRAY
The King's orders for the county militia to assemble and place themselves under the orders of his officers.

The struggle for control of the militia

The main issue now was control of the militia, the only trained military force available in the kingdom. This would require an appeal to the loyalty of local officers, together with a claim of legal authority over them. Parliament struck first by issuing the Militia Ordinance, the first time in English history that Parliament claimed the authority to issue laws without the King's approval. Just as the King had claimed that he acted from necessity in the 1620s, so Parliament now said necessity was driving it into new constitutional ground.

The King could not allow the Militia Ordinance to go unchallenged: there was no precedent for an English king surrendering command of the English army to Parliament. Charles condemned the Militia Ordinance and commanded his subjects not to obey it. On 11 June he issued his own COMMISSIONS OF ARRAY.

These events placed the militia captains throughout the kingdom in an impossible dilemma. The same was true for their soldiers, who in some places were receiving orders from two sets of officers. Sporadic fighting began breaking out in market towns across the kingdom as troops responded in different ways to the crisis.

■ 4E The struggle for control of the militia

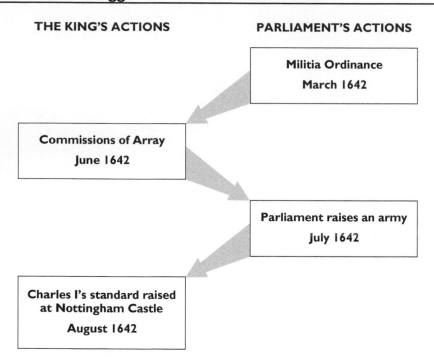

THE KING'S ACTIONS | **PARLIAMENT'S ACTIONS**

Militia Ordinance
March 1642

Commissions of Array
June 1642

Parliament raises an army
July 1642

Charles I's standard raised at Nottingham Castle
August 1642

SOURCE 4.12 Letter from Sir Thomas Knyvett to his wife, May 1642. Knyvett was a militia captain who received two sets of orders – one from Parliament and one from the King

Oh sweete hart, I am nowe in a great strayght what to doe. Waulking this other morning at Westminster, Sir John Potts, with commissary Muttford, saluted me (by vertue of an Ordinance of Parliament) my campanye and command againe. I was surprised what to doe, whether to take or refuse. Twas no place to dispute, so I tooke it and desierd sometime to advise upon it. I had not received this many howers, but I met with a declaration point Blanck against it by the King. This distraction made me to advise with some understanding men what condition I stand in, which is no other than a great many men of quality doe.

The Nineteen Propositions, June 1642

With conflict spreading across the kingdom, Parliament made one final approach to the King. The Nineteen Propositions – in effect, a declaration of Parliament's war aims – were written with public opinion in mind, as was the King's carefully drafted rejection of Parliament's terms.

Summary of the Nineteen Propositions

- Parliament to control appointments to the Privy Council and offices of state
- Policies to be arrived at not through the advice of private individuals but through discussion in Parliament
- Parliament to control the education of the King's children
- Parliament to approve the marriages of the King's children
- Anti-Catholic laws to be strictly enforced
- Catholic peers to be excluded from the House of Lords
- Parliament to reform both the government and liturgy of the Church of England
- The King to approve the Militia Ordinance
- Forts and castles to be put under the command of officers approved by Parliament
- The Five Members to be cleared of all charges.

ACTIVITY

Draft a reply from the King to the above points from the Nineteen Propositions. End your reply with this extract from the King's original response.

These being passed, we may be waited on bareheaded, we may have our hand kissed, the style of Majesty continued to us, and the King's authority declared by both Houses of Parliament may be still the style of your commands . . . but as to true and real power, we should remain but the outside, but the picture, but the sign of a King.

The call to arms

On 12 July Parliament passed a resolution raising an army and placing it under the command of the Earl of Essex. Parliament's resolution called upon the King to enter into 'a good accord with his Parliament to prevent a civil war'.

On 22 August the King raised his royal standard on Castle Hill in Nottingham, calling into existence a Royal army. The vast majority of English men and women did not want civil war, but they were powerless to prevent it. Now they had to choose between the King and Parliament. In the coming months and years, the failure of England's constitution would force them to define their loyalties in new ways, or to abandon the idea of loyalty altogether and act purely from the motives of self-interest and survival.

FOCUS ROUTE

Return to the Focus Route on page 78. Did the Militia Ordinance push England to the 'point of no return', or could a peaceful settlement have been negotiated after this?

 ## For King or Parliament?

SOURCE 4.13 Sir Benjamin Rudyerd, speaking in the House of Commons in mid-July 1642

Let us set ourselves three years back. If any man then could have credibly told us that within three years the Queen shall be gone out of England into the Low Countries for any cause whatsoever, the King shall remove from his Parliament from London to York, declaring himself not to be safe here, that there shall be a total Rebellion in Ireland, such discords and distempers both in church and state here as now we find; certainly we should have trembled at the thought of it.

On the other side, if any man then could have credibly told us, that within three years you shall have a Parliament, it would have been good News; that Ship Money shall be taken away by an Act of Parliament, the Reasons and Grounds of it so rooted out, as that neither it, nor anything like it, can ever grow up again; that Monopolies, the High Commission Court, the Star Chamber, the Bishops Votes shall be taken away, the Council Table regulated and restrained, the Forests bounded and limited; that you shall have a triennial parliament, we should have thought this a dream of happiness. Yet now we are in the real possession of it, we do not enjoy it.

ACTIVITY

Study Source 4.13.

1 In no more than ten sentences, summarise how England had reached the situation described in this source.
2 If you had been Sir Benjamin Rudyerd, which side would you have supported?

George Digby and William, Lord Russell

Both men were courtiers at Whitehall in the 1630s. Both were in the Long Parliament. Digby was married to Lord Russell's sister. When war broke out, Digby fought for the King, Lord Russell for Parliament.

The Verney family

Sir Edmund Verney's family was torn in two by the Civil War. Sir Edmund decided, after much anguish, to support the King. So did his elder son, also named Edmund. His younger son, Sir Ralph Verney, MP for Aylesbury, supported Parliament.

Sir Edmund carried the King's standard at the Battle of Edgehill, where he was killed. (The picture shows Sir Edmund and his tomb, by Van Dyck.) When Sir Ralph sent his servant to retrieve his father's body, it could not be found. All that remained was his hand, severed at the wrist.

Sir Ralph Verney served Parliament until late 1643, when he was unable to sign the treaty with the Scots. He and his family fled to France, though he continued to support Parliament's cause. Parliament, suspecting him of being a 'delinquent', sequestered (confiscated) his estate, but the sequestration was subsequently lifted and in 1653 he returned to England.

ACTIVITY

Study the example of the Verney family and Source 4.14.

1 What did Sir Edmund Verney think about the causes of the Civil War?
2 Why did he support the King?

SOURCE 4.14   Sir Edmund Verney speaking to Edward Hyde, August 1642

I will willingly join with you the best I can, but I shall act it very scurvily. My condition is much worse than yours, and different I believe from any other man's, and will very well justify the melancholic that I confess to you possesses me. You have satisfaction in your conscience that you are in the right; that the King ought not to grant what is required of him; and so you do your duty and your business together. But for my part I do not like the quarrel, and do heartily wish that the King would yield and consent to what they desire; so that my conscience is only concerned in honour and gratitude to follow my master. I have eaten his bread and served him near thirty years, and will not do so base a thing as to forsake him: and choose rather to lose my life (which I am sure to do) to preserve and defend those things which are against my conscience to preserve and defend: for I will deal freely with you, I have no reverence for the bishops, for whom this quarrel [is being fought].

Sir William Waller (1597–1668)

Sir Ralph Hopton (1596–1651)

FOCUS ROUTE: WHO'S WHO?

Make brief notes on both Sir William Waller and Sir Ralph Hopton to include in your Who's who? list.

ACTIVITY

Study Source 4.15.
Why did Waller refer to 'this war without an enemy'?

SOURCE 4.15 Letter from Sir William Waller to Sir Ralph Hopton, June 1643. Waller commanded Parliament's army in the south-west in 1643. His old friend, Hopton, was in command of the Royalist army in the same region

To my Noble friend Sir Ralph Hopton at Wells:
The experience I have had of your worth and the happiness I have enjoyed in your friendship are wounding considerations when I look upon this present distance between us. Certainly my affections to you are so unchangeable, that hostility itself cannot violate my friendship in your person, but I must be true to the cause wherein I serve. That great God which is the searcher of my heart, knows with what a sad sense I go upon this service and with what a perfect hatred I detest this war without an enemy, but I look upon it as opus Domini [God's work] which is enough to silence all passion in me. The God of peace in his good time send us peace, & in the mean time fit us to receive it. We are both upon the stage and must act those parts that are assigned to us in this tragedy. Let us do it in a way of honour and without personal animosities. Whatsoever the issue be, I shall never willingly relinquish the dear title of your most affectionate friend & faithful servant,
Bath 16th June 1643   *Wm Waller*

H Review: when did the Civil War become inevitable?

At some point after November 1640, armed conflict between Parliament and the King became inevitable. The King did not have enough support to fight in 1641; only eleven MPs and 59 Lords voted against the attainder of Strafford.

On three separate occasions – the Army Plot, the Incident, and the Attempt on the Five Members – the King tried to resort to force to break the political deadlock. Perhaps King Charles did not believe that England's problems could be resolved peacefully. By August 1642 enough Englishmen agreed with him to form a Royalist army, and it took four years for Parliament to defeat it. A substantial number of people must have blamed Parliament for the war.

The anti-royal consensus of November 1640 broke down because the King made so many concessions. By November 1641 a Royalist party was forming around Charles, convinced that Pym and his friends were going too far: men who a year before had agreed to limit the King's power were not prepared to see their King humiliated. Pym pressed ahead with demands for further concessions. Once the King had tried to arrest Parliament's leaders on a charge of treason, a struggle for control of the kingdom's military forces was bound to follow. This led on into civil war.

■ **4F The making of the Royalist party**

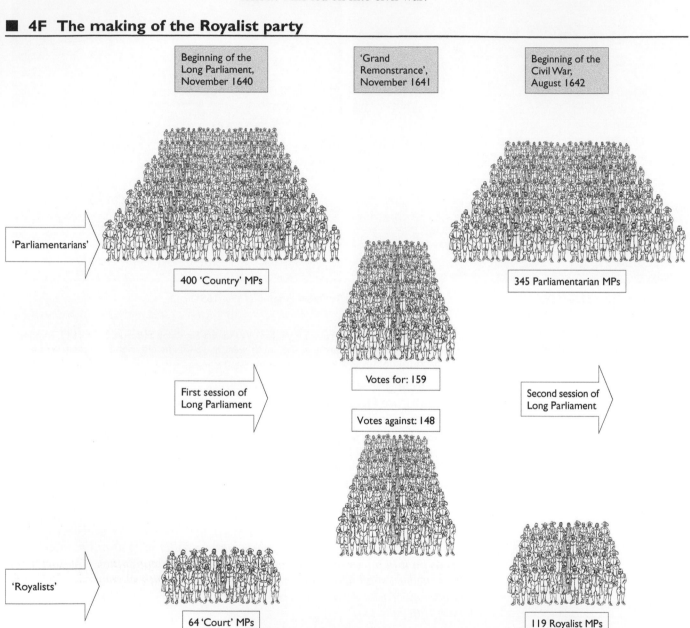

Beginning of the Long Parliament, November 1640

'Grand Remonstrance', November 1641

Beginning of the Civil War, August 1642

'Parliamentarians'

400 'Country' MPs

345 Parliamentarian MPs

First session of Long Parliament

Second session of Long Parliament

Votes for: 159

Votes against: 148

'Royalists'

64 'Court' MPs

119 Royalist MPs

FOCUS ROUTE

1 Return to the Focus Route on page 78. At what point between November 1640 and August 1642 did the Civil War become inevitable? To help you to make up your mind, you may find the activity at the top of page 101 useful.

2 Return to the Focus Route on page 79. To what extent did Parliament encroach on the King's royal prerogative between November 1640 and August 1642? The activity at the top of page 101 will help you to focus on this.

ACTIVITY

How far did the Long Parliament encroach on the King's royal prerogative between November 1640 and August 1642?

1 Divide the class into two groups. Each group is to identify evidence that could be sorted into one of the following categories:
  a) Acts of Parliament that merely ended practices which Parliament believed were already illegal (for example Ship Money)
  b) Acts and ordinances (laws) which took from the Crown power which until now had rightfully belonged to the King (for example the right to decide how often to call Parliament).
2 Use this evidence to complete a table like the one below, forming a part of your notes:

Acts of Parliament that merely ended practices which Parliament believed were already illegal (Acts which did not change the constitution)	Acts and ordinances which took from the Crown power which until now had rightfully belonged to the King (Acts which changed the constitution)
e.g. The Act prohibiting knighthood fines, August 1641	e.g. The Triennial Act, February 1641

3 How many of these Acts and ordinances occurred during the second session of the Long Parliament?
4 How can this information be used to explain the formation of a Royalist party?

Contemporary views on the origins of the Civil War

We look back on the English Civil War from the perspective of over 350 years, and this gives us knowledge and explanations that were not available at the time. But we may lack any real understanding of how contemporaries saw matters. How did the coming of war look in later years to those who looked back on it from a much closer perspective?

SOURCE 4.16 From King Charles I's speech on the scaffold, 30 January 1649

I shall begin first with my innocence. In truth I think it not very needful for me to insist long upon this, for all the world knows that I never did begin a war with the two Houses of Parliament. And I call God to witness, to whom I must shortly make an account, that I never did intend for to encroach upon their privileges. They began upon me; it is the militia they began upon. They confessed that the militia was mine, but they thought it fit for to have it from me. And, to be short, if anybody will look at the dates of commissions, of their commissions and mine, and likewise to the declarations, [they] will see clearly that they began these unhappy troubles, not I.

SOURCE 4.18 John Pym speaking to the City Fathers of London, 1642

We should never have stepped one step towards war if we might have had or hoped for such a peace as might have secured religion and liberty and the public good of the kingdom; but truly ill counsel did exclude us from such hope. We shall pursue the maintenance of our liberties, liberties that may not only be the laws and statutes, but liberties that may be in practice and in execution. For to have printed liberties, and not to have liberties in truth and reality, is but to mock the kingdom.

SOURCE 4.17 From a speech made in Parliament by Major-General Lambert, a leading Parliamentary general, in 1659

For the King, it is plain that Papists, prelates [bishops] and delinquents, all such that had places or titles, pluralists and generally all debauched people, ran with that stream. For the Parliament's party, an honest, sober, grave people, that groaned under oppressions, thirsted after grace, the reformed party of the nation, that had no ambitions and expected no advantage from the King or from the court. And these were the arguments and interests that brought the parties into the field:

1 *The papist had his toleration, and prerogative was that strength and source whence that was to proceed;*
2 *The Prelates, they had the advance and the formalities, which all flowed from the same fountain. Preferment flowed steadily on;*
3 *Dependence upon places of honour or profit engaged many and led a great way;*
4 *Debauched people expected liberty, or rather licence, to exercise their lusts and villainies without control.*

On the other side [Parliament's side] there was only a sober, quiet, reformed people.

ACTIVITY

Study Source 4.16.

1 Was King Charles correct when he said that it was Parliament which had picked a fight with him over the militia?
2 Why did King Charles focus attention on the 'short-term' argument over the militia in 1642, rather than 'long-term' causes, when claiming that the war was Parliament's fault?

Study Source 4.17.

3 General Lambert comes close in this source to blaming the Civil War on an argument between 'Court' and 'Country'. Why do you think he took a more long-term view of the war's origins than the King did?

Study Source 4.18.

4 Why did Pym argue that by going to war, Parliament was securing 'religion and liberty and the public good of the kingdom'?

■ 4G The billiard-ball effect, 1640–42: how the execution of Strafford set the ball rolling towards civil war

Was the 'British problem' responsible for the war?

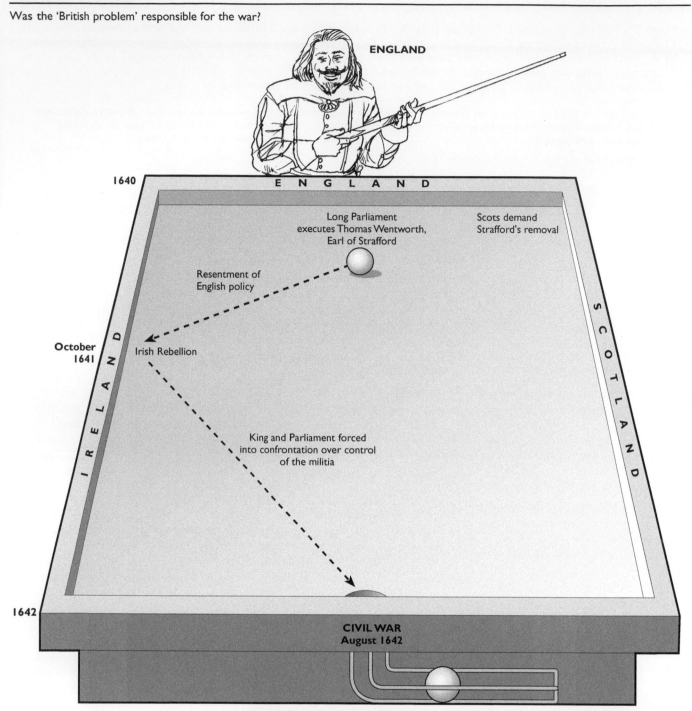

ENGLAND

1640

E N G L A N D

Long Parliament
executes Thomas Wentworth,
Earl of Strafford

Scots demand
Strafford's removal

Resentment of
English policy

October
1641

Irish Rebellion

King and Parliament forced
into confrontation over control
of the militia

1642

CIVIL WAR
August 1642

I R E L A N D

S C O T L A N D

ACTIVITY

Choose one of the following essay titles:

a) When and why did the outbreak of civil war become inevitable between November 1640 and August 1642?

b) Explain why a Royalist party formed between August 1641 and August 1642.

c) How far did the Long Parliament change the constitutional balance between Parliament and the Crown before the First Civil War broke out in August 1642?

d) How far did events in Scotland and Ireland contribute to the outbreak of civil war in England?

e) Why did civil war break out in England in 1642?

1   During the Long Parliament's first session, from November 1640 to August 1641, the King had very little support. Parliament took advantage of this to dismantle piece by piece the legal, financial and religious instruments of the Personal Rule.

2   The key event in this first period was the trial and execution of the Earl of Strafford. Strafford's death opened the floodgates to a series of Acts, all signed by the King, which ended the Personal Rule.

3   One of the most important of these was an Act which said that the King could not dissolve the current Parliament without its consent. This laid the legal foundation for the prolonged existence of the Long Parliament.

4   The King's concessions during this period won the support of many of his former critics, leading to the growth of a Royalist party. These were people who thought the time had come to work with the King instead of against him.

5   Parliament's leaders did not trust the King to honour the concessions he had already made. Pym and his supporters aimed to force the King to give up more of his prerogative powers in order to protect themselves and the kingdom against a Royalist backlash.

6   The Long Parliament's second session, from November 1641 to the outbreak of war in August 1642, was marked by the hardening of these two positions.

7   The Irish Rebellion of October 1641 forced the pace of change by calling into question the fundamental issue behind the politics: who controlled the army?

8   In early January 1642 the King tried to arrest Parliament's leaders, accusing them of treason. The failed attempt to arrest the Five Members forced the King to abandon London and travel north in search of support.

9   The next six months witnessed the gradual collapse of ordinary government. Militia captains and their soldiers were forced to choose between Parliament and the King. This led to sporadic fighting in the provinces.

10   In June 1642 Parliament issued its final offer of terms to the King – the Nineteen Propositions. When the King rejected these, both sides announced that they were raising armies for the defence of the King, Parliament, the law and religion. The Civil War had started.

Section 1 Review: Why did England have a civil war?

TALKING POINT

In what ways are the attitudes towards freedom and democracy held by Americans at the start of the twenty-first century similar to the old Whig view of history?

Theories of inevitability

Over the past two centuries there have been two major schools of thought that believed that the English Civil War – or something like it – was inevitable. These are known as the Whig and Marxist interpretations of history. Both of these interpretations are 'progressive', in the sense that they both emphasise progress in human affairs towards a better future.

The Whig interpretation

The Whig Party originated in the late seventeenth century. They wanted to exclude the Catholic Duke of York (later James II) from the throne, and thus represented the dominance of Parliament over the Crown. They came to power after the Glorious Revolution of 1688. The Whigs evolved into the Liberal Party in the nineteenth century, associated with parliamentary reform, NONCONFORMIST religion and the new wealth created by the industrial revolution.

The Whigs dominated English HISTORIOGRAPHY from the eighteenth century to the early twentieth century. They emphasised the unstoppable growth of representative government, believing that the British constitution had achieved the best possible balance between Parliament and a limited monarchy. The Whigs saw the Civil War as an unavoidable constitutional and legal conflict between a tyrannical king and a Parliament determined to protect its, and the nation's, liberties. They called the Personal Rule of Charles I the 'Eleven Years' Tyranny'.

NONCONFORMIST
Not conforming to the Anglican form of worship.

HISTORIOGRAPHY
The history of the history that has been written, in this case, about the causes of the English Civil War.

■ A The Whig interpretation of history

Tudor monarchy → English Civil War Parliament defeats royal tyranny → Glorious Revolution 1688 → **Parliamentary democracy**

The Marxist interpretation

The Marxists dominated English historiography from the 1920s until the 1970s. They were followers of the nineteenth-century German philosopher-historian Karl Marx, who wrote the *Communist Manifesto*. Marx saw all history as the struggle between classes, and predicted the eventual victory of the working masses over the capitalist 'oppressors'.

Their emphasis was on social and economic forces at work in early seventeenth-century English society, stressing the rise of capitalism from the medieval economy. The Marxists saw Parliament as the voice of the rising gentry and 'middling sort', determined to break down the existing political barriers to their economic progress. They saw the English Civil War as an inevitable political crisis, brought on as the old feudal monarchy defended its privileges against the gentry and the new economic power of the merchants. They saw the Great Rebellion as a 'bourgeois' (middle-class) revolution.

ACTIVITY

Work with a partner. Summarise each of these interpretations in three sentences and explain them orally to another pair.

'Bourgeois' revolution

FEUDALISM ⟶ CAPITALISM ⟶ COMMUNISM

'Socialist' revolution

FEUDALISM	CAPITALISM	COMMUNISM
• Monarchy • Land-owning classes rule	• Parliamentary government • Merchants, bankers and industrialists share control with the gentry	• Socialism • Working class rules • No property

■ **Learning trouble spot**

The 'inevitability' of the English Civil War

This book cannot ignore the Marxist and Whig interpretations, though it doesn't agree with either of them. Students may feel confused: if the war 'becomes inevitable' sometime between 1640 and 1642 (Chapter 4), then how could it be inevitable before 1640? It wasn't, but the circumstances in which it eventually arose were partly created by long-standing problems. Some historians have argued that these problems were insurmountable by peaceful means.

Both the Whigs and the Marxists took a long-term view of the English Civil War. Take a step back and the Great Rebellion can appear as one episode in a story that could have only one outcome – the rise of Parliament, at the expense of the Crown.

Revisionist theories

Since the 1970s belief in the inevitability of the English Civil War has gone out of fashion. Historians are now more interested in the idea that the Civil War could have been avoided than they are in its inevitability.

Even when Marxist history dominated the debate, it was rejected by historians who did not accept Marxist theories. They produced examples of individuals who did not behave in the way the Marxist model predicted. Rather than dividing one class from another, the English Civil War split every class of English society down the middle, just as contemporaries had claimed.

Recent historians have been more concerned to understand the seventeenth century in its own terms. This has thrown them back into the arguments and the language of the time, especially where religion is concerned. They have also focused attention on the interpersonal relationships of key individuals, and on the day-to-day unfolding of events as the crisis of 1640 broke and then spiralled out of control.

Inevitability revisited

If something is inevitable, it cannot be avoided. If Charles I hadn't tried to modernise the English state in the 1630s, the Civil War might not have happened. Seen from this angle, the war wasn't inevitable. But then we must ask ourselves this question: why did he do it?

Charles I was responding to pressures that could not be ignored by a responsible king. England did not exist in isolation: it was threatened by its continental neighbours, one of which – France – was soon to become the most powerful state in Europe. (The French monarchy was itself struggling with problems that were hindering France's ability to intervene effectively in the Thirty Years' War – particularly royal finance and regional diversity.) Sooner or later an English king was bound to try to strengthen his kingdom by imposing greater discipline on county government. This doesn't mean that a civil war was inevitable, but it suggests that seventeenth-century England faced some kind of unavoidable crisis.

Causes of the English Civil War

The explanation of the causes of the Civil War has to be found in the events of Charles I's reign, although they may have been driven by long-term forces.

ACTIVITY

England plc goes down the tubes

Here is a story about management that will be familiar to many people:

> 1   A new Managing Director is appointed to a firm.
>
> 2   The new MD thinks the firm needs to change to bring it up to date. The Board of Directors is anxious that other firms are getting better results. The MD knows that the changes he wants to make will be unpopular, but he is determined to carry them out. In private he thinks the previous Managing Director was lazy.
>
> 3   The MD wants his own people around him. He appoints a new Deputy to help him carry through the changes. People who don't agree with his proposals are encouraged to leave.
>
> 4   His Deputy begins scrutinising the firm, looking for weaknesses. He begins changing long-established procedures. Workers are told they must account for their performance. Staff complain about the new regime. They think they already work hard enough.
>
> At this point things could go one of two ways:
>
> **a)** SUCCESS. The workers accept the inevitability of the new regime and try to implement the changes as best they can. If the new Deputy is popular they are more likely to put up with these changes.
>
> **b)** FAILURE. The workers get up in arms about the new regime. The morale of the firm suffers. Workers consult their unions and threaten strike action. The MD may be forced to resign.
>
> And eventually the process starts all over again.

This book takes the view that the Civil War was caused by a failed attempt to make England more competitive. Charles I was appalled at the weakness of the English state in the 1620s. In the 1630s he tried to do something about it, with disastrous results. The policy of Thorough (see page 50) aimed at strengthening central government control over local government, but it backfired.

Complete the analogy by rewriting the management story above using facts from the 1620s and 1630s. Then draw and complete this spider diagram by adding detail to the problems that contributed to the failure of Charles's government.

Causes of the English Civil War

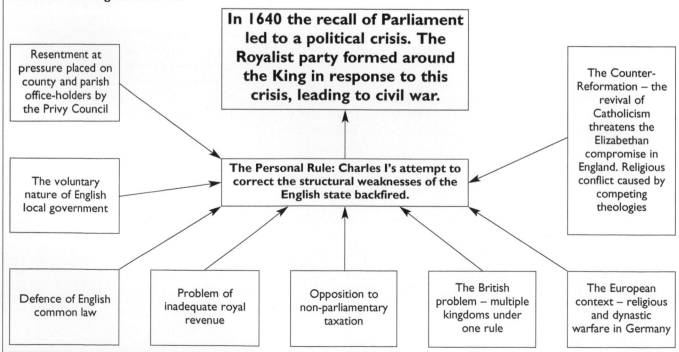

Resentment at pressure placed on county and parish office-holders by the Privy Council

The voluntary nature of English local government

Defence of English common law

In 1640 the recall of Parliament led to a political crisis. The Royalist party formed around the King in response to this crisis, leading to civil war.

The Personal Rule: Charles I's attempt to correct the structural weaknesses of the English state backfired.

The Counter-Reformation – the revival of Catholicism threatens the Elizabethan compromise in England. Religious conflict caused by competing theologies

Problem of inadequate royal revenue

Opposition to non-parliamentary taxation

The British problem – multiple kingdoms under one rule

The European context – religious and dynastic warfare in Germany

What kind of revolution did England have in the 1640s?

Death of a King

On the morning of 30 January 1649, a unique event took place in the centre of London. The King of England was led on foot along streets lined with soldiers, through a crowd of spectators, to the Banqueting House in Whitehall. During his short journey one of his guards asked the King to touch him; in the last minutes of Charles I's life, one of his enemies still believed that the King's touch could cure a person of illness.

When they arrived at the Banqueting House, the King was led up the stairs into the dining hall. On the ceiling there was a huge painting of his father being taken up to heaven to rest with the gods, but it was covered over with canvas so its message – the divinity of kings – could not be seen. The King was led out through a window onto a high wooden scaffold, where he saw an amazing scene. Thousands of people, mostly in silence, were looking up at him. They were held back from the scaffold by a squadron of armoured cavalry. On the wooden deck there was a wooden block, on one side an open coffin, and sawdust had been sprinkled on the floor around the block to catch his blood. A masked executioner stood quietly by, holding a broad-bladed axe.

King Charles stepped forward and made a short speech. He told the people that the war was not his fault. He blamed Parliament for starting the war, and then said he forgave them. He told the crowd that he wanted them to be free, but that only a King could protect their freedom. He also said that he was prepared to die for this belief – that he was their martyr. During his speech people noticed that the King, who usually stuttered, spoke easily and fluently. He did not shiver, in spite of the cold; not wanting anyone to think that he was afraid to die, he had put on two white shirts that morning.

The King then turned to the executioner and said a few words. He handed Bishop Juxon some personal effects. Then he knelt down, stretched out his hands, and with one mighty blow he was beheaded. A groan went up from the crowd as the blood gushed from his torso. The executioner picked up the King's head by the hair and held it aloft. Some of the crowd broke through the line of cavalry to the ground under the scaffold, tore off pieces of their clothing and bathed it in the King's blood.

SOURCE I The execution of Charles I, from a contemporary print

What was the English Revolution?

The death of King Charles I was one of the most dramatic events in the history of England. It was the only time a king of England was publicly executed: some other kings in the Middle Ages had been deposed and murdered, but this was done in broad daylight after a public trial. The trial was rigged, of course – there was no way that his judges were going to find the King not guilty – but even so it was a brave and desperate gesture. The men who signed the King's death warrant were consciously breaking new ground, declaring to the world that kings of England could be held to account for what they had done. This event alone might be enough to describe the events of 1649 as a 'revolution'. The death of the King, however, was not the only thing about the 1640s that was revolutionary.

■ A Road to Revolution

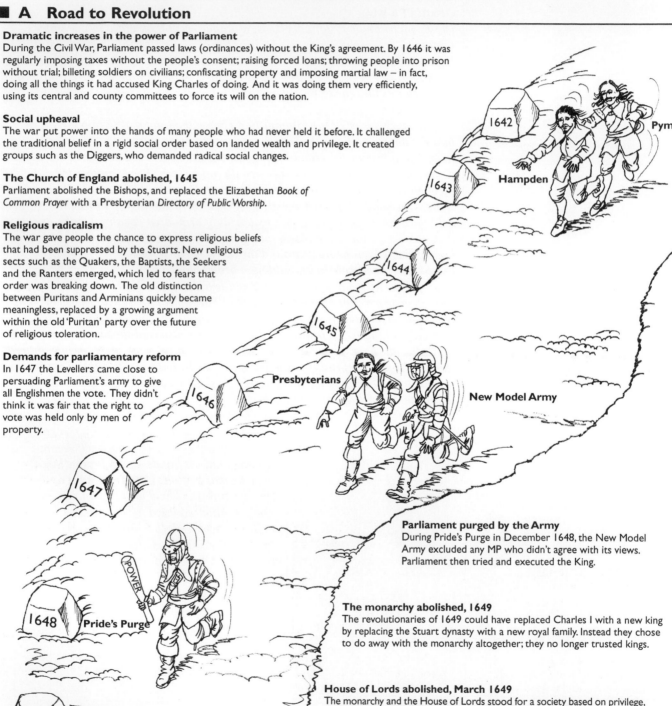

Dramatic increases in the power of Parliament
During the Civil War, Parliament passed laws (ordinances) without the King's agreement. By 1646 it was regularly imposing taxes without the people's consent; raising forced loans; throwing people into prison without trial; billeting soldiers on civilians; confiscating property and imposing martial law – in fact, doing all the things it had accused King Charles of doing. And it was doing them very efficiently, using its central and county committees to force its will on the nation.

Social upheaval
The war put power into the hands of many people who had never held it before. It challenged the traditional belief in a rigid social order based on landed wealth and privilege. It created groups such as the Diggers, who demanded radical social changes.

The Church of England abolished, 1645
Parliament abolished the Bishops, and replaced the Elizabethan *Book of Common Prayer* with a Presbyterian *Directory of Public Worship*.

Religious radicalism
The war gave people the chance to express religious beliefs that had been suppressed by the Stuarts. New religious sects such as the Quakers, the Baptists, the Seekers and the Ranters emerged, which led to fears that order was breaking down. The old distinction between Puritans and Arminians quickly became meaningless, replaced by a growing argument within the old 'Puritan' party over the future of religious toleration.

Demands for parliamentary reform
In 1647 the Levellers came close to persuading Parliament's army to give all Englishmen the vote. They didn't think it was fair that the right to vote was held only by men of property.

Parliament purged by the Army
During Pride's Purge in December 1648, the New Model Army excluded any MP who didn't agree with its views. Parliament then tried and executed the King.

The monarchy abolished, 1649
The revolutionaries of 1649 could have replaced Charles I with a new king by replacing the Stuart dynasty with a new royal family. Instead they chose to do away with the monarchy altogether; they no longer trusted kings.

House of Lords abolished, March 1649
The monarchy and the House of Lords stood for a society based on privilege, social rank and inequality – they stood or fell together. Many Lords fought for Parliament in the Civil War, but in 1649 this fact didn't save them. England was to be a republic, governed by the people's elected representatives in the House of Commons.

ACTIVITY

Take on the viewpoint of one of the characters listed below and explain whether you would be for or against the developments outlined in Chart A. Think about what effect these changes would have on your daily life and whether they would affect your beliefs.

• A landless labourer
• A gentleman farmer whose income is mostly from rent
• A merchant
• A Puritan preacher
• A Catholic

This section sets out to explore the nature and causes of the English Revolution. A level questions on this topic tend to focus on two issues, splitting the period into two parts, before and after 1646:

a) Why did Parliament win the first Civil War?

b) Why did the attempts to find a compromise settlement after 1646 fail, leading to the revolutionary events of 1648–49?

Chapters 5–7 concentrate on the first of these issues; Chapter 8 deals with the second.

You need to be aware that the events of 1642–49 were continuous, fast-moving developments that produced huge changes throughout the 1640s.

TALKING POINTS

1 What are the main features of revolutions? Think about other revolutions you may have studied:

• the Russian Revolution, 1917
• the French Revolution, 1789
• the American Revolution, 1776.

2 What did these revolutions have in common with each other? How did they differ?

FOCUS ROUTE

1 What *was* the English Revolution? You cannot explain why the English Revolution happened unless you know what it is you are trying to explain. You need to define your terms. What did this revolution consist of? Was it:

• a political revolution, with the emphasis on constitutional change, fought out between different groups within the ruling elite? This was the main thrust of Whig historians, for example S.R. Gardiner, in the nineteenth and early twentieth centuries
• a social revolution, with the 'middling sort' taking power from those above them in the social order? This was the main thrust of mid-twentieth century Marxist historians, for example Christopher Hill
• a religious revolution? The historian John Morrill has emphasised the central role played by religion in the English Civil War and in the English Revolution. In other words, are we missing the point because we live in a secular society?
• a revolution in the relationship between the state and the subject who lived in it? Recent research is emphasising the importance of 'state-building' in the context of the English Revolution
• a paradox? In the 1970s Robert Ashton called the English Revolution a conservative revolution. He meant that although the events of the 1640s saw revolutionary changes, they were controlled by men who opposed radical change.

2 Why did the English Revolution happen? What were the main forces in conflict with each other? Did these remain constant throughout the period 1642–49, or did they change?

DISCUSS

Sources 2–5 on page 110 suggest various ways in which the events of the 1640s might be described as a revolution. Study each source and discuss the way in which it illustrates changes that people at the time might have thought were revolutionary.

SOURCE 2 'The world turn'd upside down', 1647

THE
World turn'd upside down:
OR
A briefe description of the ridiculous Fashions
of these distracted Times.

By T. J. a well-willer to King, Parliament and Kingdom.

SOURCE 4 'The Quaker's dream', 1655

THE QVAKERS DREAM: 14
OR,
The Devil's Pilgrimage in England:
BEING
An infallible Relation of their severalMeetings,
Shreekings, Shakings, Quakings, Roarings, Yellings, Howlings, Trem-
blings in the Bodies, and Rhings in the Bellies: With a Narrative of
their several Arguments, Tenets, Principles, and strange Doctrine: The
strange and wonderful Satanical Apparitions, and the appearing of the
Devil unto them in the likeness of a black Boar, a Dog with flaming eys,
and a black man without a head, causing the Dogs to bark, the Swine
to cry, and the Cattel to run, to the great admiration of all that shall
read the same.

London, Printed for G. Horton, and are to be sold at the Royal
Exchange in Cornhil, 1655. April. 26.

SOURCE 3 'A great and bloody fight at Colchester', 1648

SOURCE 5 Spending Kent's weekly assessments, 1643

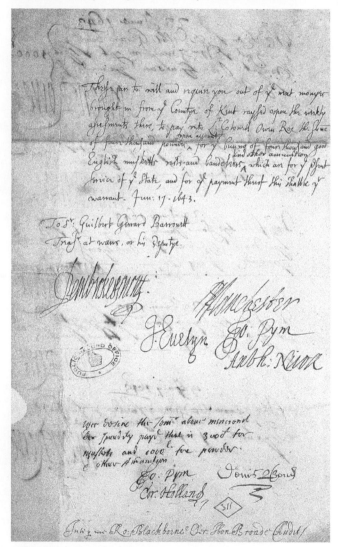

*These are to will and require you out of ye next monyes
brought in from ye Countye of Kent raysed upon the weekly
assessments there to pay unto L[ieutenant] Colonell Owen
Roe the sume of four thousand pounds upon account for ye
buying of foure thousand good English musketts rests and
bandeleers and other amunition which are for ye present
service of ye state and for ye payment thereof this shalbe
y[ou]r warrant. Jun[e] 17, 1643.*

5

Outline of the English Civil War, 1642–46

CHAPTER OVERVIEW

This chapter aims to provide a simple narrative of the main events of the war, together with some useful maps and diagrams. It should be read in conjunction with Chapter 7, and can be used to help place Chapter 6 in a broader context.

A   1642 – stalemate (pp. 112–14)

B   1643 – the Royalist 'high tide' (pp. 115–17)

C   1644 – the widening conflict (pp. 117–20)

D   1645–46 – the New Model Army (pp. 121–23)

■ 5A Main events of the Civil War, 1642–46

(Royalist successes in *italic*, Parliament's successes in **bold**)

1642	
August	King raises his standard at Nottingham
September	King raises troops in the Welsh border country
October	Battle of Edgehill – inconclusive first major battle of the war
November	Battle of Turnham Green – Royalist march on London halted by the London trained bands
December	Parliament opens peace negotiations
	Parliament establishes the Eastern Association (see Chapter 7)

1643	
February	'Oxford Treaty' negotiations begin
	Parliament's weekly Assessment Ordinance
April	'Oxford Treaty' negotiations collapse
	Parliament's Sequestration Ordinance
May	Parliament's Compulsory Loans Ordinance
July	Parliament's Excise Ordinance
	Royalists capture Bristol
	Battle of Lansdown Hill
	Battle of Roundway Down
	Westminster Assembly begins discussions on a new church settlement
August	Siege of Gloucester begins
	Parliament's Impressment Ordinance
	Solemn League and Covenant – Parliament allies with Scotland
September	**Parliament relieves the siege of Gloucester**
	King signs the Cessation Treaty with the Irish
	First Battle of Newbury

1644	
January	Royalist Parliament meets at Oxford
	Scottish army enters England
June	Siege of York
	Battle of Cropredy Bridge
July	**Battle of Marston Moor**
August	*Essex defeated at Lostwithiel, Cornwall*
October	Second Battle of Newbury
November	Political rift in Parliament between Independents and Presbyterians

1645	
February	Parliament's New Model Ordinance
April	Parliament's Self-Denying Ordinance
June	**Battle of Naseby**
July	**Battle of Langport**
August	Parliament's ordinance establishing a national Presbyterian church
September	**Parliament captures Bristol**

1646	
May	King surrenders to the Scots
June	Oxford surrenders to Parliament. End of the war

FOCUS ROUTE

1 Make a copy of the graph below to show how the war was going for Parliament.

2 As you read through this chapter, mark on the graph the following information:

• turning points in the war – when did Parliament begin to get the upper hand?

• major setbacks for Parliament.

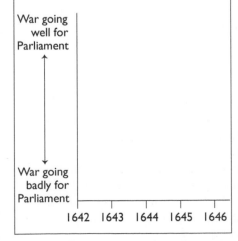

War going well for Parliament

War going badly for Parliament

1642   1643   1644   1645   1646

A 1642 – stalemate

■ 5B The Edgehill campaign

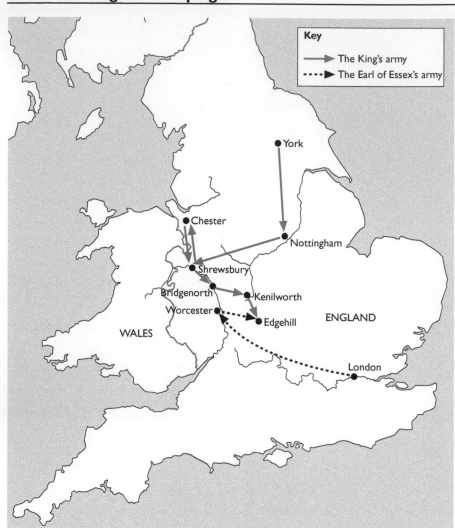

Key
→ The King's army
⇢ The Earl of Essex's army

The Battle of Edgehill, 23 October 1642

In the late summer of 1642, both sides wanted a decisive battle to bring the war to a speedy end. The King needed a quick victory before Parliament could mobilise its resources: his best chance was to march on London with as many men as he could gather from the shires and put an end to the 'Great Rebellion'.

Before he could march on London he had to gather an army. He turned for this to the Welsh borders, where he expected strong support. From Nottingham he marched to Shrewsbury, gathering a force of about 12,000 men before heading south-east towards London. He was en route to Banbury when Prince Rupert informed him that they were in contact with Parliament's army a few miles to the west.

Commanding Parliament's army was the Earl of Essex, who had helped to command the King's army in the first Bishops' War. Essex had decided to confront the Royalists immediately, marching into the Midlands to assert Parliament's power in the heart of England. When he learned that the King had left Shrewsbury, he moved to bar the Royalists' path to London; for several days the two armies marched parallel to each other, about 20 miles apart, unaware of the other's presence. Only when the quartermasters of both armies ran into each other while collecting provisions was contact made.

FOCUS ROUTE: WHO'S WHO?

Make brief notes on the Earl of Essex to include in your Who's who? list.

DISTANCES

1 mile = 1.6 kilometres

The King ordered his army to deploy on Edgehill, a high ridge overlooking the village of Kineton, hoping that Essex could be induced to attack uphill. Instead the Parliamentarians assembled on the plain 2 miles away, waiting for the King to make the first move. The armies adopted the standard deployment of the time, with the infantry regiments in the centre and the cavalry protecting the wings. They were fairly evenly matched, both sides having about 15,000 men. Realising that there would be no battle unless he forced the issue, the King moved his army down off the ridge onto the plain and attacked.

SOURCE 5.1 Prayer of Sir Jacob Astley, a Royalist commander of infantry at Edgehill

O Lord, Thou knowest how busy I must be this day. If I forget Thee, do not Thou forget me.

SOURCE 5.2 The Battle of Edgehill

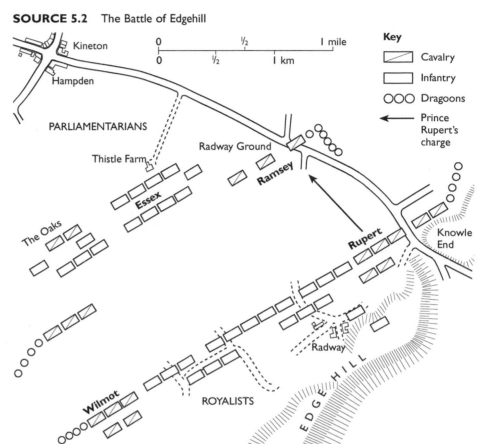

FOCUS ROUTE: WHO'S WHO?

Make brief notes on Prince Rupert of the Rhine to include in your Who's who? list.

At first the battle went badly for Parliament. Before a shot was fired, Sir Faithful Fortescue's troop crossed over to the Royalists in full view of both armies. The cavalry on the Royalist right wing, commanded by Prince Rupert, charged Sir James Ramsey's cavalry. Ramsey's men turned and fled, but in their eagerness and inexperience Rupert's reserves joined in the chase, pursuing the Roundhead horsemen all the way to Kineton. A similar scene unfolded on the Royalist left wing, where Lord Wilmot's cavalry scattered the right wing of Parliament's army.

In the centre Parliament's infantry stood fast against the Royalist advance, supported by two remaining regiments of cavalry. In spite of the Royalist successes on both wings, Parliament now had the only effective cavalry on the battlefield, and their attack drove back the left wing of the Royalist infantry with heavy loss. As Rupert's cavalry drifted back to the battlefield they found the situation greatly altered, with the King's infantry in danger of being destroyed. Charles rode among his foot soldiers, giving them encouragement. As night came on, the exhausted soldiers drew apart in confusion and shock. Some 3000 men had died, and many others were wounded or had fled.

On the following day neither army was in a fit state to continue the battle. The King resumed his march towards London, establishing his headquarters in Oxford. Essex's army reached London before Prince Rupert, but already the approach of the Royalists had galvanised Parliament into action. A new army, consisting partly of the London trained bands (militia), barred Rupert's path at Turnham Green on 13 November, after which the Royalists retreated to Oxford. Both sides ended the year consolidating their headquarters and reflecting on their first experience of battle.

The 'Oxford Treaty'

Parliament's lacklustre performance at Edgehill, together with general revulsion at the outbreak of war, led to renewed attempts at a negotiated peace. Under pressure from the House of Lords, Parliament drew up new terms and began negotiations with the King's commissioners at Oxford.

Parliament's terms were essentially a mild version of the Nineteen Propositions (see pages 96–97), with additional clauses against Papists. The fear of Catholicism was strengthened when some of the King's correspondence with the Earl of Newcastle, captured by the Parliamentarian Sir Thomas Fairfax and read out in the Commons, proved that Charles was encouraging the recruitment of Roman Catholics in his northern army. The captured letters helped to remind Parliament of what was at stake if the King should win.

Charles's reply to Parliament's initial approach made Pym's task much easier. Parliament had spent weeks drawing up the new proposals, so Lords and MPs alike were incensed when the King declared that whoever had drawn them up only wanted 'to make things worse and worse'. Negotiations dragged on into the spring of 1643, but they had little chance of success.

The reason for this was that in the spring and summer of 1643, the King thought that he was winning the war. Charles was urged to pursue outright military victory, paving the way to revoke all the concessions made to the Long Parliament. It was precisely this possibility which had led Pym and his supporters to push for further safeguards in the Grand Remonstrance of 1641.

MILITARY TERMS	
FOOT	Infantry, foot soldiers. Consisted of pikemen and musketeers
HORSE	Cavalry
DRAGOONS	Mounted infantry armed with a sword and a musket. In battle they usually fought on foot
BAGGAGE TRAIN	The supply wagons that accompanied the army
QUARTERMASTER	The officer responsible for acquiring food for the army
DISPOSITIONS	The way the army is arranged before a battle
TO DEPLOY	To place the soldiers in their dispositions
TO STAND TO	For foot soldiers to take up their weapons ready for battle

■ **5C The Royalist high tide, 1643**

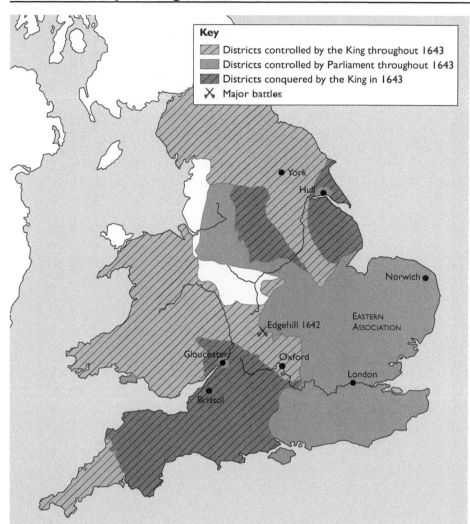

Key
- Districts controlled by the King throughout 1643
- Districts controlled by Parliament throughout 1643
- Districts conquered by the King in 1643
- ✗ Major battles

York
Hull
Norwich
EASTERN ASSOCIATION
Edgehill 1642
Gloucester
Oxford
London
Bristol

EASTERN ASSOCIATION
One of the so-called association armies formed by Parliament by grouping the militias of several counties into one regional force.

In 1643 it looked as if the King was winning the war. Parliament was shaken by a series of military defeats, high-profile desertions, and the deaths in battle of John Hampden and Lord Brooke, both leading members of the Puritan network. Parliament's resources took time to take effect, whereas the King's supporters appeared to have mobilised quickly. Some historians have spoken of a Royalist 'three-pronged strategy', advancing on London from the north, the south-west and the Midlands. By the summer, Parliament was facing a crisis of confidence. The rising panic led to demands for the resignation of the Earl of Essex as Lord General.

The war in the north

By the end of June the whole of Yorkshire, apart from Hull, was in Royalist hands. The Earl of Newcastle had fortified Newark, which commanded the Great North Road and a major bridge across the River Trent. Parliament's commanders in Yorkshire – Lord Fairfax and his son, Sir Thomas Fairfax – were unable to prevent Royalist victories at Tadcaster, Seacroft Moor and Adwalton Moor. In March the governor of Scarborough betrayed Parliament by handing over the castle to the Royalists. This was nearly followed by a worse disaster at Hull when John Hotham and his father, who had famously denied the King entry into the city in 1642 (see page 95), tried to deliver Hull and its arsenal to the Royalists. By July the Roundheads were scrambling to prevent

Newcastle's army from marching south, threatening London and the Puritan heartland in East Anglia and Lincolnshire. The continued resistance of Hull was the main factor preventing the completion of the King's conquest of the North.

The war in the south-west

Royalist progress in Cornwall, Devon and Somerset was even more dramatic. Commanded by Sir Ralph Hopton, the Royalists advanced from Cornwall through Devon, where they joined forces with Prince Maurice. Soon Plymouth was the only major factor preventing the collapse of Parliament's cause in the south-west.

As the Royalists advanced on Bath, Hopton was confronted by Parliamentary forces commanded by his old friend Sir William Waller (see page 99). Hopton's army forced its way onto Lansdown Hill outside Bath. Eight days later Waller's cavalry was destroyed at Roundway Down in Wiltshire. The King's forces in the south-west would soon be able to link up with the army at Oxford for a combined attack on London.

Before that threat materialised, Parliament was shaken to the core by the fall of Bristol. Bristol was the most important port outside London. When Parliament learned of its surrender by Nathaniel Fiennes, he was court-martialled and sentenced to death. The intervention of Lord Essex saved his life, but by this time Essex himself was being accused of incompetence. Only with great difficulty did Pym persuade Parliament to give the Lord General one more chance to vindicate his reputation. In late August 1643 Essex was sent to the relief of Gloucester, where Parliament's garrison of 1500 men was besieged by a Royalist army of 30,000, the largest force ever assembled by the King.

The siege of Gloucester

FOCUS ROUTE: WHO'S WHO?

Make brief notes on Prince Maurice of Nassau to include in your Who's who? list.

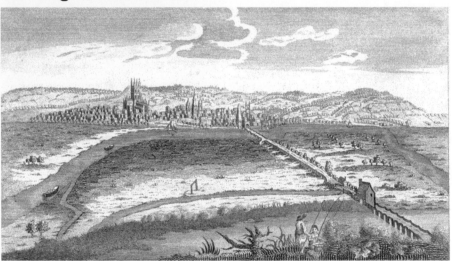

SOURCE 5.3 Gloucester – an eighteenth-century picture of the city besieged in 1643. Its strategic significance lay in the long bridge in the foreground, and its control of trade along the river Severn

The King now concentrated his forces on Gloucester. If Gloucester fell, it would create an unbroken Royalist power bloc stretching from Shrewsbury to Bristol, and from Wales to Oxford. Control of Gloucester's Severn bridge would open a direct line to Oxford from the Royalist recruiting areas in south Wales.

He confronted a city which had had a year to prepare its defences. The medieval city walls had been strengthened by the addition of earth ramparts capable of absorbing the impact of shot from cannon and mortars. The Governor of Gloucester, Sir Edward Massey, had ordered his men to pull down houses outside the ramparts in order to produce clear fields of fire for his own artillery and musketeers. The city had 40 barrels of gunpowder and a few cannon.

Meanwhile, Essex left London on 23 August with 15,000 men on a mission that would take Parliament's best force deep into enemy-held territory. He chose a route that passed to the north of Oxford, threading a path between Royalist garrisons.

FOCUS ROUTE: WHO'S WHO?

Make brief notes on Sir Edward Massey to include in your Who's who? list.

When Essex approached Gloucester, the King abandoned the siege rather than fight with his back to a hostile city. As Essex marched into Gloucester, the King's army circled around behind him to cut off his retreat to London. A war of manoeuvre followed, as Essex tried to find a way back up the Cotswold hills without having to give battle at a disadvantage. The King eventually managed to block his path to London at Newbury. In the battle that followed, Essex forced his way through the King's army to safety.

The survival of Gloucester was not a major victory for the Parliamentarians, but it was seen as a turning point in the war. The Queen criticised Charles for attacking Gloucester when he could have attacked London. Rupert thought the Royalist army should have taken Gloucester by storm instead of settling into a long siege. Such judgements are easy to make in retrospect. The King was trying to take the city with minimal loss of life. Its importance to both sides is shown by the fact that Parliament risked its main field army to save the city.

■ **5D Into the lion's den – the relief of Gloucester, August–September 1643**

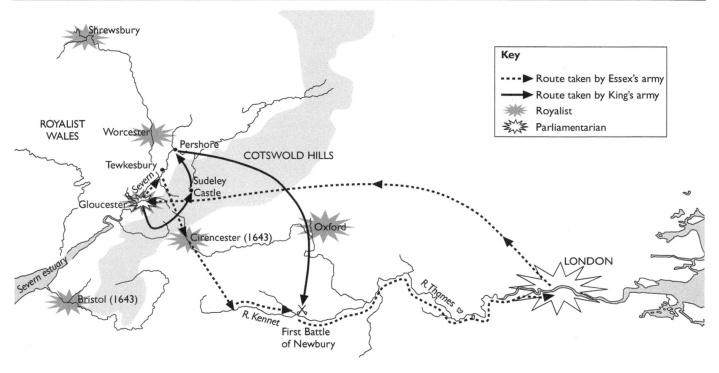

IRISH CONFEDERATION
An alliance formed in Ireland between the Irish Catholics and the English Royalists under the Duke of Ormond.

FOCUS ROUTE: WHO'S WHO?

Make brief notes on Alexander Leslie, Earl of Leven to include in your Who's who? list.

FOCUS ROUTE: WHO'S WHO?

Make brief notes on the Earl of Montrose to include in your Who's who? list.

C 1644 – the widening conflict

In January 1644 a Scottish army of 21,000 men commanded by Alexander Leslie, Earl of Leven, crossed the border into northern England as allies of Parliament. The Solemn League and Covenant (see Chapter 7, page 150) was Pym's final contribution to Parliament's war effort, but it had unforeseen consequences. The coming of the Scots altered the dynamics of the conflict, politically and militarily. In September 1643, in a direct response to Parliament's alliance with the Scots, the King signed the Cessation Treaty with the Irish rebels, and in 1644 Irish troops began appearing in England and Wales. As the Scots threatened to send an army to Ireland to protect their settlements there, so the IRISH CONFEDERATION threatened to send an army into Scotland to support the Earl of Montrose. In February 1644 the King appointed Montrose Lieutenant-General of Royalist forces in Scotland; in the summer of 1644 he began a campaign that threatened the Scottish Lowlands, forcing the Covenanters to divert resources to deal with their own civil war.

■ 5E The British archipelago disintegrates

As civil war spread through all three kingdoms, the British Isles began to break up along ethnic and/or religious lines, threatening the very concept of nationhood.

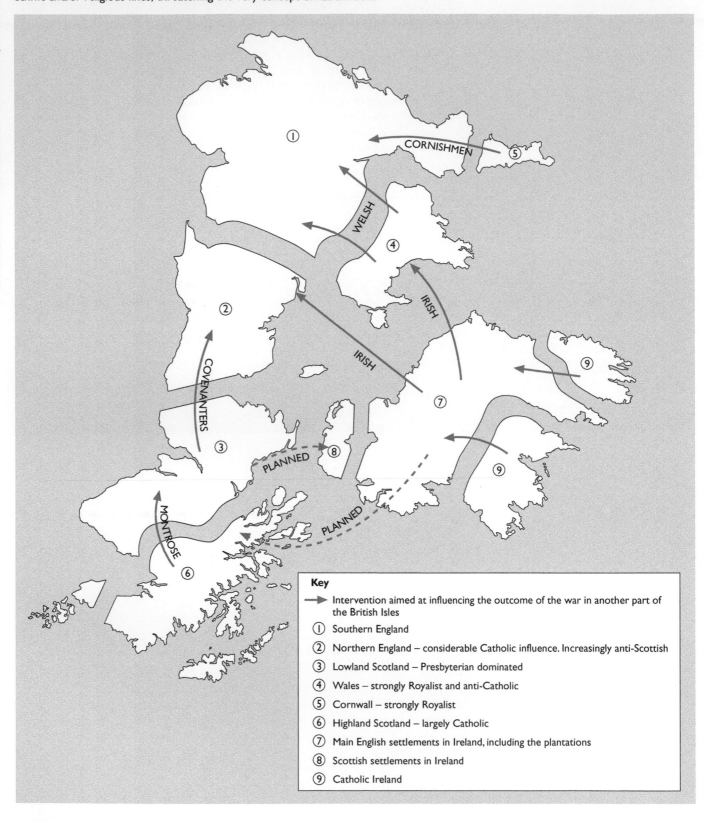

Key

→ Intervention aimed at influencing the outcome of the war in another part of the British Isles

① Southern England

② Northern England – considerable Catholic influence. Increasingly anti-Scottish

③ Lowland Scotland – Presbyterian dominated

④ Wales – strongly Royalist and anti-Catholic

⑤ Cornwall – strongly Royalist

⑥ Highland Scotland – largely Catholic

⑦ Main English settlements in Ireland, including the plantations

⑧ Scottish settlements in Ireland

⑨ Catholic Ireland

The war in the north

The coming of the Scots changed the military situation in northern England. Their first objective was to take Newcastle, which they soon occupied. The main prize in the north was York. After defeating a Royalist/Irish force at Nantwich, Sir Thomas Fairfax moved towards York from the south, linking up with the Scots to besiege the city, which was held by the Earl of Newcastle. Leslie and Fairfax were then joined by Manchester's Eastern Association army.

Newcastle's plight forced Prince Rupert to march to his relief, sweeping through the north-west gathering forces before crossing the Pennines to challenge Parliament's forces outside York. The campaign led to the Battle of Marston Moor in July 1644, the first decisive victory for Parliament, which virtually destroyed Royalist power in the north of England. The battle is analysed in Chapter 7. After Marston Moor the Scots were increasingly distracted by the campaigns of Montrose, but Parliament's alliance with the Scots continued to have a profound impact on Parliamentary politics.

■ 5F The Marston Moor campaign

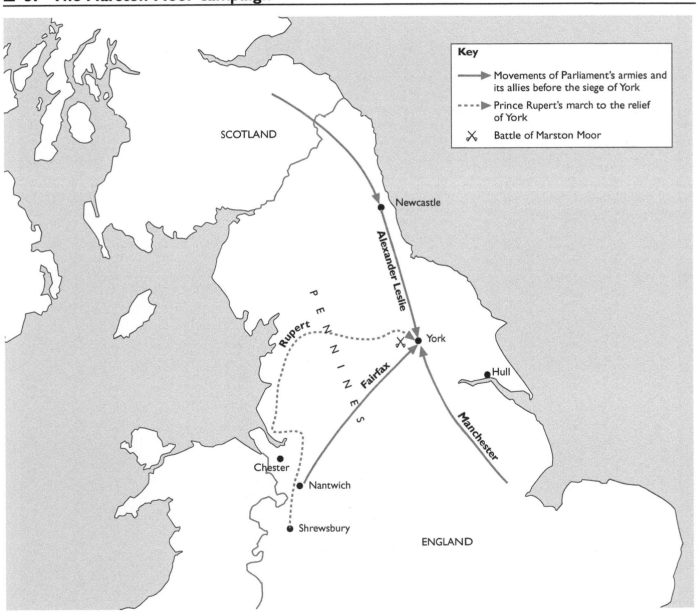

Key

→ Movements of Parliament's armies and its allies before the siege of York

⇢ Prince Rupert's march to the relief of York

✕ Battle of Marston Moor

SCOTLAND

Newcastle

Alexander Leslie

Rupert

PENNINES

Fairfax

York

Hull

Manchester

Chester

Nantwich

Shrewsbury

ENGLAND

The war in the south-west

In the summer of 1644 the Earl of Essex marched his Parliamentary army through Dorset and Devon into Cornwall, with the aim of relieving several beleaguered garrisons. His intention may have been to repeat his success at Gloucester the year before, venturing deep into enemy territory, but it was a premature move, and this time the result was disastrous. Once in Cornwall, a solidly Royalist county, he found his line of retreat blocked by the King. At Lostwithiel, at the end of August, his experienced army was forced to surrender, while Essex escaped by sea. A year earlier such a disaster would have lost the war for Parliament.

The war in the Midlands

Throughout 1644 the war in the Midlands was indecisive. The Battle of Cheriton, Sussex, prevented the Royalists from invading the south-east, but Waller's army was lucky to escape from the Battle of Cropredy Bridge, Oxfordshire. Parliament's military operations in the Thames Valley led to increasingly serious arguments between its main commanders, Waller and Essex.

During the summer and autumn there was a growing crisis of confidence in Parliament's commanders. Essex's reputation was already blighted by the loss of his army in Cornwall. Sir William Waller was not a realistic candidate for Lord General after Roundway Down and Cropredy Bridge. The lacklustre performance of these generals contrasted sharply with the Eastern Association's victory at Marston Moor. However, the Earl of Manchester, commander of the Eastern Association, seemed reluctant to follow up his victory with more decisive action. The second Battle of Newbury brought the crisis to a head, as mutual recriminations exposed the growing political rift among Parliament's officers. The crisis led directly to the SELF-DENYING ORDINANCE and the formation of the New Model Army (see Chapter 7, page 149).

By the end of 1644 the areas under Royalist control had shrunk significantly. Barring some military catastrophe or the collapse of parliamentary unity it is hard to see how Parliament could have lost the war. Contemporaries saw things differently. Parliament's unity was held together only by fear of what would follow a Royalist victory. In the north, Parliament had won, but only at the price of the Scots' demands. In the Midlands there was stalemate. The King controlled the south-west. Many Parliamentarians despaired of ever bringing the war to an end, and the King was certainly not ready to concede defeat. Parliament had to do something decisive.

SELF-DENYING ORDINANCE
A parliamentary ordinance of 1645 that forced Members of Parliament to resign their military commands.

■ **5G Parliament's victories, 1645–46**

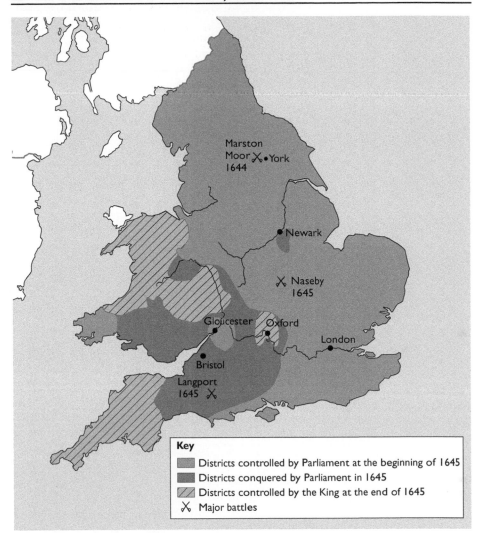

Key

Districts controlled by Parliament at the beginning of 1645

Districts conquered by Parliament in 1645

Districts controlled by the King at the end of 1645

✕ Major battles

The Battle of Naseby, 14 June 1645

In early 1645 Parliament joined its main armies into a single national force and placed it under new commanders, professional soldiers rather than political grandees. The new Lord General was Sir Thomas Fairfax. This 'new modelled army' was to be different from Parliament's previous armies in several other ways:

- Freed from the constraints of regional associations, it could search out and destroy the King's armies wherever it could find them.
- With the promise of regular pay, the army would be better disciplined and the soldiers less likely to desert.
- The army would be better trained and better equipped.

This was the theory; in practice the army's pay soon fell into arrears, and the soldiers' training consisted mostly of experience from previous campaigns. There was also concern that the army might have been fatally weakened by the purge of officers through the Self-Denying Ordinance.

However, the New Model Army quickly proved its effectiveness. In May 1645 it approached Oxford with the aim of laying siege to the King's headquarters. To draw Parliament's forces away from Oxford, the Royalists sacked Leicester. Fairfax abandoned the siege of Oxford and pursued the King's army north to Naseby, where the King decided to stand and fight.

The King's decision to give battle at Naseby requires some explanation: his army attacked a Parliamentary force nearly twice its own size, commanded by proven generals who had chosen a strong position on a ridge. The Battle of Naseby came at the end of a string of Royalist successes in Wales and the Welsh border country, which had swollen the number of Royalist troops available for active service. The King was aware of Parliament's political problems, and may have gambled on a victory in the field over the New Model Army that would split Parliament wide open.

The Battle of Naseby illustrated the importance of disciplined cavalry on a civil war battlefield. As at Edgehill, Rupert's horsemen broke the cavalry on Parliament's left flank, but instead of returning to the battle, pursued their enemy to Parliament's baggage train, which they tried to destroy. It took Rupert an hour to regroup and return to the action, by which time it was too late. On Parliament's right wing Cromwell's cavalry routed the Royalist horse, then regrouped and charged into the Royalist infantry. At the same time on the left flank Parliament's dragoons, who had deployed behind a long hedgerow, emerged from their position and attacked the right flank of the Royalist line. Without cavalry support and heavily outnumbered, the Royalist army collapsed. Parliament's victory was decisive, killing 1000 Royalists and capturing another 4500 for the loss of only 200 men.

SOURCE 5.4 The Battle of Naseby, 14 June 1645: a decisive victory for Parliament

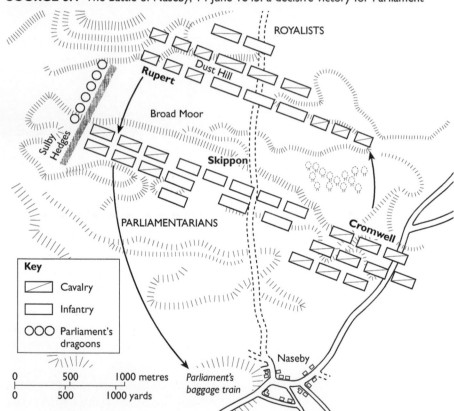

How the west was won

After Naseby, the New Model Army marched into the West Country, where it defeated another Royalist army at the Battle of Langport on 10 July. Two weeks later Fairfax's army took Bridgewater, cutting off the Royalists in the south-west from the King. By late August, Parliament's army was laying siege to Bristol, which was held by Prince Rupert. When the New Model Army's assault began in earnest, Rupert surrendered the city. In a rare show of anger, Charles sent Rupert into exile. The Royalist cause was crumbling.

Before leaving England, Rupert urged the King to make peace with Parliament in order to save his throne. Charles was not ready to admit defeat. He planned to join forces with Montrose and fight on from Scotland, but on

13 September Montrose was defeated at the Battle of Philiphaugh, south of Edinburgh. The King was rapidly running out of options.

Between October 1645 and April 1646, the New Model Army completed mopping-up operations in Somerset, Devon and Cornwall. Most of south Wales had fallen to Parliament in 1645; by this stage Royalist territory was mostly confined to isolated garrisons, falling one by one. The common fate of these Royalist castles was to be 'slighted' by Parliament, turning some of England's medieval castles into ruins.

The King's defeat

By 1646 Charles was more a fugitive than the commander of an army, scampering between loyal garrisons at Raglan, Bridgenorth, Chester, Newark and Oxford. In March 1646 a Royalist force under Sir Jacob Astley was surprised and defeated at Stow-on-the-Wold. In the same month Charles opened negotiations with the Covenanters, preferring to surrender to the Scots than to Parliament. He left Oxford in disguise at the end of April, probably hoping to take a ship to France, but when this proved impossible he surrendered to the Scottish army. Newark, which had been besieged since November, surrendered on 6 May. On 24 June Oxford surrendered, followed by Raglan Castle on 19 August 1646. The first Civil War was over.

KEY POINTS FROM CHAPTER 5

Outline of the English Civil War, 1642–46

1 Both sides expected in 1642 that one early battle would be decisive. The Battle of Edgehill, however, was a draw.

2 The prospect of fighting a long war frightened some Members of Parliament into resuming negotiations with the King. These negotiations, known as the 'Oxford Treaty', did not lead to a settlement.

3 In 1643 things went very well for the King. The Royalists captured a lot of territory and several leading Parliamentarians were killed.

4 The King's successes led to a crisis of confidence in Parliament. There were demands for the resignation of the Earl of Essex, but when the King's army besieged Gloucester, Essex commanded the army that was sent to its relief.

5 In 1644 the tide of war began to turn in Parliament's favour. The Scots joined with Parliament and the Battle of Marston Moor destroyed the King's army in the north of England.

6 During 1644 political disagreements threatened to undermine Parliament's successes. The consequence was the Self-Denying Ordinance and the formation of the New Model Army in 1645.

7 In 1645 the war turned decisively in Parliament's favour. Major victories at Naseby and Langport defeated the King's main armies and captured most of England and Wales.

8 The war ended in 1646 as Parliament captured remaining Royalist castles and strongholds, such as Newark and Oxford.

REMINDER

The purpose of Chapter 5 is to provide a simple outline narrative of the main events of the First Civil War. As you read Chapters 6 and 7, refer back to Chapter 5 to help place these chapters in a broader context.

How did the war affect people's lives? The example of Gloucestershire

CHAPTER OVERVIEW

The story of Robert Rowden

In November 1643 Robert Rowden was riding from his home in Northleach to Dursley, 20 miles across the Cotswolds. As darkness fell he got lost. Finding an inn at Nimpsfield, he had supper and went to bed.

At around eleven o'clock that night he heard a commotion downstairs. Twenty footsoldiers from the Parliamentary garrison at Eastington burst into his room with muskets and took him prisoner, saying that he was a Cavalier. They dragged Rowden out into the freezing night and marched him barefoot across the frosty hills wearing only his thin nightshirt.

Presently one of the soldiers spoke to him. Rowden takes up the story: "What is your name: whither are you travelling?" I told him my name and that my journey was to visit my mother's sister that lives in Dursley. He asked me, "What is your mother's sister's name?" I told him that her name was Bridget Everet: he said that "She was an honest woman, and one that he did respect, and that for her sake I should go back to the inn again." Seeing me in such a naked condition he went to one of the soldiers that had my doublet, he took it from him and gave it to me saying, "Put it on, you must needs be very cold and make haste to the inn again."

Rowden returned to the inn, where the maid gave him a petticoat and he warmed himself by the fire. He later heard that the soldier who saved him had spoken to his relatives in Dursley, telling them that had it not been for him, the soldiers would have beaten out his brains with their muskets and left him for dead.

DISCUSS

1 What does Robert Rowden's story tell us about the effects of the Civil War on local communities?
2 How do you think Parliament's soldiers learned that Robert Rowden was staying at the inn?

This chapter is about the impact of the Civil War on English life. Robert Rowden's story suggests that there was both change and continuity: change, because ordinary law and order had broken down; and continuity, because local family connections saved his life.

The chapter's starting point is a local study – the effects of the Civil War on the county of Gloucestershire. The county's situation was precarious. Gloucestershire lay in a strategic no-man's land, wedged between the King's headquarters at Oxford and Royalist Wales on the one hand, and Parliament's strongholds of Gloucester and Bristol on the other. Local political forces were finely balanced, so even a simple journey like Robert Rowden's could take the hapless traveller across the thin divide of conflicting loyalties into unknown dangers. The study of Gloucestershire gives us a chance to learn more about how far the civil war disrupted the continuity of life.

SOURCE 6.1 The complaint of William Hill, who managed an estate at Forthampton, Gloucestershire, in 1643

*I have lent money to both sides
Been plundered by both sides
Been imprisoned by both sides
A mad world!*

A Why was Gloucestershire divided by the war? (pp. 125–28)

B How did the war affect local communities? (pp. 129–33)

C Truth – the first casualty of war? (pp. 134–35)

D How great were the financial burdens of the war? (pp. 136–37)

E Why was looting so common? (p. 138)

F Review: how typical was Gloucestershire's experience? (pp. 139–40)

1 To what extent was the continuity of life disrupted during the Civil War?
   Prepare a report on the impact of the Civil War on Gloucestershire, focusing on
   the issue of change and continuity. As you work through the chapter, collect
   evidence for both change and continuity under the following headings.

Evidence of change	Evidence of continuity
How was life different as a result of the war? Examples: • Could people move freely around the county? • Did people pay more tax? • Did local communities stick together, or did they fight among themselves?	How did life continue as before during the war? Examples: • Did Stroud continue to make and sell cloth? • Was trade on the River Severn disrupted by the war? • Did social relations in the county survive – for example, relations between tenant farmers and landlords?

2 Alternatively, prepare a report on the impact of the Civil War on your own
   county, town or village. Local studies of the war have been written for most
   English counties and for Wales. Your local county record office may hold
   material on the Civil War, along with parish registers that might offer some
   insight into family life.

A Why was Gloucestershire divided by the war?

Choosing sides

The struggle for the militia had an immediate effect in Gloucestershire. In
February 1642 the King appointed Lord Chandos Lord Lieutenant of the
county. In August Parliament appointed its own Lord Lieutenant, Lord Saye
and Sele. In the same month Chandos arrived in Cirencester to execute the
King's Commission of Array. When his intentions became known, an angry
mob gathered in the market place. Chandos was forced to abandon his coach
and make a discreet exit through the back door of a private house. The mob
tore his coach to pieces.

SOURCE 6.2   Lucy Hutchinson, the
Puritan wife of the Parliamentarian Colonel
John Hutchinson, commenting on the Civil
War in her memoirs, written after 1663

*The King had sent forth commissions
of array, and the Parliament had
given out commissions for their
militia, and sent off their members into
all counties to put them in execution.
Between these, in many places, there
was fierce contests and disputes,
almost to blood, even at the first; for in
the progress every county had more or
less the civil war within itself.*

SOURCE 6.3   A nineteenth-century
painting by John Beacham, showing mobs
attacking Lord Chandos's coach outside
the church of St John the Baptist,
Cirencester, 1642

ACTIVITY

Draw a spider diagram to show the reasons why Gloucestershire was divided when war broke out in 1642.

Many people in the county were undecided in their sympathies, or hedging their bets against victory by either side.

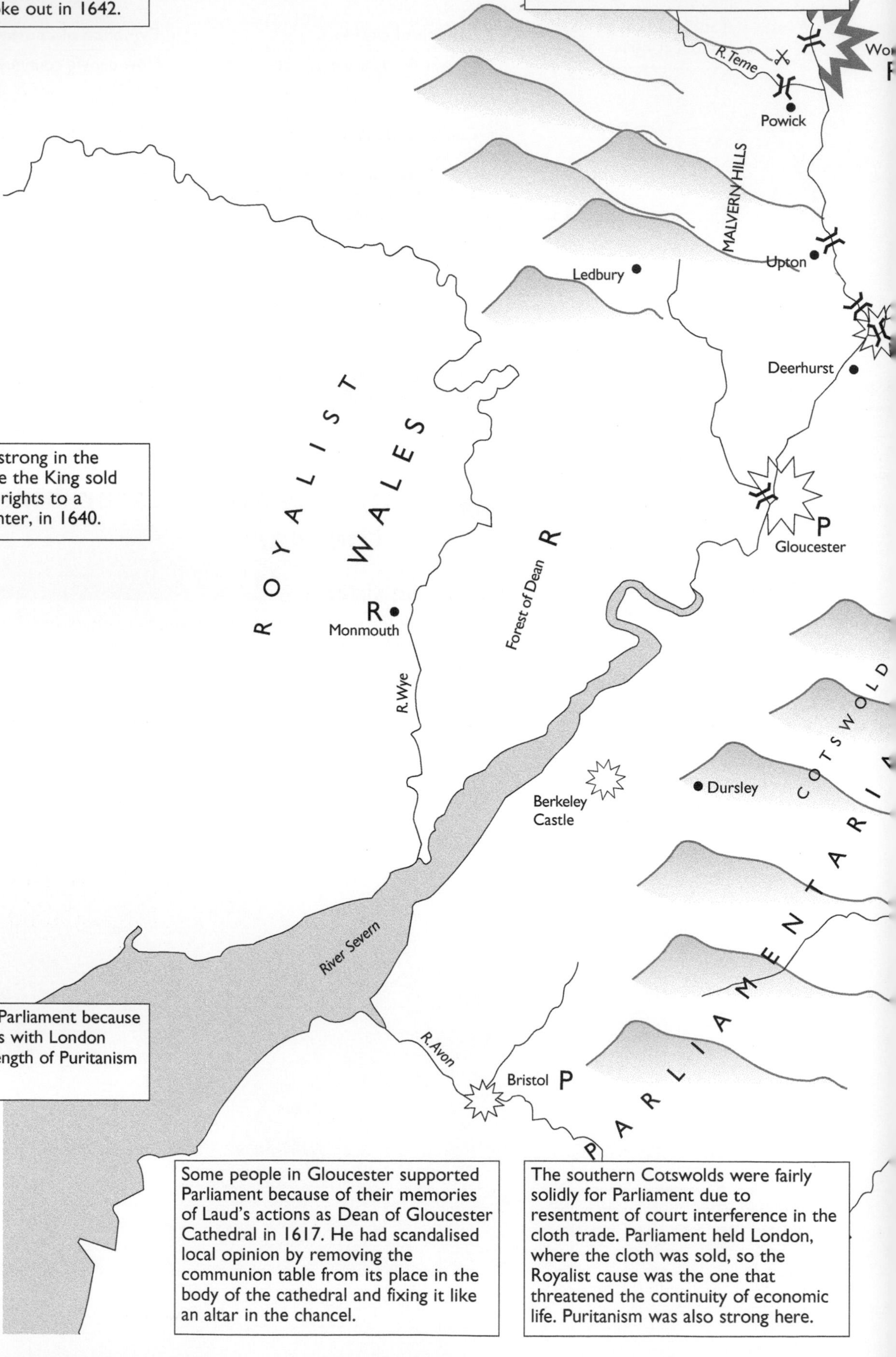

Royalist support was strong in the Forest of Dean, where the King sold property and mineral rights to a Catholic, Sir John Winter, in 1640.

Gloucester supported Parliament because of its trade connections with London merchants and the strength of Puritanism in the city.

Some people in Gloucester supported Parliament because of their memories of Laud's actions as Dean of Gloucester Cathedral in 1617. He had scandalised local opinion by removing the communion table from its place in the body of the cathedral and fixing it like an altar in the chancel.

The southern Cotswolds were fairly solidly for Parliament due to resentment of court interference in the cloth trade. Parliament held London, where the cloth was sold, so the Royalist cause was the one that threatened the continuity of economic life. Puritanism was also strong here.

R. Teme

Wor
P

Powick

MALVERN HILLS

Upton

Ledbury

Deerhurst

R O Y A L I S T
W A L E S

P
Gloucester

R
Monmouth

R.Wye

Forest of Dean R

R. Severn / River Severn

Berkeley
Castle

Dursley

C O T S W O L D

R.Avon

Bristol P

P A R L I A M E N T A R I A N

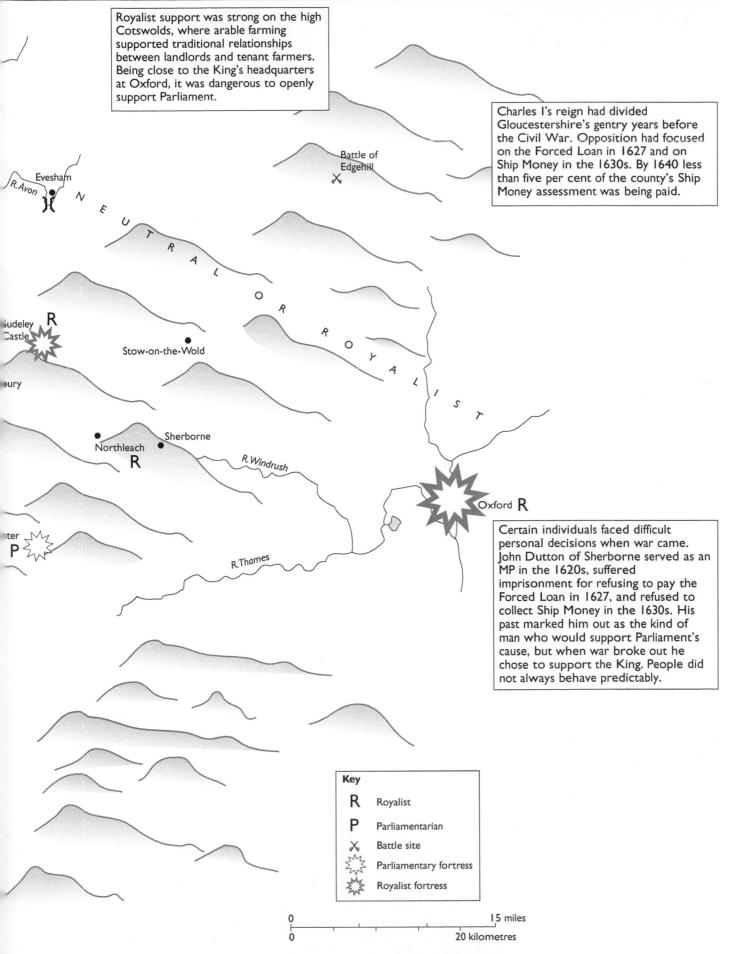

Royalist support was strong on the high Cotswolds, where arable farming supported traditional relationships between landlords and tenant farmers. Being close to the King's headquarters at Oxford, it was dangerous to openly support Parliament.

Charles I's reign had divided Gloucestershire's gentry years before the Civil War. Opposition had focused on the Forced Loan in 1627 and on Ship Money in the 1630s. By 1640 less than five per cent of the county's Ship Money assessment was being paid.

Certain individuals faced difficult personal decisions when war came. John Dutton of Sherborne served as an MP in the 1620s, suffered imprisonment for refusing to pay the Forced Loan in 1627, and refused to collect Ship Money in the 1630s. His past marked him out as the kind of man who would support Parliament's cause, but when war broke out he chose to support the King. People did not always behave predictably.

Evesham

R.Avon

Battle of Edgehill

N E U T R A L   O R   R O Y A L I S T

Sudeley Castle R

Stow-on-the-Wold

bury

Northleach R

Sherborne

R.Windrush

Oxford R

R.Thames

ter P

Key

R Royalist

P Parliamentarian

X Battle site

Parliamentary fortress

Royalist fortress

0   15 miles

0   20 kilometres

■ 6B The Civil War in Gloucestershire, 1642–46

	Events in Gloucestershire	National events
1642		
March		Parliament's Militia Ordinance
July	Parliament grants Gloucester permission to train volunteers	
August	Gloucester establishes a Committee of Defence	Parliament asks for donations known as 'propositions'
	Lord Chandos fails to enforce the King's Commission of Array in Cirencester	King raises his standard at Nottingham
	Parliament sends officers to co-ordinate Gloucestershire's defence	
October		Battle of Edgehill
November	Parliament establishes a county committee to co-ordinate the county's war effort	King's headquarters established at Oxford
December	Bristol falls to Parliament	
	Colonel Edward Massey takes over the defence of Gloucester	
1643		
January		Parliament gives county committees power to tax those who refused to donate to its cause
February	Prince Rupert takes Cirencester	Parliament establishes the Western Association under Sir William Waller to organise the war in the West Country
	Parliament appoints local tax collectors	
	Royalists take Tewkesbury	
	Parliament orders Gloucestershire to pay £750 per week as its weekly assessment	Parliament's weekly assessments begin
March	Parliament takes Tewkesbury	Parliament sets up county committees to confiscate estates of Royalists
July	Royalists capture Bristol	Battle of Lansdown
August	Royalists take Tewkesbury	Parliament introduces conscription
	Siege of Gloucester begins	
September	Essex's army relieves Gloucester	First Battle of Newbury
	Parliament takes Tewkesbury	Scottish alliance with Parliament signed
October	Royalists take Tewkesbury	
1644		
February	Parliament sends armed supply convoy to Gloucester	
May	Lord Chandos of Sudeley Castle defects to Parliament	
June	Parliament takes Tewkesbury	
July		Battle of Marston Moor
August	Parliament's assessment on Gloucestershire increased to £1000 per week	
September	Colonel Massey captures Monmouth	
1645		
February		Parliament's New Model Army Ordinance
April	Prince Rupert and Prince Maurice terrorise the Forest of Dean	Parliament's Self-Denying Ordinance
June		Battle of Naseby
July		Battle of Langport
September	Parliament establishes control throughout Gloucestershire	Parliament takes Bristol
1646		
May		King Charles I surrenders

ACTIVITY

Study Chart 6B.

1 Which side was the first to set up a co-ordinated military system in Gloucestershire? Why do you think this was?
2 Which side appears to have been more organised in raising tax money from Gloucestershire to support its war effort?

PARISH
The smallest division of local and church government.

DISCUSS

Study the map on pages 126–27. Why was control of Tewkesbury so important to both sides? (Study the timeline, Chart 6B, to see how many times it changed hands.)

ACTIVITY

The Civil War comes to Deerhurst
This role-playing activity is designed to help you to understand the impact of the English Civil War on local communities.

Three miles (5 kilometres) south of Tewkesbury lies the parish of Deerhurst, shown on the map in Chart 6A. The local community in Deerhurst was used to doing things its own way, and sorting out its own affairs. The people of Deerhurst enjoyed considerable freedom to regulate and police their PARISH. The King, the court and the Privy Council in London seemed a long way away. Local people called their county their 'country', and decided for themselves how to apply the law in their parish. They called this their liberty.

Few people in Deerhurst were able to vote in parliamentary elections, but many people at one time or another held one of the many unpaid offices of government at parish level – churchwardens, overseers of the poor, constables, and so on. By sharing the workload of local government, the people had a sense of community and common purpose. They called this the 'commonwealth'.

Unfortunately for the people of Deerhurst, both sides in the Civil War wanted to hold the nearby town of Tewkesbury. When war broke out in 1642, Deerhurst, like Tewkesbury, chose to support Parliament. Deerhurst church had been the scene of one of the altar controversies of the 1630s, like the one at Beckington, Somerset (described in Chapter 3, page 64), an indication of the strength of Puritan sympathies in the village. However, Parliament's hold on this area was insecure: Tewkesbury and Deerhurst lay roughly the same distance from Gloucester (Parliamentarian) and Worcester and Sudeley Castle (both Royalist), and was not far from the Royalist Welsh border country. Every time Tewkesbury changed hands during the Civil War, Deerhurst changed hands as well.

Instructions
1 Before attempting this activity, the teacher should photocopy the role cards and event cards on pages 130–33 so they can be handed out.
2 The teacher takes the role of referee.
3 Two class members assume the roles of the Royalist army and the Parliamentary army.
4 The rest of the class members each assume one of the roles described in the role cards.
5 The game progresses through a series of 'event cards'. These event cards are based on actual events that took place during the Civil War.
6 At each game turn, an event card is presented to the Deerhurst village council by either
   a) the teacher
   b) the Royalist army
   c) the Parliamentary army.
7 As a result of the event cards, one of three things will happen:

   • The players are faced with a **group decision**, and must discuss the situation before deciding on a course of action by a show of hands.
   • The players are faced with a **personal decision**. When forced to make a **personal decision**, the players all write their decisions down on a piece of paper and hand them in to the teacher/referee. These pieces of paper must have their role-card names on them. These decisions are kept secret from the other players.
   • The teacher/referee pauses the game to discuss the event and its implications.

8 A new game turn then begins and a new event card is presented to the village council.

Further advice for the teacher before the game begins can be found on page 292.

ROLE CARDS

- **Teacher/referee**

Your job is to present Deerhurst parish council with the first two event cards; to collect written notes when the game turn requires it; and generally to manage the simulation (see page 292). Event 6 is also in your care.

ROLE CARDS

- **Parliamentary army**

You represent Parliament's armed forces. Your task is to ensure that Parliament's instructions are carried out. You have military force at your disposal when you are in possession of Deerhurst.

ROLE CARDS

- **Royalist army**

You represent the King's armed forces. Your task is to ensure that His Majesty's commands are obeyed. You have military force at your disposal when you are in possession of Deerhurst.

ROLE CARDS

- **Sir Walter Bressingham, Lord of Priory Manor**

Your landlord, Thomas, Lord Coventry, is an ardent Royalist. You are a committed Anglican of Puritan sympathies. You hold the advowson to Deerhurst church (the right to appoint the minister of the parish).

ROLE CARDS

- **Henry Cassey of Wightfield Manor**

You are a Roman Catholic. You refused to attend church services at Deerhurst until the Puritan minister in 1634 was forced to restore the Communion table and rail it off with altar rails. Since then you have been a regular attender. Being a Catholic, you have always stressed your loyalty to the King of England as a way of reassuring your neighbours of your loyalty to the Crown. However, because you cannot take the oath required by the Act of Supremacy, you are barred from holding office, despite your considerable wealth.

ROLE CARDS

- **William Troughton, Puritan minister of Deerhurst Church**

Deerhurst parish has a long history of Puritan sympathies. Your two predecessors were reprimanded for baptising children without making the sign of the cross, and for refusing to wear a surplice. You describe yourself as a 'godly' minister.

ROLE CARDS

- **Thomas Clutterbuck, Constable of Deerhurst**

You are a yeoman farmer, owning your own farm with an income large enough to sustain your economic independence, but too small to admit you to the ranks of the gentry. You and your fellow yeomen think of yourselves as 'free Englishmen', the salt of the earth. You are currently serving as the Constable of the parish, a responsibility you perform for no pay, but out of a sense of responsibility.

ROLE CARDS

- **Giles Hawker, Overseer of the Poor**

You are a yeoman farmer, owning your own farm with an income large enough to sustain your economic independence, but too small to admit you to the ranks of the gentry. You and your fellow yeomen think of yourselves as 'free Englishmen', the salt of the earth. You are currently serving as Overseer of the Poor, a responsibility you perform for no pay, but out of a sense of responsibility. *Note*: the Overseer of the Poor was someone whose duty it was to enforce the Poor Law by, for example, putting poor people to work and providing them with shelter.

ROLE CARDS

- **John Powell, Churchwarden of Deerhurst**

You are a tenant farmer, renting your land from Thomas Clutterbuck. You are currently serving as one of the two churchwardens in Deerhurst, responsible for maintaining the fabric of the church building, keeping an eye on attendance at church services and generally assisting the minister in his parish work.

ROLE CARDS

- **John Fluck**

You are a tenant farmer, renting land from Sir Walter Bressingham of Priory Manor. You owe Sir Walter £20, but there is little prospect of your being able to find the money to repay him.

ROLE CARDS

- **Edmund Mortimer**

You are a yeoman farmer, owning your own farm with an income large enough to sustain your economic independence, but too small to admit you to the ranks of the gentry. You and your fellow yeomen think of yourselves as 'free Englishmen', the salt of the earth.

ROLE CARDS

- **Walter King**

You are a tenant farmer, renting your land from Giles Hawker, the Overseer of the Poor. You were recently found to be responsible for an illegitimate child born in the parish, and you have been ordered by Giles Hawker to pay the mother a regular income until the child comes of age.

EVENT CARDS

1 Teacher/referee

August 1642. Civil War has broken out between the King and Parliament.

The following letter has been received from the High Constable of Tewkesbury Hundred:

To the constables of all the parishes in Tewkesbury Hundred:

Be advised that the situation in Tewkesbury is very uncertain. The Borough Corporation is solidly for Parliament, whereas most people of quality in the town say they support the King. In order to prevent bloodshed, I hereby order all parish constables to collect together all arms and ammunition in their parishes and send them to Tewkesbury for safe keeping.

Group decision: Do we obey his instructions? What are:
a) the possible benefits
b) the possible risks?

EVENT CARDS

2 Teacher/referee

August 1642. The following letter has been received from the Governor of Worcester:

You will be aware of the rebellion that has recently broken out in London. In order to secure the King's Peace amongst His Majesty's loyal subjects, upon receipt of your declaration of loyalty to His Majesty, a troop of horse under the command of a trusted officer will be sent to maintain peace and security against disaffected elements that might attempt to take advantage of the current rebellion in London. All arms, armour and ammunition will be handed over to the appointed officers to enable them to carry out their work.
Signed: Sir William Russell, Governor of Worcester

Group decision: How should we respond?

- Should we reply declaring our loyalty to the King and accepting his offer of protection?
- Should we reply affirming our loyalty to 'King and Parliament'? If we do this, he may attack us.
- Should we draft a positive reply to Sir William Russell's letter, but send a copy of both his letter and our reply to Gloucester to find out their response before sending it?

EVENT CARDS

3 Parliamentary army

August 1642. Parliament has established a defence association for Gloucestershire. All loyal subjects are invited to make a voluntary contribution to Parliament's cause.

Individual decision: Will you donate money to Parliament? Each member of the council writes down their decision – Yes or No – on a piece of paper with their role name on it and gives it to the teacher/referee.

EVENT CARDS

4 Royalist army

February 1643. The Royalists have taken Tewkesbury. Sir William Russell demands that Tewkesbury donate £500 for the King, on the grounds that it previously donated £500 to Parliament. Similarly, he now demands that Deerhurst parish contribute money to balance the figure previously donated to Parliament.

Individual decision: Will you donate money to the King? Each member of the council writes down their decision – Yes or No – on a piece of paper with their role name on it and gives it to the teacher/referee.

EVENT CARDS

5 Parliamentary army

March 1643. Parliamentary forces have taken Tewkesbury. Parliament is demanding a weekly tax on all property owners. Catholics are to pay double. Anyone who failed to contribute to Parliament's cause in Event 3 is to be charged treble the normal amount, on the grounds that they are 'delinquents' – that is, Royalist sympathisers. (Teacher/referee now gives the names of those who DID contribute in Event 3 to the Parliamentary army player).

Group decision: Do we identify Henry Cassey of Wightfield Manor as a Catholic to the Parliamentary army?
Teacher intervention: At this point the teacher pauses the game to consider the latest event.

- How has Parliament's decision to demand a weekly property tax affected people's attitudes towards Parliament? Do you still feel that Deerhurst's decision to support Parliament at the beginning of the war was the right one?
- How do you feel about Parliament's decision to force Catholics to pay double the rate?
- How do you feel about the way the decision some of you took to donate money to Parliament is now being used to identify as 'delinquents' those people who didn't make this donation?

EVENT CARDS

6 Teacher/referee

April 1643: the Battle of Ripple Field, a mile or two north of Tewkesbury. Volleys of musketry can plainly be heard in Deerhurst, punctuated by the much louder sound of artillery gunfire and explosions. Everyone is frightened, and praying that the fight will not spread into Deerhurst.

Teacher intervention: How are you affected by the sounds of battle? In particular:

- Which side do you hope will win?
- Why do you want this side to win?
- Point of information: Parliament's forces came off worse during the battle, but the Parliamentarians retained control of Tewkesbury.

EVENT CARDS

7 Parliamentary army

July 1643. Parliament has imposed a sales tax on basic commodities such as salt (needed to preserve food), beer (better than water – most people drink at least six pints a day!), and bread. A county committee has been established by Parliament to oversee its enforcement.

Teacher intervention: You have no choice but to pay this tax, as long as Parliament is in control of Deerhurst.

Individual decision: Does the new tax make anyone feel differently about Parliament? Is it an imposition? Is it in a good cause?

EVENT CARDS

10 Teacher/referee

October 1643. The Royalist Sir William Vavasour has taken Tewkesbury with 400 Welsh soldiers. He has been joined by Prince Rupert with a powerful force of cavalry. Rupert has threatened to burn the houses of any people known to have supported Parliament's cause. Deerhurst council is ordered to identify all those who have actively assisted Parliament.

Teacher intervention: How do you feel now about the way the war is going?

- Which side do you want to win, and why?
- Which side do you think is going to win, and why?
- Why is the war becoming more violent?

EVENT CARDS

11 Parliamentary army

June 1644. Colonel Edward Massey has taken Tewkesbury for Parliament. The tide of war has turned in favour of Parliament. Parliament has set up a committee to investigate allegations of tax abuses in Gloucestershire, with extra penalties against Royalist delinquents. Anyone who knowingly protects a Royalist or a Catholic from the full penalty of the law is to be regarded as a delinquent.

Group decision: Do we identify all the Royalists and Catholics in Deerhurst?

EVENT CARDS

8 Royalist army

August 1643. The Royalists have taken control of the whole county of Gloucestershire, including Bristol and Tewkesbury. The only town holding out for Parliament is Gloucester. It appears that the King is winning the war. The commander of the Royalist force in Tewkesbury has threatened to destroy the house of anyone known to have actively assisted Parliament. (Teacher/referee now gives the names of those who *did* contribute in Event 4 to the Royalist army player).

Individual decision: Do you now wish to declare openly for the King? This must now be done publicly by a show of hands.

EVENT CARDS

9 Parliamentary army

September 1643. The Earl of Essex has taken Tewkesbury and Cirencester for Parliament. Parliament has passed a sequestration ordinance – the estates and property of all Royalist 'delinquents' are to be confiscated and placed in the hands of Parliament men. Anyone failing to comply with this ordinance is assumed to be a Royalist delinquent.

Individual decision: Do you now wish to identify the Royalist delinquents in Deerhurst? If so, you must do so publicly.

Group decision: Do we want to throw all Royalist delinquents into jail?

EVENT CARDS

12 Parliamentary army

August 1644. Parliament has passed an ordinance to deal with people who have hidden their assets from its tax collectors. You are ordered to investigate allegations that some residents of Deerhurst parish have hidden their money, or taken other measures to avoid complying with the law. Anyone reported as having made comments in support of the King is to be arrested.

Personal decision: Do you wish to inform Parliament about any member of Deerhurst village council whose loyalty has been suspect? Each player writes down on a piece of paper anything they wish to report to Parliament and hands it in to the teacher/referee.

EVENT CARDS

13 Teacher/referee

End of game. The teacher reads out the final statements of all the players.

End of role play. The teacher can now turn to page 292 for notes on discussion points.

ACTIVITY

What have you learned from this activity?

1 Why was it impossible for Deerhurst to keep out of the Civil War?
2 What effects did the war have on the local community in Deerhurst? Why did it have these effects?
3 What did the people of Deerhurst hope to achieve by supporting Parliament at the beginning of the war?
4 By the time the war ended, had the people of Deerhurst achieved what they had hoped to achieve at the beginning? If not, why not?
5 Why will it be difficult to make Deerhurst work together again as a community in the future?

Truth – the first casualty of war?

The storming of Cirencester, 2 February 1643

In early 1643 the Royalists decided to capture Cirencester, a parliamentary town dangerously isolated and close to the King's headquarters at Oxford. The task of taking Cirencester was given to Prince Rupert. On 2 February Rupert's army launched an assault. After two hours of fighting the Royalists took the town.

Two anonymous accounts of the battle – one Royalist, one Parliamentarian – were published. They were part of the propaganda war, intended by both sides to convince people of the justice of their cause, the wickedness of the enemy, and the valour of their own forces. Close comparison of these accounts provides us with an opportunity to view the same event through the eyes of the opposing forces.

SOURCE 6.4 The Royalist account

The Prince (after some shots of cannon made at Him) now returning to His Troopes, and prayers now ended through all the Regiments, led on beyond the Towne, arranging his Battaglions in the Barton-field at the West end of Cyrencester.

'Tis a town of many streets . . . Tis more than half encompassed with water, a great part with a high wall; the rest by strong works secured. The Gardens and backsides, be divided by many low dry stone walls, as good as breastworks; and one so serving for retreats unto the other, that had the defendants the courage to maintain a second, after they were put to retreat out of the first, we must have disputed every wall and garden with them. The streets were barricaded up with chains, harrows and wagons of bavins or risebushes [faggots of brushwood]. Each end of the high street leading through the town was secured against Horse with strong slaght-boomes, which our men call Turnpikes. Two Cavaliers or batteries they had. The town (as appears by the slain and the prisoners) had some 2,000 men in it.

The word was Queen Mary: which given, the order of the assault was thus. First were thirty musketeers drawn out of Colonel Kirks men . . . led by Lieutenant St. Johns, who performed his part bravely. At that (first) hedge and the low wall beyond it, was the skirmish began; St. Johns giving fair fire to beat the enemies out of it. After this the whole regiment came down the hill, to attack their designed post: which was Giffords Barton house and garden wall coming forwards, after some hot volleys beat the enemy from the hedge to the garden wall aforesaid. By this time were Colonel Usser and my Lord Wentworth come into this work so that the enemy beaten out of the house, works and wall, retired, with more haste than order, through Cecily hill to their first turnpike; our pursuing the retreat upon them, in blood and execution.

But here I find some difference, who should first brake open this turnpike. Some say a sergeant of Colonell Duncomb's brake off the horse-lock: others, that a soldier of Colonell Usser's, filled it with powder, and blew it open. But, doubtless, many valiant men at once assisting, may equally share the glory of it. But being opened, Lieutenant Colonel Russell riding foremost, cried, the town is ours, follow, follow . . .

In the mean time, the enemy at the Spittle gate, continued skirmishing but hearing the town was taken; they flung down their arms and ran away.

Now were the enemy all in flight; and ours in chase. Those that fled towards Cricklade, were by the Prince's command pursued by Sir John Byron: whose men remembering Burford; killed above one hundred, and took as many prisoners. Among the rest, two Ministers, one Mr. Stanfield armed back and breast, with sword and pistols.

Thus have you here related, what was acted by the King's Army, upon every part of the town. [And thus] was the confident Cirencester in an hour and half's fight, and with the loss of less than twenty men, on our side, fully taken in on all parts: (though diverse of them be since dead of poisoned bullets). Slain of theirs, those that think fewest, judge three hundred, others think more. The truth is, we could see but few men left at all in the town; plainly they hid their dead and wounded men in their houses; whereof we heard many since buried in one night: but most falling in the fields in the chase, we could get no precise notice of the numbers. Prisoners we brought away about twelve hundred: which shows the Princes and the Cavaliers mercy, as the Captives themselves acknowledge. Among the Prisoners were some 160 wounded: whom the Prince next day send his Surgeon and Doctor, and chaplains to dress and visit.

DISCUSS

'These sources demonstrate the impossibility of uncovering the objective truth about incidents during wartime.' Do you agree or disagree with this view?

ACTIVITY

Compare Sources 6.4 and 6.5.

1 How does the description of Cirencester's defences in Source 6.4 make the capture of the town sound all the more impressive?
2 How do the two sources differ in their descriptions of the bravery of the attacking force?
3 Why do you think Source 6.4 focuses on the role played by named individual soldiers, whereas Source 6.5 does not?
4 How do the two accounts differ when describing the defence of the town once the Royalists had broken into it?
5 How do the two accounts differ in their description of the treatment of prisoners by the Royalists?
6 Why would the memory of what happened in Cirencester make it more difficult for the two sides to make peace?
7 Despite the differences in these accounts, what can you deduce from them about the likely impact of the war on the town's economy and wealth, and on the people's attitude towards civil war?

SOURCE 6.5 The Parliamentary account

On Thursday morning, Febru. 2 . . . About twelve a clock, two or three regiments of foote being kept in, and forced on by the horse behind them, began a furious assault on the Barton, a great farm which lay not far from the Town westward, where they were valiantly entertained by some hundred musketeers that lay under the Garden wall . . . the Welshmen were seen to drop down apace but still the horsemen behind them, cried On, On, and drove them forward till they had got quite under the Garden wall. But before that, the enemy had fired some barns and ricks of corn and hay that lay behind those hundred musketeers, so that the enemy being at the wall, and breaking it down, and the fire so behind them and they being so few our men were forced out of that worke after two hours' valiant resistance . . .

Our men retreating to the second work, which was hard by, being so hotly pursued by the enemy, fire and smoke, which the wind drove directly upon them; they and the Guards of that work without any resistance made, very disorderly fled into the town, and were furiously pursued by the enemy, who without quarter killed those they met withall or overtook: which so desperately enraged our men, that in the market place, and from the windows they shot at the enemy almost an hour together, purposing to sell their lives and their liberties as dear as they could.

While the enemy was assaulting the Towne on the West side at the Barton, The Earl of Carnarvon and his forces sought to enter it on the North side, where there was a sore charge valiantly received by our men with little loss, who yielded not, till the enemy, who had entered the town on the other side, was on their backs. Thus about four of the clock the town was wholly won, and the shooting was ended on all sides, and then they took prisoners, and fell to plundering that night, all the next day, and on Saturday, wherein they shared all the barbarous insolence of a prevailing enemy . . . they spared not to plunder their best friends; for I can assure you, some of the notorious Malignants was the most notably plundered of all the Towne.

I tremble to write of their Blasphemies, they tauntingly asked some godly people, Where is now your God (you Roundhead Rogues?) you prayed to the Lord to deliver

you, and you see how he hath delivered you, ye Rebels etc.

The number that the enemy lost, is altogether unknown, by reason none durst go forth to see the slain. Of the town forces, both townsmen and countrymen, there were not above twenty killed, as can yet be learned.

The number of prisoners that they took and carried to Oxford was betwixt eleven and twelve hundred, amongst which there were some Gentlemen of eminent estates and affections to their Country. Two very godly Ministers, divers Commanders, and others, which were very religious and of good account.

They stripped many of the prisoners, most of them of their outmost garments. They were all turned that night into the Church, and though many of them were wounded and weary, yet their friends were not suffered to bring them a cup of water into the Church that night, but what they had thrust into the backside of the Church, having broken the windows.

They tied all the prisoners, Gentlemen, Ministers, and all in ropes, and made them go afoot through the dirt in the streets and way to Oxford, which in regard of the many horses, was up to their knees sometimes.

They shamefully abused the two Ministers, reproachfully imitating their manner of preaching etc. The Captain who took the Ministers, upon earnest solicitation of their friends for their releasement, promised that for fifty or sixty pounds apiece he would release them: which money being procured and paid them, he scoffingly answered, that they might as well pay as much more to him for not killing them, as he might have done, and they deserved.

The value of the pillage of the town is uncertain, but very great, to the utter ruin of many hundred families. On Friday they went into the country, and took away all the horses, sheep, oxen, and other cattle of the well-affected that inhabited near Cirencester.

On Saturday, Febru. 4 they took away cloth, wool, and yarn, besides other goods from the Clothiers, about the Stroudwater, to the utter undoing, not only of them and theirs, but of thousands of poor people, whose very livelihood depend on that trade.

D How great were the financial burdens of the war?

The war subjected the people of Gloucestershire to unprecedented financial burdens. Troops were often quartered on local people, who had to bear the costs of supporting them.

A good example is the case of John Chamberlayne of Maugersbury. Chamberlain was a Royalist whose estate near Stow-on-the-Wold placed him in the line of march of both armies as they fought for control of the Cotswolds. At the end of the war he faced the SEQUESTRATION of his estate by Parliament as a 'delinquent'. In an attempt to prevent this, he submitted to Parliament an account of exactly what the war had cost him.

> **SEQUESTRATION**
> The process by which Parliament confiscated the estates of Royalists ('delinquents'), appointed their own commissioners, and used the profits to support its war effort.

SOURCE 6.6 Extracts from the Expenses of John Chamberlayne of Maugersbury. These figures show how much money Chamberlayne lost during the entire war

A note of quartering contribution and provisions sent to the Armies for the lands I hold of Sir Nicholas Bainton in Maugersbury

	£	s	d
Firstly quartered upon the coming up of Marquiss Hartford with the Welshmen 120 men and 20 Horses 5 days which at £5 days and nights came to	25	00	00
Item paid to Colonel Gerard's regiment. My Lord Percy's regiment. 14 months' contribution at £3 03s 04d the month which comes to	44	06	08
Quartered of my Lord Percy's regiment. A Scotch lieutenant of Horse and 7 Horse and men more at several times 7 weeks and two days which at 4d per day man and horse comes to	28	00	08
Item when my Lord of Essex came to relieve Gloucester: they spent me in Household provision of Bread and beer cheese and meat and Provender to the value of £6 at the least	6	00	00
Quartered upon the Breaking up of Gloucester siege 20 Men and Horses of the King's army 3 days which came to	4	00	00
And upon the return from Newbury fight I quartered a captain and 12 men and horse, ten days which comes to £8 00s 00d	8	00	00
Paid to Sir Thomas Aston's Regiment. two months' contributions at £3 03s 04d p. month	6	06	08
I had Corn upon the ground spoiled by the King's army and my Lord of Essex, when Prince Rupert faced him at Stowe to the value of £40 00s 00d at the least	40	00	00
Paid more to Sir William Vavasour 5 months' contributions which came to	15	06	08
Quartered of His men Captain and 13 men and Horses 5 days which comes to	4	06	08
Quartered more of Sir Wm. Vavasour's men a major and 23 Horse 2 days which comes to	3	00	04
Quartered Sir William Clarke, his Major and 32 Horse more of his regiment two nights	4	05	04
When my Lord Wilmot lay at Morton in the Marsh for the stopping of Gloucester's convoy I quartered my Lord Wentworth and 30 men and Horse at two times a fortnight there lay with Him the Earl of Down and my Lord Goring's Brother this comes to at the former rate	28	00	00
Quartered Lieutenant Colonel Hurleston and Captain Norwood's and 7 Horses and 52 foot soldiers one night which comes to	2	02	00
Quartered Captain Flower and 10 men and Horses 3 days which comes to	2	04	00
When Sir William Waller chased the King's army towards Worcester I quartered of the King's army 43 Horse and Men one night which comes to	2	17	04
The next day I quartered of Sir William Waller's army Colonel Birch and 30 Officers and 40 Horses and 120 foot 5 days which comes to	27	10	00
About ten days after the King returned and then His army spent me in provision for Horse and men at the least	6	00	00
Then Sir William Waller lay at Stowe the Carriage Horses were turned in my Corn and did me at the least 30 Pounds worth of Hurt	30	00	00

MONEY

There were 12 pence (d) to the shilling, and 20 shillings (s) to the pound. A typical country gentleman at this time might have had an income of around £150–£300 per year.

ACTIVITY

Using Source 6.6, calculate the following.

1 How much money had Chamberlayne spent?
2 How many officers, men and horses had Chamberlayne accommodated during the war?
3 What was the largest group of soldiers Chamberlayne accommodated, and from which army?
4 How many times did Chamberlayne accommodate soldiers from:
   a) the King's army
   b) Parliament's army?
5 What different kinds of costs did Chamberlayne incur during the course of the war?

As Gloucestershire was controlled by neither side, it was subjected to tax demands by both armies. Both sides asked for voluntary contributions, but quickly moved towards compulsory payments backed up by the threat of force. The process all but destroyed the 'ancient liberty' enjoyed by local communities to order their affairs according to local circumstances.

SOURCE 6.7 The tax burden on Gloucestershire (from Barry Coward and Chris Durston, *The English Revolution*, 1997, pp. 74 and 77). These figures do not include the purchase tax called the excise

Ship Money (Amount charged to Gloucestershire annually in the 1630s)	Yearly Assessments (Parliamentarian) (The amount Parliament ordered to be collected each year from Feb 1643)	Yearly Contributions (Royalist) (The amount the King ordered to be raised in tax from 1643)
£5,500	£42,250	£72,000

ACTIVITY

Study Source 6.7.

1 Expressed as a percentage, how much higher were the tax duties imposed on Gloucestershire during the Civil War than the Ship Money assessments in the 1630s?
2 In the 1630s there had been great opposition to the King's tax policies, especially to Ship Money. Charles was frustrated by this opposition. Do the figures in Source 6.7 help to explain why the King was so frustrated?

E Why was looting so common?

Civilians complained about the impact of the armies on local communities. Looting, requisitioning and rape were common. Acts of violence were inevitable when soldiers went unpaid and were expected to fend for themselves in a countryside ravaged by war. Horses were requisitioned by both sides, making the ploughing and sowing of fields difficult. In desperation, individuals sometimes tried to protect their assets by purchasing 'protection orders'; during the siege of Gloucester in 1643 Prince Rupert sold protection orders to raise ready cash.

ACTIVITY

How many items can you identify in Source 6.8 that the soldier has looted?

SOURCE 6.8   A contemporary picture of a pillaging soldier. This picture reflects the revulsion felt by ordinary people at the plundering by both sides

SOURCE 6.9   A royal proclamation against looting, 10 August 1643

ACTIVITY

Study Source 6.9.

1 What does this source tell you about the way the King's army was supplied with food?
2 What do the King's instructions of 10 August tell you about his concerns over the effects of looting?
3 What do the King's instructions suggest about the impact on the local community of the presence of a large army in the county?

We being enforced to sit down with our Army before the City of Gloucester now in Rebellion against us and to reduce the same to their due obedience have for the ease and good of our Army commanded that there should be daily Market kept in our Camp where our soldiers may provide themselves with all manner of Victualls for their relief, paying reasonably for the same. If any soldier or other of our Army shall at any time during our stay at or before our City of Gloucester rob, spoil or take away from any person or persons coming to Market to our Camp any of their goods or victuall of what kind or quality so ever, that upon Complaint made such soldier shall be forthwith apprehended and hanged without mercy as justly deserving the same.

We being informed that divers soldiers both of horse and foot and others pretending to be of our Army do wander about the Country robbing and spoiling our subjects and taking away provision of victuall coming for the use of our Army before Gloucester do strictly require and Command the chief officers of our horse to cause all such as shall be found so offending to be apprehended and hanged without mercy.

CLUBMAN MOVEMENTS

Many local communities formed groups of local citizens to defend themselves. They armed themselves with primitive weapons, such as clubs and pitchforks. Clubman movements appeared in Wiltshire, Somerset, Dorset, Shropshire, Worcestershire, Herefordshire, Sussex, Berkshire, Hampshire and South Wales – all counties which had experienced severe disruption, plunder and the quartering of troops. Most of these groups sprang from the spontaneous efforts of local farmers and cattlemen to defend their land and produce from plunder. In some cases the local gentry adopted the movement to reassert the traditional county relationships, laws and customs: the Clubmen wanted to return to the old ways. They regarded both sides as enemies, and tried to arrange local ceasefires between hostile garrisons. In response to invasion, local communities were rebuilding their militias for the purpose for which they were originally intended.

The Clubmen were powerful enough to force commanders to consider how to deal with them. Attempts were made to win them over, and to infiltrate their meetings. In the end they failed to force an end to the war, and Parliament's victory restored a kind of law and order. They were a stark reminder that the English people wanted nothing more than peace, and the continuity of their ancient laws and customs.

F Review: how typical was Gloucestershire's experience?

Gloucestershire was not the only county to experience the violence and destruction of the First Civil War. Indeed, the only counties to be spared were those firmly controlled by Parliament – Kent, Essex, parts of Sussex, most of East Anglia – but they too suffered from the fiscal (tax) burdens and the disruption of trade.

In many counties civil war broke out among the inhabitants long before the major armies appeared. A case in point is Somerset, where the cathedral town of Wells clashed with the nearby wool town of Shepton Mallet. A spontaneous armed uprising temporarily forced the Royalists to retreat, but they reappeared when a large Royalist army entered the county.

Many English towns and villages changed hands on several occasions. People were drawn into the war by force of circumstances as they tried to protect their interests. The longer the war went on, the more difficult it became to make peace.

Compared to some towns, Cirencester seems to have got off quite lightly. In 1644 Prince Rupert's soldiers sacked Bolton, Lancashire, killing perhaps as many as 1800 soldiers and civilians. When Cromwell's soldiers forced their way into Basing House in Hampshire in 1645, 100 Royalists were killed, including women of the household. In 1645 the Royalists sacked Leicester and murdered prisoners of war. At Barthomley, Cheshire, in 1643 Lord Byron ordered his men to slit the throats of twenty Parliamentarians.

SOURCE 6.10 'The Bloody Prince': a picture of Prince Rupert and his dog Boy during the storming of Birmingham, taken from a parliamentary pamphlet of April 1643. This woodcut illustrates the growth of Rupert's reputation for ruthlessness

The most Illustrious and High borne PRINCE RUPERT, PRINCE ELECTOR, Second Son to FREDERICK KING of BOHEMIA, GENERALL of the HORSE of His MAJESTIES ARMY, KNIGHT of the Noble Order of the GARTER.

Neutralism – the example of Cheshire

In August 1642 several counties tried to avoid the conflict by drawing up neutrality pacts. In 1642 Cheshire declared neutrality and tried to create a 'third force' to defend the county from any army that crossed its borders.

In late September the King rode north from Shrewsbury to secure Chester's loyalty. The arrival of the King encouraged the Royalists to come out of the woodwork and presented the neutralists with the ultimate dilemma – if they tried to fight off the King, they would be branded as rebels. Cheshire's first attempt to keep out of the Civil War had failed.

As the Royalist army moved away towards London, the pressure on Cheshire receded. In December a further attempt was made to turn the county into a demilitarised zone, but the cat was out of the bag. Cheshire's ability to speak with one voice was hopelessly compromised by the harsh realities of war, and by the attempts of rival factions in the county to take advantage of the opportunities it offered to settle old scores.

Casualties

How many people died? The best recent estimate places the death toll of the Civil War conservatively at 180,000, including deaths from combat, disease, accidents and the Bishops' Wars. This represents 3.4 per cent of the estimated total population of 5.2 million. By comparison, the First World War killed 2.6 per cent of the population of the United Kingdom, and the Second World War 0.6 per cent.

DISCUSS

Do these comparative death rates surprise you? If so, why? What does this tell you about your preconceptions about the seventeenth century?

FOCUS ROUTE

Presenting your report
You could present your report (see the Focus Route on page 125) as an oral report. If possible, use PowerPoint to illustrate your presentation with maps and to outline the key features of your report.

1 Begin with a brief outline of the Civil War, 1642–46, and the position of Gloucestershire (or your own county) in it.
2 Focus more sharply on how the county was affected by the outbreak of war. Which parts of the county supported Parliament or the King, and why?
3 Present your evidence for change.
4 Present your evidence for continuity.
5 Explain how this evidence relates to the key question of the section introduction, what was the English Revolution? In what ways did the changes in Gloucestershire (or your own county) either:
   a) bring about revolutionary changes in the lives of the people, or
   b) set up conditions in the county which might lead to civil unrest at a later date?

KEY POINTS FROM CHAPTER 6 **How did the war affect people's lives? The example of Gloucestershire**

1 The English Civil War divided friends, families, parishes, hundreds, towns, cities and counties. It killed thousands of people. It led to plunder, rape, the interruption of trade, the destruction of property and economic catastrophe.

2 The Civil War drove a wedge into local communities. It exposed personal rivalries, disputes between neighbours, and economic and social differences that in normal times might lie just under the surface of everyday life.

3 During the 1630s Charles I's Personal Rule and his efforts to increase central government control over the traditional system of English local government had provoked great resentment. The Civil War led to a far greater tax burden, and a far greater degree of centralisation, than Charles I ever achieved. Parliament went to war to defend 'ancient liberties', but in order to win it had to destroy the sort of liberty that, arguably, meant the most to most Englishmen – the liberty to govern themselves.

4 Sooner or later there would be a reaction against this. Local communities expected the country to return to normal when the war ended.

7

Why did Parliament win the Civil War?

CHAPTER OVERVIEW Parliament's victory in the First Civil War was not inevitable. It took four years to defeat the Royalists. Not until their victory at Naseby in June 1645 did the Parliamentarians begin to feel confident that they would win. The King, for his part, did not concede defeat until he surrendered in May 1646. In this chapter, you must try to explain not only why Parliament won the war, but also why the King lost it.

FOCUS ROUTE

Why did Parliament win the Civil War? At the end of this chapter you will write an essay to explain your answer to this question. Collect evidence that can be used to help you to answer it.

Factor that would decide the outcome of the war	What the Royalists did about this, and with what success	What Parliament did about this, and with what success
Resources		
Building armies		
Making alliances		
Political struggles		
Winning battles		

A Resources (pp. 142–43)

B Building armies (pp. 143–49)

C Making alliances (pp. 149–51)

D Political struggles (pp. 152–59)

E Winning battles (pp. 159–65)

F Review: why did Parliament win the Civil War? (p. 166)

A Resources

In August 1642 the kingdom was facing its worst nightmare. Civil war was breaking out throughout the country. The government had failed in its first duty – to maintain domestic order – and consequently the kingdom was disintegrating into chaos.

The King had lost London, but everything else was up for grabs. Neither side had an army, though, with which to grab it. It was left to local communities to decide whether to declare their allegiance and, if so, to whom. The potential assets available to both sides was nothing less than the entire kingdom of England and Wales, and so each side faced the appalling prospect of trying to make some sense of the chaos confronting them.

■ 7A Resources needed to fight the war – England and Wales at the end of 1642, showing principal areas of Royalist and Parliamentary control

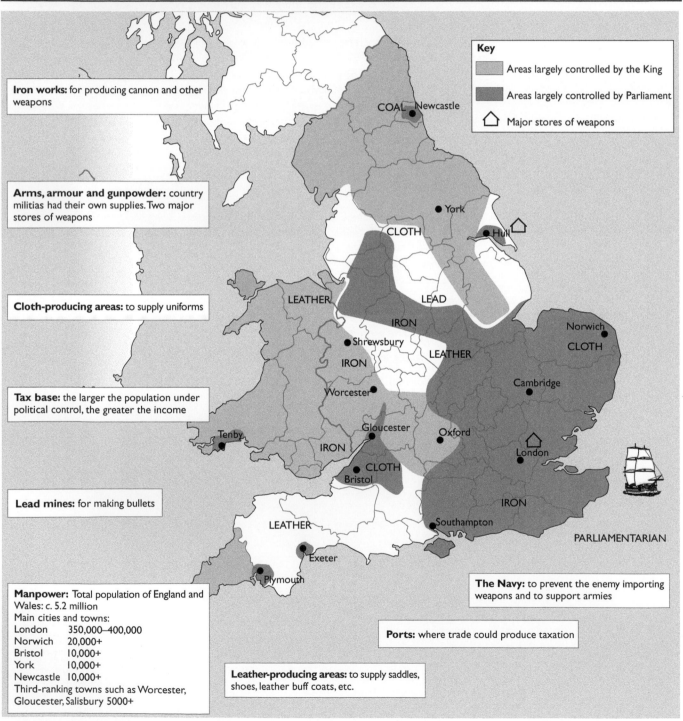

Key

- Areas largely controlled by the King
- Areas largely controlled by Parliament
- Major stores of weapons

Iron works: for producing cannon and other weapons

Arms, armour and gunpowder: country militias had their own supplies. Two major stores of weapons

Cloth-producing areas: to supply uniforms

Tax base: the larger the population under political control, the greater the income

Lead mines: for making bullets

Manpower: Total population of England and Wales: c. 5.2 million
Main cities and towns:
London   350,000–400,000
Norwich   20,000+
Bristol   10,000+
York   10,000+
Newcastle   10,000+
Third-ranking towns such as Worcester, Gloucester, Salisbury 5000+

The Navy: to prevent the enemy importing weapons and to support armies

Ports: where trade could produce taxation

Leather-producing areas: to supply saddles, shoes, leather buff coats, etc.

Resources	The King	Parliament
Manpower		
Arms, armour and gunpowder		
Iron works		
Lead mines		
Cloth-producing areas		
Leather-producing areas		
Ports		
The Navy		
Tax base		

It was important for the King to win the war quickly. The longer it lasted, the more Parliament's greater resources would come into play.

Building armies

Both sides during the Civil War faced the same problem – how to build an efficient army out of chaos. Parliament and the King had very different conceptions of how the country should be organised for war. King Charles turned instinctively to tradition and personal contacts, building his war effort around local aristocrats with regional power. Parliament was more impersonal and arbitrary, using its legislative powers to create a tax-collecting bureaucracy supporting, eventually, a professional standing army. In the process, Parliament achieved what Charles I had failed to achieve in the 1630s – a Thorough government.

	Royalists Key: relying on traditional loyalties and the regional powers of local aristocrats and gentry	Parliamentarians Key: creating a tax-collecting bureaucracy wielding impersonal, arbitrary powers
Raising money		
Raising and equipping troops		
Establishing clear lines of command		
Overcoming regionalism		

The Royalists

The King's war effort began with the Commissions of Array issued from York in June 1642, ordering wealthy local gentlemen to raise their counties' forces for the King. This was the system the Stuarts had inherited from the Tudors, a joining together of local defence forces. From the middle of 1642, loyal subjects were fortifying their castles and manor houses and trying to seize control of disputed towns.

By 1643 a more systematic organisation emerged. County committees of the wealthier gentry were formed to raise money and recruit soldiers. Their task was to liaise with the commanders of local garrisons so their needs could be supplied out of local taxation. They could also confiscate the estates of local Parliamentarians, though the King was reluctant to seize personal property. At this stage the Royalist war effort was still based on the county and its traditional office-holders.

During 1643 the King grouped counties into military districts and placed them under the command of regional aristocratic governors ('grandees'). The country was divided into six military zones, each commanded by a Royalist grandee (see Chart 7B). This could only be done in those parts of the kingdom that were not under firm Parliamentary control.

■ 7B The evolution of Royalist military organisation, 1642–43

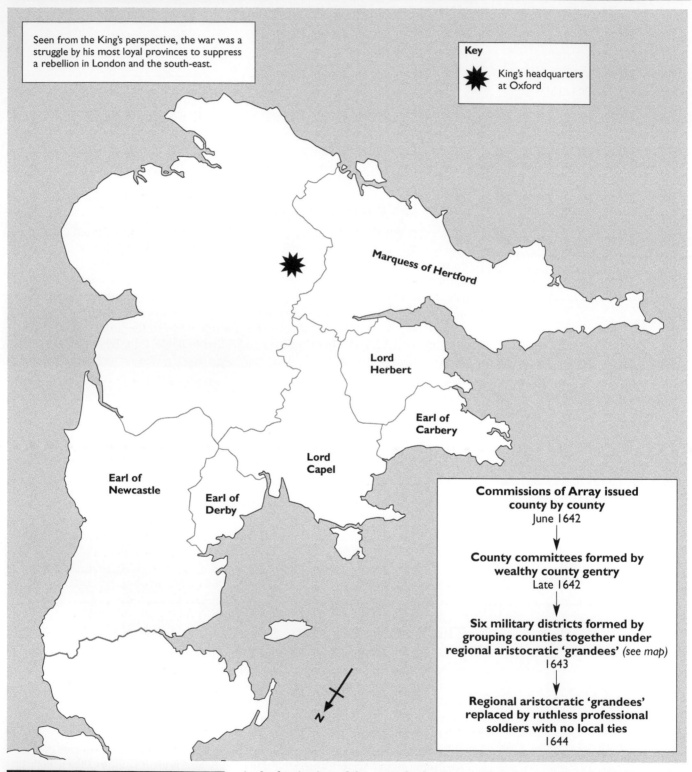

Seen from the King's perspective, the war was a struggle by his most loyal provinces to suppress a rebellion in London and the south-east.

Key

★ King's headquarters at Oxford

Marquess of Hertford

Lord Herbert

Earl of Carbery

Lord Capel

Earl of Newcastle

Earl of Derby

Commissions of Array issued county by county
June 1642
↓
County committees formed by wealthy county gentry
Late 1642
↓
Six military districts formed by grouping counties together under regional aristocratic 'grandees' *(see map)*
1643
↓
Regional aristocratic 'grandees' replaced by ruthless professional soldiers with no local ties
1644

DISCUSS

If the Civil War was partly caused by 'Country' opposition to the 'Court', how do you explain the fact that most of the King's support came from the provinces?

At the beginning of the war, the business of raising money and troops was in the hands of local gentry and wealthy lords such as the Earl of Newcastle, who raised and equipped a regiment of infantry – the 'Whitecoats' – out of his own pocket. In the summer of 1642, loans and gifts poured in to the King's treasury as gentlemen pledged their loyalty.

By 1643 the county committees began to create a more orderly system for the collection of taxes. The King relied on local men to raise local taxes, and therein lay several disadvantages. They expected local money to be spent on local defence; proper accounting for the money raised was almost unheard of; and, being local men, they were prepared to let their friends and neighbours off the hook. The problems which had undermined Charles's military system throughout his reign therefore re-surfaced, made worse by the fact that Parliament disputed his control of these localities.

Late in the war the Royalists learned that a more draconian, less traditional system was needed. The King's army began pressing men into service to replace losses due to desertion, disease and casualties of war. In 1644 the OXFORD PARLIAMENT (see also page 152) passed a bill legalising conscription, along with an excise tax on basic commodities. By this time Parliament had been collecting its own excise for a whole year.

Creating a national Royalist war effort was almost impossible. In 1643 it looked as if the King had a national strategy for a 'three-pronged attack' on London, but no hard evidence for such a strategy exists. The strategy was probably simply the result of the geographical isolation of the King's armies and the temporary success gained in all three areas by the Royalists' methods.

The Royalists should have enjoyed an immediate advantage of a clear command structure. Instead Charles's armies were riddled with personal rivalries, confused command structures and wounded pride. On the evening before the Battle of Edgehill, the King gave Prince Rupert independent command of the cavalry out of the hands of its Lord General, the Earl of Lindsey. Lindsey was so upset that he quit his post and fought with the infantry, where he died.

The King learned by hard experience that his original notion of fighting the war by traditional means was fatally flawed. Gradually a more ruthless system emerged, in which strangers squeezed taxes from the counties with brutal objectivity. By this time Parliament was ahead of the game.

OXFORD PARLIAMENT

The Parliament called at Oxford by the King in 1644 to act as a rival to Parliament at Westminster.

SOURCE 7.1 King Charles's speech to the Gentlemen, freeholders and other inhabitants of the county of Shropshire, given at Shrewsbury, 28 September 1642

Gentlemen,
It is some benefit to me, from the insolencies and misfortunes which have driven me about, that they have brought me to so good a part of my kingdom, and to so faithful a part of my people. I hope neither you nor I shall repent my coming hither. I will do my part that you may not, and of you I was confident before I came.

The residence of an army is not usually pleasant to any place, and mine may carry more fear with it, since it may be thought, being robbed and spoiled of all my own, and such terror used to fright and keep all men from supplying me, I must only live upon the aid and relief of my people. But be not afraid, I would to God my poor subjects suffered no more by the insolence and violence of that army raised against me (though they have made themselves wanton even with plenty) than you shall do by mine; and yet I fear I cannot prevent all disorders. I will do my best; and this I'll promise you, no man shall be a loser by me, if I can help it.

I have sent hither for a mint, I will melt down all my own plate, and expose all my land to sale or mortgage, that if it be possible, I may bring the less pressure on you. In the mean time I have summoned you hither, to invite you to do that for me, and yourselves, for the maintenance of your religion and the laws of the land, by which you enjoy all that you have, which other men do against us. Do not suffer so good a cause to be lost for want of supplying me with that which will be taken from you by those who pursue me with this violence. Assure yourselves, if it please God to bless me with success, I shall remember the assistance every particular man here gives me, to his advantage. However, it will hereafter (how furiously soever the minds of men are now possessed) be honour and comfort to you, that with some charge and trouble to yourselves, you did your part to support your King, and preserve the kingdom.

ACTIVITY

Study Source 7.1.

1 How does the King's speech appeal to the loyalty of the people of Shrewsbury?
2 How does the speech appeal to their self-interest?

The Parliamentarians

Parliament's war effort began with the Militia Ordinance of March 1642. In the race to gain control of the county militias, Parliament was first off the starting line. In July Parliament appointed a Committee of Safety to oversee the conduct of the war and voted to raise an army. In August officers were sent from London to co-ordinate county defences, and soon county committees were formed. Initially, therefore, it appeared that Parliament was following the same traditional path as the King.

But Parliament quickly introduced innovations that went beyond the scope of traditional methods. In 1643 it passed a series of ordinances (see Chart 7C) aimed mainly at securing funding as the basis for future victory, assuming that it could survive long enough for the ordinances to take effect. Alongside this fiscal revolution was a bureaucratic one: the county committees were authorised to enforce these ordinances, reporting to central committees in London. These measures laid the foundations for the 'military-fiscal state', a government raising taxes based more closely on the actual wealth of individuals, supported by an administrative system that did not depend on the goodwill of local men.

■ 7C Parliamentary Ordinances, 1643

Ordinance	Date	Description
Assessment Ordinance	February	Weekly assessments imposing a specific sum of tax from each county. Unlike the old parliamentary subsidy, the assessments were based on the Ship Money returns of the 1630s, and therefore reflected more accurately the country's actual wealth.
Sequestration Ordinance	March	Confiscated the property of Royalists. Their estates were managed by local commissioners, who used the profits to support Parliament's war effort.
Compulsory Loans Ordinance	May	Everyone worth £10 a year from land or £100 a year in goods to lend one-fifth of the revenue of their estate or half of their value in other forms of property to Parliament.
Excise Ordinance	July	A sales tax on a wide range of essential commodities and foodstuffs, including beer and salt.
Impressment Ordinance	August	Introduced conscription, thus ending Parliament's reliance on volunteers. This helped to counteract the effects of desertion and enabled Parliament to build larger armies.

DISCUSS

How similar were these measures to those taken by Charles I during the Personal Rule?

Parliament's armies continued to evolve in response to changing circumstances. The most deeply-rooted problem was the regional bias of its first armies – soldiers were reluctant to leave their counties vulnerable by embarking on national campaigns. By grouping its county militias into association armies, Parliament made strategic sense of its forces: for example, the East Anglian counties formed the Eastern Association (see Chart 7D).

Superficially this was similar to the Royalists' grouping of counties into military districts, but Parliament took the process a step further. In August 1643 the Eastern Association was reorganised, giving its commander, the Earl of Manchester, power to impress a further 20,000 men. In January 1644 Parliament gave Manchester direct control of the tax assessments raised in the eastern counties. The Army of the Eastern Association became Parliament's most effective force.

In another sense, too, the Eastern Association became the beating heart of Parliament's war effort, its 'engine of victory'. The Royalists never managed to invade East Anglia. Consequently, Parliament enjoyed an advantage denied to the King: a populous, wealthy and sizeable geographical base where taxes could be raised and arrears of tax collected without impediment.

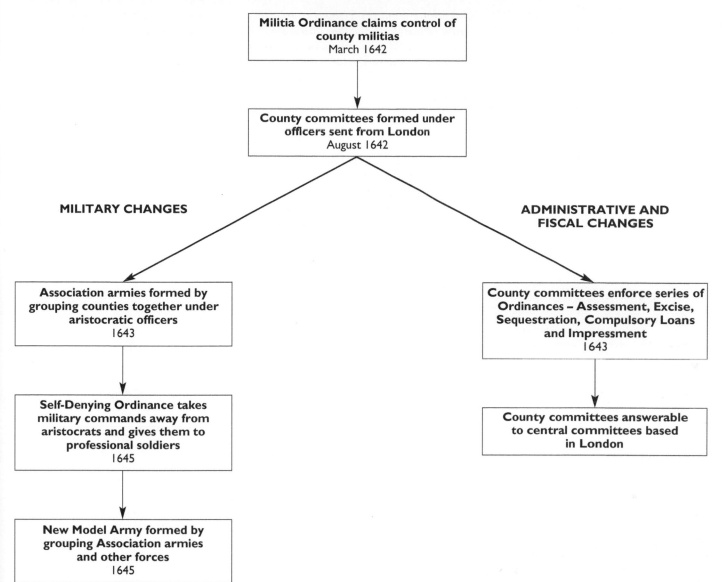

Militia Ordinance claims control of county militias
March 1642

↓

County committees formed under officers sent from London
August 1642

MILITARY CHANGES

ADMINISTRATIVE AND FISCAL CHANGES

Association armies formed by grouping counties together under aristocratic officers
1643

↓

Self-Denying Ordinance takes military commands away from aristocrats and gives them to professional soldiers
1645

↓

New Model Army formed by grouping Association armies and other forces
1645

County committees enforce series of Ordinances – Assessment, Excise, Sequestration, Compulsory Loans and Impressment
1643

↓

County committees answerable to central committees based in London

---

■ **Learning trouble spot**

East Anglia

Many students underestimate the importance of East Anglia to Parliament's war effort because their assumptions about which areas of Britain were the wealthiest and poorest are based on situations in later periods, rather than the situation in the 1600s. In the seventeenth century, East Anglia held a much more important position in England's economy than it does today. Norwich was the second largest city in England, with a population twice as large as that of any other city outside London. The region's wealth was based on the cloth industry and on farming. East Anglia had close trade connections with Holland, a Calvinist republic, and Puritanism was well established in the region.

THE
SOULDIERS
CATECHISME:

Compoſed for
The Parliaments Army:

Conſiſting of two Parts : wherein
are chiefly taught :

1 The Iuſtification ⎱ of our Souldiers.
2 The Qualification ⎰

Written for the Incouragement and In-
ſtruction of all that have taken up Armes in
this Cauſe of God and his People; eſpe-
cially the common Souldiers.

2 Sam. 10.12. *Be of good courage, and let us
play the men for our people, and for the Cities of our God, and the Lord do that Which
ſeemeth him good.*

Deut. 23.9. *When the Hoſt goeth forth againſt
thine enemies, then keepe thee from every
wicked thing.*

Imprimatur. JA. CRANFORD.

Aprill. 8ᵗʰ
Printed for J.Wright *in the Old-Baily.* 1644

SOURCE 7.2 Extracts from 'The Soldier's Catechism', 1644, a Parliamentary pamphlet widely distributed to encourage 'especially the common souldiers'

Question: What profession are you of?
Answer: I am a Christian and a soldier.
Q. *Is it lawful for Christians to be soldiers?*
A. *Yea doubtless: we have arguments enough to warrant it.*
   1. *God calls himself a man of war, and Lord of Hosts.*
   2. *Abraham had a Regiment of 318 trained men.*
   3. *David was employed in fighting the Lord's battles.*
   4. *The Holy Ghost makes honourable mention of David's Worthies.*
   5. *God himself taught David to fight . . . .*
Q. *What side are you of, and for whom do you fight?*
A. *I am for King and Parliament: or, in plainer terms;*
   1. *I fight to recover the King out of the hands of a Popish Malignant Company, that have seduced His Majesty with their wicked Counsels, and have withdrawn him from his Parliament.*
   2. *I fight for the Laws and Liberties of my Country, which are now in danger to be overthrown by them that have long laboured to bring into this Kingdome an Arbitrary, and Tyrannical Government.*
   3. *I fight for the preservation of our Parliament, in the being whereof (under God) consists the glory and welfare of this Kingdome; if this Foundation be overthrown, we shall soon be the most slavish Nation in the Christian World.*
   4. *I fight in the defence and maintenance of the true Protestant Religion, which is now violently opposed, and will be utterly suppressed in this Kingdom; and the Popish Religion again advanced, if the Armies raised against the Parliament prevail.*
Q. *But is it not against the King that you fight in this Cause?*
A. *No surely: yet many do abuse the world with this base and absurd objection . . .*
   4. *If the King will join himself with them that seek the ruin of his people, and the overthrow of Religion, surely both we and all good Subjects, may lawfully stand in the defence of both . . .*
Q. *But is it not a lamentable thing that Christians of the same Nation, should thus imbrue [stain] their hands in one another's blood?*
A. *I confess it is: But as the case now stands, there is an inevitable and absolute necessity of fighting laid upon the good people of the Land . . .*

ACTIVITY

Study Source 7.2.

1 How does the Soldier's Catechism try to reassure Parliament's soldiers that it was lawful for Christians to be soldiers?
2 Why did the Soldier's Catechism go to such lengths to do this?
3 What can you learn from the Soldier's Catechism about Parliament's war aims?
4 How does the Soldier's Catechism justify fighting against the King?
5 How effective do you think the Soldier's Catechism would have been in mobilising support for Parliament? What sort of people do you think it would have appealed to the most?
6 Compare Sources 7.1 (page 145) and 7.2. What difference can you see in the way the King and Parliament appealed for support? Why do you think this was so?

FOCUS ROUTE: WHO'S WHO?

Make notes on Sir Thomas Fairfax to include in your Who's who? list.

Sir Thomas Fairfax (1612–71)
Fairfax was given command of the New Model Army in 1645 in order to heal the political divisions in Parliament. An experienced general who had commanded the Yorkshire cavalry since 1642, Fairfax was neither an MP nor a member of the House of Lords. He came from a wealthy and respected Yorkshire family – his father, Lord Fairfax, commanded a regiment of foot. Married to a Presbyterian, he was well placed to maintain good relations between the New Model Army and its Scottish allies. He was widely respected for his ability, his modesty and his humanity.

The New Model Army

In February 1645 Parliament passed the New Model Ordinance, bringing together the armies of the Earls of Essex and Manchester and Sir William Waller into a national army under professional officers. The regional association armies were replaced by an army that would seek out and fight the King's forces wherever they could be found. The House of Lords gave up its powers of command and control. This was not an easy decision, but one that emerged from the unimpressive performance of Parliament's forces after their success at the Battle of Marston Moor in 1644 (see pages 162–65).

Four months after it was created, the New Model Army destroyed the King's main field army at Naseby. It is sometimes seen as the magic ingredient in Parliament's victory, but it should be seen as part of an ongoing process of military reform. Its 22,000 men, composed of 14,400 foot, 6600 horse and 1000 dragoons, were paid for by a fixed allocation of £53,000 from the monthly assessments. In fact it never quite achieved its theoretical size, or its theoretical regular pay. Other Parliamentary armies continued to exist: separate commands in the West Country and in the North had around 10,000 men each, while the Scots' army numbered around 22,000. There may not, therefore, have been much that was 'new' about the New Model Army apart from its victories.

FOCUS ROUTE

Returning to the Focus Route at the beginning of the chapter, make notes on the way the King and Parliament organised their respective war effort. How successfully did they deal with the two problems of **a)** finance and **b)** the regional bias of their armies?

C Making alliances

Both sides during the Civil War made alliances to increase their military power in England. The crisis of the three kingdoms did not stop with the outbreak of war in 1642; the billiard-ball effect (see Charts 3E and 4G) continued until both Celtic kingdoms – Scotland and Ireland – were not only drawn into the English conflict but were also locked in civil wars of their own.

The Royalists

In September 1643 the King signed a Cessation Treaty with the Irish Catholics. The cessation was a ceasefire, offering no immediate political settlement but enabling the King – in theory – to bring back the English soldiers from Ireland. Rumours soon spread that the King was planning to introduce Irish Catholic soldiers into the war in England. If Charles I won the war, he would be beholden to Catholic forces. The treaty raised again the old Protestant fears of a Catholic plot, and led some Royalists to defect to the Parliamentary cause.

The Battle of Naseby handed Parliament a major propaganda victory. Parliament captured the correspondence between the King, the Catholic Earl of Digby, and the Irish Confederation. It was clear that Charles was seeking support from the Confederation's Catholic forces. In exchange, he was promising to govern Ireland with a Catholic Lord Lieutenant, to introduce

Catholic bishops into the Irish House of Lords, and to make Catholicism the official religion of Ireland. The correspondence was published, and even those men in Parliament who defended the King's integrity were appalled.

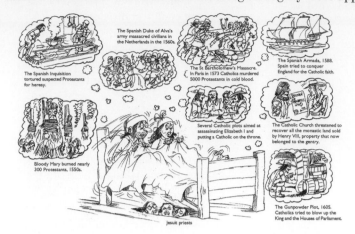

The Spanish Inquisition tortured suspected Protestants for heresy.

The Spanish Duke of Alva's army massacred civilians in the Netherlands in the 1560s.

The St Bartholomew's Massacre. In Paris in 1573 Catholics murdered 5000 Protestants in cold blood.

The Spanish Armada, 1588. Spain tried to conquer England for the Catholic faith.

Several Catholic plots aimed at assassinating Elizabeth I and putting a Catholic on the throne.

The Catholic Church threatened to recover all the monastic land sold by Henry VIII, property that now belonged to the gentry.

Bloody Mary burned nearly 300 Protestants, 1550s.

Jesuit priests

The Gunpowder Plot, 1605. Catholics tried to blow up the King and the Houses of Parliament.

Did the King's Irish negotiations contribute anything to the Royalist war effort? Many Irish troops brought into England were captured or killed at Nantwich, Cheshire, in January 1644. For a time Irish troops helped to secure the Welsh border country. But the 'Irish peace dividend' never really materialised for the King. Parliament's control of the Navy prevented large numbers of Irish forces from being transferred to England, and the numbers of English and Irish troops available for such service were smaller than was generally believed.

Could the King have received help from the Continent? In February 1642 Henrietta Maria departed for Europe in search of assistance, returning a year later with weapons and money. None of the continental powers had any intention, however, of intervening in England's troubles. They had troubles of their own.

The Parliamentarians

The Solemn League and Covenant

In August 1643 Parliament formed an alliance with the Scots called the Solemn League and Covenant. The Scots would send an army of 22,000 men into England to help defeat the King. In return, the English Parliament had to take the Solemn League and Covenant, meaning that Parliament's MPs and officers were expected to swear an oath to uphold the treaty or alliance. This committed England to a Presbyterian settlement. Cementing the alliance was the Committee of Both Kingdoms, creating a joint command over the Scottish and Parliamentary armies.

The alliance quickly proved its worth. In January 1644 the Scottish army, commanded by Alexander Leslie, Earl of Leven, crossed the border into England, forcing the Earl of Newcastle to shift his army northwards from the Midlands to meet the new threat. By June, Newcastle's army was besieged at York by a combination of Scottish and Parliamentary forces. Prince Rupert's army forced its way through to York, only to be destroyed at the Battle of Marston Moor.

Marston Moor was Parliament's first great victory. It enabled Parliament to redeploy its armies to the Midlands and the south, boosted Parliament's morale, and enhanced the reputations of Alexander Leslie and Oliver Cromwell. Rupert's reputation as the King's ablest general was damaged, and the Earl of Newcastle went into exile.

Cromwell was critical of the Scots' performance at Marston Moor, but the battle would never have been fought if they hadn't threatened York. Victory at Marston Moor placed the terms of the Solemn League and Covenant at the centre of a growing controversy over the Scots' contribution to Parliament's war effort.

DISCUSS

Why did the Cessation Treaty seem to confirm fears of a Catholic conspiracy? Refer back to this illustration on page 9.

DISCUSS

In the 1630s, Charles I tried to bring about uniformity of religion in England, Scotland and Ireland. Was the Solemn League and Covenant trying to achieve the same thing?

■ **Learning trouble spot**

Scotland during the First Civil War

Many students find it difficult to follow the changing fotunes of the leading figures in Scotland. Chart 7E is intended to clarify the situation. Make sure you study it carefully.

FOCUS ROUTE: WHO'S WHO?

Make notes on the Earl of Newcastle to include in your Who's who? list.

EARL OF MONTROSE

Montrose became the Royalist leader in Scotland despite being a Covenanter in the 1630s. Like many English Royalists, Montrose chose to support the King because he believed the opposition was encroaching too far on the royal prerogative. Personal rivalry with the Marquess of Argyll also played a part in his decision. Most of his support came from the Highlands, which were largely Catholic. After a brilliant campaign that forced the Covenanters to divert forces from England, he was finally defeated at Philiphaugh in September 1645 and went into exile.

Post-script: In 1650 Montrose returned to Scotland to raise the Royalists for Charles II. He was defeated at Carbisdale, captured and executed.

MARQUESS OF ARGYLL

Argyll was a leading Covenanter in the 1630s. When civil war broke out in England, he pressed for the alliance with the English Parliament which led to the Solemn League and Covenant. He believed that only a Parliamentary victory in England could secure the Presbyterian faith in Scotland; if the King won, he would then have overwhelming military force with which to crush the Covenanters in Scotland.

Post-script: Like many Scots incensed by the English execution of Charles I, Argyll supported Charles II's coronation as King of Scotland. In 1652 he submitted to Parliament's forces, and in 1658 he sat as an MP in Cromwell's Second Protectorate Parliament. After the restoration of Charles II in 1660, he was executed for high treason.

Map labels:
- HIGHLANDS (Catholic)
- HIGHLANDS (Catholic)
- Main area of Montrose's campaign 1644–45
- LOWLANDS (Protestant)
- Edinburgh
- Philiphaugh
- 1644 Covenanter army
- BORDER COUNTRY
- ENGLAND
- Threat of intervention from Ireland

DUKE OF HAMILTON

Hamilton was a close friend of the King and had accompanied Charles on his visit to Madrid in 1623. The events of the late 1630s strained their relationship: Charles sent Hamilton to negotiate on his behalf with the Covenanters, but he was never sure where Hamilton's true loyalties lay. In 1643 Hamilton tried to keep Scotland out of the English Civil War, arguing that the King would eventually win and that, when he did, Scotland's loyalty would be the only way to keep the Presbyterian faith and the Covenant intact. The King was not impressed by Hamilton's failure to support Montrose, and imprisoned him from 1644 to 1646.

Post-script: In 1648 Hamilton led the army of the Scottish Engagers (see Chapter 8) into England during the Second Civil War. He was defeated at Preston by Cromwell, captured and executed.

FOCUS ROUTE: WHO'S WHO?

Make notes on the Marquess of Argyll and the Duke of Hamilton to include in your Who's who? list.

D Political struggles

Throughout the Civil War, both sides faced the problem of internal divisions and political arguments. Both sides had men of widely differing views, held together with great difficulty by their political leaders. The King was obviously the political leader of the Royalists and had the final say when choices had to be made. With Parliament the task was more complicated, because no single person could claim the right to make decisions.

In each case the political coalition covered a spectrum of thought ranging from moderates, who wanted peace at almost any price, to hard-liners, who wanted complete military victory. Today we might call such groupings 'doves' and 'hawks'. The Civil War had its own names for these groups.

The Royalists

Charles I tended to side with the CAVALIERS against the moderate Royalists. The moderates certainly noticed this tendency in their King. It may have contributed to Lord Falkland's suicide at the First Battle of Newbury (he charged through a hedge knowing that he was likely to get shot), and Edward Hyde (Earl of Clarendon) wrote despairingly of it. However, there were times when moderate royalism prevailed. The King's replies to both the Grand Remonstrance and the Nineteen Propositions were masterpieces of moderation, designed to split the opposition and isolate Pym and his supporters.

In 1643 the King pronounced that Parliament was an illegal assembly. In 1644 Hyde persuaded the King to open the 'Oxford Parliament', a Royalist alternative to the rebel Parliament at Westminster. The idea was to show that Charles intended to work hand in hand with a loyal Parliament once the war was over. This might persuade Parliamentarians to change sides and join the King in Oxford. The Oxford Parliament also aimed at giving legitimacy to the emergency measures being introduced to raise money and troops for the war.

The King promised that there would be no return to Personal Rule, and that the extraordinary taxes being raised during wartime would not be continued when the war ended, nor would they be regarded as having established any kind of legal peacetime precedent. The Oxford Parliament drew the support of around 175 MPs and 82 peers. In public, the strategy appeared to achieve some success at a time when many Parliamentarians were having second thoughts about the war. In private, the King wrote disparagingly of the initiative as the 'mongrel Parliament'.

CAVALIERS
The Royalist 'hawks', who argued against the advice of the moderate Royalists. The Cavaliers wanted nothing less than a complete military victory over Parliament.

LORD FALKLAND'S SUICIDE

Lord Falkland was one of the moderate Royalists. It is thought that he committed suicide at the First Battle of Newbury because he was depressed by the failure of peace negotiations. He may also have been taunted by Cavaliers as a coward, which he was not. His death isolated Edward Hyde and made the Cavaliers' influence over the King even stronger.

ACTIVITY

The Royalist 'tug-of-war'

In the table opposite are some of the key decisions taken by Charles I during the English Civil War and in the period leading up to it. Each of these decisions represents a victory for either the Cavaliers or the moderates among the King's advisers.

1 On a copy of the table, explain in the appropriate column why each decision was a victory for either the Cavaliers or the moderates.
2 Explain whether you think this decision had good or bad results for Charles.
3 Add any further evidence you can find to the table.
4 On balance, do you think the King listened more frequently to the Cavaliers or to the moderates, and with what results?

Cavaliers	Decisions taken by the King	Moderates
Lord Digby The Queen The Earl of Newcastle		Edward Hyde Lord Falkland (killed 20 September 1643)
	The King's reply to the Grand Remonstrance, December 1641	
	The Attempt on the Five Members, January 1642	
	The King's reply to the Nineteen Propositions, June 1642	
	After the Battle of Edgehill, the King's decision to march on London instead of offering terms for negotiation, October 1642	
	Prince Rupert's brutal attack on Brentford, which strengthened the 'war party' in Parliament at a moment when many MPs were having second thoughts about the war, November 1642	
	The King's rejection of Parliament's terms during the 'Oxford Treaty', March 1643	
	The decision to lay siege to Gloucester rather than take it by assault, August 1643	
	When three peers – the Earls of Holland, Bedford and Clare – defected from Parliament and joined the King at Oxford, they were given such an unfriendly reception by Charles that they returned to London, August 1643	
	The decision to negotiate with the Irish Catholics, leading to the Cessation Treaty, September 1643	
	The Oxford Parliament, 1644	

FOCUS ROUTE: WHO'S WHO?

Make brief notes on Lord Digby to include in your Who's who? list.

The Parliamentarians

The crisis of 1643–44

By definition, those MPs and Lords who stayed at Westminster in 1642 were 'Parliamentarians', but there were always differences of opinion about what they were fighting for, and what would constitute victory. We have already seen how, during the year before the outbreak of war, the Royalist party was created as more and more people began supporting the King (see Chart 4F, page 100). This process continued after war was declared, gathered momentum during the winter of 1642/43, and threatened to undermine Parliament's war effort. It took great skill to keep Parliament focused on the task of winning the war.

From 1642 until 1644, politics were polarised between the 'war' and 'peace' parties at Westminster. The problem facing Pym and his allies was how to maintain Parliament's resolve to finish what it had started.

There was also a smaller but highly influential third group of radicals, led by the republican Henry Marten. This group argued for permanent changes to the English constitution, including the possibility of abolishing the monarchy. Their existence contributed to a sense of unease among many MPs and Lords, notably Parliament's two most important generals – the Earl of Essex and the Earl of Manchester.

To win the war, the leaders of the 'war party' had to:

- convince moderates that the radicals would not drive the country into revolution
- prevent the 'peace party' from persuading Parliament to conclude a dishonourable peace with the King
- prevent substantial numbers of Lords and MPs from defecting to the Royalists.

And they had to do all this while forcing through Parliament the radical legislation needed to achieve victory.

R
O
Y
A
L
I
S
T
S

PARLIAMENTARIANS			

'Peace party'	**Non-aligned majority**	**'War party'**	**Radicals**
Aim: to end the war as quickly as possible through negotiation, without losing the achievements of 1641		Aim: to negotiate terms from a position of strength, without going much beyond the achievements of 1641	Aim: permanent constitutional changes
Membership: Denzil Holles* John Maynard Sir Simmonds D'Ewes Earl of Northumberland Earl of Holland	Membership: the majority of MPs at Westminster	Membership: John Pym* (d. Dec 1643) John Hampden* (d. June 1643) Lord Saye and Sele Lord Brooke Earl of Essex Earl of Manchester* Earl of Bedford Earl of Warwick Oliver Cromwell	Henry Marten Henry Vane the Younger Sir Arthur Haselrig* William Strode*

44 MPs defected to the Royalists after August 1642, mostly during the crisis of 1643

*The Five Members (six, including the Earl of Manchester) whom the King tried to arrest in January 1642

We must end the war as quickly as possible. Parliament is passing laws that threaten to undermine our liberties more surely than the King ever did. The King is a man of his word, but if he wins the war we can expect no mercy.

We must prepare for war while negotiating for peace. The nature of war is incompatible with the ordinary rules of a peaceable government. When the King realises that we can win, he will be more inclined to accept terms that are also acceptable to us.

We must fight and we must win. The King will never negotiate in good faith, so we must dictate terms to him. If he persists in rejecting our terms, then we must consider radical proposals – perhaps a change of dynasty, or even a republic.

Denzil Holles   **John Pym**   **Henry Marten**

PARLIAMENTARIANS

The Scottish alliance is a mistake. By introducing a foreign army into England, we give the King an excuse to bring in troops from Ireland, or even France and Spain. This is a move that will anger the King and make it more difficult to end the war by negotiation.

The Scots are not a 'foreign army' – like us, they are the King's subjects, fighting to rescue him from his evil advisors. We need their help, especially in the north. By forming an alliance with them, we prevent them from making a deal with the King and intervening on his side.

The Scottish alliance is essential to our victory. When the time comes we may decide not to honour our promise to create a Presbyterian church – but for the moment the promise is a price worth paying.

Denzil Holles

John Pym

Henry Marten

The Earl of Essex is losing the war, so we must make peace. If he can't win the war for Parliament, no one can.

Essex is doing a good job in difficult circumstances. To take away his command at this point would sow panic in Parliament. We need the Earl to lead our armies, to reassure conservative country gentlemen and to maintain good relations with the Lords.

Essex is incompetent. Let us replace him with someone who will fight more vigorously – or at least give Sir William Waller an independent command in the west.

Denzil Holles

John Pym

Henry Marten

FOCUS ROUTE: WHO'S WHO?

Make brief notes on Henry Marten to include in your Who's who? list.

ACTIVITY

Some historians believe that Pym's greatest achievement was to steer Parliament through its darkest hours in 1643. Using the information on these two pages make notes on the main areas of Pym's work and write a short assessment of his importance to the Parliamentary cause. Focus on Pym's:

• persuading Parliament to pass laws imposing new taxes and other measures vital to military success, while overcoming the objections of those who feared that Parliament was acting illegally
• giving the Earl of Essex the opportunity to restore his damaged reputation at Gloucester and Newbury
• persuading Parliament to agree to the Solemn League and Covenant, thereby bringing the Scots into the war against the King.

What evidence can you find that Pym performed a balancing act between the 'peace' and 'war' parties?

In the summer of 1643 Parliament faced its greatest test during the siege of Gloucester. Parliament was losing the war, and as a result the performance of the Earl of Essex as Lord General of Parliament's armies was being called into question. While Pym defended Essex's reputation, he pushed through Parliament the measures that ultimately gave it victory. Essex's march to the relief of Gloucester, followed by his success at the first Battle of Newbury, marked a turning point in the politics of Parliament's war effort.

Independents vs. Presbyterians, 1644

John Pym and John Hampden both died in 1643. Their deaths robbed the House of Commons of two of its most important political managers. In 1644 Parliament polarised into two new factions – the Independents and the Presbyterians. These groups could trace their origins back to the old 'war' and 'peace' parties, but were also driven by new pressures.

The chief of these was the alliance with Scotland. Parliament had agreed to impose a Presbyterian church settlement on England when the war ended. But many English officers and soldiers were not happy about this.

In the long run, the impact of the Scottish alliance on Parliament's politics was greater even than its impact on the war against the King. The coming of the Scots led to a complete change in the way the 'war' and 'peace' parties viewed the alliance. Having objected to it on the grounds that it would prolong the war, the old 'peace party' now saw in Scottish Presbyterianism a way of bringing the war to a rapid end, preventing further social upheaval. The 'war party' was coming to regret its alliance with the Scots, with its assumption that the Scots were somehow more religious than the English. After Marston Moor, the 'war party' was confident that Parliament could win the war on its own. Consequently, the 'peace party' became known as the 'Presbyterians', while the 'war party' evolved into the 'Independents' (see Chart 7G).

■ 7G The impact of the Scottish alliance on Parliament's politics

Opposed to Scottish intervention   1643   In favour of Scottish intervention

'Peace party'   'War party'

SOLEMN LEAGUE AND COVENANT AUGUST 1643

Scottish army crosses into England, 1644

Independents
Former 'war party' now sees Scottish Presbyterianism as a threat to religious liberty and to an acceptable settlement with the King.

1644

Presbyterians
Former 'peace party' now sees Scottish Presbyterianism as the best way to control religious radicals and reach agreement with the King.

FOCUS ROUTE: WHO'S WHO?

Make brief notes on the Earl of Manchester to include in your Who's who? list.

ACTIVITY

Work with a partner to carry out the following role plays.

1 One of you represents the 'peace party' and the other the 'war party'. Explain to each other how your policy has been affected by the Solemn League and Covenant.

2 One of you represents the Earl of Manchester and the other Cromwell. Re-enact the clash between you, but in your own words.

Trouble was already brewing over relations between Scottish officers serving in the Eastern Association (under the Earl of Manchester) and Cromwell. The Scots accused Cromwell of promoting Independents in preference to Presbyterians. At first Manchester agreed with Cromwell that the religious beliefs of their soldiers were secondary to their willingness to serve. In 1643 Manchester had spoken of his willingness to enlist men 'differing in judgement to what I profess'. Early in 1644 Cromwell argued with Lawrence Crawford, a Scottish officer serving with the Eastern Association, for punishing two soldiers for their radical religious beliefs.

Manchester's overriding concern was to maintain good relations with the Scots. Marston Moor confirmed his opinion that the Scottish alliance was central to Parliament's war effort. Cromwell drew a different conclusion: in his opinion the Scots' performance on the battlefield that day was disappointing. He ascribed victory to the godly soldiers under his command. Many of these soldiers were motivated by religious beliefs incompatible with the Presbyterian faith. Cromwell's reputation as a fighting general was enhanced enormously at Marston Moor, and with greater self-confidence he became more critical both of the Scottish army and its intolerance and of Parliament's willingness to sacrifice his soldiers' religious freedom to please the Scots. His outspokenness brought him into conflict with Manchester.

Tension between Manchester and Cromwell exploded into open argument after the Second Battle of Newbury, where the combined armies of Manchester and Waller failed to defeat a Royalist army half their size. Cromwell was angry that the King had escaped when Manchester failed to press home his attack. Parliament demanded an enquiry into allegations that the battle was mismanaged, and this triggered a confrontation between the two officers.

① The Earl of Manchester has deliberately avoided battles that might have placed the King at a greater disadvantage. At Newbury he failed to press his attack, allowing the King to escape.

② Lieutenant-General Cromwell is insubordinate. The commanders at Newbury – and he was one – must share collective responsibility for any failings in the Army's performance. It was Cromwell's cavalry that allowed the King to escape at Newbury.

Earl of Manchester

Oliver Cromwell

③ **6 December 1644**
If we beat the King ninety-nine times, yet he is King still, and so will his posterity be after him; but if the King beat us once we shall all be hanged, and our posterity made slaves.

④ **6 December 1644**
My Lord, if this be so, why did we take up arms at first? This is against fighting ever hereafter. If so, let us make peace, be it never so base.

	'Peace party'		'War party'
	POLITICAL PRESBYTERIANS	G R O U P	POLITICAL INDEPENDENTS
Leading members of the 'party'	Denzil Holles Earl of Manchester Earl of Essex		Oliver Cromwell Henry Ireton Lord Saye and Sele Oliver St John
War aims	To end the war through negotiation		To win the war
Promotion from the lower ranks	To be discouraged. The war threatens social disorder		*'The State, in choosing men to serve them, takes no notice of their opinions. If they be willing faithfully to serve them, that satisfies'* (Cromwell speaking to Lawrence Crawford)
Post-war religious settlement	A national Presbyterian church to replace the Church of England. Compulsory attendance will prevent the kingdom descending into religious anarchy	MIDDLE	Liberty of conscience should be granted to all Protestants. *'We look for no compulsion but that of light and reason.'* (Cromwell in a letter to Parliament after capturing Bristol, 1645)
The Scottish alliance	A Presbyterian church settlement will consolidate our alliance with Scotland. In time it could even pave the way for the unification of the two kingdoms		The Scots entered the war for their own reasons. We are glad to have them as allies, but they must not expect to dictate to us the terms on which we settle the kingdom when the war ends

The Self-Denying Ordinance, April 1645

The political crisis of 1644 was resolved by the Self-Denying Ordinance, proposed in the House of Lords by Lord Saye and Sele and in the Commons by Oliver Cromwell. On 9 December 1644 Cromwell suggested that all members of both Houses of Parliament resign their commissions, handing over military command of Parliament's armies to professional soldiers. The idea of self-denial, like fasting and prayer, appealed to the godly as a way of regaining God's favour, which had shone so brightly at Marston Moor. The practical benefits were just as important: at a stroke the ordinance would sweep away the group of aristocratic commanders who had led the armies since 1642. It would also pave the way for the New Model Army by placing the private regiments raised by wealthy politicians under centralised command.

SOURCE 7.3 Oliver Cromwell, speaking in a Grand Committee meeting in the House of Commons, 9 December 1644

It is now a time to speak, or forever hold the tongue. The important occasion now, is no less than To save a Nation, out of a bleeding, nay almost dying condition: which the long continuance of this War hath already brought it into; so that without a more speedy, vigorous and effectual prosecution of the War we shall make the kingdom weary of us, and hate the name of a Parliament.

For what do the enemy say? Nay, what do many say that were friends at the beginning of the Parliament? Even this, That the Members of both Houses have got great places and commands, and the sword into their hands; and, what by interest in Parliament, what by power in the Army, will perpetually continue themselves in grandeur, and not permit the War speedily to end, lest their own power should determine [end] with it. This 'that' I speak here to our own faces, is but what others do utter abroad behind our backs. I am far from reflecting on any. I know the worth of those Commanders, Members of both Houses, who are yet in power: but if I may speak my conscience without reflection upon any, I do conceive if the Army be not put into another method, and the War more vigorously prosecuted, the People can bear the War no longer, and will enforce you to a dishonourable Peace.

Continued

But this I would recommend to your prudence, Not to insist upon any complaint or oversight of any Commander-in-chief upon any occasion whatsoever; for as I must acknowledge myself guilty of oversights, so I know they can rarely be avoided in military affairs. Therefore waiving a strict enquiry into the causes of these things, let us apply ourselves to the remedy; which is most necessary. And I hope we have such true English hearts, and zealous affections towards the general weal [welfare] of our Mother Country, as no Member of either House will scruple to deny themselves, and their own private interests, for the public good; nor account it to be a dishonour done to them, whatever the Parliament shall resolve upon in this weighty matter.

One major problem stood in the way of the Self-Denying Ordinance. Marston Moor had turned Cromwell into a national figure – at last, Parliament had a general who could win battles. But Cromwell would have to resign his commission under the terms of the Ordinance.

Much research has focused on the question of whether some premeditated plan existed for excluding Cromwell from the provisions of the Self-Denying Ordinance (see Chapter 9, pages 209–11), but the outcome is not disputed. When Parliament appointed Sir Thomas Fairfax as Lord General of the New Model Army and Philip Skippon as Major-General of the infantry, the post of Lieutenant-General of Horse was left vacant. This was Cromwell's particular skill, and after twice extending the deadline for his resignation, Parliament approved a request from Fairfax that Cromwell be given command of the New Model cavalry.

Parliament therefore survived two major political crises between 1642 and 1645. The success of the 'war party' in 1644–45 was something of a compromise: Fairfax had a Presbyterian wife and may have sympathised with the Scots. Nevertheless, Parliament could now concentrate on the task of winning the war, which could only be done by searching out the King's armies and annihilating them on the battlefield.

ACTIVITY

Study Source 7.3.

1 What was the main point of Cromwell's speech?
2 According to Cromwell, why was Parliament losing support?
3 How does this speech demonstrate Cromwell's political skill?

FOCUS ROUTE

1 In 1643 John Pym worked hard to protect the Earl of Essex as Lord General of Parliament's armies. In late 1644, however, Essex was removed from command alongside the Earls of Manchester and Warwick (the Navy) and Sir William Waller, under the provisions of the Self-Denying Ordinance. What had changed between August 1643 and December 1644 to turn Essex from a political asset to a political liability?
2 Return to the Focus Route at the beginning of the chapter. How successfully did the King and Parliament deal with their political problems?

E Winning battles

All the effort by both sides would come to nothing unless they could achieve victory on the battlefield. Months of careful preparation raising money, recruiting and training soldiers, buying weapons, organising supplies and marshalling armies could be thrown away in a day on the battlefield. Many civil war battles were relatively small, and sieges consumed many of the armies' resources. Nevertheless, on several occasions the kingdom's fate rested in the hands of the officers commanding the main field armies of the King and Parliament.

SOURCE 7.4 The Battle of Naseby, 14 June 1645 – a contemporary plan of the battle

ACTIVITY

Study Source 7.4.

1 Find the following individuals:
   a) on the King's side: King Charles I; Prince Rupert; Prince Maurice
   b) on Parliament's side: General Fairfax; Oliver Cromwell; Henry Ireton.

2 Find the following military units:
   a) on the King's side: The King's Lifeguards; Prince Rupert's Regiment of Foot; the King's Baggage.
   b) on Parliament's side: the Forlorn Hope; the Dragoons in Sulby Hedges; Lt. Colonel Pride's Rear Guard; the (baggage) train guarded by Fire-Locks.

3 How are the infantry regiments on both sides organised? What weapons are they carrying, and in what proportion? What does this tell you about their effectiveness and the way they might have been used?

4 Parliament has placed a 'Forlorn Hope' of musketeers in front of its army. What do you think this was for?

5 How is the artillery on both sides deployed?

6 Dragoons were mounted infantry – horsemen armed with muskets. During battles they would dismount to use their weapons while their horses were held behind the firing line. You can see this in the picture. Parliament's army has placed its dragoons along Sulby Hedges on its left flank. What would they be used for, firing from this position?

7 The armies have chosen to fight on a broad patch of ground known as a 'battaglia' between Sulby Hedges and the Rabbit Burrows. Why do you think they wanted the battle to be fought on a patch of open ground in between hedges and woodland?

8 Roughly what proportion of the armies is made up of infantry (foot) and cavalry (horse)?

9 Explain why the armies are deployed in the following way:
   a) the cavalry on the wings and in several rows
   b) the infantry regiments in two or three rows, with the pikemen in the second row guarding the gaps between the musketeers in the first row, and so on.

10 How important is this source as evidence of the way civil war battles were fought?

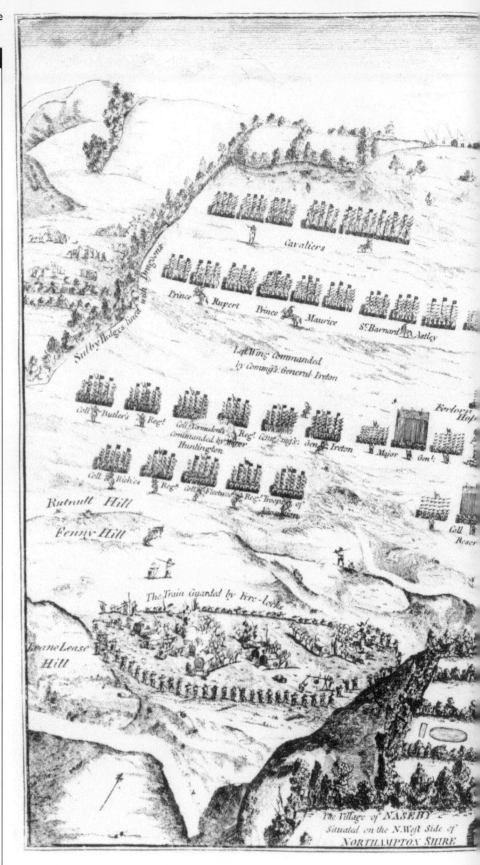

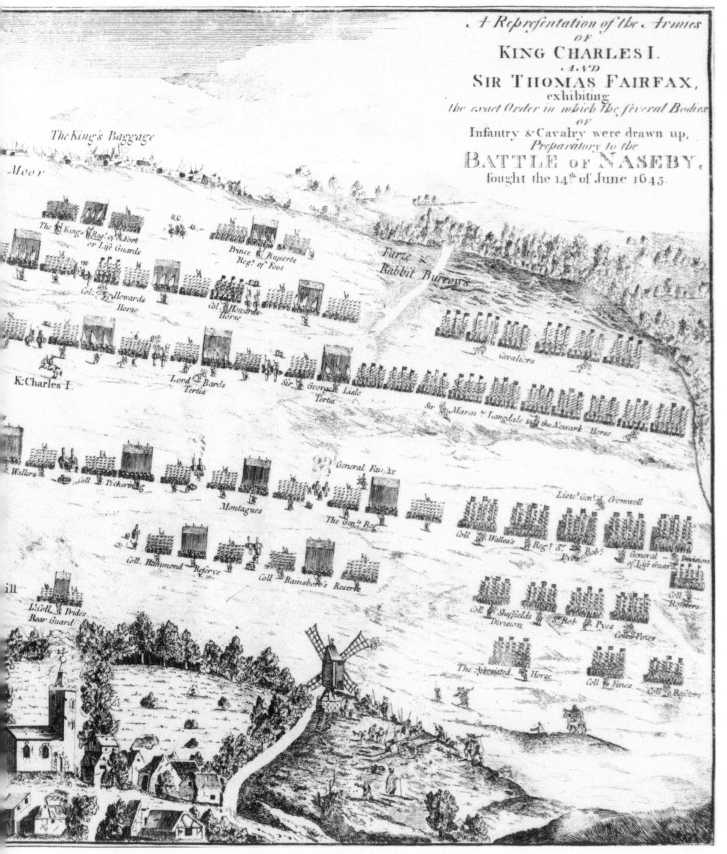

A Reprefentation of the Armies OF KING CHARLES I. AND SIR THOMAS FAIRFAX, exhibiting the exact Order in which the feveral Bodies OF Infantry & Cavalry were drawn up, Preparatory to the BATTLE OF NASEBY, fought the 14th of June 1645.

The King's Baggage

Moor

The Kings Reg.t of Foot or Life Guards

Prince Ruperts Reg.t of Foot

Furze & Rabbit Burrows

Coll. Howards Horse

Col. Howards Horse

Cavaliers

K: Charles I.

Lord Bards Tertia

Sir George Lisle Tertia

Sir Marm. Langdale with the Newark Horse

Wallers

Coll. Pickering

General Fairfax

Lieu.t Gen.l Cromwell

Montagues

The Gen.ls Reg.t

Coll. Walles's Reg.t Sr. Rob.t Pye

General of Life Guard

Division

Coll. Hammond Reserve

Coll. Rainsboro's Reserve

Coll. Sheffields Division

Sr. Rob. Pyes

Coll. Rositers

Li. Coll. Prides Rear Guard

The Affociated Horse

Coll. Fines

Coll. Pittes

Coll. Rejeters

Learning from experience

The Battle of Edgehill (see Chapter 5) was a panic-stricken, amateur business, which both sides deserved to lose. Royalists and Parliamentarians both assumed that the other side would give in after the first sight of blood, but this didn't happen. Looking back on Edgehill, both sides drew their conclusions about what had gone wrong. Future battles would depend on whether they were willing and able to learn from their mistakes. Eyewitnesses on both sides concluded that the performance of their cavalry was crucial, though for different reasons.

SOURCE 7.5 Oliver Cromwell, who commanded a Parliamentary troop of cavalry at Edgehill, describing a conversation he had with John Hampden after the battle. (Cromwell's troop arrived part way through the action)

At my first going into this engagement, I saw our men were beaten at every hand and I told him I would be serviceable to him in bringing such men in as I thought had a spirit that would do something in the work. 'Your troopers', said I, 'are most of them old decayed servingmen and tapsters and such kind of fellows; and', said I, 'their troopers are gentlemen's sons, younger sons and persons of quality; do you think that the spirits of such base and mean fellows will be ever able to encounter gentlemen that have honour and courage and resolution in them? You must get men of a spirit that is likely to go on as far as gentlemen will go, or else I am sure you will be beaten still.'

SOURCE 7.6 Sir Philip Warwick, who fought among the Royalist infantry

But as if a fate had attended all we did, though Prince Rupert entirely routed the left wing of Essex's Horse, which being perceived, Wilmott [the commander of the Royalist cavalry on Parliament's right] had very little to do with the right ... but both reserves pursuing the chase, contrary to all discipline of war, left the King and his Foot so alone, that it gave Essex a title unto the victory of that day; which might have been his last day, if they had done their parts, and stood their ground.

ACTIVITY

Both sides claimed victory at Edgehill, but in private both Royalists and Parliamentarians were critical of their performance.
Read Sources 7.5 and 7.6.

1 Both sources are critical of the role their cavalry played in the battle, but for different reasons. What did **a)** Cromwell and **b)** Warwick think had gone wrong at Edgehill?
2 Which of these problems do you think should have been easier to put right, and why?

The plan of the Battle of Naseby (Source 7.4) suggests that armies were arranged before battle in a disciplined and organised way. Once battle was joined, however, order could quickly collapse. When this happened a great deal depended on the discipline of the soldiers, and on the qualities of leadership of their officers. The most instructive battle is Marston Moor, where order quickly collapsed, and where either side could have won.

The Battle of Marston Moor

At seven o'clock on the evening of 2 July 1644, a Royalist army of 18,000 men commanded by Prince Rupert faced a Parliamentary and Scottish army of 27,000 men on Marston Moor, 10 miles west of York. The two armies adopted the standard deployment of the time, with the infantry in the centre and the cavalry on the wings. They were unusually close, the front lines standing only 400 yards apart. Separating them was a narrow road running the length of the battlefield between Long Marston and Tockwith, with a ditch and broken hedge on the Royalist side to the north. Rupert, whose army was deployed on the flat moor, was relying on the ditch to slow down Parliament's cavalry if it charged.

DISTANCES

1 mile = 1.6 kilometres
1 yard = 0.9 metre

Parliament's army was drawn up in a position chosen by Cromwell, on a long ridge and rolling farmland to the south of the road. It was a strong position: not only did the army have the advantage of height, but seen from the Royalist lines much of Parliament's army was invisible, tucked away between folds in the hills. The road and ditch offered protection from Rupert's famous cavalry. Cromwell had chosen his ground well.

Rupert was outnumbered, facing the largest Parliamentary army ever assembled, serving under veteran commanders – Alexander Leslie, the Earl of Manchester, Oliver Cromwell and Sir Thomas Fairfax. With the evening sun low in the sky under storm clouds, dazzling the Royalists as they peered into the gathering gloom at the indistinct host across the road, Prince Rupert did an extraordinary thing. He went back to his tent to have dinner. Taking its cue from its commanding officer, the Royalist army began to relax, preparing psychologically to stand to before dawn for battle the following morning.

■ 71 Why did Prince Rupert go to dinner?

Rupert's decision to return to his tent and stand down (withdraw) the army in the face of the enemy seems bizarre.
To make sense of it, we must understand that all was not well in the Royalist ranks. Several factors contributed to his decision.

Lord Eythin, the Earl of Newcastle's Chief of Staff, was criticising Rupert's dispositions. He said they were fine on paper, but chaotic on the ground. Eythin had fought alongside Rupert on the Continent and didn't think much of him as a commander.

Rupert thought it was too late in the day to begin a large battle, and that the enemy would think so too. In the morning the sun would be in the enemies' eyes.

Newcastle's soldiers were still arriving from York and needed time to move into position and rest. Newcastle was urging delay.

After a day of heavy rain another storm was about to sweep across the moor. Wet weather made the musketeers' job almost impossible, trying to keep their powder dry and their matches lit.

The Battle

SOURCE 7.7 The Battle of Marston Moor

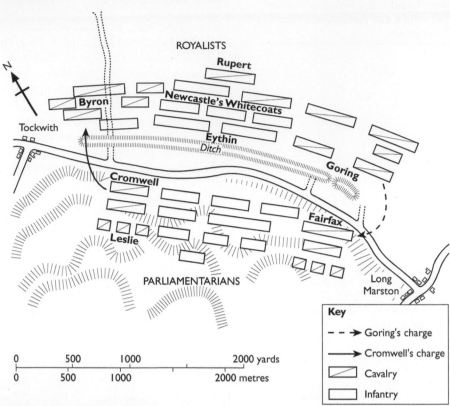

On the hilltop overlooking the battlefield, General Leslie saw the enemy relaxing and seized his opportunity. Quoting an old legend that 'a summer's night is as long as a winter's day', he ordered an attack along the entire front. On Parliament's left wing, Cromwell's cavalry swept down the hillside, crossed the road and ditch, and attacked the Royalist right wing. Lord Byron's Royalist cavalry counterattacked, but in doing so they blocked the line of fire of their own musketeers. Rupert led his own reserve of horse to support Byron, and soon a large cavalry battle was being fought on the outskirts of Tockwith.

On Parliament's right wing, Sir Thomas Fairfax also led his cavalry down the slope, but ran into trouble. The ground was covered with gorse, and narrow lanes and hedges lined with Royalist dragoons stopped his charge. He was counterattacked by Lord Goring's cavalry, and after a fierce battle Fairfax's men were broken, some fleeing from the field while others fell back into their own infantry, creating panic and confusion.

The crisis of the battle was at hand. On the left of Parliament's centre, Crawford's infantry stormed across the ditch and attacked the right wing of the Royalist infantry, which was driven slowly backwards. Behind Eythin's infantry were Newcastle's 'Whitecoats', the finest infantry in Rupert's army, ready to take up the battle. On Parliament's right wing, the collapse of Fairfax's cavalry had exposed the flank of the Scottish infantry, who were also falling back. The battle was twisting clockwise like a great tropical storm.

On the western side of the battlefield, Cromwell was knocked from his horse, stunned by a sword blow to the neck. David Leslie took control until Cromwell regained his senses and re-entered the battle. Cromwell's cavalry now regrouped and charged again, driving their enemies from the field before turning onto the exposed flank of the Royalist infantry. Rupert was forced to take refuge in a field of beans (see Source 7.9). Sir Thomas Fairfax gathered his remaining cavalry and, riding around the back of the Royalist army, attacked their infantry from the rear. As darkness fell, the desperate struggle on Parliament's right wing gave way to chaos as the Royalist army disintegrated. Last to fall were Newcastle's 'Whitecoats', who refused to surrender and were slaughtered where they stood. The Royalist army had been annihilated.

SOURCE 7.8 Extract from a letter from Oliver Cromwell to Colonel Valentine Walton, 5 July 1644

Truly England and the Church of God hath had a great favour from the Lord, in this great Victory given unto us, such as the like never was since this War began. It had all the evidences of an absolute Victory obtained by the Lord's blessing upon the Godly Party principally. We never charged but we routed the enemy. The Left Wing, which I commanded, being our own horse, saving a few Scots in our rear, beat all the Prince's horse. God made them as stubble to our swords.

SOURCE 7.9 Rupert does a runner: a Parliamentary cartoon showing Rupert hiding in a bean field. His poodle 'Boy' lies dead on the battlefield, as Parliamentary soldiers discover Catholic images in the Royalist baggage. Parliament was quick to poke fun at the reputation of the Royalists' most feared general. Parliament's propaganda suggested the Royalist army was full of Catholics

ACTIVITY

Why did Parliament win the Battle of Marston Moor?

1 Copy and complete the table below to evaluate the relative importance of the various factors that contributed to Parliament's victory.

Factors	How they affected the battle	Relative importance to Parliament's victory
Size of the armies	• The Royalists had 18,000 men • Parliament and the Scots had 27,000 men	
Choice of battlefield	• Rupert chose Marston Moor as a battlefield • Cromwell held the high ground and recalled the army to accept battle on that ground	
Quality of the cavalry	• Lord Goring's horse defeated Sir Thomas Fairfax, but played no further part in the battle • Cromwell's horse defeated Byron and Rupert, then regrouped and attacked the Royalist infantry	
Leadership	• Prince Rupert – how do you rate his performance? • Oliver Cromwell – what qualities of leadership did he display at Marston Moor? • Alexander Leslie – it was his decision to launch the attack	
The Scots	• How did Cromwell rate the Scots' performance? (See Source 7.8) • What reasons might he have had for emphasising the role played by his own cavalry?	

2 You are Prince Rupert the day after the Battle of Marston Moor. Write a letter to King Charles I, telling him what has happened and why. Outline the policies you think he should now pursue.

FOCUS ROUTE

Return to the Focus Route at the beginning of the chapter. Make sure that you have collected evidence from all five sections for both the Royalists and the Parliamentarians.

F Review: why did Parliament win the Civil War?

ACTIVITY

Choose one of the following essay titles:

a) Why did Parliament win the First Civil War, 1642–46?

b) How important was the New Model Army in the victory of Parliament in the First Civil War?

c) Discuss the view that the King lost the First Civil War primarily due to financial problems.

d) How valid is the view that Parliament was bound to win the First Civil War because its resources were greater than the King's?

Note: The first essay in this list is the 'open' form of the question, inviting you to discuss the relative importance of all the various factors which led to Parliament's victory in 1646. You are free in this question to decide how much weight to give to each factor.

All the other essay titles present the same question in a different way, forcing you to consider the relative importance of one particular factor compared to the rest. Ultimately your essay will have to consider all the factors, but you must give special attention to the one factor that has been picked out for you. The simplest way to do this is to deal with that factor first, before setting it in the context of all the others. If you do this, you must return to that factor in your conclusion and explain how much weight you give it compared with the others.

KEY POINTS FROM CHAPTER 7

Why did Parliament win the Civil War?

1 In 1642 Parliament's resources were of a type that held out hope for victory in the long run. There was every possibility that the King might win the war in the short run.

2 The King organised his war effort along traditional lines to begin with, believing that victory depended on giving local communities their traditional control over the processes of raising resources and organising local defence.

3 Parliament followed the same strategy as the King to begin with, but nearly lost the war in 1643. This forced Parliament to rethink its entire approach. It developed a more centralised bureaucracy and a national standing army paid for by taxation.

4 In 1644 and 1645 the Royalists lost several major battles. This forced them to rethink their approach, developing a more impersonal system for raising resources.

5 Parliament's uncontested control of London and East Anglia gave it a reliable source of revenue and manpower.

6 The closest the King could come to matching this was his uncontested control of Wales.

7 Parliament overcame two major political crises, which enabled it to take the practical steps necessary to win the war.

8 Parliament was more successful than the King in making alliances to introduce 'foreign' soldiers into the English war.

9 In the course of the war, Parliament found commanders capable of winning major battles.

8

Who was to blame for the King's execution in 1649?

CHAPTER OVERVIEW

SOURCE 8.1 'England's Miraculous Preservation', 1646 – a picture celebrating Parliament's victory in the First Civil War. The verse above the Ark says:

> Though England's Ark has furious storms endured
> By plots of foes and power of the sword,
> Yet to this day by God's almighty hand
> The Ark is preserved and almost safe at land

ACTIVITY

Study Source 8.1.

1 What is the message of this source?
2 By 1646 it was already clear that making peace would be difficult. When the picture was made it was already out of date. Why, then, was this picture published? Who might have drawn it, and for what purpose?

Study Source 8.2 (page 168).

3 How does this picture show despair at the way things were turning out?
4 Why were pictures like these such a popular way of expressing political ideas in the late 1640s?

SOURCE 8.2 England in 1649 – an allegory of regicide

Source 8.1 celebrates Parliament's victory in the First Civil War. Parliament is shown as Noah's Ark, preserving the kingdom through the Deluge of civil war. The Royalists – the Earl of Newcastle (waving a sword); Archbishop Laud; the Earl of Strafford (firing a gun); Prince Rupert (over Laud's right shoulder); a bishop clutching a mitre – are shown drowning in the sea. In 1646 there was great optimism that England's troubles were over. Parliament had won the war. Surely the King would now accept defeat and make peace on Parliament's terms? Soon, it was hoped, everything would be back to normal.

By 1649, however, things looked very different. Source 8.2 shows how the optimism of 1646 had given way to confusion and despair. The 'ship of state' is being shipwrecked in a storm. The King – the ship's pilot – is being thrown overboard. Lightning is striking the House of Commons, which should be acting as a lighthouse but is signalling in the wrong direction. The people are fighting among themselves while the Army idly watches.

The expectations of 1646 had not been fulfilled. England had endured religious and social upheaval, political anarchy, a second civil war and revolution, resulting in the death of the King.

This chapter covers the period 1646–49, addressing question **b)** in the section introduction (page 109). It aims to help you explain why Parliament's victory in 1646 turned into revolution and regicide by 1649.

FOCUS ROUTE

1 At the end of this chapter you must explain why the King was tried and executed. Who was to blame for the failure to reach a settlement after 1646? There are five main possible answers to this question – the five 'key players'.

   a) The King refused to accept the logic of defeat. He wasn't sure which version of a parliamentary settlement he could safely agree with. His refusal to accept any of the terms offered pushed the country further and further into crisis. His execution was the only way to achieve peace.

   b) Parliament was deeply divided over the kind of settlement it wanted. The division between Presbyterians (the majority) and Independents meant that Parliament could not speak with one voice.

   c) The New Model Army was not willing to stand aside while Parliament imposed a settlement that the soldiers didn't agree with. The Army intervened and used the threat of force to protect its interests.

   d) The Levellers (see page 180) were the only key player with revolutionary aims. The kind of revolution they wanted is a subject of great debate among historians – were they restoring lost liberties or creating new ones?

   e) The Scots expected the war to end with a Presbyterian settlement that would enhance Scotland's importance throughout the British Isles. In 1648 another Scottish army invaded England to try to force the English to reach such a settlement. Was 'Scottish imperialism' to blame for England's revolution?

2 Construct a spider diagram similar to the one below. Working out from the centre, add further information about the King, Parliament, the Army, the Scots and the Levellers – their aims, concerns and motives. Some headings have been included to get you started.

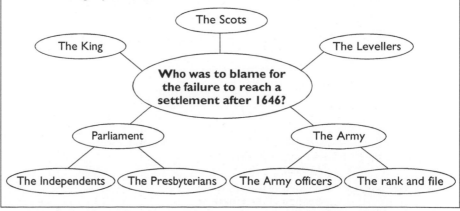

■ 8A Timeline of the English Revolution, 1646–49

(Documents referred to in the text are highlighted in **bold** type. The numbered asterisks refer to the models in Chart 8B)

			The King's movements	Negotiations and general events	New Model Army's intervention in politics	The Levellers
	1646	May	King surrenders to the Scots			
*1		July		**Propositions of Newcastle**	Army mutinies break out	
		October		Parliament abolishes bishops		
	1647	January	King Charles handed over to Parliament	Scottish army returns to Scotland		
		February			Parliament proposes to reduce the New Model Army	
*2		March			**New Model Army petition** to Parliament, which condemns it as treason	Large Petition condemned as treason by Parliament **An Apology of the Soldiers** protests against the imprisonment of Leveller leaders
		May		Parliament accepts the King's third reply to the Propositions of Newcastle	Parliament votes to disband the Army with only eight weeks' pay Fairfax orders a general rendezvous of the Army at Newmarket	
		June	King taken to the Army at Newmarket		Cornet Joyce seizes the King from Holdenby House **A Solemn Engagement of the Army** and **A Representation of the Army** published	
		August		**Heads of the Proposals**	Army occupies London and impeaches eleven MPs	
		October			**The Case of the Army Truly Stated**	Putney Debates **An Agreement of the People** (first version)
		November	King escapes to the Isle of Wight		Army mutiny at Ware suppressed	
*3		December	King signs the Engagement with the Scots	**The Four Bills**		**An Agreement of the People** (second version)
	1648	January		**The Vote of No Addresses**		
		April–June		Rebellions in south Wales, Kent and Essex	Second Civil War	**An Agreement of the People** (third version)
		July		Scottish army invades England	Second Civil War	
*4		August		Battle of Preston – Scots defeated The Vote of No Addresses is revoked	Second Civil War	
		September		Parliament begins negotiations with the King		
		November		'Treaty of Newport' negotiations	New Model Army rejects further negotiations with the King	
*5		December			Pride's Purge	
	1649	January	Trial and execution of Charles I			
		February	Abolition of the monarchy Abolition of the House of Lords			

Use the numbers to place them correctly in the timeline in Chart 8A

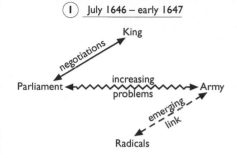

① July 1646 – early 1647

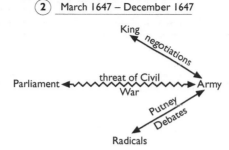

② March 1647 – December 1647

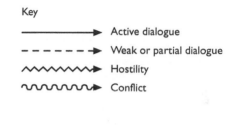

③ December 1647 – August 1648

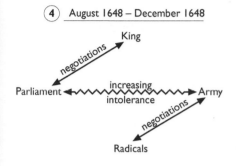

④ August 1648 – December 1648

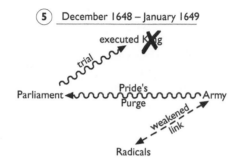

⑤ December 1648 – January 1649

Key

⟶	Active dialogue
- - -⟶	Weak or partial dialogue
∿∿∿⟶	Hostility
∿∿∿⟶	Conflict

FOCUS ROUTE

Was the failure to reach a settlement the King's fault? Add notes to your spider diagram to show evidence of the King's stubbornness and its effects.

PROPOSITIONS OF NEWCASTLE
The peace treaty offered to Charles I in July 1646, at the end of the First Civil War. Its terms were essentially the same as the Nineteen Propositions of 1642. (See Chart 8C.)

ACTIVITY

Study Source 8.4.

1 What does this source tell us about Charles's attitude towards the Propositions of Newcastle?
2 What light does this letter throw on the wider problem of making a peace treaty with the King?

TALKING POINT

Historians use their empathetic skills to understand why Charles did not agree to any peace proposals after the first Civil War. What do we mean by 'empathy' in history, and why is empathy an important part of historical explanation?

A Was it impossible to make peace with Charles I?

SOURCE 8.3 'The Bilton snake'. This image of Charles I was carved by Parliamentary soldiers on the church door at Bilton, near Marston Moor

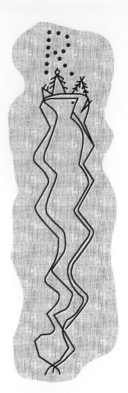

The image of the King as a devious, slippery snake illustrates the way many Parliamentary soldiers viewed Charles I. They saw him as the serpent that tempted Adam and Eve, a man who could never be trusted. The King's refusal to accept the military verdict of 1646 contributed to the political instability of England after 1646. If the King had accepted the PROPOSITIONS OF NEWCASTLE in July 1646, much of what happened next might have been avoided.

SOURCE 8.4 Letter from Charles I to Henrietta Maria, written from Newcastle where he was in the custody of the Scots, 1 July 1646

Dear Heart,
I had the contentment to receive [your letter] of the 28th of June upon Saturday last. The same day I got a true copy of [the Propositions of Newcastle] which ('tis said) will be here within ten days, and now do assure thee that they are such as I cannot grasp without loss of my conscience, crown, and honour; to which, as I can no way consent, so in my opinion a flat denial is to be delayed as long as may be, and how to make an handsome denying answer is all the difficulty...

Why was the King so obstinate?

We saw in Chapter 4 how Charles was forced to take responsibility for the Earl of Strafford's death. Charles blamed himself for signing Strafford's death warrant. He had made up his mind never again to betray those who were most loyal to him, and refused any terms that didn't pardon all the Royalists.

As King, Charles had the responsibility to protect the monarchy's prerogative. It was his duty to reject any proposals for a settlement that diminished the authority of the Crown. He had no way of knowing whether he was negotiating with a group that was stable enough to speak for Parliament.

Experience had taught Charles that the longer he held out, the deeper the divisions became among his enemies. In the short term, the nation faced chaos. Eventually his enemies would have to turn to him to save the nation from turmoil.

It wasn't just the King's rejection of peace terms that filled Parliament's soldiers with alarm: it was his willingness to spin out the negotiations, holding out the prospect of a settlement without ever accepting one. The soldiers lost patience with him long before the House of Commons did. In September 1648 the New Model Army lost patience with Parliament as well.

Issues	Nineteen Propositions June 1642	Oxford proposals March 1643	Uxbridge proposals January 1645	Propositions of Newcastle July 1646	Heads of the Proposals August 1647	Four Bills December 1647
New Parliaments	Every three years (Triennial Act of 1641)	Every three years	Every three years	Every three years	Every two years	Every two years
Militia	King to accept the Militia Ordinance	King to settle with Parliament's advice	To be settled by commissioners named by Parliament	Parliament to control for twenty years	Parliament to control for ten years	Parliament to control for twenty years
Privy Councillors	Parliament to approve	—	—	—	—	—
Officers of State	Parliament to approve sixteen	—	Parliament to nominate thirteen	Parliament to nominate thirteen	Parliament to nominate for ten years	—
The King's children	Parliament to approve teachers and governors	—	—	—	Royal family to be restored without personal constraints	—
Church government	Reformed with Parliament's advice	Bishops etc. abolished	Bishops etc. abolished; Westminster Assembly to reform	Bishops etc. abolished; Presbyterian church for three years' trial	Bishops cannot coerce; No Presbyterian church	Bishops etc. abolished; Presbyterian church for three years' trial
Catholics	Existing laws to be enforced	Existing laws to be enforced	Existing laws to be enforced	Existing laws to be enforced	Existing laws to be enforced	Existing laws to be enforced
Royalists not to be pardoned	—	Two	58	58	Seven	58
Dismissals from office	—	Two for life	48 for life	48 for life	Parliament's enemies for five years	48 for life

ACTIVITY

Study Chart 8C.

1 Which of the six peace proposals outlined do you think offers the King the best deal?
2 Which specific terms of which treaties do you think Charles would have found particularly unacceptable, and why?

SOURCE 8.5 Sir John Berkeley, a former Royalist general, describes an incident that occurred at Reading in July 1647 while he was trying to help the King and the Army reach an agreement. Cromwell was upset over accusations that he was not sincere in trying to reach a settlement with the King

I met with [Cromwell] about three days after I came to Reading, as he was coming from the King. He told me, that he had lately seen the tenderest sight that ever his eyes beheld, which was the interview between the King and his children, and wept plentifully at the remembrance of it, saying, that never man was so abused as he, in his sinister opinions of the King, who, he thought, was the uprightest and most conscientious man of his three kingdoms; that they, of the Independent party (as they are called) had infinite obligations to him, for not consenting to the Scots' Propositions at Newcastle, which would have totally ruined them, and which his Majesty's interest seemed to invite him to; and concluded with me, by wishing, that God would be pleased to look upon him according to the sincerity of his heart towards his Majesty.

I immediately acquainted his Majesty with this passage; who seemed not well edified by it [who did not seem to learn anything from it], and did believe, that all proceeded out of the use Cromwell and the army had of his Majesty, without whom, he thought, they could do nothing.

ACTIVITY

Study Source 8.5.

1 What had Cromwell witnessed that made him cry?
2 Why was Cromwell glad that the King had rejected the Propositions of Newcastle?
3 How did the King react when told about Berkeley's meeting with Cromwell?
4 What light does this incident throw on the King's attitude towards the peace negotiations?

SOURCE 8.6 Lord Astley, a Royalist general, speaking to some Parliamentary soldiers after being captured at Stow-on-the-Wold, 1646

You have done your work, boys. You may go play, unless you fall out among yourselves.

The Presbyterians

During the war the peace party evolved into the Presbyterian party, mainly as a result of the Scottish alliance. Their leader was Denzil Holles, one of the Five Members of 1642 and a long-time critic of Charles I. The Earls of Essex and Manchester came to support the Presbyterian view. At the end of the war, the Presbyterians were the dominant group in the House of Commons.

B What issues divided Parliament by 1646?

■ 8D What happened to the Church of England? (The progress of Presbyterianism)

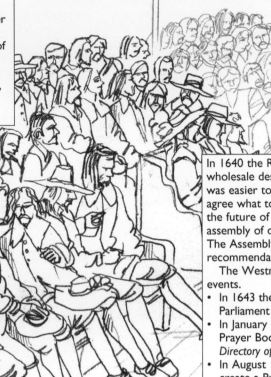

In 1640 the Root and Branch Petition called for the wholesale destruction of the Church of England. It was easier to destroy the old church than it was to agree what to replace it with. In 1643 Pym referred the future of the English church to an Anglo-Scots assembly of divines called the Westminster Assembly. The Assembly would report back to Parliament with recommendations when the war was over.

The Westminster Assembly was soon overtaken by events.
- In 1643 the Solemn League and Covenant committed Parliament to a Presbyterian religious settlement.
- In January 1645 Parliament replaced the Elizabethan Prayer Book with a Presbyterial service book, the *Directory of Public Worship*.
- In August 1645 Parliament passed an ordinance to create a Presbyterian system of church goverment.
- In October 1646 bishops were abolished.
- In spite of these official changes, most parishes continued to use the old Prayer Book.

Earl of Essex

The King is indispensable. Now that his 'evil advisers' have been defeated, Charles I must be given the benefit of the doubt, and returned to power on minimal terms.

The Scots are our allies. The Solemn League and Covenant is the best guarantee of social and religious stability.

Lower taxes. The nation needs to get back to normal as quickly as possible. We must limit the power of the county committees and return the country to traditional forms of government.

Earl of Manchester

Denzil Holles

A Presbyterian church for the whole country. This offers the best chance of restoring religious unity, stamping out the radical sects and restoring social order. It will build religious unity in the three kingdoms of England, Scotland and Ireland.

Disband the New Model Army. The nation cannot bear the cost of maintaining it. The Army is dangerous – a hotbed of radical religious sects; it has been infiltrated by the Levellers; and it has nothing to do. Complaints are coming in from all over the country about the soldiers' lack of discipline.

■ Learning trouble spot

Presbyterian and Independent 'parties'

When we talk about the Presbyterian and Independent 'parties', we do not mean political parties in the modern sense of the word. Modern parties have several characteristics: a party manifesto outlining their policies; a membership of committed party activists, and rigid party discipline. The Presbyterians and Independents had none of these things. We should think of them as 'groupings', with supporters coming and going over individual issues.

FOCUS ROUTE

Why did the division of Parliament into Presbyterians and Independents make it more difficult to reach a settlement after 1646? Add further information to your spider diagram to show why the two groups differed.

■ **Learning trouble spot**

The Church of England
Many students do not have a clear understanding of what happened to the Church of England at this time. Chart 8D summarises the dominance of the Presbyterians in Parliament and how this affected the church in England.

The Independents
The Independent party evolved from the 'war party' of 1643. Ironically they were a reaction against the Scottish alliance, which the 'war party' negotiated. Their name came from their support for 'independent' religious sects and from their opposition to Scottish interference. Their leaders were men such as Lord Saye and Sele, Henry Ireton, Sir Arthur Haselrig and Oliver Cromwell. The main power of the Independents was not in Parliament but in the New Model Army.

In 1645 Parliament began holding new elections to seats left vacant either by death or by expelled Royalists. By 1647 some 235 new MPs had joined the Long Parliament – nearly half its membership. Many were elected in former Royalist counties such as Cornwall. These elections strengthened the Presbyterians and increased the tension between them and the Independents.

The King cannot be trusted. He must be forced to accept further limits on his sovereign powers. Parliament must not surrender its advantage in its haste to reach a settlement.

Higher taxes will have to be endured for the time being. We must not falter at the last hurdle. Failure to reach a settlement is not the Army's fault. The committees set up during the war are full of corruption and prolong the nation's agony – they need to be brought to heel.

The New Model Army is like no other army in history. Its professionalism and discipline are exemplary. The Army has a better claim to represent the people than the Long Parliament does. Some Presbyterian MPs are misrepresenting the Army in Parliament. They should be excluded.

The Scots are interfering in England's affairs. They are opposed to religious freedom.

Religious toleration for Protestants. It is presumptuous to assume that there is only one right way to worship. Parliament has accepted the sacrifices of many soldiers who fought to free the nation from religious intolerance.
The Presbyterians threaten to replace one kind of tyranny with another – 'New Presbyter is but old priest writ large'.

Lord Saye and Sele   **Sir Arthur Haselrig**   **Henry Ireton**   **Oliver Cromwell**

ACTIVITY

(This activity can only be done by those classes that have previously done the Chapter 6 activity, 'The Civil War comes to Deerhurst', on page 129.)

It is time to hold another meeting of the Deerhurst parish council. How will Deerhurst be affected by the political dispute in Parliament? Discuss the views of the Presbyterian and Independent parties, in the light of the way your parish has been affected by the Civil War.

Consider particularly:

• taxation
• the future of former Royalists
• religion
• the power of the central government, exercised through the county committee.

Group decision: Who do we want to win the dispute in Parliament, the Presbyterians or the Independents?

■ **Learning trouble spot**

Religious radicalism

How widespread was religious radicalism? Despite the publicity these groups received at the time, and since, their numbers were never very large. It is possible that the Ranters never really existed at all except in anti-radical propaganda. What really mattered, though, was that people believed the radicals were a threat.

Why did religion lie at the heart of the dispute?

SOURCE 8.7 Richard Baxter, a Puritan minister, describes what he found after the Battle of Naseby in 1645 when he became a chaplain in the New Model Army (from Baxter's autobiography, published in 1696)

We that lived quietly in Coventry did keep to our old principles, and thought all others had done so too, except a very few inconsiderable persons. We took the true happiness of king and people, Church and State, to be our end, and when the Court newsbooks told the world of swarms of Anabaptists in our armies, we thought it had been a mere lie. But when I came to the army among Cromwell's soldiers I found a new face of things I never dreamt of. A few proud self-conceited, hot-headed sectaries had got into the highest places and were Cromwell's chief favourites, and by their very heat and activity bore down upon the rest or carried them along with them, and were the soul of the army. I perceived that they took the king for a tyrant and an enemy, and really intended absolutely to master him or to ruin him.

■ **8E Presbyterianism and some other religious beliefs in the late 1640s**

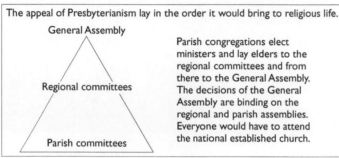

The appeal of Presbyterianism lay in the order it would bring to religious life.

General Assembly

Regional committees

Parish committees

Parish congregations elect ministers and lay elders to the regional committees and from there to the General Assembly. The decisions of the General Assembly are binding on the regional and parish assemblies. Everyone would have to attend the national established church.

Anglicans: By 1647 Anglicanism was widely regarded as a Royalist faith. Parliament had taken steps to destroy it by abolishing bishops and replacing the Elizabethan *Book of Common Prayer* with a Presbyterian *Directory of Worship*. However, in many parishes the Elizabethan Prayer Book continued to be used.

Quakers: In 1647 George Fox began preaching that every man was enlightened by the divine light of Christ. It was the duty of every person to follow their 'inner light' – their conscience. The Quakers rejected formal church services, ministers, creeds and the taking of oaths. They got their name from the 'trembling' they experienced during meetings, when moved by the Holy Spirit.

ERASTIAN
Thomas Erastus was a sixteenth-century Swiss theologian. His name is used to describe those who supported the idea of the supremacy of the state in church affairs.

DISCUSS

How was the argument between English Presbyterians and the Scots in the 1640s similar to the argument between the Puritans and Archbishop Laud ten years earlier?

Baxter's first impressions of the New Model Army (Source 8.7) help us to explain why many MPs favoured a quick peace settlement based around a Presbyterian national church. Consider the following facts.

1 The Scots were insisting on a Presbyterian settlement in England.
2 By 1646 many people believed that social order was breaking down. The Presbyterian church offered structure, hierarchy and discipline at a time when the country seemed to be descending into religious anarchy.
3 Most seventeenth-century Englishmen regarded religious unity as an essential aspect of an orderly national life.

The relationship between the Scots and English Presbyterians had its problems, too. The Scots claimed that the Presbyterian church was based on Divine Law. Parliament made it clear to the Scots that any religious settlement in England would be ERASTIAN, owing its legal and moral authority to Parliament.

Anabaptists: Believers in adult baptism who were regarded as dangerous radicals. In the seventeenth century calling someone an 'Anabaptist' was an insult, like calling someone a 'Commie' in 1950s' America. People still recalled an incident in Munster, Germany, in the 1530s when a group of Anabaptists seized control and began a reign of terror. In 1646 Thomas Edwards, a Presbyterian minister, reported an incident at Yately, Huntingdonshire: 'In contempt of baptism, some of the soldiers got into the church, pissed in the font, and went to a gentleman's stable in the town, and took out a horse, and brought it into the church, and there baptised it.'

[Ant]inomians: An offshoot of Calvinism that criticised [the] constant searching of your life for signs that you [ar]e one of the Elect. Played down the idea of [pr]edestination, and with it the importance of obeying [the] moral laws of the church, in order to emphasise [God]'s ability to transform the Elect. Never more than [a] handful of individuals.

Seekers: People who tried various churches and found them all disappointing. They were widely regarded as sceptics and atheists.

Ranters: A small sect that received an enormous amount of publicity. They took the Calvinist belief in predestination to extremes: if a person was of the Elect, then they could do no sin. People were therefore free to do whatever they wanted. The Ranters denied the sinfulness of swearing, fornication and adultery.

FOCUS ROUTE: WHO'S WHO?

Make brief notes on Cornet Joyce to include in your Who's who? list.

FOCUS ROUTE: WHO'S WHO?

Make brief notes on Henry Ireton to include in your Who's Who list.

C Why did the New Model Army intervene in politics?

The New Model Ordinance of 1645 was supposed to take the politics out of the army by forcing MPs to give up their army commissions. The Presbyterians believed that the New Model Army would take its orders from the politicians. But the New Model Army was an Independent army; when the war ended, it returned to the political arena in the only way open to it – by direct intervention in the peace-making process.

■ 8F The Army intervenes in politics, 1647–48

The Army Revolt happened in three distinct phases.

PHASE 1

Phase 1: Revolt of the rank and file, May–June 1647
A spontaneous revolt by the rank and file, who rebelled at their treatment by Parliament after the war. On **2 June 1647** a troop of cavalry from the New Model Army, led by Cornet George Joyce, seized the King from his Parliamentary guards at Holdenby House in Northamptonshire and placed him in the protective custody of the Army at Newmarket. Parliament could no longer negotiate with Charles without the Army's approval.

The 'First Big Presbyterian Mistake', spring 1647
Parliament tried to launch a pre-emptive strike against the New Model Army. Fearful of the Army's militancy, it tried to disband the Army as cheaply and as quickly as possible. The plans (below) nearly triggered another civil war – they politicised the Army and engaged it with constitutional issues.
- The Army to be purged of Independent officers.
- The Army to be sent to Ireland under Presbyterian officers to suppress the Irish Rebellion.
- All New Model regiments that refused to go to Ireland to be disbanded.
- A new army to be formed from the London trained bands, to defend the capital against the New Model Army.
- Disbanded New Model soldiers to be given only eight weeks' arrears of pay. Many soldiers were owed much more than this.

When the soldiers responded with a **New Model Army Petition** in **March**, the petition was condemned by Parliament as an act of treason (the Declaration of Dislike).

Grievances and demands of the soldiers
In **April** the regiments elected Agitators to speak to the officers on their behalf. Their demands included a mixture of national and personal issues:
- Indemnity for actions committed during the war
- Arrears of pay
- Freedom from conscription
- Soldiers not to be forced to serve in Ireland
- The right of soldiers to petition against their grievances
- Freedom of worship
- Reform of the law
- Ex-Royalists to be purged from office
- Quartering of the troops on civilians to be curbed
- Army pensions to be paid to war widows and disabled soldiers
- Apprentices whose training had been interrupted by the war to be given freedom to practise their trades
- Civilian corruption to be investigated.

Where is your commission?

Behind

Cornet Joyce

It is as fair a commission, and as well written as I have seen a commission in my life; a company of handsome proper gentlemen.

PHASE 3

The 'Second Big Presbyterian Mistake', August 1648
As soon as the war was over, Parliament revoked the Vote of No Addresses and voted to reopen negotiations with the King. The Army's patience with Parliament now snapped.

Second Civil War
Parliament and the Army temporarily reunited in order to defeat the new threat.

Pride's Purge, 6 December 1648
On the morning of 6 December 1648 soldiers of the New Model Army commanded by Colonel Thomas Pride blocked the entrance to the House of Commons. As MPs turned up as usual to attend the House their names were checked against a list of MPs regarded as hostile to the Army. About 110 were excluded, with 47 arrested and held as prisoners. Many more withdrew in protest at this clear breach of parliamentary privilege. This event led to the trial and execution of

Phase 3: the Second Civil War, 1648
The Second Civil War led to a hardening of the Army's attitude. When the war ended, Parliament tried yet again to open negotiations with Charles. This was too much for the Army, which now intervened decisively by purging Parliament of its political enemies, mostly Presbyterians.

PHASE 2

Phase 2: Intervention of the Army officers, June 1647
Many officers felt that the soldiers' grievances were justified. They were torn between loyalty to their men and loyalty to Parliament, which gave them their commissions. They were worried that if they tried to enforce Parliament's orders to disband the Army, they would not be able to control the rank and file. To assert their authority, the officers adopted the soldiers' case and intervened in the negotiations between Parliament and the King.

Army's slow march on London, June–October 1647

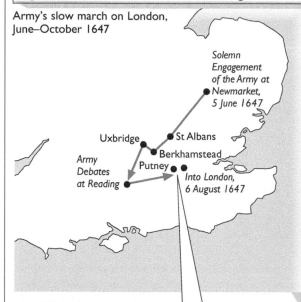

Solemn Engagement of the Army, 5 June 1647
General Fairfax called a general rendezvous of the New Model Army at Newmarket, where he spoke to the regiments. The Army promised not to obey Parliament's order to disband until its grievances were met.

SOURCE 8.8 The Army's Declaration (Representation of the Army), 14 June 1647. This was probably drafted by Henry Ireton

We were not a mere mercenary army, hired to serve any arbitrary power of a state, but called forth and conjured by the several declarations of Parliament, to the defence of our own and the people's just rights and liberties. And so we took up arms in conscience to those ends, and have so continued them, and are resolved to assert and vindicate the just power and rights of this kingdom in Parliament, for those common ends against all arbitrary power, violence and oppression, and against all particular parties or interests whatsoever.

Putney Debates with the Levellers, October 1647

Vote of No Addresses, January 1648
In **December 1647** the King signed the Engagement with the Scots (see page 184), who agreed to invade England to defeat the New Model Army, paving the way for a settlement between the King and the Presbyterians in Parliament. The plan backfired: Parliament and the Army came together to defeat the new Royalist threat. In **January 1648** Parliament passed the Vote of No Addresses: there would be no more negotiations with the King.

Heads of the Proposals, July 1647: a set of proposals for a settlement with the King, approved by the Army General Council
The King to return on the following conditions:
• The Long Parliament to dissolve itself within one year
• Parliament to be elected every two years, with guarantees against early dissolution
• Reform of parliamentary constituencies to reflect changes in population and wealth
• Parliament to appoint the great officers of state for ten years
• Former Royalists to be barred from holding public office for five years
• Parliament to control the militia for ten years
• Religion: a national church with bishops stripped of their coercive powers. Freedom of worship for Protestants
• An Act of Obilivion (general amnesty) with only seven Royalist exceptions

FOCUS ROUTE

Was the New Model Army to blame for the failure to reach a settlement after 1646? As you work through this section, add further information to your spider diagram, showing the three stages of the Army's intervention. What factors, at each stage, drove the process forward?

DISCUSS

Pride's Purge was denounced by the Presbyterians as 'the highest and most detestable Force and Breach of Privilege and Freedom ever offered to any Parliament in England'. How does Pride's Purge compare with the Attempt on the Five Members of January 1642?

FOCUS ROUTE

Were the Levellers responsible – directly or indirectly – for the failure to reach a settlement after 1646? Try to identify ways in which the Levellers helped to push the country towards revolution. Consider not only the Levellers' ideas but also:

a) the impact they had on the unity of the New Model Army, and

b) the effect this had on the King and his view of peace negotiations.

When you have reached some conclusions about these points, add further points to your spider diagram.

DISCUSS

1 Why were the Levellers' ideas likely to provoke strong opposition in the 1640s?

2 By 1900 the demand for universal male suffrage made by the Levellers had been achieved. Why was this demand no longer revolutionary?

FOCUS ROUTE: WHO'S WHO?

Make notes on John Lilburne to include in your Who's who? list.

D What impact did the Levellers have on the search for settlement?

Negotiations between the Army officers and the King aroused suspicion among some soldiers that a deal was being struck behind their backs. Many soldiers thought the terms of the *Heads of the Proposals* were too lenient. In the autumn of 1647 the Army's occupation of London brought it into closer contact with city radicals, whose printing presses ensured a wide distribution of their ideas. One group in particular – the Levellers – had a profound impact on the course of events.

Who were the Levellers?

The Levellers were one of the radical groups active in London in the late 1640s. They were popular among London's artisans and apprentices, men of the 'middling sort' whose skills and professionalism went largely unrewarded in seventeenth-century English political life. They got their name from their belief in religious and political equality. Their leaders – John Lilburne, Richard Overton and William Walwyn – were prolific pamphleteers. Because they believed in religious toleration and a fair deal for the common soldier, their ideas could not be dismissed easily by the officers. Cromwell was moved by their earnest desire to make England a land fit for heroes. But the Levellers also campaigned against social distinctions that brought political advantage. Their main aim was to replace the monarchy and the House of Lords with a single representative chamber (the House of Commons) elected by the male heads of households; up until this point only a handful of men such as Henry Marten had openly supported the creation of an English Republic. The Levellers also demanded law reform, the abolition of tithes and the curbing of the power of county committees.

The Putney Debates

In October 1647 Leveller influence in the Army was growing visibly stronger. In the *Case of the Army Truly Stated*, the Levellers took Parliament and the officers to task for failing to address any of their complaints. On 27 October they published their manifesto, the *Agreement of the People*. The next day the Army General Council agreed to meet with the Levellers' representatives to hear their arguments in full.

For a week members of the Army General Council met with Leveller spokesmen in the parish church at Putney. Cromwell and Ireton spoke for the officers; the Levellers were represented by two soldiers, Colonel Rainborough and the Agitator Sexby. The debates ended in deadlock, but they convinced the Army Council that the time had come to break the back of rank-and-file agitation. On 15 November a mutiny at Ware, Hertfordshire, was quickly crushed. Four days earlier the King had escaped from Hampton Court to the Isle of Wight, where he made the political blunder that was to cost him his life. His escape played into the hands of the Army Council by giving it the best reason possible for restoring discipline among the rank and file.

John Lilburne (1614–57)

Lilburne was a controversial figure throughout the civil war period. In 1638 he was punished by the Court of Star Chamber for writing pamphlets attacking the bishops. In 1640 he was released from prison to a hero's welcome. He fought for Parliament in the Civil War, but resigned his commission over the Solemn League and Covenant. A constant irritant to the authorities, he was frequently imprisoned for demanding religious and political liberty. After the King's execution, Lilburne became a bitter opponent of the Commonwealth, publishing *England's New Chains Discovered* in 1649. He continued to suffer periodic imprisonment and banishment until his death, a converted Quaker, in 1658.

This image shows an earlier picture of Lilburne with prison bars superimposed over it, made in protest at his imprisonment by the Commonwealth.

Using primary sources

'Doing history' is a bit like trying to complete a jigsaw puzzle with some of the pieces missing. The study of history is often made difficult by gaps in the source material. Occasionally, however, the historical record is fairly complete, giving us a rare chance to explore the thoughts and feelings of the people involved in great detail. This is the case with the Levellers, because a complete record was kept of the Putney Debates. This activity, using Sources 8.9–8.13, aims to help you to get inside the mind of the Levellers and their opponents.
Study Source 8.9, paragraph 1 and articles 1–4.

1 What did the Levellers mean when they said 'it cannot be imagined that so many of our countrymen would have fought for the other side if they had understood their own good'?

2 What changes did the Levellers want to make to the way MPs were elected? Why did they want to make these changes? (See articles 1 and 3.)

3 According to article 4, where did ultimate political authority (sovereignty) in England lie?

Study Source 8.9, points **a)** to **d)**. This is a statement of human rights.

4 Why have the Levellers included a statement of human rights in the *Agreement*?

5 Which of these points do you think would have been most unacceptable to
   a) the Army
   b) the Presbyterians
   c) the House of Lords?

For discussion:

6 Which of these points, if any, do we take for granted in our political system today?

7 What problems can you foresee in trying to enforce point **d)**?

Study Source 8.10 overleaf.

8 Why did Cromwell say that the *Agreement* 'does contain in it very great alterations of the very government of the kingdom'?

9 Do you get the impression that Cromwell approved of this or not?

10 Explain in your own words the basis of the argument between Rainborough and Ireton on the second day of the Putney Debates.

For discussion:

11 Within fourteen months of making these statements, Cromwell had taken the lead in abolishing the monarchy and turning England into a republic. Does this mean that he was lying when he spoke in the Putney Debates?

Study Sources 8.12 and 8.13 (page 183). In the six months following the Putney Debates, the Levellers produced two more versions of the *Agreement of the People*. Compare these versions with the first version of the *Agreement*, and answer the following questions.

12 In what ways did the Levellers' views on voting become more radical with the passage of time? Why do you think this might have happened?

13 In what other ways do these two sources show the Levellers' ideas becoming more radical?

SOURCE 8.9 Adapted from the first *Agreement of the People*, 28 October 1647. The language of the text has been modernised to make the Levellers' ideas more clear to the reader

By fighting in the recent war we have shown the world how highly we value our freedom. We must now take the best care we can for the future to avoid the danger of returning into a condition similar to slavery that would lead to another war. It cannot be imagined that so many of our countrymen would have fought for the other side if they had understood their own good. Therefore we are sure that, when our common rights and liberties are made clear, those who try to make themselves our masters will be disappointed . . . In order whereunto we declare:

1. *That the people of England, being very unequally distributed for the election of their deputies in Parliament, ought to be more fairly proportioned according to the number of the inhabitants.*

2. *That to prevent the many inconveniences arising from the long continuance of the same persons in authority, this present Parliament be dissolved upon the last day of September 1648.*

3. *That the people choose themselves a Parliament once in two years, for example upon the first Thursday in every second March to begin to sit upon the first Thursday in April following at Westminster and to continue till the last day of the next September, and no longer.*

4. *That the power of Parliaments of this nation is inferior only to those who choose them, and extends without the consent of any other person, to enacting, altering and repealing laws; erecting and abolishing offices and courts; to the appointing, removing and calling to account magistrates and officers of all degrees; to the making of war and peace; to the treating with foreign States; and generally to whatever is not reserved by the people to themselves.*
                    Which are as follows:

a) *That matters of religion and the ways of God's worship are not at all entrusted by us to any human power, because otherwise we may be forced to go against the dictates of our conscience: nevertheless the public way of instructing the nation (so it be not compulsive) is referred to their discretion.*

b) *That the matter of impressing and constraining any of us to serve in the wars is against our freedom.*

c) *That in all laws made or to be made every person may be bound alike, and that no tenure, charter, degree, birth or place do confer any exemption from the ordinary course of legal proceedings whereunto others are subjected.*

d) *That as the laws ought to be equal, so they must be good, and not evidently destructive to the safety and well-being of the people.*

These things we declare to be our native rights, and we are resolved to maintain them against all opposition; being compelled to do so by the example of our ancestors, whose blood was often spent in vain for the recovery of their freedoms, but also by our own woeful experience . . .

SOURCE 8.10 Extracts from the Putney Debates, October 1647

First day, 28th October

Sexby: *The cause of our misery [is] upon two things. We have laboured to please a King, and I think, except we go about to cut all our throats, we shall not please him; and we have gone to support the parliament, which consists of a company of rotten members ...*

Ireton: *I shall declare it again that I do not seek the destruction either of Parliament or King.*

Cromwell: *Truly this paper* [Agreement of the People] *does contain in it very great alterations of the very government of the kingdom, alterations from that government that it hath been under, I believe I may almost say, since it was a nation.*

Second day, 29th October

Rainborough: *For really I think that the poorest he that is in England has a life to live, as the greatest he; and therefore truly, sir, I think it's clear, that every man that is to live under a government ought first by his own consent to put himself under that government.*

Ireton: *I think that no person has a right to an interest or share in the disposing of the affairs of the kingdom that hath not a permanent fixed interest in this kingdom. But that by a man's being born here he shall have a share in that power that shall dispose of the lands here, and of all things here, I do not think it a sufficient ground. Those that choose the representatives for the making of laws are the persons who, taken together, do comprehend the local interest of this kingdom; that is, the persons in whom all land lies, and those in corporations in whom all trading lies.*

SOURCE 8.11 A meeting of the Army Council, 1647

SOURCE 8.12 Extracts from the second *Agreement of the People*, 15 December 1648. This was the Levellers' second manifesto

The Parliament of the whole nation shall consist of 300 persons, and in each county there shall be chosen to make up the said Parliament the numbers here following.

[Here follows the distribution of seats for the counties, cities, boroughs and universities.]

That the electors shall be natives of England, not persons receiving alms, but such as are assessed towards the relief of the poor; not servants to, or receiving wages from, any particular person. They shall be men of one-and-twenty years old or upwards, and householders.

That every Parliament shall appoint a Council of State for managing public affairs until the first day of the next Parliament.

So that all officers of state may be accountable, and no factions made to maintain corrupt interests, no member of a Council of State, nor any officers in the army or garrisons, shall be elected to a Parliament.

SOURCE 8.13 Extracts from the third *Agreement of the People*, 1 May 1649

That the supreme authority of England shall be in a Parliament consisting of four hundred persons, in the choice of whom all men of one-and-twenty years and upwards shall have their voices.

That no member of the present Parliament shall be capable of being elected to the next, nor shall any member of any future Parliament be chosen for that succeeding it.

For the preservation of the supreme authority entirely in the hands of such persons as shall be chosen thereunto, all Parliaments shall continue in power for one year, and when adjourned shall not erect a Council of State but refer the managing of affairs to a committee of their own members, giving and publishing such instructions as shall not contradict this Agreement.

GROUP ACTIVITY

Now that you have considered in detail the Levellers' ideas, consider how the Army officers might have tried to rebuff them.

1 Hold a meeting in which all members of the class take the role of officers in the Army General Council. Choose a chairman to take the role of General Fairfax.
2 Discuss each of the eight points made in the first *Agreement of the People* (see Source 8.9). After discussing each point, try to reach agreement about a single sentence that will best explain the Army's reaction to it.
3 Choose a person in your class to act as secretary. The secretary's role is not to write down everything that is said in the meeting, but to write down the single sentence agreed by the Council about each of the *Agreement*'s eight points.

TALKING POINT

Today politicians use opinion polls to measure public opinion. Why was it much more difficult to measure public opinion in the seventeenth century? What problems does this create for historians?

E Why was there a Second Civil War?

In 1648 public anger at the failure to reach a settlement boiled over into a Second Civil War. The people's grievances were an indictment (criticism) of Parliament's failure to solve any of the many problems left from the first war. High taxation, especially the excise on necessities such as beer and salt, was deeply unpopular. There had been no settlement of the church. Parliament's failure to restore traditional county government focused anger on the continuing power of county committees, which were run by men who were 'outsiders', often of lower social standing. Many people assumed this was Parliament's fault. They associated the monarchy with order and tradition, so the return of the King was a common theme running through the rebels' demands.

The King had anticipated such a backlash. Deep divisions had opened within the Parliamentary cause, and now the tide of public opinion seemed to be running in favour of a Royalist settlement. Charles felt that the nation had learned its lesson – only a King, with the full sovereign rights of his predecessors, could govern successfully. Much of the public's anger was directed towards the Army, which appeared to be the main obstacle to a return to normality. It only remained for the 15,000 men of the New Model Army to be overwhelmed before a settlement acceptable to the King, the nation and the majority in Parliament could be reached. For this, Charles needed military force – the Scots.

■ Learning trouble spot

The Scots and the Engagement, December 1647

The Scots' decision to make a deal with the King often causes confusion. In 1643 their decision to ally with Parliament was a political victory for the Marquess of Argyll, who feared the consequences for Scotland if the King won the war. However, by 1647, the main threat to the Scottish church seemed to come from the Independents.

In 1647 the Scots saw an opportunity to restore the political power of the Presbyterian party in Parliament. The Duke of Hamilton, who had opposed the alliance with Parliament in 1643, persuaded the Scottish Parliament that their best chance of safeguarding Presbyterianism in Scotland was to enlist the support of the King, who was willing to give it a 'trial run' in England, though he refused to take the Covenant. The agreement between Charles and the Scots was called the Engagement.

The Engagement split Scotland. The church denounced it, and Alexander Leslie refused to make war on his former allies. The army that Hamilton led into England in 1648, therefore, was not the same army that Leslie had led into England in 1644. It was much weaker.

The Engagement threatened to isolate the New Model Army. Charles hoped to encourage the Presbyterians in Parliament to strike once more at the Army, its unity fatally weakened by the Levellers. The King was gambling that Scottish intervention would force the Presbyterians to support the Engagement or face political oblivion. When Parliament offered him new peace proposals, the Four Bills, the King turned them down. There was reason for optimism: if the combined weight of the King, the Scots, the 'people' and the majority in Parliament wanted a settlement, who were the Army to disagree?

The King had miscalculated. His alliance with the Scots drove the Independents and the Presbyterians back together to defeat the revived Royalist threat. In January 1648 Parliament passed the Vote of No Addresses – there would be no further negotiations with the King. The rebellions which broke out in the spring of 1648 were not as widespread as the King had hoped. In the war that followed, the Royalists never really stood a chance.

Main terms of the Engagement:

- A Scottish army to invade England to restore the King to the throne
- Presbyterianism to be established in England for a three-year trial
- The Independents to be suppressed

THE KING'S MOVEMENTS

Charles I was a difficult man to imprison. After surrendering to the Scots in 1646 he was held prisoner in Newcastle. When the Scots handed him over to Parliament, he was moved to Holdenby House in Northamptonshire. It was here that he was seized by Cornet Joyce, who took him to join the New Model Army at Newmarket. He travelled south with the Army to Reading, where he negotiated with Cromwell. As the Army approached London, he was imprisoned in Hampton Court. In November 1647 he escaped through a window of Hampton Court and made his way to the Isle of Wight, where he was again arrested and imprisoned in Carisbrooke Castle. It was from Carisbrooke that he negotiated the Engagement with the Scots that led to the Second Civil War. When this war ended, he was brought to London to face trial and execution.

SOURCE 8.14 King Charles imprisoned at Carisbrooke Castle on the Isle of Wight. When the King arrived at Carisbrooke, the governor, Colonel Hammond, placed him under arrest. Without Hammond's knowledge, the King was able to negotiate the Engagement with the Scots

SOURCE 8.15 The end of the war: the destruction of Colchester

ACTIVITY

1 Do you think Source 8.14 was drawn by a Parliamentarian or a Royalist?
2 Do you think Source 8.15 was drawn by a Parliamentarian or a Royalist?
3 Choose a modern political cartoon from a newspaper and show it to someone in your class. Ask them to tell you what it means. Is this easy or difficult for them?
4 What special problems do historians face when trying to interpret cartoons from the past?

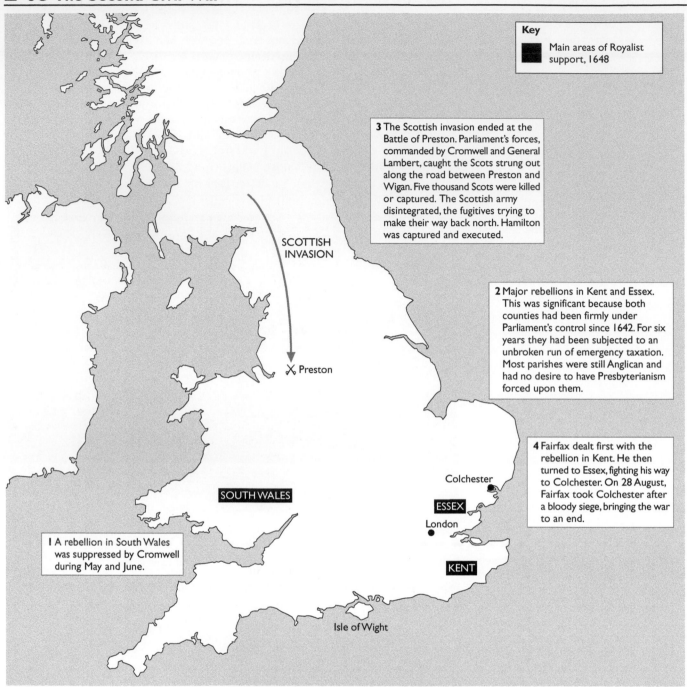

Key

Main areas of Royalist support, 1648

3 The Scottish invasion ended at the Battle of Preston. Parliament's forces, commanded by Cromwell and General Lambert, caught the Scots strung out along the road between Preston and Wigan. Five thousand Scots were killed or captured. The Scottish army disintegrated, the fugitives trying to make their way back north. Hamilton was captured and executed.

SCOTTISH INVASION

2 Major rebellions in Kent and Essex. This was significant because both counties had been firmly under Parliament's control since 1642. For six years they had been subjected to an unbroken run of emergency taxation. Most parishes were still Anglican and had no desire to have Presbyterianism forced upon them.

✗ Preston

4 Fairfax dealt first with the rebellion in Kent. He then turned to Essex, fighting his way to Colchester. On 28 August, Fairfax took Colchester after a bloody siege, bringing the war to an end.

Colchester

SOUTH WALES

ESSEX

London

1 A rebellion in South Wales was suppressed by Cromwell during May and June.

KENT

Isle of Wight

The Second Civil War had a profound effect on the New Model Army. In April 1648 the Army held a three-day prayer meeting at Windsor.

SOURCE 8.16   The words of William Allen, an eyewitness to the Windsor prayer meeting

[God] did direct our steps, and presently we were helped to a clear agreement amongst ourselves, not any dissenting, that it was our duty of our day . . . to go out and fight against those potent enemies, which that year in all places appeared against us [and] that it was our duty to call Charles Stuart, that man of blood, to an account for that blood he had shed . . .

FOCUS ROUTE

What effect did the Scots' intervention have on the situation in England? Add notes to your spider diagram.

The Army had reached a turning point. One civil war was fair enough: the contest had been fairly fought, and God had judged against the King. A second civil war was unforgivable, for it challenged God's judgement. The scales had fallen from their eyes: there was no more talk of evil advisers, but of a King who, like the Bilton Snake, could never be trusted.

DISCUSS

'The Second Civil War demonstrated the weakness more than the strength of Parliament's position.' Do you agree with this statement?

 # Why was King Charles I tried and executed?

In September 1648 a remarkable scene took place on the Isle of Wight. Lord Saye and Sele, the central figure in the old Puritan network, a leading Independent and one-time member of the 'war party', had come to offer the King terms for a settlement. In a gesture which must have given the King great satisfaction, the old man got down on his knees and begged Charles to accept Parliament's terms.

Lord Saye and Sele was reduced to pleading with the King because the Independent party in Parliament had collapsed. The Second Civil War had been too much for it. The rebellions in the Puritan heartland of Essex and Kent were a stark warning that a settlement had to be reached quickly. A number of Royalists in the Second Civil War had been Parliamentarians in the first, including Colonel Massey (who defended Gloucester in 1643) and the leaders of the rebellion in Wales.

The Presbyterians had always been convinced that the country needed a quick settlement. Now many Independents in Parliament had reached the same conclusion, and were throwing in the towel. On 28 April 1648, the House of Commons voted by 165 to 99 not to alter 'the fundamental Government of the Kingdom, by King, Lords and Commons'. The King was still central to any settlement.

Parliament would therefore have to negotiate. In August it revoked the Vote of No Addresses and began a new round of negotiations – the 'Treaty of Newport'. Parliament's terms were no longer non-negotiable, but a starting point for further discussions, to be completed within 40 days. On 5 December, when the 40 days had expired, Parliament again voted to continue negotiations. But time, and the Army's patience, had run out for Parliament.

Pride's Purge

FOCUS ROUTE: WHO'S WHO?

Make brief notes on Colonel Pride to include in your Who's who? list.

The 'Treaty of Newport' was the trigger that led to Pride's Purge. The Army General Council faced a stark choice. It could either watch Parliament betray the cause for which the Army had fought, or it could act. On 16 November, Ireton persuaded the Council to issue a remonstrance (a formal protest) accusing the King of tyranny and calling for his trial. The Army Remonstrance was presented to Parliament on 20 November. Parliament put off discussion of it for a week, hoping to rush through a last-minute deal with the King. A week later, Fairfax ordered Cromwell to return to London from Lancashire, where he had lingered after the defeat of the Scots. The Army was gathering its forces.

By the time Cromwell returned, Pride's Purge had already happened. The excluded MPs were held under armed guard to prevent them taking part in the debate which led Parliament once again to adopt the Vote of No Addresses. Forty-seven of the excluded MPs were arrested. The others mostly kept away for fear of being arrested, or stayed away in protest.

A last-minute effort was made to avoid Charles's martyrdom by offering to make his second son, the Duke of Gloucester, REGENT. The King would have none of it. On 1 January, the Commons voted to establish a High Court of Justice for the trial. The next day the House of Lords threw it out. Two days later the Commons excluded the Lords from the trial. The way was clear for the trial and execution of the King, but the revolution didn't stop there. It was followed by the abolition of both the monarchy and the House of Lords. Three of England's most important political institutions – the Crown, the Lords and the Church of England – had been destroyed by the great constitutional crisis of the 1640s. In 1649 it wasn't at all clear that the road ahead would lead to their restitution.

REGENT
Someone who rules on behalf of the King.

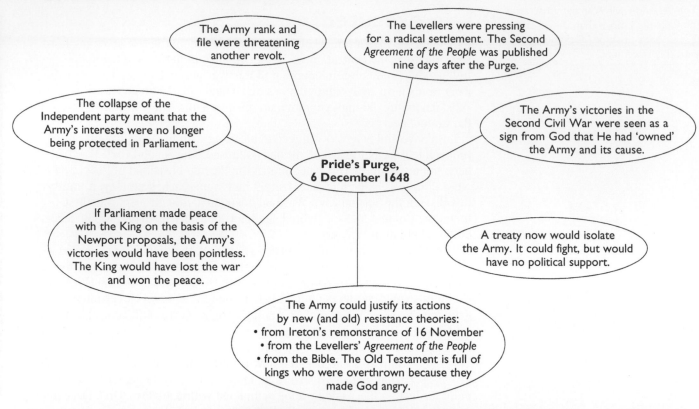

The Army rank and file were threatening another revolt.

The Levellers were pressing for a radical settlement. The Second *Agreement of the People* was published nine days after the Purge.

The collapse of the Independent party meant that the Army's interests were no longer being protected in Parliament.

The Army's victories in the Second Civil War were seen as a sign from God that He had 'owned' the Army and its cause.

Pride's Purge, 6 December 1648

If Parliament made peace with the King on the basis of the Newport proposals, the Army's victories would have been pointless. The King would have lost the war and won the peace.

A treaty now would isolate the Army. It could fight, but would have no political support.

The Army could justify its actions by new (and old) resistance theories:
• from Ireton's remonstrance of 16 November
• from the Levellers' *Agreement of the People*
• from the Bible. The Old Testament is full of kings who were overthrown because they made God angry.

ACTIVITY

Study Chart 8H.

1 Working individually, prioritise the Army's reasons for purging Parliament, starting with what you think was the most important reason.
2 When everyone in the class has done this, compare notes.
3 Which of the following statements best summarises the outcome of your discussion?
   a) Pride's Purge was motivated by exasperation at Parliament's lack of resolve.
   b) Pride's Purge was an act of desperation by the Army.
   c) Pride's Purge was driven by religious beliefs within the Army.

FOCUS ROUTE: WHO'S WHO?

Make brief notes on John Bradshaw to include in your Who's who? list.

ACTIVITY

Study Source 8.17 on page 189.

1 Why do you think there were musketeers in the hall, shown near the bottom of the picture?
2 Why was the public admitted to watch the trial? What problems did this lead to during the trial?
3 What has been done in Westminster Hall to make the trial look like a proper, legal trial?
4 Do you think this picture was drawn simply to give an accurate image of the way the trial looked, or has it been drawn in such a way as to convey either sympathy for the King, or sympathy for those who had put him on trial?
5 Do you think it was brave/foolish/ necessary to give the King a public trial?

The trial of Charles I

The trial of the King began on 20 January 1649, in Westminster Hall. He was tried in open court, and tiers of seats had been built in the Hall to accommodate the public. It was a bold decision, and potentially a very embarrassing one. When Fairfax failed to answer to his name, his wife, sitting in the public gallery, called out that 'he hath more wit than to be here'. The President of the High Court wasn't taking any chances either: during the trial John Bradshaw wore an armour-plated hat.

The charge against the King was that he had attempted to set up an unlimited power to rule according to his own wishes, and that by doing away with Parliament he had deprived the people of their ancient right to have their grievances heard and addressed. Twice he had made war on Parliament, and was therefore guilty of all the killing and destruction those wars had brought to his people.

For three days the King sat before the court, refusing to enter a plea, refusing even to take off his hat. When the charge was read out against him, he poured scorn on the authority of the court. Pride's Purge and the exclusion of the House of Lords gave an edge to his arguments. Only when sentence was passed, and the court refused to let him have the final word, did the King's composure slip.

SOURCE 8.17 The King's trial in Westminster Hall, January 1649

SOURCE 8.18 Extract from the King's comments on the third and final day of the trial, 23 January 1649

For the charge, I value it not a rush. It is the liberty of the people of England that I stand for. For me to acknowledge a new Court that I never heard of before, I that am your King, I that should be an example to all the people of England for to uphold justice, to maintain the old laws; indeed I do not know how to do it.

SOURCE 8.19 The sentence of the court, 27 January 1649

You have, Sir, spoken of a precious thing called Peace. It is to be wished that God had put it into your heart to effectively and really endeavour to study and preserve the peace of the kingdom, as now in words you pretend to have done.

A King is placed above the people for their preservation and safety; if he goes contrary to that end, then he must understand that he is only an Officer in trust, to be punished by the people if he should pervert the ends for which he is placed in power. This is no new law, but an ancient law and principle of the kingdom, and the King's Oath of Coronation implies as much . . .

Sir, as King you have sought to destroy Parliament. Caligula, the great Roman Tyrant, was heard to have said he wished the people of Rome had but one neck, so that at one blow he might cut it off. Your own proceedings have been somewhat like this, for the body of the people of England is nowhere represented but in the Parliament. Could you have but confounded that, you would soon have cut off the Head and Neck of England.

For all which Treasons and Crimes this Court doth adjudge, that the said Charles Stuart, as a Tyrant, Traitor, Murderer and a public enemy, shall be put to death, by the severing of his head from his body.

REGICIDES
The men who signed Charles I's death warrant.

SOURCE 8.20 The death warrant of Charles I. Persuading the judges to sign the death warrant was not easy. One hundred and thirty-five commissioners had been named, of which 67 took their seats as judges. It took all of Cromwell's considerable powers of persuasion to cajole 59 of these to do it. When they started signing, the tension in the room broke as Cromwell flicked ink at some of his fellow REGICIDES

The making of a royal martyr

In the final days of his life, Charles did everything in his power to influence the way posterity viewed his death. His trial and execution gave him an opportunity to win sympathy for himself and his family. His eldest son, Charles, Prince of Wales, would carry on the Royalist cause from exile. By dying well, the King could reach out from beyond the grave and help his son regain the throne for the Stuarts.

SOURCE 8.21   The execution of Charles I – a contemporary Dutch print

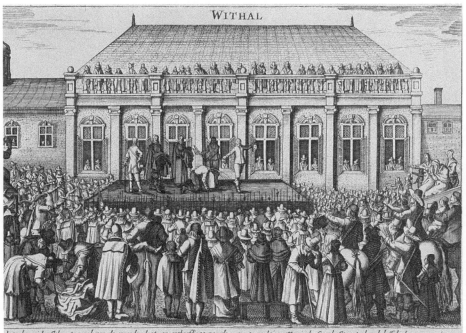

het droevich Schou-tonneel van de wreede doot en onthoofdinge van den groot machtigen Koningh Carel Stuart, hooch loffelycker memorie gewesen Koningh van Engelant, Schotlant en Yrlant, beschermer des Geloofs, openlyck onthooft voor zyn eygen Koninchlyck Pallays van withal binnen Londen, op dingsdach den 10 February 1649 tusschen twee en dryen s achtermiddachs.   F. v. Beusekom exc.

SOURCE 8.22   Extract from the King's speech on the scaffold, 30 January 1649

For the people. And truly I desire their liberty and freedom as much as anybody whomsoever. But I must tell you that their liberty and freedom consists in having of government; those laws by which their life and their goods may be most their own. It is not for having a share in government, Sir, that is nothing pertaining to them. A subject and a sovereign are clean different things . . . Sirs, it was for this that now I am come here. If I would have given way to an arbitrary way, for to have all the laws changed according to the power of the sword, I needed not to have come here. And therefore I tell you, and I pray God it be not laid to your charge, that I am the martyr of the people.

SOURCE 8.23 The frontispiece of the *Eikon Basilike: The Portraiture of his sacred Majesty in his solitudes and sufferings*, 1649. The King probably wrote the *Eikon Basilike*, describing his suffering at the hands of his enemies. The first edition of this book was published within a week of his death. Within one year it had gone through 35 editions, including miniature versions that could be hidden from the authorities. During the 1650s it kept the King's image alive in the people's memory.

The King also helped to design the frontispiece. At the King's feet is his earthly crown, but his eye is fixed on a celestial crown as he passes from a corruptible to an incorruptible realm. He is holding a crown of thorns, symbolically linking his suffering to that of Christ. Behind him are symbols of his strength and resilience: a rock withstanding a storm at sea, and a palm tree that cannot be crushed under weights

DISCUSS

1 How powerful do you think the imagery of 'Charles the Martyr' was?
2 In Source 8.22 why did Charles say he was 'the martyr of the people'?
3 What effect do you think this martyr imagery might have had on the following people:
   • the Leveller John Lilburne
   • the Independent Lord Saye and Sele
   • the Presbyterian Denzil Holles
   • the republican Henry Marten
   • General Fairfax
   • Oliver Cromwell.
4 What problems would the image of 'Charles the Martyr' create for the republic – the Commonwealth – that followed the abolition of the monarchy?

FOCUS ROUTE

Who were the key players in the tragedy that unfolded during 1646–49, and who was most at fault for the King's death?
Return to the spider diagram you began at the beginning of this chapter. Make sure that you have added points taken from all the sections of the chapter. The further away your diagram goes from the centre of the circle, the more depth you have reached. Make sure you complete the spider diagram by considering the following points:

• **The King** Was it the King's fault for trying to take advantage of the divisions among his former enemies? Why did he judge that the time was right to begin a second civil war?
• **Parliament** Was it Parliament's fault for allowing itself to split into two 'parties', the Presbyterians and the Independents, when it needed to speak with one voice? Why did Parliament split into these groups?
• **The New Model Army** Was it the Army's fault for preventing Parliament from reaching a moderate settlement with the King? Why did the Army intervene in politics?
• **The Levellers** Was it the Levellers' fault for dividing the Army at a critical moment? Why did the Levellers push for radical change at such a sensitive time?
• **The Scots** Was it the Scots' fault for intervening in England's domestic problems? Why did they do it?

ACTIVITY

Refer to the Learning Trouble Spot on writing essays on the failure to reach a settlement, 1646–49. Then choose one of the following essay titles:

a) Why did the victors of the First Civil War fall out among themselves after 1646?

b) Assess the relative responsibility of the King, the New Model Army and Parliament for the failure to reach a constitutional settlement during the years 1646–49.

c) Why was there no peaceful settlement between Charles I and his enemies in the period 1646–49?

d) Why was the New Model Army so important in the search for a settlement during the period 1646–49?

e) What impact did the Leveller movement have on the failure to reach a settlement between 1646 and 1649?

■ Learning trouble spot

Writing essays on the failure to reach a settlement, 1646–49

An essay title on this period is likely to ask you to make a judgement about the relative importance of the key players. The King's execution was not due to just one of these factors, but to a combination of all of them. You need to decide which factors were the most important, and how they interacted to lead to revolution and the King's death.

Try looking at the five key players in a different way. Turn the question of responsibility on its head, and ask yourself: what alternative did each of the five key players have? For example:

- Given what the King believed, what else could he have done? Could he have accepted any of the terms he was offered without betraying his fundamental beliefs?
- If you were a Leveller, what else could you have done? Given that you believed in fundamental changes in England's political system, could you have let the opportunities of 1647/48 pass you by?

This should help you clarify your ideas about who was responsible for what, and whether it could have been avoided. This in turn should make it possible to reach some conclusions about responsibility for the way things turned out in 1649.

KEY POINTS FROM CHAPTER 8 — Who was to blame for the King's execution in 1649?

1 In 1646 most people thought that the King would accept the terms offered to him by Parliament.

2 The King refused to accept any of the terms offered to him. He thought that if he held out long enough his enemies would have to restore him to the throne on his own terms.

3 The King probably would have been restored with minimal conditions if Parliament had spoken with one – Presbyterian – voice.

4 The Independents and the Army were the real winners of the first Civil War. They prevented the majority in Parliament from imposing a 'Scottish' peace treaty on England.

5 The Army Revolt of 1647 greatly complicated the peace-making process. The Army General Council was forced to adopt many of the soldiers' demands or face a New Model Rebellion.

6 The Levellers influenced events in several ways. They helped to stir up the revolt among the Army rank and file. The *Agreement of the People* outlined a republican system of government that was partly adopted by the Army in 1649. The signs of a split in the Army also encouraged the King to make the Engagement with the Scots.

7 In this the King miscalculated. When he signed the Engagement with the Scots he went too far. Parliament and the Army temporarily reunited to defeat the invasion. However, the Independent party in Parliament collapsed in response to the public's demands for a speedy settlement with the King.

8 The Second Civil War angered the Army so much that it was prepared to smash the Long Parliament in order to kill the King. It accomplished this through Pride's Purge.

9 The English Revolution did not stop with the trial and execution of the King. It also led to the abolition of the monarchy and of the House of Lords, which were replaced by a republic – the Commonwealth.

10 It is important to remember that none of the 'key players' in this period spoke with one voice, with the exception of the King. The Army, Parliament and the Scots were all caught up in turmoil. This was a genuine revolution, in which events were running out of control.

Section 2 Review: What kind of revolution did England have in the 1640s?

Today 'revolution' means the violent and sudden overthrow of a government, changing the political system of an entire country. The French and Russian revolutions were world-changing events, which helped to create our modern view of what a revolution is.

Many things happened in the 1640s that could be described as revolutionary. In Chapters 5–8 we have encountered many ways in which the normal lives of the English people were shattered. Some were sudden, dramatic events such as the trial of the King; others were more gradual changes. Nevertheless, there is something about the English Revolution that is very different from those in France or Russia. Nobody really doubts that the French and Russian revolutions had long-term causes. In England's case, there is no such consensus. Nor is there consensus that England's troubles should even be described as a 'revolution'. No one would describe the French and Russian revolutions as 'rebellions', but England's troubles were known for many years afterwards as the 'Great Rebellion'.

To explain why England had a revolution you have to decide what it is that you are trying to explain. You have to define your terms. With the English Revolution this is essential, not only to understand what happened in the 1640s, but also to understand what was going to happen in the 1650s.

ACTIVITY

1 Read Sources 1–5 overleaf. Match each source with one of the following summaries of the interpretations. Explain briefly why you have matched the source to the description.

Summaries of the interpretations expressed in the sources
a) The English Revolution was a conflict between social classes.
b) The English Revolution failed to satisfy those who saw the King's execution as the first step towards more radical changes.
c) The English Revolution was ultimately about religion.
d) The English Revolution was conservative, looking back into ancient history for its justifications.
e) The English Revolution marked a dramatic increase in the ability of the state to harness the wealth of the country for military purposes.
Check your answers on page 291.

2 Return to the introduction to Section 2 and study the illustrations on page 110. Compare them to Sources 1–5 below. Which illustrations a) did and b) did not come to pass in the 1640s?

3 In no more than 100 words, describe what you think the English Revolution actually was. (*Note:* The ideas expressed in Sources 1–5 are not mutually exclusive. You do not have to base your answer on just one of them. Feel free to combine ideas or to offer your own opinion.)

TALKING POINT

Why do historians offer different interpretations of the same events?

FOCUS ROUTE

1 In Chapter 3 you began keeping a police file on the leading members of the Puritan network. You should now have gathered evidence on the following people:

• Lord Saye and Sele
• John Pym (died 1643)
• Oliver St John
• John Hampden (died 1643)
• Sir Arthur Haselrig
• Oliver Cromwell.

2 Report back to the class on your findings. To what extent, if any, do you think that Charles I was the victim of a conspiracy? Did the behaviour of these individuals remain consistent throughout the period c.1635–49, or were there significant changes? Did disagreements emerge between them that cast light on their original intentions?

SOURCE 1 Michael J. Braddick, 'The Rise of the Fiscal State', in Barry Coward, ed., *A Companion to Stuart Britain*, 2003, pp. 69 and 79

Before the Civil War perhaps three-quarters of [royal] revenues were not under the control of parliament, and the proportion was declining. After the Civil War non-parliamentary revenues provided only about 10 per cent of total income . . . This transformation was associated also with a great increase in the scale of public revenues which, according to the best current estimate, doubled as a proportion of national wealth during the 1640s . . .

Although England was not the principal military power in Europe after [1660] it was a much more significant military power than it had been before the civil wars. The small standing army and the increasingly impressive, professional and effective state navy represented a significant change in the nature of the military resources of the state.

SOURCE 2 Blair Worden, *The Rump Parliament*, 1974, p. 40

Pride's Purge, the execution of the king and the abolition of the House of Lords excited widespread optimism among radicals outside parliament. A regime capable of such actions, it was believed, would be anxious to instigate changes still more revolutionary. The act of regicide was celebrated as a symbol of liberation, as the triumph of a newly won freedom over immemorial slavery. The cleansing of political institutions, it was held, would be followed by the cleansing of society at large . . . Such hopes were to be sadly disappointed. The inauguration of the Commonwealth proved to be the end, not the beginning, of the Long Parliament's revolutionary measures, and the regime left in its wake a trail of disillusionment and resentment among the advocates of social and religious reform.

SOURCE 3 Robert Ashton, *The English Civil War*, 1978, p. 349

It was only to very few, if any, that the establishment of the Commonwealth marked a new dawn. For far more it was the return to pristine English freedoms which had been usurped by innovating kings . . . Nor was this basic conservatism confined to the political establishment . . . Revolutionaries in most ages have derived strength from seeing themselves as agents of an historical process. For the revolutionaries of seventeenth-century England, almost without exception, the aim of that process was to return to ancient ways, not to innovate.

SOURCE 4 Christopher Hill and Edmund Dell, *The Good Old Cause*, 2nd edition, 1969, p. 27

Civil war produced general social unrest, riots against enclosures, criticism of established institutions, the rise of sectarian congregations free from the supervision and control either of a state church or of Parliament. Many of the wealthier classes on the Parliamentary side began to get anxious. They worked for a compromise settlement with the King rather than complete victory . . . The conservatives had been right to fear the growth of the sects. In their congregations and in the Army the middling and lower classes were now discussing politics in a way that had never before been possible for them . . .

The King was tried and executed; the House of Lords abolished; a republic was proclaimed, which was in effect a dictatorship of the Army. This was . . . a political rather than a social revolution. New men were in power, but the republican government broke with the extreme left – the Levellers and Diggers. The achievements of the Commonwealth . . . benefited above all the commercial classes.

SOURCE 5 John Morrill, *The Nature of the English Revolution*, 1993, p. 394

Perhaps the most extraordinary development of the 1640s and 1650s is how a civil war that began as a struggle between two authoritarianisms became a revolution for religious liberty. This is what Cromwell meant when he said that 'religion was not the thing first contended for, but God hath brought it to that issue at last' . . . For Cromwell, above all, religious toleration was a means to effect a deeper and elusive unity which was part of his fierce vision of England as the new Elect Nation being led on by God to a new Promised Land.

Oliver Cromwell – Caesar or Cincinnatus?

In the early seventeenth century school children such as Cromwell were taught a curriculum which emphasised classical studies. Greek and Roman history provided models of behaviour and warnings of how liberty could fall into tyranny in the hands of unscrupulous men.

In the 1650s Cromwell was aware of the accusation that he was ambitious. In a speech to Parliament in 1654 (see Source 2) he tried to show that the accusation was false. The facts of his life, he said, did not bear out this view. He portrayed himself as a private man who wanted to retire to his home and family, but circumstances would not let him do it.

■ A Cromwell – Caesar or Cincinnatus?

Roman history provided two models of behaviour in the wake of military success.

JULIUS CAESAR – AN EXAMPLE OF DANGEROUS AMBITION

- Caesar's military career began in his forties.
- Caesar conquered Gaul (France) for Rome.
- When Caesar crossed the Rubicon river, separating his province in northern Italy from that of his rival in Rome, he was taking a step that he knew would lead to civil war.
- The civil wars made Caesar the most powerful man in Rome.
- Caesar was assassinated by a group of senators who were afraid that he was planning to make himself king.

OLIVER CROMWELL

SOURCE I
A portrait of Cromwell in 1649 by Samuel Cooper

SOURCE 2   Cromwell speaking to the first Protectorate Parliament, 12 September 1654

That which I drive at is this; I say to you, I hoped to have had leave to have retired to a private life, I begged to be dismissed of my charge, I begged it again and again, and God be judge between me and all men if I lie in this matter. That I lie not in matter of fact is known to very many, but whether I tell a lie in my heart, I say, the Lord be judge. Let uncharitable men that measure others by themselves, judge as they please; as to the matter of fact, I say it is true.

LUCIUS QUINCTIUS CINCINNATUS – A MODEL OF REPUBLICAN VIRTUE

- Rome was threatened with defeat.
- Cincinnatus was called from his farm to command the army.
- To save Rome he was made dictator.
- When the war was over, he gave up power and returned to his farm.

Cromwell's rise to power – plot or providence?

In April 1653 Cromwell expelled what remained of the Long Parliament, known as the Rump. (This is described in some detail at the beginning of Chapter 10.) The expulsion of the Rump placed enormous political power into Cromwell's hands. Eight months later, in December 1653, that power was confirmed when he became Lord Protector. Cromwell was now both chief executive and head of state, to all intents and purposes as powerful as a king.

To many people Cromwell's rise to power looked like the well-executed plot of an ambitious man. No one, they thought, could rise from relative obscurity to a position of supreme power without intending to do it. The expulsion of the Rump was simply the most blatant of a long series of episodes which brought Cromwell closer to the heart of government. Looking back over his career, it seemed obvious that he had wanted power for its own sake. At the very least, he had been an opportunist, taking advantage of situations for his own benefit.

■ B Two views of Cromwell's rise to power

View 1: a hostile view of Cromwell

Cromwell called for the resignation of all officer Members of Parliament, but contrived to have himself excluded from its provisions.	Cromwell met Cornet Joyce on 31 May, four days before Joyce seized the King from Holdenby House. After Joyce seized the King, he wrote to Cromwell asking for instructions. This proves that Cromwell was behind the move.	Cromwell led the Levellers to believe that he was interested in their ideas, but the Putney Debates were a sham. He was merely going through the motions of consulting with the Levellers to give the Army General Council time to negotiate a settlement with the King.	Cromwell engineered the King's escape from the custody of one of Cromwell's kinsmen into the custody of another. This paved the way for the Second Civil War, in which General Cromwell reinforced his military reputation and his political power.
THE SELF-DENYING ORDINANCE, DECEMBER 1644	**THE SEIZURE OF THE KING BY CORNET JOYCE, JUNE 1647**	**THE PUTNEY DEBATES WITH THE LEVELLERS, OCTOBER 1647**	**THE KING'S ESCAPE FROM HAMPTON COURT, NOVEMBER 1647**
When Cromwell supported the Self-Denying Ordinance he did not expect to be excluded from its provisions. Parliament extended his commission because Fairfax asked it to.	The evidence linking Cromwell to the seizure of the King is merely circumstantial. There is no evidence that he ordered this to happen, or knew about it in advance.	Cromwell was genuinely interested in many of the Levellers' demands. In the course of the debates, however, it became clear that they wanted more radical changes than the nation could accept. Cromwell was a realist and didn't want to encourage false hopes.	Cromwell had nothing to do with the King's escape to the Isle of Wight. In fact, he was still hoping that the King would accept the *Heads of the Proposals*. He was appalled by the Second Civil War.

View 2: a sympathetic view of Cromwell

Not everyone agreed with this view. The 'godly party' believed Cromwell was elevated by God through a series of providential events. These were not of his making, and neither was the role he played in them. Each step along the road to power was unforeseen, but God had consistently placed Cromwell at the critical time and place. Accusing Cromwell of opportunism was a form of blasphemy. If Cromwell never lost a battle it was because the Lord of Hosts had owned his cause. To many of his contemporaries he was the human instrument of Divine Providence, a godly man for whom ambition was a deadly sin.

You do not have to believe in God to agree with the 'godly' judgement that Cromwell was not personally ambitious. His rise to power may have been the product of circumstances which forced him to take a leading role in order to prevent unacceptable outcomes. It is possible, through a secular reading of his career, to conclude that Cromwell was not ambitious. It is also possible to arrive at the opposite conclusion.

DISCUSS

What are your first thoughts before you look at Cromwell's career in detail? Do you have any prejudices for or against Cromwell? If so, where do they come from?

Cromwell used brute force to expel the Rump, the last remaining link with due legal process. He destroyed the evidence of the bill for a new parliament because he didn't want people to know there were about to be new elections.

...well's son-in-law, ...Ireton, was the ...mover behind the ...purge of Parliament. ...well pretended not ...nvolved, but he ...d London the same ...d took control of the ...trial.

It was Cromwell who persuaded the regicides to sign the King's death warrant.

Cromwell betrayed the Levellers to win support from the gentry after the revolution of 1649. When he no longer needed their support he destroyed them.

Cromwell was toying with the idea of becoming King a whole year before he became Lord Protector.

Cromwell was made Lord Protector by the Army, not by Parliament. He was the Lord General of that Army, and readily accepted supreme power when it was offered to him.

| ...IDE'S PURGE, ...CEMBER 1648 | THE TRIAL AND EXECUTION OF THE KING, JANUARY 1649 | THE SUPPRESSION OF THE LEVELLERS, MAY 1649 | CROMWELL DISCUSSED THE IDEA OF BECOMING KING WITH THE MP BULSTRODE WHITELOCKE, DECEMBER 1652 | EXPULSION OF THE RUMP PARLIAMENT, APRIL 1653 CROMWELL INSTALLED AS LORD PROTECTOR, DECEMBER 1653 |

...Ireton may have ...romwell's son-in-law, ...t doesn't mean that ...took orders from ...romwell was still in ...rth of England ...ng order after the ...h invasion when the ...cisions were made ...d to Pride's Purge.

Cromwell tried to avoid the King's execution in late December 1648 by negotiating for a REGENCY, but the King would not accept it. Only when he became convinced that the King's trial was providential (of God's doing) did Cromwell support it decisively.

Cromwell suppressed the Levellers in 1649 because they mutinied. It was essential to maintain discipline within the Army.

Cromwell's conversation with Whitelocke is evidence not that he wanted to be King, but that he was looking for a way to restore stability to England's government. It would have been odd if Cromwell hadn't considered this possibility.

Cromwell expelled the Rump Parliament because it had failed the nation. The Rump MPs were planning to secure automatic re-election for themselves. Cromwell replaced the Rump not with a military junta but with the Nominated Assembly.

When the Nominated Assembly failed, Cromwell chose to limit his own power with a written constitution.

REGENCY
The idea was that Charles's second son would succeed to the throne while his father and older brother were still alive. His older brother, Charles Stuart, Prince of Wales, was too deeply involved in the Royalist cause to be trusted with the crown.

How far can Cromwell's life and career until 1654 support his assertion that he was driven by necessity towards the centre of power? Did Cromwell abandon this life reluctantly, or did he relish the excitement of parliamentary affairs? When Civil War came in 1642, how did he respond? What were the crucial steps which brought him towards the heart of government?

This section sets out to explore the career and reputation of Cromwell from his birth until December 1653 when he was installed as Lord Protector. Cromwell's rise to power was highly controversial, giving rise to many different interpretations in the three and a half centuries since his death. Was he a revolutionary? Was he ambitious? A-level questions tend to focus on the reasons why Cromwell's career continues to divide historians. To examine these issues, Section 3 is divided into two chapters, Chapter 9 covering the period from 1599 to 1649 and Chapter 10 focusing on Cromwell and the Commonwealth, 1649–53.

FOCUS ROUTE

At the end of Section 3 you are going to put Oliver Cromwell on trial. The charge will be that he took advantage of the Civil War and the revolution that followed in order to raise himself up to a position of supreme power. The trial will take the form of a class debate.

As you work through Section 3, gather evidence that can be used in the trial at the end of the section. Along with Cromwell's religion, specific incidents (see Chart B, pages 198–99) will form the core of the evidence – where these occur in the text, they are referred to as 'Cromwell's controversies'. Use a copy of the table below to record your evidence.

Cromwell as Caesar – the case *against* Cromwell	Cromwell's controversies	Cromwell as Cincinnatus – the case *for* Cromwell
	Was Cromwell sincere about his religious beliefs?	
	The Self-Denying Ordinance, December 1644	
	The seizure of the King by Cornet Joyce, June 1647	
	The King's escape from Hampton Court, November 1647	
	Pride's Purge, December 1648	
	The trial and execution of the King, January 1649	
	The suppression of the Levellers, May 1649	
	Cromwell's conversation with Bulstrode Whitelocke, December 1652	
	The case of the missing bill, April 1653	
	Cromwell installed as Lord Protector, December 1653	

9

Cromwell in Civil War and Revolution, 1599–1649: was Cromwell a revolutionary?

WESTMINSTER ASSEMBLY
The Anglo-Scots committee established in 1643 to reach a new religious settlement.

On 2 December 1644 the Earl of Manchester wrote a letter to the House of Lords accusing Cromwell of hoping 'to live to see never a nobleman in England'. Cromwell, he said, held the WESTMINSTER ASSEMBLY in contempt. As for Parliament's allies, the Scots, 'he told me that he could as soon draw his sword against them as against any in the King's army'. Manchester's letter was written in self-defence, and so we might expect him to counter Cromwell's charges with more serious ones of his own. But given the fact that Cromwell played a significant part in the revolution of 1649, in which both the monarchy and the House of Lords were abolished, should we dismiss Manchester's comments?

Cromwell's opponents called him the 'darling of the sectaries', a man whose religious beliefs threatened to undermine the religious and social fabric of England. His promotion of soldiers from humble origins challenged the assumption that only gentlemen should be officers, just as the Self-Denying Ordinance challenged the automatic right of the lords to hold the supreme commands in Parliament's armies.

On the other hand, many radicals were disappointed by Cromwell's refusal to adopt their cause. Cromwell recoiled instinctively from actions that might alienate the traditional political nation. He refused to allow himself to be cast in a role written for him by any particular faction or interest group. For this reason he can readily be accused of being either a radical revolutionary or a reactionary hypocrite. It is difficult to make either accusation stick.

DISCUSS

What policies or ideas would make someone a revolutionary in the 1640s? Why might the definition of a 'revolutionary' depend on your social position, your religious beliefs or your political views?

At the end of this chapter you must reach some conclusions about Cromwell's role in the revolutionary events of 1640–49. You will need to consider several aspects of his life:

- his background and early life before 1640
- his military career, 1642–48
- his involvement in politics, 1640–49.

A   Cromwell's early life, 1599–1640 (pp. 202–03)

B   What was Cromwell's role in the Long Parliament, 1640–42? (pp. 204–05)

C   Why was Cromwell promoted so rapidly during the Civil War? (pp. 205–07)

D   Why did Cromwell oppose the Presbyterian party? (pp. 208–11)

E   Cromwell and the search for settlement, 1646–48 (pp. 211–14)

F   What part did Cromwell play in the trial and execution of the King? (pp. 215–16)

G   Review: Cromwell in Civil War and Revolution, 1599–1649 (pp. 216–17)

A Cromwell's early life, 1599–1640

SOURCE 9.1   Cromwell speaking to the first Protectorate Parliament, 12 September 1654

I was by birth a gentleman, living neither in any considerable height, nor yet in obscurity.

Cromwell was born in 1599, into a family that had profited greatly from the Protestant Reformation. Like many gentry families, the Cromwells had purchased monastic land taken from the Catholic Church, but by the turn of the century the benefits of this windfall were starting to wear off and the Cromwells were facing hard times. Sir Oliver Cromwell, the head of the family, was living beyond his means at Hinchingbrook House, the family seat near Huntingdon. His younger brother Robert, Oliver's father, had ten children to feed, clothe and educate. Large families were not unusual but, without further injections of cash through marriage or trade, their wealth was likely to dissipate through several generations.

SOURCE 9.2
The grammar school Cromwell attended in Huntingdon. It is now the Cromwell Museum

Cromwell's education was a common one for gentlemen's sons. He attended Huntingdon grammar school, founded on confiscated monastic wealth, where he was taught by Dr Thomas Beard, a schoolmaster and vicar whose anti-Catholic views were commonplace at that time. In 1616 he went to Sidney Sussex College, Cambridge, another institution that owed much of its wealth to the dissolution of the monasteries. Cromwell grew up in a world that equated Catholicism with darkness, ignorance and superstition, among people who treasured the English Reformation for transforming monastic wealth into schools and colleges. In the reign of Henry VIII his distant relative, Thomas Cromwell, had been largely responsible for this change.

When his father died in 1617, Cromwell left Cambridge. He returned home to become the head of the family, looking after his mother and seven sisters.

In August 1620 he married Elizabeth Bourchier, daughter of a prosperous London furrier, and settled with her in Huntingdon. In the 1620s Cromwell was a family man,

raising six children, looking after his mother and his unmarried sisters, and managing his estate as best he could. If he was ambitious, his ambition probably focused on economic survival.

In 1628 family connections got Cromwell elected to Parliament as MP for Huntingdon, but the family fortunes were taking a turn for the worse. It was a difficult year for Cromwell. Hinchingbrook House had to be sold by his uncle's family, an event which dealt a severe blow to Cromwell's prestige and social standing. Suffering from 'melancholia' (depression), he consulted a physician in London. In 1630 came Cromwell's disastrous outburst at the mayor of Huntingdon and his decision to move to St Ives (see page 3). Denied the status and respect of a gentleman in his home town, he slipped below the income of the gentry into the position of a tenant farmer. The next few years were far from easy, filled with the birth of more children (nine in all by 1638) and hard physical labour.

Two events in the 1630s transformed Cromwell's private life. At some time before 1636 he experienced a religious conversion that left him in a state of spiritual euphoria. The influence of a Puritan preacher was probably behind his conversion, which broke through Cromwell's depression and infused him with a sense of well-being. From this time on he counted himself among the godly, certain of salvation and full of hope.

In 1636 Cromwell's material well-being was transformed by the death of his maternal uncle, who left him a house in Ely along with TITHE INCOME and some land. The family moved to Ely, where Cromwell was employed by the cathedral as an administrator. He was not rich but, as the financial pressure eased, his social standing, mental health and sense of purpose recovered. In 1640 he was elected as an MP for Cambridge to sit in both the Short and Long Parliaments.

SOURCE 9.3   Cromwell's house in Ely

Searching Cromwell's early life for signs of ambition is pointless. He was born in a time when most people did not pursue careers, enter professions or work for salaries. Ambitious men looked to the court for advancement, and Cromwell was no courtier. The gentry aspired to play a significant role in local, not national affairs, finding self-fulfilment in the respect of their friends and neighbours. Cromwell's early life conformed to this pattern.

203

CROMWELL IN CIVIL WAR AND REVOLUTION, 1599–1649: WAS CROMWELL A REVOLUTIONARY?

SOURCE 9.4 Extract from a letter written by Cromwell to his cousin, the wife of Oliver St John, 13 October 1638

I thankfully acknowledge your love in your kind remembrance of me upon this opportunity. Alas, you do too highly prize my lines, and my company. I may be ashamed to own your expressions, considering how unprofitable I am, and the mean improving of my talent.

Yet to honour my God by declaring what he hath done for my soul, in this I am confident, and I will be so. Truly, then, this I find: That He giveth springs in a dry and barren wilderness where no water is. I live (you know where) in Meshek, which they say signifies Prolonging; in Kedar, which signifieth Blackness: yet the Lord forsaketh me not. Though He do prolong, yet He will (I trust) bring me to His tabernacle, to His resting place. My soul is with the congregation of the firstborn, my body rests in hope, and if here I may honour my God either by doing or by suffering, I shall be most glad.

Truly no poor creature hath more cause to put forth himself in the cause of his God than I. I HAVE HAD PLENTIFUL WAGES beforehand, and I am sure I shall never earn the least mite. The Lord accept me in His Son, and give me to walk in the light, as He is the light. He it is that enlighteneth our blackness, our darkness. He giveth me to see the light in His light. One beam in a dark place hath exceeding much refreshment in it. Blessed be His name for shining upon so dark a heart as mine! You know what my manner of life hath been. Oh, I have lived and loved darkness, and hated the light. I was a chief, the chief of sinners. This is true: I hated godliness, yet God had mercy on me. O the riches of His mercy! Praise Him for me, pray for me, that He who hath begun a good work would perfect it to the day of Christ.

Salute all my good friends in that family whereof you are yet a member. I am much bound to them for their love. I bless the Lord for them; and that my son, by their procurement, is so well. Let him have your prayers, your counsel; let me have them. Salute your husband and sister from me. He is not a man of his word! He promised to write about Mr. Wrath of Epping; but as yet I received no letters. Put him in mind to do what with conveniency may be done for the poor cousin I did solicit him about.

Once more farewell. The Lord be with you; so prayeth.
Your truly loving cousin,
Oliver Cromwell

'I HAVE HAD PLENTIFUL WAGES'
'I have sinned a lot.'

TITHE INCOME
Income originally intended for the church which had, since the Reformation, become the property of the landed gentry in many parishes.

ACTIVITY

Study Source 9.4.

1 What evidence is there in this letter that Cromwell believed he had led a sinful life before his conversion?
2 What evidence can you find that Cromwell was well connected through his family to other godly and political networks?
3 Why is this letter an important source of evidence about Cromwell's early life?

B What was Cromwell's role in the Long Parliament, 1640–42?

SOURCE 9.5 Extract from Sir Philip Warwick, *Memoirs of the Reign of King Charles I,* 1701. Warwick's memoirs were written shortly after the Civil War, but were not published until 2001. Here he describes his first encounter with Cromwell in the Long Parliament. Warwick fought for the King in the Civil War

[Cromwell was] very ordinarily appareled in a plain cloth suit made by an ill country tailor, with plain linen, not very clean, and a speck or two of blood upon his little band; his hat without a hatband; his stature of a good size; his sword stuck close to his side; his countenance [face] swollen and reddish; his voice sharp and untunable, his eloquence full of fervour. I sincerely profess it lessened much my reverence unto that great council [Parliament], for this gentleman was very much hearkened unto.

Sir Philip Warwick's description of Cromwell poses a problem that has puzzled historians ever since. Cromwell was neither wealthy nor sophisticated, yet in the Long Parliament he was near the heart of the opposition to the King's government. Nothing in Cromwell's early life suggests that he suffered great personal hardship from the Personal Rule, yet he acted with 'fervour' to destroy it.

A lot is known about what Cromwell did in the Long Parliament. He sat on many committees. He acted as a messenger between the Commons and the Lords, helping to keep open personal contacts between the two Houses.

In addition, several specific incidents are documented.

1 Within six days of the first meeting of the Parliament, Cromwell presented a petition against the sentence which the Court had handed down against John Lilburne in 1638 for attacking the bishops.
2 On 30 December 1640 Cromwell moved the second reading of the bill for annual parliaments, which led to the Triennial Act.
3 In February 1641 Sir John Strangeways defended the bishops by saying that 'if we made a parity in the church we must at last come to a parity in the Commonwealth'. Cromwell launched an attack on Strangeways so violent and personal that the Commons reprimanded him.
4 In May 1641 Cromwell supported the Protestation, warning the nation to be on its guard against plots and conspiracies.
5 In August 1641 Cromwell proposed that Lord Saye and Sele and the Earl of Bedford be appointed guardians for Charles Stuart the Prince of Wales, who was next in line of succession to the throne.
6 In September 1641 Cromwell made a speech criticising the Elizabethan Prayer Book and in support of more sermons.
7 In October 1641 Cromwell made a fool of himself during the struggle over the bishops' presence in the House of Lords. With Parliament facing a vote over whether or not to deny the bishops the vote, Cromwell naively suggested that they could be excluded while this vote was taken, then be readmitted; the whole point of the vote was to exclude the bishops permanently from the Lords.
8 In the autumn of 1641 Cromwell proposed that the Earl of Essex should be made commander of the militia by a parliamentary ordinance – that is, without the King's agreement. This was several months before Parliament passed its first ordinance.
9 When the Grand Remonstrance was proposed, Cromwell predicted that few MPs would oppose it. The Remonstrance provoked one of the bitterest debates in the Long Parliament's history. Cromwell said afterwards that if the Remonstrance had failed, he would have moved to New England.

10 Shortly after the Attempt on the Five Members (January 4, 1642), Cromwell proposed the motion to establish a committee to consider the means of putting the kingdom into a 'posture of defence'.

11 In the spring of 1642 Cromwell invested £2050 in the reconquest of Ireland.

12 In July 1642 Cromwell asked for authority to raise two companies of volunteers in Cambridge.

DISCUSS

Revolutionaries are usually driven by fervent zeal for an ideological cause. Is there any evidence that Cromwell was driven by such zeal during the Long Parliament?

ACTIVITY

This activity is designed to help you to place Cromwell's actions during the Long Parliament into the context of the main events leading to the outbreak of civil war.

1 Draw a timeline running from November 1640 to August 1642 (the opening of the Long Parliament to the formal declaration of war).

2 Place the following main events of the Long Parliament in their correct place on the timeline.

- Root and Branch Petition
- Triennial Act
- Trial of the Earl of Strafford
- Irish Rebellion
- Grand Remonstrance
- Attempt on the Five Members
- Militia Ordinance
- Nineteen Propositions
- Bill to exclude bishops from House of Lords.

3 Place Cromwell's actions on the timeline in a separate column. Where his actions had an impact on national events, show this by drawing lines to connect them.

4 Look back at Chart 3B on page 59. Does this diagram help you to explain:
   a) Cromwell's opposition to the Personal Rule
   b) the sudden and unexpected appearance of Cromwell as an activist in the Long Parliament?

5 Cromwell played no known part in Strafford's trial, the Grand Remonstrance or the Nineteen Propositions. Can you suggest why not?

C Why was Cromwell promoted so rapidly during the Civil War?

Cromwell's military ability is often taken for granted. His enemies readily acknowledged it: it was Prince Rupert who christened Cromwell's cavalry the 'Ironsides'. During the Civil War Cromwell was rapidly promoted. How far did Cromwell owe his promotion to his political allies, the personal and religious network to which he was linked in the Long Parliament?

Criticism of Cromwell's methods came more from his allies than from his enemies. Cromwell was committed to military victory. This worried those Parliamentarians who saw military force merely as a lever to force the King to negotiate. Cromwell used methods that were politically unorthodox, promoting men from humble origins over less able officers from better families. He was prepared to sacrifice anything or anyone that was holding back Parliament from achieving outright victory. He saw that only a decisive result could bring the misery of civil war to an end.

1642: Captain of his own troop of horse

Cromwell began preparing for war even before the war broke out. In early August 1642 he returned to Cambridge and placed his constituency on a war footing. He seized the weapons in Cambridge Castle and intercepted the university's plate silver, which was being sent to the King in York. By the end of the month he had raised a troop of horse cavalry from local volunteers.

1643: Colonel of a regiment of horse, Army of the Eastern Association

During 1643 Cromwell served as Colonel of a regiment of horse in the Eastern Association. The strategic problem was to keep Royalist forces out of East Anglia. In a series of sieges and skirmishes Cromwell helped first to establish Parliament's superiority and then to create a defensive line along the river Ouse, running through his old home towns of Huntingdon, St Ives and Ely. In October he achieved his first notable success at the Battle of Winceby, Lincolnshire, forestalling an invasion by the Earl of Newcastle's Royalist army.

1644: Lieutenant-General of Horse and second-in-command of the Army of the Eastern Association

In 1644 Cromwell was again promoted. He was also a member of the Committee of Both Kingdoms, linking the political and military management of the Anglo-Scottish war effort. In 1644 East Anglia was secure enough for the army to range further afield. In July Cromwell's national reputation was established at the Battle of Marston Moor. Thereafter he became increasingly critical of the way the war was being fought, and of the attitude of the Scots and English Presbyterians. The year ended with his important argument with the Earl of Manchester (see Chapter 7 page 157) and the passing of the Self-Denying Ordinance.

1645: Lieutenant-General of Horse, New Model Army (Here in a portrait of the late 1640s, probably by Robert Walker.)

On 10 June 1645, at the request of Fairfax, Cromwell was appointed second-in-command of the New Model Army. Four days later he helped Fairfax to crush the King's army at Naseby. This was followed on 10 July by victory at Langport. The rest of the Civil War was spent mopping up Royalist strongholds. Cromwell was now the only man in England to combine military command with direct political power in Parliament, looked on with awe and wonder by fellow MPs on the rare occasions when he visited Westminster.

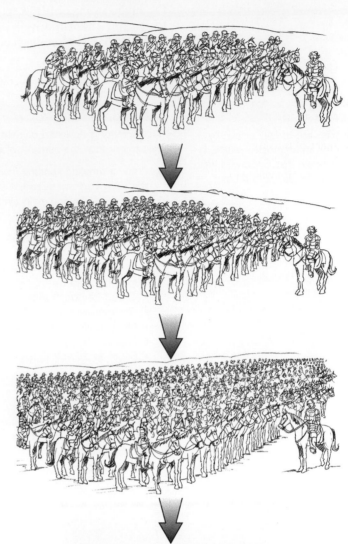

207

CROMWELL IN CIVIL WAR AND REVOLUTION, 1599–1649: WAS CROMWELL A REVOLUTIONARY?

ACTIVITY

What were Cromwell's strengths as an officer? Read Sources 9.6–9.14. They are primary sources providing evidence of different aspects of Cromwell's military abilities.

1 Match each of the quotations with one or more of the qualities listed below.

- leadership
- political awareness
- discipline
- recruitment of troops
- courage
- collaboration with fellow officers
- resolution
- networking
- strategic vision
- raising money
- administration
- religious faith
- promoting men of ability.

2 Compare these qualities with the first three stages of Cromwell's military career (Chart 9A). Which qualities do you think would have played a vital part in his promotion:
   a) from Captain of a single troop to Colonel of a regiment of horse
   b) from Colonel of a regiment to Lieutenant-General of the Army of the Eastern Association?

DISCUSS

What, if anything, was revolutionary about Cromwell's approach to war?

SOURCE 9.11 General William Waller describing how Cromwell served under his command in 1645

Although he was blunt he did not bear himself with pride or disdain. As an officer he was obedient and did never dispute my orders nor argue upon them.

SOURCE 9.12 Cromwell speaking to the Suffolk county committee, 1643

If you choose honest godly men to be captains of horse, honest men will follow them, and they will be careful to mount such. I had rather have a plain russet-coated captain that knows what he fights for, and loves what he knows, than that which you call a gentleman and is nothing else. I honour a gentleman that is so indeed.

SOURCE 9.6 A Parliamentary news report, 1643

As for Cromwell, he hath 2,000 brave men, well disciplined: no man swears but he pays his twelve pence; if he be drunk he is set in the stocks, or worse; if he call the other 'Roundhead' he is cashiered; in-so-much that the countries where they come leap for joy of them, and come in and join with them. How happy were it if all the forces were thus disciplined.

SOURCE 9.7 Cromwell speaking in support of the Self-Denying Ordinance, 9 December 1644

I can speak this for my own soldiers, that they look not upon me, but upon you; and for you they will fight, and live and die in your Cause; and if others be of that mind that they are of, you need not fear them. They do not idolise me, but look upon the Cause they fight for.

SOURCE 9.8 John Vicars, a Parliamentary propagandist, praising Cromwell's courage in 1646

As for that famous and magnanimous commander, Lieutenant-General Cromwell, whose prowess and prudence . . . in this fight [Marston Moor] have crowned him with the never withering laurels of fame and honour, who with so lion-like courage and impregnable animosity, charged his proudest adversaries again and again, like a Roman Marcellus indeed . . . even to the end of the fight; and at last came off, as with some wounds, so with honour and triumph inferior to none.

SOURCE 9.9 Edward Hyde, Earl of Clarendon, describing Captain Cromwell's orders to his troop of horse in 1642 (quoted in *History of the Rebellion and Civil Wars in England*, 1702)

[Cromwell] told them, that if the King chanced to be in the body of the enemy that he was to charge, he would as soon discharge his pistol upon him as at any other private person, and if their conscience would not permit them to do the like, he advised them not to list themselves in his troop or under his command . . .

SOURCE 9.10 Cromwell writing to the congregation of the parish church of Fen Drayton, Cambridgeshire, 8 March 1643

Having in part seen your good affections to the Cause, and now standing in need of your further assistance to the perfecting of the said Fortifications, which will cost at least two thousand pounds, We are encouraged as well as necessitated to desire a Freewill Offering of a Liberal Contribution from you . . . knowing that every honest and well-affected man, considering the vast expenses we have already been at . . . will be ready to contribute his best assistance.

SOURCE 9.13 Cromwell writing to defend the actions of one of his officers, September 1643

I hear there hath been much exception taken to Captain Margery and his Officers, for taking of horses. I am sorry you should discountenance those who (not to make benefit to themselves, but to serve their Country) are willing to venture their lives, and to purchase to themselves the displeasure of bad men, that they may do a Public benefit. If these men be accounted 'troublesome to the Country', I shall be glad you would send them all to me. I'll bid them welcome. And when they have fought for you, and endured some other difficulties of war which your 'honester' men will hardly bear, I pray you then let them go for honest men. Gentlemen, it may be it provokes some spirits to see such plain men made Captains of Horse.

SOURCE 9.14 Cromwell writing to Colonel Hacker, 25 December 1650

Truly I think he that prays and preaches best will fight best. I know nothing will give like courage and confidence as the knowledge of God in Christ will . . .

D Why did Cromwell oppose the Presbyterian party?

Some of the qualities that made Cromwell an effective officer brought him into conflict with his superiors. His willingness to promote men from humble social origins raised concerns that his army posed a threat to social order. During 1643 he appealed to Parliament to consider the risks his men were taking for its cause. After Marston Moor, Cromwell was famous enough to take the political offensive. As he did so, his promotion of plain men became bound up with the larger issues of the Scottish alliance and the religious war aims of Parliament.

The Scots demanded a Presbyterian settlement. Parliament accepted this as a price worth paying, and its officers – including Cromwell – took the Solemn League and Covenant. But Scottish Presbyterianism was intolerant of other Protestant sects, a fact that became more obvious as time went on. Cromwell opposed such intolerance, defending the right of his soldiers to worship according to their conscience. He could not accept the cynical way his soldiers were being used by English Presbyterians.

By late 1644 the Presbyterians in Parliament were closely associated with the 'peace party' led by Denzil Holles. They were concerned at the damage the war was inflicting on local communities. They were particularly disturbed by the apparent collapse of religious and social order. Scottish-style Presbyterianism appeared to them to offer the best way of reconstructing English society after the war, with the obvious advantage that it pleased the Scots. But pleasing the Scots was not, in Cromwell's opinion, what the English Civil War was about – at least not at first. As he said years later, 'Religion was not the thing first contested for, but God brought it to that issue at last.'

Was Cromwell sincere about his religious beliefs? Not everybody thought so. It seemed too easy for him to use Providence to justify everything he did. He made many enemies, and it suited some of them to accuse him of insincerity. Most modern historians believe that Cromwell cannot be understood unless his belief in Providence is accepted as genuine.

■ Learning trouble spot

What were Cromwell's religious beliefs?

SOURCE 9.15 Cromwell writing to Parliament after the capture of Bristol, 21 September 1645

As for being united in forms, commonly called Uniformity; every Christian will for peace-sake study and do, as far as conscience will permit; and from brethren, in things of the mind we look for no compulsion, but that of light and reason.

Little is known of Cromwell's religious practices. There is no direct evidence of the kind of services he attended after the 1630s, or whether and when he used either the *Book of Common Prayer* or the *Directory of Public Worship* that replaced it in 1645. Our knowledge of Cromwell's religious beliefs has to be constructed from the evidence of what he said and did.

From his letter to Mrs St John (Source 9.4, page 203), we know that he had gone through some sort of conversion experience. After this he felt that he had been saved (chosen by God to go to Heaven when he died). This had a liberating effect and may have contributed to his personal bravery – if he were killed in battle, it wouldn't matter. It may help to explain also his willingness to speak his mind freely.

Linked to this was a strong belief in Providence – nothing happened unless God wanted it to happen. Things that seemed impossible to men were not impossible to God. Cromwell's God was the God of the Old Testament, a living God who constantly intervened in human affairs. People could find themselves called upon to be the instruments of Providence. The power of God was not an excuse for people to do nothing. It was man's responsibility to examine events for signs of God's intentions, and then to help them come to pass. Anything that helped to focus the spirit – fasting, prayer, self-denial – could help in this.

It was therefore sinful – and dangerous – to take the credit for things that were achieved. 'Wherever anything in this world is exalted, or exalts itself,' Cromwell said after the Battle of Preston, 'God will pull it down.' After Naseby, he praised Fairfax for giving all the glory of the victory to God. Attributing his own victories to God became a standard theme in Cromwell's dispatches (official reports).

From the soul-searching that accompanied his faith in Providence sprang Cromwell's belief in liberty of conscience. For the State to require a single form of compulsory worship was an impious act, since no one could know for certain the mind of God. Only through the free transfer of beliefs and ideas could people test those beliefs and come towards a greater understanding of God's intentions. There were limits to this liberty – Catholicism could not be tolerated, because it was the ideology of Anti-christ – but Cromwell consistently defended liberty of conscience for his soldiers.

It was not government's place to hinder this search for spiritual truth. In the days before Archbishop Laud, there had been considerable freedom within the Anglican church to worship according to local preference. Laud had tried to snuff this out by rigidly enforcing the Act of Uniformity. Now the Presbyterians were planning to replace one intolerant State church with another. In the 1650s Cromwell argued for a national church that would lead by example rather than by force.

209

CROMWELL IN CIVIL WAR AND REVOLUTION, 1599–1649: WAS CROMWELL A REVOLUTIONARY?

DISCUSS

Were Cromwell's religious beliefs revolutionary? Consider the following issues:

• Did his ANTI-FORMALISM pose a threat to social order?
• Was Cromwell trying to introduce something new in English worship, or was he trying to get back to something that had existed before the Laudian policies of the 1630s?

ANTI-FORMALISM
The belief that the precise details of doctrine and worship are less important than the fact that a person believes in Christ and tries to live by Christian principles.

FOCUS ROUTE

Study Sources 9.16–9.19.
What do these sources tell us about the way some contemporaries regarded Cromwell's professions of faith? Look back at the Learning Trouble Spot on Cromwell's religious beliefs. Now return to the Focus Route on page 200 and record the case for and against Cromwell's sincerity.

ACTIVITY

Study Sources 9.16, 9.17 and 9.18.

1 What did Robert Ward and Giovanni Sagredo make of Cromwell's religious faith?
2 Does Source 9.18 support the evidence of Sources 9.16 and 9.17? Explain your answer.

Study Source 9.19.

3 Why did John Milton think Cromwell was 'our chief of men'?
4 What dangers did Milton foresee for the future?
5 Why was there so much opposition to the idea of religious freedom at this time?

FOCUS ROUTE

Look back at the Focus Route on page 200. Remember to take notes on evidence to use in the class 'trial'.

Cromwell's controversies: was Cromwell sincere about his religious beliefs?

Was Cromwell sincere about his religious beliefs? Or did he use religion cynically to build support for himself within the Army? Not everyone thought that he was sincere.

SOURCE 9.16   Robert Ward, *The Hunting of the Foxes*, 1649. Ward was a Leveller who believed Cromwell had betrayed their cause

You shall scarce speak to Cromwell about any thing, but he will lay his hand on his breast, elevate his eyes, and call God to record, he will weep, howl and repent, even while he doth smite you under the first rib.

SOURCE 9.17   The Venetian Ambassador, Giovanni Sagredo, reporting to his government in 1655

[Cromwell] makes a great show of his zeal . . . and then goes every Sunday to preach to the soldiers and exhort them to live after the Divine law. He does this with fervour, even to tears, which he has ready at a moment's notice, and this way he stimulates the troops to second his designs.

SOURCE 9.18   A 'statement by an opponent of Cromwell', made during the argument between Cromwell and the Earl of Manchester

Colonel Cromwell [chooses] his officers not such as were soldiers or men of estate, but such as were common men, poor and of mean parentage, only he would give them the title of godly, precious men. I have heard him often say that it must not be soldiers nor Scots that must do this work, but it must be the godly. When any new Englishman or some new upstart Independent did appear there must be a way made for them by cashiering others, some honest commander or other, and those silly people put in their command. If you look upon his own regiment of horses see what a swarm there is of those that call themselves the godly. Some of them profess they have seen visions and had revelations.

SOURCE 9.19   John Milton, 'To the Lord General Cromwell', 1652

Cromwell, our chief of men, who through a cloud,
Not of war only, but detractions rude,
Guided by faith and matchless fortitude,
To peace and truth thy glorious way has ploughed . . .
    Yet much remains
To conquer still; peace hath her victories
No less renowned than war: new foes arise,
Threatening to bind our souls with secular chains;
Help us to save free conscience from the paw
Of hireling wolves whose gospel is their maw.

Cromwell's controversies: the Self-Denying Ordinance, December 1644

In Chapter 7 we examined the part played by the Self-Denying Ordinance in helping Parliament to win the war (see pages 158–59). Now we must focus on the controversy surrounding Cromwell's unique exemption from the terms of the Ordinance.

Cromwell's exemption would not appear so sinister if he himself hadn't suggested the Ordinance to the House of Commons, on 9 December 1644. The fact that he did lays him open to the charge that the whole thing was a plot. Denzil Holles, Cromwell's parliamentary opponent, and the Royalist Edward Hyde later accused him of subterfuge (being deceitful in trying to avoid blame). We cannot easily dismiss their accusations as partisan propaganda. We need to examine in detail the events by which Cromwell was exempted from the Ordinance (see Chart 9B).

210

CROMWELL IN CIVIL WAR AND REVOLUTION, 1599–1649: WAS CROMWELL A REVOLUTIONARY?

■ 9B Events leading to Cromwell's exemption from the Self-Denying Ordinance

1644

November	December
25 November Parliament fails to destroy the King's army in the Second Battle of Newbury. This provokes the Commons to demand a report on the disaster from Cromwell and Waller, both members of the Committee of Both Kingdoms. Cromwell's report criticises Manchester's failure to press his attack. What begins as mutual accusations of military incompetence escalates into arguments over war aims. **28 November** Manchester accuses Cromwell of having said that he hoped 'to live to see never a nobleman in England' while replying to Cromwell's attack in the Lords.	**9 December** In a speech before a parliamentary committee investigating the argument, Cromwell raises the idea of the Self-Denying Ordinance, a mutual sacrifice to restore peace between the Lords and the Commons. **14 December** The Self-Denying Ordinance is introduced as legislation in the Commons. The charges between Manchester and Cromwell are dropped. Is Cromwell making a noble sacrifice of his career for the good of the 'Cause', or is he dodging embarrassing revelations about his own military record? **19 December** The Ordinance is sent to the Lords. Immediately the question arises of whether an exception to the Ordinance can be made – not for Cromwell, but for the Earl of Essex. The motion to exempt Essex fails by seven votes.

1645

January	February	March	April
13 January The Lords rejects the first version of the Ordinance. **18 January** The Commons agrees to reorganise the Army. **21 January** Commanders are appointed for the New Model Army. Sir Thomas Fairfax is appointed General; Sir Philip Skippon Major-General of Foot; the Lieutenant-General of Horse is left vacant.		**Early March** Cromwell returns to active campaigning, marching to the relief of Taunton.	**3 April** The Lords pass a second version of the Ordinance, which enables the noble commanders to resign, thereby avoiding the dishonour of being dismissed. Essex and Manchester lay down their commissions. Cromwell does not.

May	June	July	August
12 May The official deadline by which Cromwell has to resign his commission. Just before this date a motion is proposed that Cromwell should be granted a permanent exemption. Parliament extends his commission by 40 days.	**14 June** Battle of Naseby. Cromwell's reputation is enhanced by the victory. **18 June** The official deadline by which the extension of Cromwell's commission is due to expire. A second 40-day extension is granted.	**Summer** Two more 40-day extensions are granted, followed by an extension of six months, which sees Cromwell to the end of the war.	

SOURCE 9.20 Extract from Cromwell's letter to Parliament after the Battle of Naseby, 14 June 1645. The part in *italics* was censored by Parliament

Sir, this is none other but the hand of God; and to Him alone belongs the glory, wherein none are to share with Him. [Fairfax] served you with all faithfulness and honour: and the best commendation I can give him is, That I daresay he attributes all to God, and would rather perish than assume to himself. *Honest men served you faithfully in this action. Sir, they are trusty; I beseech you, in the name of God, not to discourage them. I wish this action may beget thankfulness and humility in all that are concerned with it. He that ventures his life for the liberty of his country, I wish he trust God for the liberty of his conscience, and you for the liberty he fights for.*

ACTIVITY

211

CROMWELL IN CIVIL WAR AND REVOLUTION, 1599–1649: WAS CROMWELL A REVOLUTIONARY?

History's 'dark matter'

Physicists now believe that there is something in the universe called dark matter – matter which we know is there, but which we cannot see. Its existence would explain things about the behaviour of the universe that cannot be explained otherwise.

History has its dark matter too – events which took place behind the scenes but which never got recorded. History's dark matter is probably many times greater than the historical record. There are times when the surviving evidence is not enough to prove that one interpretation is correct and another incorrect.

The Self-Denying Ordinance is a case in point. The surviving evidence can be interpreted in different ways. The way we interpret it depends largely on how we perceive the dark matter interacting on the events that did leave evidence behind.

Cromwell was the only officer-politician to be exempted from the Ordinance. Was this unforeseen, or was it put forward knowing that he would probably survive the purge and retain his command? Answering the following questions will help you understand why the Self-Denying Ordinance has been interpreted in different ways.

Questions raised by the evidence	Your answers to these questions
On 21 January 1645, why was the newly created post of Lieutenant-General of Horse in the New Model Army left vacant? Could Cromwell have known he would be exempted from the Ordinance when he proposed it?	
If Cromwell and his allies thought he might be exempted, then why was he permitted to propose it? Wouldn't this expose him to charges of hypocrisy?	
Did Cromwell have enough friends in the two Houses of Parliament to know that his exemption would probably be secured?	
Was Cromwell already so famous that he knew Parliament needed his services in the field?	
Did the military situation change in some way in early 1645 to change Parliament's mind about Cromwell?	
What were relations like between Parliament and Cromwell after he retained his command? (Consider Source 9.20.)	

E Cromwell and the search for settlement, 1646–48

In 1646 Cromwell expected a political settlement to be reached quickly. He hoped to see the King return to the throne with safeguards to protect Parliament's privileges. He expected Parliament to do right by its Army, paying the soldiers their back-pay, taking care of its widows and orphans, and ensuring that the Cause was not betrayed. Cromwell wanted his men to continue to enjoy the same liberty of conscience in peacetime that they had enjoyed in war.

Not everyone in Parliament shared Cromwell's vision of a fair settlement. When the Army intervened in politics, Cromwell was forced to accept that it might not be possible to achieve the kind of settlement he wanted. He tried to prevent an open breach between the Army he commanded and the Parliament he served. He also tried to reach an agreement with the King. When both of these efforts ended in failure, Cromwell was forced to protect the Cause as he understood it – the Army itself.

We do not know exactly when or how Cromwell became disillusioned with the political process. His wartime experiences alerted him to the dangers and pitfalls of politics, which he found distasteful compared to the honest simplicity of a military campaign. In 1645 the 'war party' had outmanoeuvred the 'peace party' to press for a decisive victory. Now that the war was over, the 'peace party' and its Presbyterian allies were reasserting their authority at Westminster. Their attacks on the Army dismayed Cromwell: in January 1647 he was ill with an 'impostume of the head'. Parliamentary records suggest that he either stayed away from Westminster for much of March and April 1647, or that he listened in silence to the debates in which Parliament planned the demobilisation of the Army.

This chart should be studied together with Chart 8F on pages 178–79.

At the start of 1647, Cromwell was still insisting that the Army must obey Parliament. By the end of the year, he had taken decisive steps to support the Army in its quarrel with Parliament. Cromwell's role in the events leading up to the revolution in 1649 have always provoked controversy. One view sees him as an 'agent provocateur', manipulating events from behind the scenes while taking care to cover his tracks. An alternative view sees him as indecisive, reluctant to commit himself until forced to do so by events.

PHASE 1

Phase 1: Revolt of the rank and file, May–June 1647

When the Army regiments were drawing up their lists of grievances, electing Agitators and organising petitions, Cromwell tried to prevent an open breach between them and Parliament. He still believed that only a parliamentary settlement could work, and argued against any military revolt. In May he was sent by Parliament to assure the Army of Parliament's good intentions.

- **21 May** Cromwell assured Parliament that the Army would remain loyal and follow its orders.
- **27 May** Cromwell took the full £2000 arrears of back-pay he was owed, at a time when Parliament was offering his soldiers a fraction of what was owed to them.
- **29 May** Fairfax held a Council of War. The officers warned Fairfax that the army could not be disbanded without disorder. Cromwell remained in London, apparently undecided on a course of action.

(In 1656 during a conversation with Cromwell, Sir Gilbert Pickering reminded him that 'the third letter came to you from them [the Army officers] wherein they peremptorily told you that if you would not forthwith … come and head them, they would go their own way without you.')

Cornet Joyce seizes the King from Holdenby House, 3–4 June 1647

Cromwell may or may not have known what Joyce was about to do. It is possible that he encouraged Joyce without wanting to take responsibility for giving the order to seize the King.

Cornet Joyce

PHASE 3

Cromwell's controversies: Pride's Purge, 6 December 1648

After the Battle of Preston, Cromwell did not rush back to London. He remained in the North, mopping up remnants of the Scottish and Royalist forces.

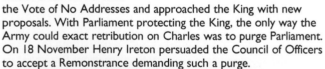

The Army was deeply affected by the Second Civil War. It was appalled when Parliament revoked the Vote of No Addresses and approached the King with new proposals. With Parliament protecting the King, the only way the Army could exact retribution on Charles was to purge Parliament. On 18 November Henry Ireton persuaded the Council of Officers to accept a Remonstrance demanding such a purge.

Was Cromwell behind Pride's Purge? Circumstantial evidence suggests that he was. Ireton, the mover and shaker of the Purge, was his son-in-law. When Fairfax ordered Cromwell to come south, it took him six days to reach London from Pontefract, entering London on the day of the Purge. There is no direct evidence linking him to the decision to launch Pride's Purge, but there is evidence that he was considering the merits of such a coup.

Phase 3: Second Civil War

In 1648 Cromwell commanded his own army for the first time. While Fairfax dealt with the rebellions in Kent and Essex, Cromwell crushed the Royalist uprising in South Wales. From Wales he went north to intercept the Scottish invasion. At the Battle of Preston, Cromwell caught the Scots strung out along the road. By attacking their flank, he achieved local superiority against a larger enemy and defeated them. The Second Civil War had a profound effect on Cromwell:

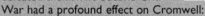

- He demanded vengeance on those who had conspired to start a second civil war. By doing so they had 'sinned against so much light, and against so many evidences of Divine Presence going along with and prospering a righteous cause …'
- His wrath was directed particularly at those parliamentarians of the First Civil War who had switched sides. When Parliament let off Colonel Humphrey Matthews with nothing more than a fine, Cromwell was amazed 'to see such manifest witnessings of God … no more reverenced'.
- He blamed the victors in the First Civil War for showing too much leniency. The same mistake would not be made again.

SOURCE 9.21 Cromwell writing to Colonel Robert Hammond, 25 November 1648. Hammond had expressed his anxiety that the Army might be about to purge Parliament, and his unhappiness at finding himself caught up in these events

Authorities and powers are the ordinance of God. This or that [kind of authority] is of human institution, and limited, some with larger, some with stricter bands, each one according to its constitution. But I do not therefore think the Authorities may do anything, and yet such obedience is due. All agree that there are cases in which it is lawful to resist. If so, your ground fails … Indeed, dear Robin, not to multiply words, the query is, Whether ours be such a case? This ingenuously is the true question.

To this I shall say nothing, though I could say very much; but only desire thee to see what thou findest in thy own heart to two or three plain considerations … thirdly, Whether this Army be not a lawful Power, called by God to oppose and fight against the King upon some stated grounds; and being in power to such ends, may not oppose one Name of Authority [Parliament], for those ends, as well as another Name [the King], – since it was not the outward Authority summoning them that by its power made the quarrel lawful, but the quarrel was lawful in itself?

213

CROMWELL IN CIVIL WAR AND REVOLUTION, 1599–1649: WAS CROMWELL A REVOLUTIONARY?

PHASE 2

Phase 2: Intervention of the Army officers, June–December 1647

As the Army began its slow march on London, Cromwell was still trying to reach a settlement acceptable to the King, Parliament and the Army.

- **7 June** Cromwell met Charles I for the first time near Cambridge. During the summer and autumn Cromwell was involved in intensive negotiations with the King, particularly at Reading, after the publication of the *Heads of the Proposals*.
- **28 October – early November** Cromwell chaired the Putney Debates between the Army Council and the Levellers. While giving the Levellers a chance to air their views, he probably hoped that they could be persuaded to drop their more radical demands.
- **15 November** Cromwell was present at the general Army rendezvous at Ware, where he helped to suppress an incipient Leveller mutiny, riding among the defiant regiments and plucking copies of the *Agreement of the People* out of their hats.

**OLIVER CROMWELL:
AGENT OF PROVIDENCE,
OR *AGENT PROVOCATEUR*?**

Heads of the Proposals, July 1647

The Army officers' terms for a settlement with the King aroused suspicion among the rank and file. On 16–17 July representatives from the Army Council debated the merits of the *Heads of the Proposals* with the regimental Agitators, in an attempt to win them over. The Agitators wanted the Army to march on London, purge Parliament of its Presbyterian MPs and impose more radical terms. Cromwell was against this, arguing that only a parliamentary settlement, freely arrived at, could work. He feared that military intervention would undermine the Army's friends in Parliament.

**Vote of No Addresses,
January 1648**

- **23 November 1647** Cromwell spoke in the Commons, describing his negotiations with the Levellers. He urged Parliament to suppress the Levellers and restore order.
- **3 January 1648** Cromwell spoke in Parliament to support the Vote of No Addresses. He urged Parliament to face up to the coming conflict: 'Expose not the honest party of the Kingdom, who have bled for you, and suffer not misery to fall upon them, for want of courage or resolution in you, else that honest people may take such course as nature dictates to them.'

Cromwell's controversies: King's escape to the Isle of Wight, November 1647

On 11 November 1647 the King escaped from Hampton Court to the Isle of Wight, where he was rearrested and imprisoned in Carisbrooke Castle. He was still able to negotiate the Engagement with the Scots, which led to the Second Civil War.

The King's escape simplified Cromwell's task. It showed that Charles was untrustworthy, and forced an end to the Putney Debates. It brought the Army and Parliament closer together, at least temporarily. Some historians have suggested that Cromwell was behind the King's escape. Consider the following facts:

- The King's gaoler at Hampton Court was related to Cromwell. Before the King escaped, he was shown a letter written by Cromwell warning his guards that an attempt was about to be made on his life.
- The governor of the Isle of Wight who rearrested the King, Colonel Robert Hammond, was also related to Cromwell.
- On 19 November, in a speech before Parliament, Cromwell blamed the kingdom's crisis on the NORMAN YOKE and the Stuart monarchy that was descended from it. Cromwell's attitude was now hardening against the King, a fact that would be difficult to explain if he were behind the King's escape.

NORMAN YOKE

The idea that England's troubles could be traced back to the Anglo-Saxons' loss of freedom during the Norman Conquest in the eleventh century.

ACTIVITY

Read Source 9.21.

1 Cromwell was discussing in this letter the question of whether it was ever legal to resist authority – not the King this time, but Parliament. Summarise his argument briefly in your own words.
2 Why did Cromwell write, 'To this I shall say nothing, though I could say very much'?
3 How likely was it that the Army would go ahead with Pride's Purge without Cromwell's knowledge?
4 What could be described as 'revolutionary' about Source 9.21?

ACTIVITY

1 Divide the class into two parts. One part should draw up a diagram similar to Chart 9C, based on the assumption that throughout this period Cromwell was the agent of Providence, reacting to events that were outside his control.
2 The other part should draw up a similar diagram, based on the assumption that Cromwell was an agent provocateur, actively steering events this way and that, but very cleverly leaving no evidence of his direct involvement.
3 Compare the two diagrams. Which of these views do you find more convincing?

214

CROMWELL IN CIVIL WAR AND REVOLUTION, 1599–1649: WAS CROMWELL A REVOLUTIONARY?

Cromwell's controversies: Cornet Joyce seizes the King from Holdenby House, 3–4 June 1647

The seizure of the King by Cornet Joyce is an example of how conspiracy theories thrive when there is no direct evidence to support them. Was Cromwell involved in a plot to seize the King? Joyce believed Parliament was plotting to seize control of Charles and move him to London. In these circumstances of plot and counterplot, is it likely that Cromwell would have done nothing? Most historians think that it is.

■ 9D Events surrounding the seizure of the King by Cornet Joyce

31 May	Cornet Joyce, on his way from Oxford to Holdenby House, Northamptonshire, visits Cromwell in London. No record of their discussion survives
3 June	Cromwell leaves London for Newmarket, where Fairfax has called a general rendezvous of the Army
	Cornet Joyce seizes the King at Holdenby House
4 June	Cornet Joyce writes to Cromwell for instructions
7 June	Cromwell's first meeting with Charles I near Cambridge

SOURCE 9.22   Letter written by Cornet Joyce to Cromwell on 4 June 1647, the day after the King was taken into the Army's custody (Joyce refers to Graves, who was probably the officer in charge of the guards that Parliament had placed at Holdenby House to watch over the King)

Sir, we have secured the king. Graves is run away. He got out about one o'clock in the morning and so went his way. It is suspected he is gone to London; you may imagine what he will do there. You must hasten an answer to us, and let us know what we shall do. We are resolved to obey no orders but the general's; we shall follow the commissioner's directions while we are here, if just in our eyes. I humbly entreat you to consider what is done and act accordingly with all the haste you can. We shall not rest night nor day till we hear from you.
Yours and the kingdom's faithful servant till death.
George Joyce
Holdenby this 4th of June at 8 of the clock in the morning.

FOCUS ROUTE

How closely involved do you think Cromwell was in the actions of Cornet Joyce? Do you find the evidence conclusive one way or the other? Consider the following questions.

• Why did Cornet Joyce stop off for a meeting with Cromwell on 31 May?
• Is it likely that Joyce would not have told Cromwell of his intentions?
• If Cromwell knew what Joyce was about to do, and did nothing to stop him, does that mean that Cromwell was involved in the plot to capture the King?
• Does hindsight lead us to focus on Joyce's accountability to Cromwell when Fairfax was the Lord General of the Army?
• Use this event to add evidence to use in Cromwell's trial at the end of Section 3.

TALKING POINTS

Consider other examples of historical events that have led to conspiracy theories (for example, President John F Kennedy's assassination; Princess Diana's death; the American moon landings).

a) In your opinion, were these conspiracies?
b) Assuming that they were not conspiracies, why is it so difficult to disprove the conspiracy theories surrounding them?

215

CROMWELL IN CIVIL WAR AND REVOLUTION, 1599–1649: WAS CROMWELL A REVOLUTIONARY?

F What part did Cromwell play in the trial and execution of the King?

CROMWELL IN CIVIL WAR AND REVOLUTION, 1599–1649: WAS CROMWELL A REVOLUTIONARY?

SOURCE 9.23 Cromwell's reaction to Algernon Sydney's objections to the idea of putting the King on trial for his life

I tell you we will cut off his head with the crown on it.

In 1660, at the time of the restoration of the monarchy, some of the men who had been involved in Charles I's trial and execution tried to blame these events on Cromwell. Two years after Cromwell's death, lurid stories of his behaviour were circulating in a kingdom that was anxious to demonstrate its loyalty to its new sovereign, Charles's eldest son, Charles II. Some of these stories came from the regicides. Their anecdotes were eagerly taken up by Royalists to blacken Cromwell's name.

Some of the most colourful stories of Cromwell's role in the events of the English Revolution must therefore be suspect, because of the dubious motives of the people who told them. Many of these stories focus on the actual signing of the death warrant. An example can be seen in Source 9.25 – but Ingoldsby's signature (Source 9.24) shows no sign of the struggle supposed to have taken place over the document. Some of the stories may be true: as the tension broke and men began to sign, Cromwell is supposed to have got into an ink fight with Henry Marten. This interest in the signing of the death warrant presupposes that the King's death could have been avoided at this moment, just as it assumes that Cromwell made no effort to save the King. Both assumptions are incorrect.

SOURCE 9.24 Ingoldsby's signature on the King's death warrant

SOURCE 9.25 Edward Hyde, Earl of Clarendon, describes an incident supposed to have happened during the signing of the King's death warrant (*History of the Rebellion and Civil Wars in England*, 1702)

[Colonel Richard Ingoldsby] seeing what it was, refused with great passion, saying he knew nothing of the business, and offered to go away. But Cromwell and others held him by violence; and Cromwell, with a loud laughter, taking his hand in his, and putting the pen between his fingers, with his own hand writ Richard Ingoldsby, he making all the resistance he could . . .

In January 1649 Cromwell did support the trial and execution of Charles I. He attended 21 of the 23 sessions of the High Court during the trial, his signature is the third one on the death warrant, and he tried to persuade as many members of the High Court as possible to sign. But during the three weeks between Pride's Purge (6 December) and Bulstrode Whitelocke's decision to leave London for the sanctuary of his estate (26 December), Cromwell was undecided what to do for the best. Even after the Army's decision to put the King on trial (15 December), Cromwell continued searching for a way to avoid the calamity of regicide. According to Whitelocke's diary, he and Cromwell spent Christmas in fruitless negotiations to have Charles abdicate in favour of his younger son, the Duke of Gloucester. The failure of these discussions led to Whitelocke's decision to distance himself from the trial. Cromwell resigned himself to the inevitability of the King's execution, and accepted it as the righteous judgement of God. Thereafter he appears to have had no qualms about it, and accepted his instrumentality in that which God was bringing to pass.

SOURCE 9.26 Cromwell, speaking to the Army Council on 23 March 1649, defends the decision to execute the King

God hath brought the war to an issue here, and given you a great fruit of that war, to wit, the execution of exemplary justice upon the prime leader of all this quarrel into the three kingdoms, and upon divers persons of very great quality who did co-operate with him in the destruction of this kingdom.

SOURCE 9.27 Cromwell, speaking in 1650, defends the decision to execute the King

[Parliament], true to the ends of the Covenant, did, in answer to their consciences, turn out a tyrant, in a way which the Christian in aftertimes will mention with honour, and all tyrants in the world look at with fear . . .

DISCUSS

Study Sources 9.26 and 9.27.

1 Do you agree with Cromwell that Charles I was 'the prime leader of all this quarrel'?
2 What did Cromwell mean in Source 9.26 when he spoke of 'persons of very great quality'?
3 Why was Cromwell proud of the way the King had been brought to justice?
4 How might a Royalist have responded to Cromwell's statement in Source 9.27?

FOCUS ROUTE

Look back over Section F and reach your own conclusions about Cromwell's involvement in the King's trial and execution. Then return to the Focus Route on page 200 and record the case for and against Cromwell. Which case do you find more convincing?

DISCUSS

When Caesar crossed the Rubicon river into Italy he provoked a civil war. It was his point of no return. What was Cromwell's point of no return?

Cromwell's controversies: the trial and execution of the King, January 1649

Cromwell's role as a regicide was the most serious of all his controversies. If he wanted to be king himself, then clearly Charles I and his family had to be removed. His enemies claimed that Cromwell was the chief instigator of the trial and execution that followed, but was this really so, and did he support these events for selfish reasons?

The King's execution was not the end of the revolution. Several other prominent Royalists, including the Duke of Hamilton, followed Charles I to the scaffold. The King's death presaged the abolition of the monarchy, followed by that of the House of Lords. Cromwell may have argued against this, but their refusal to support the Commons' trial of the King placed the peers (Lords) outside the revolution, and they had to go. As always, Cromwell made a virtue of necessity and embraced the radicalism of the move as another providential act.

The consequences of the King's execution could not have been more serious for Cromwell. Whitelocke was not the only person in his network of friends and associates to distance himself from the regicide. The Lords refused to have anything to do with it. Cromwell's old ally Lord Saye and Sele returned to his home at Broughton Castle (see Source 3.2, page 60). Fairfax abandoned the trial after the first day. Of the 135 commissioners nominated to attend the High Court trial of the King, only 59 signed the death warrant. For Cromwell the King's execution was the breaking of the mould, a point of no return not only for the nation but for himself personally. The Commonwealth would have to go forward conscious of what failure might mean for all its members.

G Review: Cromwell in Civil War and Revolution, 1599–1649

Was Cromwell a revolutionary? If by a 'revolutionary' we mean someone who set out deliberately to undermine the political and social fabric of the society he or she lived in, then the answer is that he was not. Cromwell was trying to save England, not destroy it. His opposition to Charles I sprang from the conviction that the King was responsible for 'the destruction of this kingdom' (Source 9.25). Like Pym, Cromwell was persuaded that a conspiracy lay at the heart of government which, if left unchallenged, would lead to the destruction of the law and liberties of the English people and the ruin of religion.

Yet there was something revolutionary about Cromwell that drove him to confront those on his own side who had doubts about the righteousness of their cause. By December 1648 Cromwell was attacking not only the King but also the Parliament that was protecting him. Like some modern revolutionaries, Cromwell often acted with the single-mindedness of a zealot. His religious convictions cut a path through the fog of doubt that clouded the judgement of many on his side. He was less troubled than some by the many ironies thrown up by the war: by, for example, the fact that a war to defend ancient liberties had ended up furthering the tendency towards the centralisation of government. Cromwell was quite relaxed about the spilling of blood if the blood in question belonged to his enemies: when 'God made them as stubble to our swords', it was all in a good cause. Perhaps he saw with greater clarity than most that once the hounds of war had been unleashed, only further bloodshed could bring them to heel.

Throughout the search for settlement that followed the First Civil War, Cromwell was either extremely cunning or very undecided. Perhaps in a nation of only 5 million people, we should not make too much of the kind of coincidences and accidents that can make Cromwell's motives appear so sinister. Most current historians are inclined to give him the benefit of the doubt.

217

CROMWELL IN CIVIL WAR AND REVOLUTION, 1599–1649: WAS CROMWELL A REVOLUTIONARY?

FOCUS ROUTE

By now you should have accumulated a considerable amount of evidence, both for and against Cromwell, to use in his 'trial' at the end of section 3. Check back over your notes to make sure that you have considered each of 'Cromwell's controversies' before 1649 (see the Focus Route on page 200).

ACTIVITY

Choose one of the following essay titles.

a) How far does Cromwell's career to 1649 suggest that he was motivated by personal ambition?

b) How consistent was Cromwell's behaviour during the search for a political settlement between 1646 and 1649?

c) To what extent can it be argued that Cromwell rose from obscurity to the heart of political power because he was seen by others as an instrument of God's Providence?

d) 'A reluctant revolutionary' – is this an appropriate description of Oliver Cromwell in the 1640s?

KEY POINTS FROM CHAPTER 9

Cromwell in Civil War and Revolution, 1599–1649

1 The first 41 years of Cromwell's life were unexceptional.

2 Cromwell was not, however, living in total obscurity. He had family connections which placed him on the fringes of a powerful network of opponents to the Personal Rule.

3 Sometime in the 1630s Cromwell experienced a religious conversion that left him assured of God's grace. From this moment onwards he believed he was one of the Elect, a godly man living in the belief that he had been saved.

4 During the Long Parliament Cromwell acted with zealous certainty about the righteousness of Parliament's cause. The main controversy about this period focuses on whether he was acting independently or whether he was being used by more powerful men, such as Lord Saye and Sele, John Pym, John Hampden and others, who took the lead themselves during the major crises.

5 Cromwell began the First Civil War as one of a large number of junior provincial officers, helping to organise the defence of East Anglia. He was rapidly promoted, becoming within two years the second-in-command of the Army of the Eastern Association.

6 His willingness to promote men from humble backgrounds and unorthodox religious beliefs drew Cromwell into arguments with some of his fellow officers. After Marston Moor he became more outspoken in criticising the Scots for their intolerance. After the Second Battle of Newbury, he became highly critical of his commanding officer, the Earl of Manchester.

7 In the crisis which led to the Self-Denying Ordinance and the New Model Army, Cromwell showed that he had lost the political naivety of his Long Parliament days. His exemption from the Ordinance forms one of the most controversial aspects of his career.

8 When the war ended in 1646, Cromwell anticipated a settlement in which the King returned to power under conditions that would safeguard Parliament's privileges.

9 The failure of the search for such a settlement forced Cromwell to make uncomfortable choices. His actions between 1647 and 1649 have been the subject of much argument and are open to widely differing interpretations.

10 The Second Civil War forced Cromwell to confront the issue of resistance to authority – not only the King's authority, but Parliament's. Convinced of the justice of the Army's case, Cromwell accepted Pride's Purge as providential. Thereafter he helped to bring the King to trial and execution.

10

Cromwell and the Commonwealth, 1649–53: was Cromwell ambitious?

CHAPTER OVERVIEW   *The wrath of Cromwell*

On 20 April 1653 Cromwell made his way to the House of Commons and sat down to listen to a debate. Dressed in plain black clothes with a large grey felt hat, he listened in silence while the MPs discussed a bill for new elections. When the Speaker was about to put the bill to the vote, Cromwell turned to Colonel Harrison and said, 'This is the time. I must do it.' Taking off his enormous hat, he got to his feet and began speaking. Quietly at first, he commended the good work of the Long Parliament and the Rump. Then the tone of his speech changed to anger. Pacing the floor of the House, he berated the MPs for their failure to fulfil the nation's expectations of reform. With mounting rage, he accused the Rump of corruption and of placing personal interests before those of the nation.

One or two MPs protested at Cromwell's tirade. They merely succeeded in provoking him to further outrage.

'It is not fit that you should sit here any longer!' Cromwell shouted. 'You have sat too long here for any good you have been doing lately. You shall now give place to better men.' With that he turned to Colonel Harrison and said, 'Call them in!'

To the astonishment of the MPs, the doors opened and 30 musketeers with loaded guns marched into the chamber.

'You call yourselves a Parliament,' Cromwell continued. 'You are no Parliament; I say you are no Parliament! Some of you are drunkards, some of you are whore-masters, living in open contempt of God's Commandments, following your own greedy appetites, and the Devil's Commandments. Corrupt unjust persons, scandalous to the profession of the Gospel: how can you be a Parliament for God's People? Depart, I say, and let us have done with you. In the name of God, go!'

Most of the MPs went. As they filed out, Cromwell approached the mace, the ancient symbol of the Commons' authority. 'What shall we do with this bauble?' he asked. Then to a soldier he said, 'Take it away.'

The Speaker lingered in his chair. 'Fetch him down,' Cromwell said to Harrison, who guided the Speaker off the dais and out of the chamber. 'It's you that have forced me to this,' he said as the remaining MPs left. 'I have sought the Lord night and day, that He would rather slay me than put me upon the doing of this work.'

As Cromwell left the House, he scooped up the bill for new elections in his hand and walked off with it. The door of the House was locked, and the bill was never seen again.

SOURCE 10.1 Cromwell expelling the Rump Parliament – a contemporary Dutch picture

A. *General Olivier Cromwel.* B. *Maior Lambert.* C. *Capiten Cuyper.* D. *Ceron Strickland.* E. *Worstley.* F. *Herison.* G. *Orator in Parlement.*

DISCUSS

Look at Source 10.1. The artist who drew this was not an eyewitness to the event. Does the picture show Cromwell in a critical or a positive light?

Cromwell's expulsion of the Rump Parliament was one of the most important events of the English Revolution. He never escaped the accusation that he had taken control of the nation by force. Perhaps he was a Caesar after all, tearing up the English constitution in the ruthless pursuit of personal power.

Yet, as always with Cromwell, there is another way to see this event. The expulsion of the Rump may not have been a deeply-laid plot, but a decision taken reluctantly when he felt that there was no other choice. Cromwell may have acted not from personal ambition, but from a sense of duty. Perhaps if he had felt that England were in safe hands, then Cromwell, like Cincinnatus, would have retired from public life.

SOURCE 10.2 The statue of Oliver Cromwell by Sir William Thorneycroft, outside the Palace of Westminster. This statue was paid for in 1899 by Lord Rosebery, the former Liberal Prime Minister, who had failed to persuade Parliament to allow it to stand inside the palace along with other Parliamentary heroes. Cromwell's statue was 'locked out' of Parliament, just as he locked out the Rump in 1653. Ironically, because most people never see inside Westminster, it gives the impression that Parliament owes its liberties to Cromwell

■ 10A Timeline of Cromwell and the Commonwealth, 1649–53

1649	
January	Trial and execution of King Charles I
February	Act abolishing the monarchy
	Act abolishing the House of Lords
	Leveller leaders arrested
March	Parliament asks Cromwell to lead the expedition to Ireland
April	Digger communities established in Surrey
	Sale of estates formerly owned by the Crown and by cathedral Dean and Chapters begins
May	Act declaring England a republic
	Cromwell suppresses Leveller mutiny at Burford
August	Cromwell's Irish campaign begins
September	Parliament orders censorship of the press
	Massacre at Drogheda
October	Massacre at Wexford

1650	
January	Oath of Engagement to the English Republic instituted
April	Cromwell returns from Ireland
June	Cromwell appointed to lead the army against Scotland
September	Battle of Dunbar
	Compulsory church attendance abolished by Parliament

1651	
July	Parliament passes an Act for the sale of lands of leading Royalists
September	Battle of Worcester
	Charles Stuart escapes to France
October	Navigation Act

1652	
May	First Anglo-Dutch War begins
September	Admiral Blake victorious in the English Channel
November	Dutch victory over the English fleet off Dungeness

1653	
February	Anglo-Dutch naval battle off Portland
April	Cromwell expels the Rump Parliament
	New Council of State appointed
July	Nominated Assembly meets for the first time
August	Nominated Assembly votes to abolish the Court of Chancery
	Civil marriages legalised
November	Nominated Assembly votes to abolish tithes and lay patronage of church livings (advowsons)
December	Nominated Assembly resigns its power to Cromwell
	Instrument of Government
	Oliver Cromwell installed as Lord Protector

FOCUS ROUTE

Continue to make notes on 'Cromwell's controversies' started in the introduction to Section 3 on page 200.

FOCUS ROUTE

Did the Commonwealth face insurmountable problems or was it coping reasonably well when Cromwell destroyed it? This is an important question, which came back to haunt Cromwell in the parliaments of the Protectorate later in the 1650s. Make notes on:
• the problems facing the Commonwealth in 1649
• the political divisions among the revolutionaries of 1649
• the reasons why the Rump Parliament failed to satisfy the Army's expectations by 1653.

The Commonwealth period from 1649 to 1653 saw the new English Republic struggling to protect itself from its enemies both at home and abroad. In Ireland and Scotland, Cromwell's armies dealt with the most immediate threats to the new regime. In England, the government strove to reassure the nation that the revolutionary events of 1648 and 1649 did not threaten the very fabric of English society. Yet in 1653 it was Cromwell himself who overthrew the Rump Parliament. This chapter explores the tensions that undermined the Commonwealth almost from the start, and the reasons behind Cromwell's decision to use force against Parliament.

A How fragile was the Commonwealth? (pp. 222–23)

B 'England's New Chains Discovered'? (pp. 224–25)

C The Irish campaign (pp. 226–27)

D The Scottish campaign: Cromwell's greatest triumph? (pp. 228–31)

E Why did Cromwell expel the Rump Parliament? (pp. 232–35)

F The Nominated Assembly: Cromwell's greatest folly? (pp. 235–37)

G Review: Cromwell and the Commonwealth, 1649–53 (pp. 238–39)

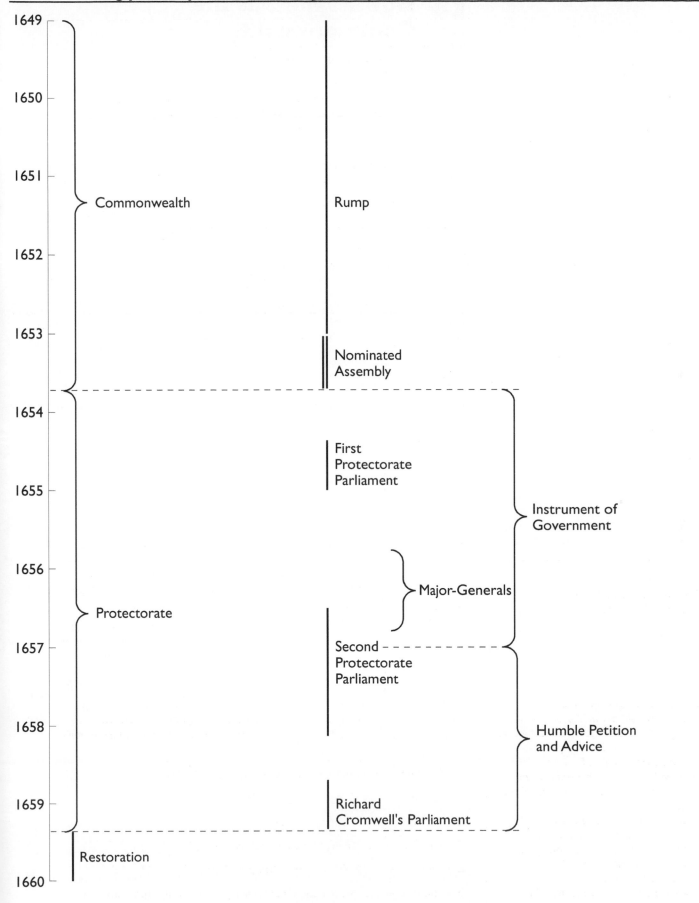

1649

1650

1651 — Commonwealth — Rump

1652

1653 — Nominated Assembly

1654 — First Protectorate Parliament

1655 — Instrument of Government

1656 — Major-Generals

Protectorate

1657 — Second Protectorate Parliament

1658 — Humble Petition and Advice

1659 — Richard Cromwell's Parliament

Restoration

1660

A How fragile was the Commonwealth?

■ 10C Threats facing the Commonwealth

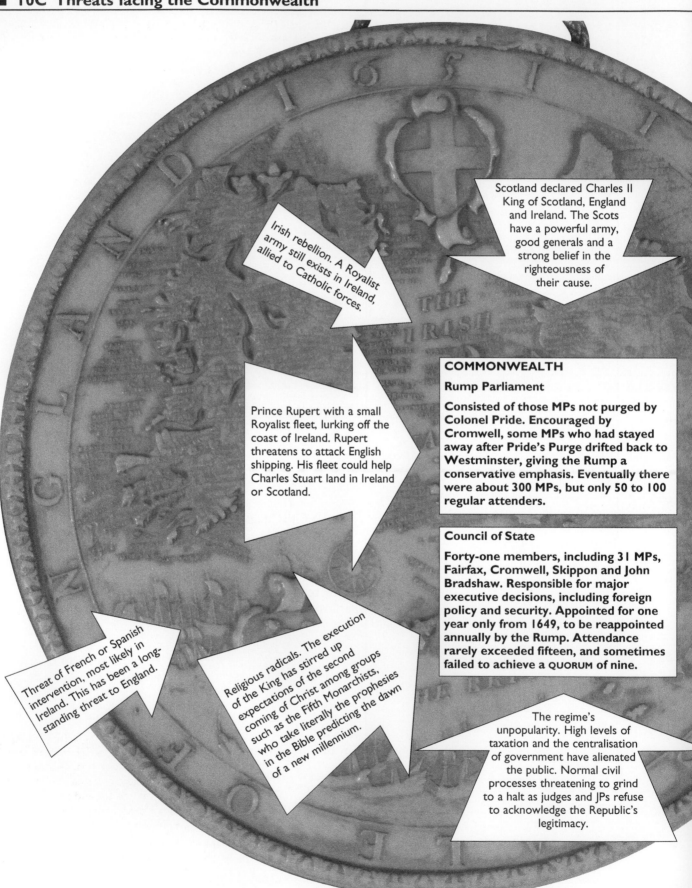

Scotland declared Charles II King of Scotland, England and Ireland. The Scots have a powerful army, good generals and a strong belief in the righteousness of their cause.

Irish rebellion. A Royalist army still exists in Ireland, allied to Catholic forces.

Prince Rupert with a small Royalist fleet, lurking off the coast of Ireland. Rupert threatens to attack English shipping. His fleet could help Charles Stuart land in Ireland or Scotland.

COMMONWEALTH

Rump Parliament

Consisted of those MPs not purged by Colonel Pride. Encouraged by Cromwell, some MPs who had stayed away after Pride's Purge drifted back to Westminster, giving the Rump a conservative emphasis. Eventually there were about 300 MPs, but only 50 to 100 regular attenders.

Council of State

Forty-one members, including 31 MPs, Fairfax, Cromwell, Skippon and John Bradshaw. Responsible for major executive decisions, including foreign policy and security. Appointed for one year only from 1649, to be reappointed annually by the Rump. Attendance rarely exceeded fifteen, and sometimes failed to achieve a QUORUM of nine.

Threat of French or Spanish intervention, most likely in Ireland. This has been a long-standing threat to England.

Religious radicals. The execution of the King has stirred up expectations of the second coming of Christ among groups such as the Fifth Monarchists, who take literally the prophesies in the Bible predicting the dawn of a new millennium.

The regime's unpopularity. High levels of taxation and the centralisation of government have alienated the public. Normal civil processes threatening to grind to a halt as judges and JPs refuse to acknowledge the Republic's legitimacy.

Universal condemnation of the regicide. Not one foreign state has recognised the Commonwealth's legitimacy.

The Levellers. Political radicals demanding further constitutional changes. The Levellers have a loyal following within the Army, which has presented *An Agreement of the People* to the Rump as a possible basis for a political settlement.

Threat of a naval war with the Dutch over trade.

Royalist uprisings fuelled by sentiment over the King's death.

ACTIVITY

Prioritising the threats to the Commonwealth

Complete a copy of the following table, filling each row with your own comments about the nature and seriousness of the threats posed to the Commonwealth.

Threat	How likely is this threat to develop into something serious?	How serious a threat will this be if it does develop?	Is this threat likely to join with other threats?	Order of priority: in which order (1–9) should the Commonwealth deal with these threats?
Prince Rupert				
Scotland's declaration that Charles Stuart is King of Great Britain				
Naval war with the Dutch				
The Levellers				
Religious radicals				
Threat of foreign intervention by France or Spain				
Irish Rebellion				
Royalist forces of reaction				
Unpopularity of the new regime				

QUORUM
The minimum attendance needed to give legitimacy to the decisions taken by the Council of State.

DISCUSS

1 Were the greatest threats to the Commonwealth internal or external?
2 Why were internal and external threats closely connected?
3 What did the Commonwealth have in its favour?
4 How likely was the Commonwealth to survive these threats?

FOCUS ROUTE: WHO'S WHO?

Make brief notes on Gerard Winstanley to include in your Who's who? list.

B 'England's New Chains Discovered'?

The main threat to the regime's security came from within England. The Republic was pulled in two directions. Radical groups expected further reform, but a growing number of MPs and Army officers were recoiling from further revolution.

Cromwell was the physical embodiment of the contradictions inherent in the Commonwealth. Early in 1649 he tried to persuade former friends and allies, who had deserted him over the King's execution, to support the new regime. Yet Cromwell was committed to further radical reform, especially liberty of conscience and toleration for Protestant sects – the very issues that alienated conservative opinion.

■ 10D Revolution or reaction? Cromwell was delicately balanced between the two

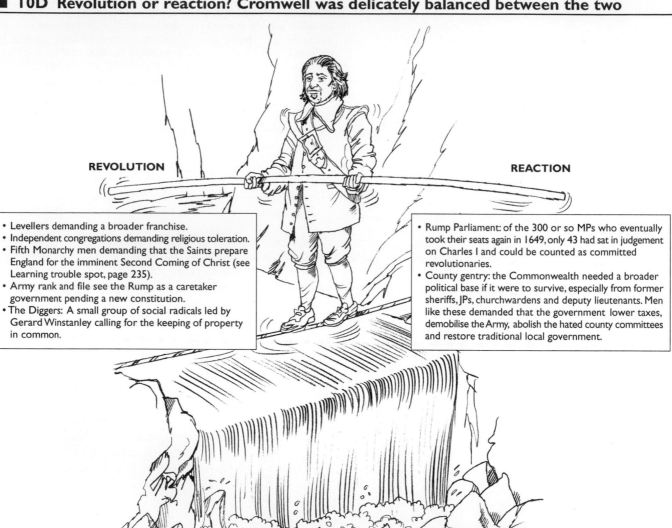

REVOLUTION

REACTION

- Levellers demanding a broader franchise.
- Independent congregations demanding religious toleration.
- Fifth Monarchy men demanding that the Saints prepare England for the imminent Second Coming of Christ (see Learning trouble spot, page 235).
- Army rank and file see the Rump as a caretaker government pending a new constitution.
- The Diggers: A small group of social radicals led by Gerard Winstanley calling for the keeping of property in common.

- Rump Parliament: of the 300 or so MPs who eventually took their seats again in 1649, only 43 had sat in judgement on Charles I and could be counted as committed revolutionaries.
- County gentry: the Commonwealth needed a broader political base if it were to survive, especially from former sheriffs, JPs, churchwardens and deputy lieutenants. Men like these demanded that the government lower taxes, demobilise the Army, abolish the hated county committees and restore traditional local government.

FOCUS ROUTE

Study Source 10.3 and the text that follows. You may also want to return to page 180 in Chapter 8 to consider Cromwell's role in the Putney Debates of 1647. When you have studied this material, record the case for and against Cromwell and his role in bringing the Leveller movement to heel. (See the Focus Route on page 200.) Which case do you find more convincing?

■ Learning trouble spot

The Levellers and the Army

Leveller influence among the Army rank and file was never easy to judge. There were certainly Levellers in the Army, but there were also Levellers among the apprentices of London. Not all the soldiers were Levellers, but many of them had grievances that had been taken up in Leveller pamphlets.

DEAN AND CHAPTERS
Chapters were cathedral councils. The Dean was the head of the Chapter.

Cromwell's controversies: the suppression of the Levellers

Did Cromwell betray the Levellers? In early 1649, when the Rump cracked down on petitioning and agitation within the Army, a series of Leveller pamphlets accused Cromwell of betraying the revolution.

SOURCE 10.3 Cromwell speaking to the Council of State about the Levellers, as recorded by John Lilburne, a leading Leveller, who was listening at the door

Lt. General Cromwell (I am sure of it) very loud, thumping his fist upon the Council table, till it rang again, and heard him speak in these very words or to this effect . . . Sir, let me tell you that which is true, if you do not break them, they will break you; yea, and bring all the guilt of the blood and treasure shed and spent in this kingdom upon your heads and shoulders, and frustrate and make void all that work that . . . you have done . . . to be broken and routed by such a despicable, contemptible generation of men.

The Council of Officers and the Rump needed the Levellers' help during the trial and execution of the King. The Levellers were the only group with a coherent revolutionary programme, a draft constitution, and an ideology that looked beyond the overthrow of Old Testament tyrants to natural law and human rights. The King's death exposed the fragility of this political alliance.

The core of the problem was public opinion. Gauging the nation's mood was far from easy. The Levellers claimed to know what the nation wanted, but the Rump could not follow them any further down the road of popular sovereignty. Offering the vote to all male householders who contributed to poor relief was not an option for a Parliament that needed support from the gentry. To dissolve Parliament and hold new elections was too risky. The Levellers would accept nothing less.

In 'England's New Chains Discovered', Lilburne accused the Army of returning England to slavery. A number of Leveller leaders, including Lilburne, Overton, Prince and Walwyn, were arrested on a charge of sedition (encouraging people to rebel). One by one they were hauled before the Army Council and examined. Their arrest provoked a minor mutiny in one of the Army's cavalry regiments. One of the troopers, Roger Lockyer, was sentenced to death. Cromwell tried to spare him, but was overruled by Fairfax; an example had to be made. Over 4000 people followed Lockyer's coffin through the streets of London.

As in 1647, the prospect of service in Ireland provoked further discontent amongst the Army rank and file. In May a larger mutiny broke out in some of the regiments. Cromwell and Fairfax caught up with the mutineers at Burford in Oxfordshire. They were arrested and imprisoned overnight in Burford church. The following day three of the ringleaders were shot in the churchyard. The rest were promised arrears of pay (back-pay) and pardoned. A small Leveller uprising in Oxfordshire was also suppressed and its leader, William Thompson, killed in a shoot-out in the woods.

Lilburne's arrest was embarrassing for Cromwell. Lilburne was a popular hero who had once idolised Cromwell. His arrest added a touch of personal betrayal to the political argument: however, Cromwell had never made any promises to the Levellers. To his mind, it was vital to preserve what had already been achieved by building support among the traditional governing classes. It was necessary to establish command and control over the rank and file as the Army faced imminent campaigns across the British Isles.

The mutinies reminded the Rump that the Army had to be paid. Further taxes, however, would drive away much needed support. The government needed a windfall. It found one in the sale of Crown lands: since the monarchy had been abolished, the Crown's assets were up for grabs. In June Parliament allocated Crown lands to individual regiments to sell off and pay themselves from the proceeds. The sale of DEAN AND CHAPTER lands supplemented their income, and taxes raised from specific counties were also allocated to certain regiments. Paying the Army was becoming part of the English constitution!

C The Irish campaign

On 23 March 1649, Cromwell spoke to the General Council of the Common-wealth. The Rump's Council of State was offering him command of the army it was planning to send to Ireland. Before he accepted, he wanted to clarify his position. He began by saying that he was acting not from personal ambition, but out of consideration for the expedition's importance. The Irish Rebellion had been running unchecked for eight years, threatening to uproot the English interest in Ireland. Mindful of the Army's previous refusal to serve in Ireland under commanders it did not trust, Cromwell felt it his duty to lead his soldiers in the new campaign.

Behind Cromwell's words was a concern that lay at the heart of the civil war crisis. England's weakness in the 1630s had destabilised the British Isles. Unless the Commonwealth acted decisively to stamp its authority on the Celtic kingdoms (Ireland, Wales, Scotland), the cycle of war and rebellion was set to continue indefinitely.

Ireland was the Commonwealth's priority. This was the likeliest route for an attempted back-door invasion of England. The atrocities that had swept Ireland in 1641 (see Chapter 4) also played a part: England expected these to be avenged. A successful campaign might help rally support for the Commonwealth. Everything pointed to the need for a quick, decisive victory in Ireland.

SOURCE 10.4 Cromwell speaking to the General Council at Whitehall, 23 March 1649, on being asked to accept command of Parliament's army in Ireland

I had rather be over-run with a Cavalierish interest than a Scotch interest; I had rather be over-run with a Scotch interest than an Irish interest; and I think of all, this is the most dangerous, and if they shall be able to carry on this work they will make this the most miserable people in the earth. For all the world knows their barbarism.

ACTIVITY

Looking at Ireland from the Commonwealth's viewpoint, brainstorm a cost-benefit analysis of the Irish campaign. Consider the possible benefits of the campaign for England. Set against this the likely financial cost of the campaign, and the possibility that other dangers might become more pressing in the next year.

■ Learning trouble spot

Ireland in the 1640s

Ireland in the 1640s can be compared to a highly unstable geological formation, with 'fault lines' dividing the main parties. A series of political earthquakes causes these fault lines to shift, creating an ever-changing spectrum of parties and alliances. In Chart 10E, the horizontal lines show the fault lines between parties; the vertical lines represent the political earthquakes that cause the faults to shift.

Throughout the decade two major issues are competing with each other to dominate the political scene. The first is religion. In 1640 the main problem in Ireland is the Catholic/Protestant divide. The Irish Rebellion in 1641 polarises opinions, hardening religious attitudes and squeezing the Old English Catholics and Anglicans, who are now torn between their loyalty to England and their religious faith (A). In 1642 the Civil War in England introduces the second major issue of King versus Parliament, splitting the English Protestants into two parties (B).

The King's Lord Lieutenant in Ireland, the Earl of Ormond, succeeds in forming an alliance between the English Protestant Royalists and the Catholic Confederacy (C). The situation is further complicated by the existence in Ulster of a native Irish Catholic force under Owen Roe O'Neill (D), and a Presbyterian Scottish army under Colonel Monroe (E). In 1643 the Scots and Parliamentarians form an alliance (F). In 1645 the Pope's envoy, Rinuccini, tries to convert the conflict into a straightforward war of religion. All he succeeds in doing is to drive a wedge between O'Neill and the Catholic Confederacy (G).

Whenever Catholic victories threaten to unleash further massacres of English Protestants, Royalist officers are likely to throw in their lot with Parliament. However, the Second Civil War drives a wedge between the Scots and the Parliamentarians (H). The King's execution converts a number of Parliamentarians – including Inchiquin - into Royalists (I). Cromwell's campaign of 1649–50 brings the war to an end by establishing an English Protestant ascendancy across the island (J).

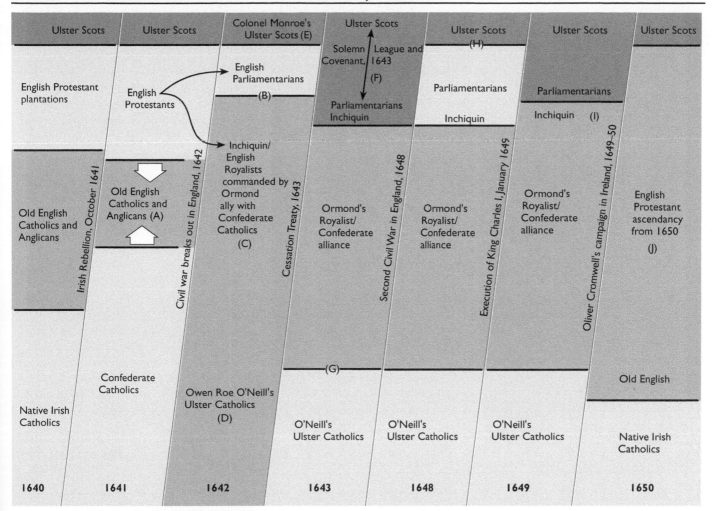

The following is a timeline diagram spanning 1640 to 1650 showing shifting alliances during the Irish Rebellion:

1640	1641	1642	1643	1648	1649	1650
Ulster Scots	Ulster Scots	Colonel Monroe's Ulster Scots (E)	Ulster Scots	Ulster Scots (H)	Ulster Scots	Ulster Scots
English Protestant plantations	English Protestants	English Parliamentarians (B)	Solemn League and Covenant, 1643 (F)	Parliamentarians	Parliamentarians	
			Parliamentarians Inchiquin	Inchiquin	Inchiquin (I)	
Old English Catholics and Anglicans	Old English Catholics and Anglicans (A)	Inchiquin/English Royalists commanded by Ormond ally with Confederate Catholics (C)	Ormond's Royalist/Confederate alliance	Ormond's Royalist/Confederate alliance	Ormond's Royalist/Confederate alliance	English Protestant ascendancy from 1650 (J)
	Confederate Catholics	Owen Roe O'Neill's Ulster Catholics (D)	(G)			Old English
Native Irish Catholics			O'Neill's Ulster Catholics	O'Neill's Ulster Catholics	O'Neill's Ulster Catholics	Native Irish Catholics

Timeline markers: Irish Rebellion, October 1641; Civil war breaks out in England, 1642; Cessation Treaty, 1643; Second Civil War in England, 1648; Execution of King Charles I, January 1649; Oliver Cromwell's campaign in Ireland, 1649–50.

FOCUS ROUTE: WHO'S WHO?

Make brief notes on the Earl of Ormond to include in your Who's who? list.

SOURCE 10.5 Cromwell's report to Parliament after the taking of Wexford

And indeed it hath not without cause been deeply set upon our hearts, that we intended better to this place than so great a ruin, ... yet God would not have it so; but, by an unexpected providence, in his righteous justice, brought a just judgement upon them, causing them to become a prey to the soldier, who in their piracies had made preys of so many families, and made with their blood to answer the cruelties which they had exercised upon the lives of divers poor Protestants.

DISCUSS

Study Source 10.5.
1 What was the driving force behind Cromwell's anger towards his enemies during the Irish campaign?
2 To what extent was Cromwell's view of Ireland's recent history an oversimplification?

The key to victory was finance. Cromwell demanded that the Army be properly funded and his soldiers paid. He made thorough logistical preparations. On his arrival in Ireland he issued an order that there should be no plundering by his troops, which he enforced by executing two soldiers for theft. He also issued a declaration denying that the campaign was motivated by the financial interests of the City of London.

Cromwell's strategy involved hitting the rebels hard in the opening sieges of the campaign, to terrorise other enemy garrisons into submission and so bring the war to a rapid conclusion. This he accomplished at the siege of Drogheda, but in circumstances that led to accusations of indiscriminate slaughter (see the introduction to Section 4, page 243).

Drogheda was swiftly followed by another bloody incident at Wexford, where nearly 2000 Irish soldiers were killed. Cromwell spent ten days trying to negotiate terms for the town's surrender. While negotiations were in progress, an enemy officer surrendered Wexford castle without the knowledge of the town's garrison, which found itself being stormed unexpectedly. In the scramble to escape, a number of civilians died when their overcrowded boats sank as they tried to cross the estuary. Cromwell had tried to avoid great loss of life at Wexford, but when events there spiralled out of control he interpreted it as another act of God.

Within nine months Cromwell's army had broken the back of resistance in Ireland. The campaign was not without its problems, however. Dysentery affected most of the army, at times reducing the effective force to one-fifth its original size. Stubborn resistance was encountered at Clonmel, where 2000 of Cromwell's men were killed, and at Waterford. Nevertheless, by April 1650 Cromwell felt secure enough to return to England to face the challenge of war with Scotland.

D   The Scottish campaign: Cromwell's greatest triumph?

Why did Cromwell invade Scotland?

By the time Cromwell returned from Ireland to a hero's welcome, Parliament faced war with Scotland. The Scots had declared Charles Stuart, eldest son of Charles I, King not only of Scotland but of Britain. Charles Stuart was prepared to go to any lengths to win their support:

- He denounced his parents' religious beliefs.
- He betrayed Montrose by ordering him to disband his forces.
- He disowned Ormond's treaty with the Catholic Confederates in Ireland.
- He signed the National Covenant, committing himself to a Presbyterian settlement.

With the King at their head, the Scots prepared to invade England for the third time in eleven years.

The Rump decided to launch a pre-emptive strike, but Fairfax refused to make war against his old allies. After failing to persuade him of the justice and necessity of the war, Cromwell accepted his command, thereby becoming Lord General – supreme commander of the Army of the Commonwealth. One month after returning from Ireland he embarked on a new campaign to settle the British problem once and for all.

Scotland was a tougher proposition than Ireland, both militarily and emotionally. These were not the Duke of Hamilton's Scots who had invaded England in 1648, but their opponents – England's former allies. Their commander was David Leslie, who had fought alongside Cromwell at Marston Moor. The Scottish army was disciplined, large and well equipped. The Scots were utterly convinced of their righteousness, and they would be defending their country against an invading army.

Cromwell made extensive use of propaganda throughout the campaign. He viewed the Scots, unlike the Irish, as 'people of the Book', fellow godly Christians who might be helped to see the error of their ways. It was painful for godly Englishmen to fight against Scottish Presbyterians, but it might be equally painful for the Scots to fight English Puritans. Then again it might not: the Scots were remarkably confident in their own righteousness.

Things started to go wrong for Cromwell from the start. Leslie employed a scorched earth policy, destroying everything that might be of use to the English while falling back towards his own supplies at Edinburgh and Leith. Cromwell had arranged to be supplied by sea, but this strategy forced him to hug the coastline and failed to deliver adequate supplies. In appalling weather, Cromwell's army was depleted by sickness. After trying unsuccessfully to bring Leslie to battle, Cromwell retreated to Dunbar. Leslie seized his opportunity and cut off the English line of retreat. Expecting a major defeat, Cromwell began evacuating his sick and wounded by sea and warned Sir Arthur Haselrig at Newcastle to prepare to defend England against a Scottish invasion.

The Battle of Dunbar

Leslie's position appeared impregnable. The Scots outnumbered the English by two to one, with 22,000 men to Cromwell's 11,000. They were deployed on high ground overlooking Dunbar, their front protected by the natural entrenchment of Spott Burn. From this position they could observe all the movements of Cromwell's forces, though Leslie moved his army forward off the highest slopes to bring Dunbar within range of his artillery and began to bombard Cromwell's army. Late in the afternoon of 2 September, Cromwell and his senior officers rode forward to reconnoitre the enemy position. They concluded that the Scottish army could be attacked successfully.

> **FOCUS ROUTE: WHO'S WHO?**
>
> Make brief notes on David Leslie to include in your Who's who? list.

SOURCE 10.6 The Battle of Dunbar, 3 September 1650

Key
A Dunbar
B English camp
C Spott Burn
D English dragoons
E Cromwell's cavalry
F English infantry
G Scottish baggage train
H Scottish infantry
I Scottish soldiers fleeing from the battle

The Battle of Dunbar was Cromwell's tactical masterpiece. Cromwell saw that Leslie had failed to secure the half-mile gap between his right flank and the sea. The gap was too narrow to try to slip past the Scots to safety – but under cover of darkness there was enough room to aggressively outflank Leslie's army. While the Scots slept, Cromwell worked through the night to manoeuvre his forces into position. When the Army attacked before dawn it achieved total surprise and local superiority, both unheard of in seventeenth-century warfare. Disorientated and unprepared, the Scottish army disintegrated as one regiment after another panicked and ran. That night Cromwell was seen laughing hysterically.

ACTIVITY

To understand the significance of Dunbar to Cromwell, we need to pass the facts of the battle through the prism of Cromwell's mind. Study Sources 10.7–10.9 and answer the questions that follow on page 230.

SOURCE 10.7 Facts of the Battle of Dunbar

	The Scots	**The English**
Size of the armies at the start of the battle	22,000	11,000
Prisoners captured	10,000	None
Weapons captured	15,000, including 30 artillery pieces	None
Casualties (killed)	3,000	20 (Cromwell's estimate)
Cromwell's battle cry – quoted from the Book of Psalms	*Now let God arise, and his enemies shall be scattered.*	

SOURCE 10.8 Book of Judges 7: 15–21 (adapted from the King James Bible). This tells of Gideon's miraculous victory for the people of Israel over the vastly superior army of the Midianites

Gideon returned into the host of Israel, and said, Arise; for the Lord hath delivered into your hands the host of Midian . . . So Gideon, and the hundred men that were with him, came unto the outside of the [enemies'] camp in the beginning of the middle watch [i.e. in the middle of the night] . . . and they blew the trumpets . . . and they cried, The sword of the Lord, and of Gideon. And they stood every man in his place round about the camp: and all the host ran, and cried, and fled.

SOURCE 10.9 Extract from Cromwell's official report to Parliament, 4 September 1650

Thus you have the prospect of one of the most signal mercies God hath done for England and His people, this War: and now may it please you to give me the leave of a few words. It is easy to say, The Lord hath done this. It would do you good to see and hear our poor foot to go up and down making their boast of God. But, Sir, it's in your hands, and by these eminent mercies God puts it more into your hands, To give glory to Him . . . We that serve you beg of you not to own us, but God alone. We pray you own His people more and more; for they are the chariots and horsemen of Israel. Disown yourselves, but own your Authority; and improve it to curb the proud and the insolent. Relieve the oppressed, hear the groans of poor prisoners in England. Be pleased to reform the abuses of all professions – and if there be any one that makes many poor to make a few rich, that suits not a Commonwealth.

ACTIVITY

1 What evidence is there that Cromwell genuinely believed God was present with him during the Battle of Dunbar?
2 What was the purpose of Cromwell's report to Parliament (Source 10.9)? In what sense was his report a warning to the Rump?
3 Ireland and Scotland were both Celtic kingdoms that had contributed to the coming of civil war in England. How do you account for the differences in the way Cromwell treated them in 1650 and 1651?

The 'crowning mercy' – the Battle of Worcester

For six months after Dunbar there was little fighting. Leslie retreated beyond Edinburgh to Stirling where, with the Highlands at his back, he continued raising troops and avoided giving battle. Cromwell occupied Edinburgh but held back from the risks of a major winter campaign; he became dangerously ill and was incapable of taking the field.

The strategic problem was how to lure Leslie out of his stronghold to give battle. In July an English victory at Inverkeithing opened the way to an invasion of Fife. Cromwell moved his army north of Stirling and occupied Perth, cutting Leslie off from his supplies. This manoeuvre left an open door for the Scots to invade England, and gave them little choice but to do so. Charles Stuart hoped that his appearance at the head of a Scottish army would encourage a Royalist uprising in England, so the decision was made to march on London. The invasion is sometimes called the 'Third Civil War' for this reason but, unlike in 1648, there was no Royalist uprising in England.

The speed with which Cromwell's army moved to intercept the Scots suggests that Cromwell had anticipated the invasion and may even have wanted it: a pitched battle in the heart of England was preferable to a campaign of manoeuvre in the Highlands. Cromwell caught up with Charles's army at Worcester where, in a complex battle lasting over five hours, the Scottish/Royalist army was destroyed.

Worcester was Cromwell's last battle. In his despatch to Parliament, he referred to Worcester as 'a crowning mercy', one that should inspire Parliament 'to do the will of Him who hath done His will for it' – a warning to the Rump to get on with the job of reform.

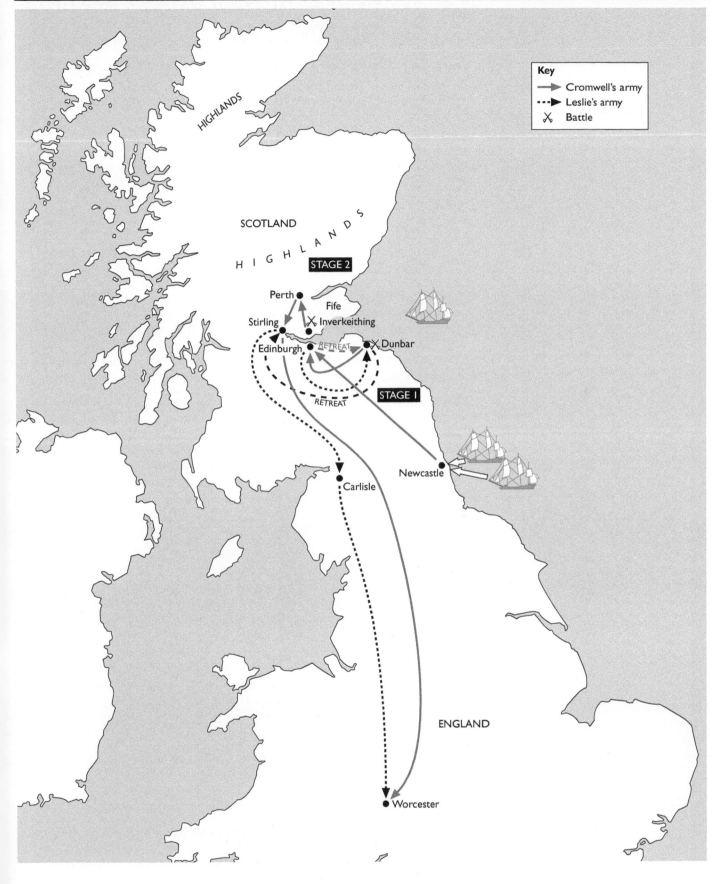

Key
→ Cromwell's army
---▶ Leslie's army
✗ Battle

HIGHLANDS

SCOTLAND

HIGHLANDS

HIGHLANDS

STAGE 2

Perth

Fife

Stirling

✗ Inverkeithing

Edinburgh

RETREAT

✗ Dunbar

STAGE 1

RETREAT

Newcastle

Carlisle

ENGLAND

Worcester

FOCUS ROUTE

Why did Cromwell expel the Rump in March 1653? Make notes on why the Army ran out of patience with the Rump. Note in particular the controversy surrounding the events that triggered Cromwell's 'dissolution', and the disappearance of the crucial piece of evidence that might explain why he decided to dissolve the Rump.

E Why did Cromwell expel the Rump Parliament?

Why did the Army lose patience with the Rump?

SOURCE 10.10 John Dury speaking to Hermann Mylius, envoy of a small German principality, 27 September 1651

Things will shortly happen which have been unheard of, and above all would open the eyes of those who live under Kings and other Sovereigns, and lead to great changes. Cromwell alone holds the direction of political and military affairs in his hands. He is one who is worth all the others put together, and, in effect, King.

By 1652 Cromwell's personal importance was enhanced by three developments.

1 His victories against the Irish and the Scots confirmed him as the greatest general of his time.
2 The resignation of Fairfax in 1650 and the death of Ireton in 1651 strengthened Cromwell's authority within the Army.
3 In the course of his campaigns, Cromwell gained a unique insight into the opinions, beliefs, interests and fears of all three kingdoms. By 1653 Cromwell had more direct knowledge of the British Isles than any monarch had ever had.

Cromwell was disturbed by the Rump's lack of progress. After the battles of Dunbar and Worcester, he urged the Rump to do more to fulfil the nation's expectations of reform, and his letters briefly stung the Rump into action. Their efforts were always short-lived however, the problems they faced seemed insurmountable, and their conservatism meant that sweeping social and political change was never really likely. To make matters worse, by mid-1652 England was at war with the Dutch.

THE COUNCIL OF OFFICERS' DEMANDS

In August 1652 the Council of Officers issued a list of demands that included the following:

• Replacement of unworthy parish ministers
• Abolition of tithes
• Legal reform
• Purge of corrupt officials
• Provision for war widows, orphans, wounded soldiers and the poor
• Reform of the tax system. Abolition of the hated excise tax
• New elections that would ensure that only decent men would sit in Parliament.

THE ANGLO-DUTCH WAR

England and the United Provinces went to war in 1652. The war was mainly over commercial rivalry and a growing number of incidents on the high seas. The Dutch claimed exclusive rights to fishing in the North Sea, while England demanded recognition of its sovereignty in the English Channel. The Dutch also resented the new English Navigation Act, which threatened Dutch trade.

This was a naval war between the English and Dutch fleets. Both sides had some initial success, but under Admiral Blake's command the Commonwealth's investment in new warships turned the war in England's favour. By 1653 both sides were looking for a way out, but England's political problems led to a diplomatic paralysis until the beginning of 1654. One of Cromwell's first tasks as Lord Protector was to negotiate an end to the war.

The Army, too, was running out of patience with the Rump. The cost of England's military establishment forced the Rump to maintain high taxes, crippling its popularity. The Rump was unpopular anyway, but the Army didn't seem to understand that new elections could return a Parliament hostile to the Commonwealth.

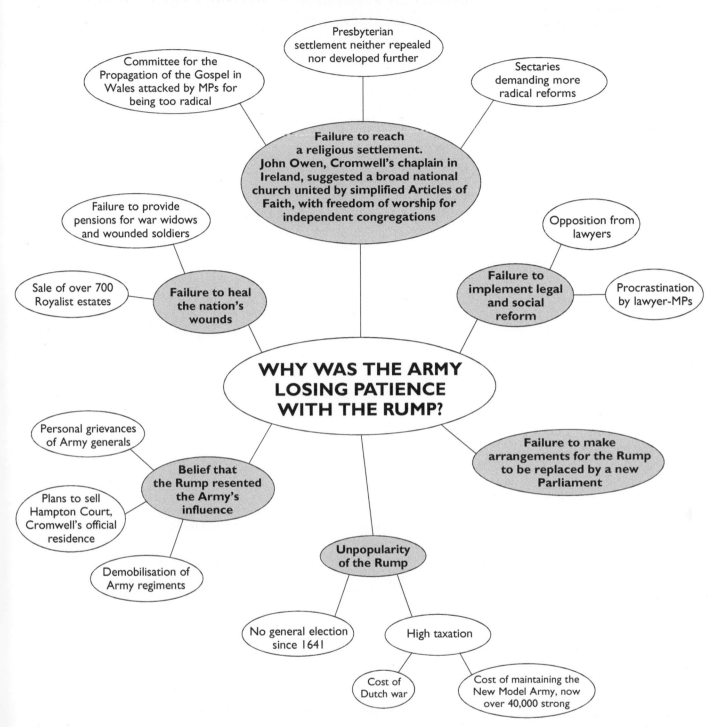

FOCUS ROUTE: WHO'S WHO?

Make brief notes on John Owen to include in your Who's who? list.

What had the Rump achieved?

- An Oath of Engagement, 1650, required every man to swear allegiance to the Commonwealth, but failed to promote genuine loyalty.
- The Act of Oblivion, 1651, aimed to reconcile former Royalists to the Commonwealth, but there were so many exceptions that it failed to achieve this.
- Minor legal reforms: abolished the use of Latin and stylised handwriting; abolished legal privileges of Members of Parliament; transferred from church to common-law courts the power to grant probate of wills.
- Victories in Ireland and Scotland, but the Army took the credit for this.

FOCUS ROUTE: WHO'S WHO?

Make brief notes on Bulstrode Whitelocke to include in your Who's who? list.

FOCUS ROUTE

Return to the Focus Route on page 200. Add notes on Cromwell's conversation with Bulstrode Whitelocke. Did Cromwell really want to be king, or was he thinking out loud about the advantages to the nation of a return to more familiar political relations?

ACTIVITY

Study Source 10.11.

1 Interrogate the source using a source matrix (see page 61).
2 What does the source tell us about Cromwell's thinking at this time?
3 Why is this an important source for the interpretation of Cromwell's motives and actions?
4 Why does this source need to be used with caution?

Cromwell's controversies: his conversation with Bulstrode Whitelocke, December 1652

The conversation between Cromwell and Whitelocke has sometimes been used as evidence that Cromwell wanted to be king. Source 10.11 is the only evidence in existence that the conversation took place.

SOURCE 10.11 Bulstrode Whitelocke's account of a conversation he had with Cromwell in December 1652 in St James's Park (from Whitelocke's *Memorials*, published in 1682)

> *[Cromwell and Whitelocke discuss the Rump's failings and the problem of how to deal with them.]*
>
> Cromwell: *What if a man should take upon him to be king?*
> Whitelocke: *I think that remedy would be worse than the disease.*
> Cromwell: *Why do you think so?*
> Whitelocke: *As to your own person the title of king would be of no advantage, because you have the full kingly power in you already . . .*
> Cromwell: *[But] surely the power of a king is so great and high, and so universally understood and reverenced by the people of this nation, that the title of it might not only indemnify, in a great measure, those that act under it, but likewise be of great use and advantage in such times as these . . .*
> *[Cromwell then asks Whitelocke for his advice.]*
> Whitelocke: *Pardon me, Sir, in the next place, a little to consider the condition of the King of Scots [Charles Stuart]. By a private treaty with him you may secure yourself, and your friends and their fortunes; you may make yourself and your posterity as great and permanent . . . as ever any subject was, and provide for your friends. You may put such limits to monarchical power, as will secure our spiritual and civil liberties, and you may secure the cause in which we are all engaged . . .*

Cromwell's controversies: the case of the missing bill April 1653

On 20 April 1653 Cromwell expelled the Rump in scenes described at the beginning of this chapter. The trigger was a bill that the Rump was debating for a new Parliament. Since Cromwell had been urging the Rump for months to do this, it is strange that he chose this moment to use force to shut it down.

The mystery is deepened by the fact that the crucial piece of evidence – the bill itself – was carried off by Cromwell and never seen again. Was there something in the bill that Cromwell wanted to hide? Since the bill no longer exists, we cannot examine it for clues, but we may be able to draw some conclusions from the context in which the Rump was expelled.

■ 10H Key facts about the missing bill

1 For several weeks before 20 April, Cromwell stayed away from Parliament. He had done this sort of thing before – just before Pride's Purge, for example.

2 On 19 April, Cromwell held a meeting with Oliver St John and a group of MPs. The Army wanted the Rump to dissolve itself and hand over power to a group of officers and MPs – a provisional government – to arrange fresh elections and call a new Parliament. At the end of the meeting, Cromwell thought he had the MPs' agreement to suspend discussions of the bill until this idea could be considered.

3 The following morning, Cromwell was taken by surprise by the news that the Rump was trying to rush the bill through before the Army could stop it. He raced to the House of Commons in his casual clothes, listened until the motion for the bill was about to be put to the vote, called in the soldiers and expelled the MPs.

SOURCE 10.12 Notice found nailed to the door of the House of Commons after the Rump's expulsion

> This House
> is to be let,
> now unfurnished

DISCUSS

On 3 May 1653 Cromwell published a letter denying that his use of military force against the Rump had destroyed the people's liberty. He explained that Parliament's power 'is only suspended; 'tis a sword taken out of a mad man's hand, till he recover his senses'.
How was Cromwell's explanation similar to/different from Charles I's explanation of his decision to rule without Parliament in 1629? (You may wish to refer back to Chapter 1.)

SOURCE 10.13 Extract from Cromwell's speech at the opening session of the Nominated Assembly

I confess I never looked to see such a day as this – it may be nor you neither – when Jesus Christ should be so owned as He is, at this day, and in this work ... I say, you are called with a high call. And why should we be afraid to say or think, that this may be the door to usher in the things that God has promised; which hath been prophesied of; which He hath set the hearts of His people to wait for and expect? ... Indeed I do think something is at the door; we are at the threshold.

FOCUS ROUTE: WHO'S WHO?

Make brief notes on Colonel Harrison to include in your Who's who? list.

JEWISH SANHEDRIN
The supreme council of the Jews in ancient Israel. The Sanhedrin had jurisdiction over Jewish religious, civil and criminal law. It was made up of 71 'sages'.

FOCUS ROUTE

Until the 1970s most historians assumed that the bill provided not for a general election, but for by-elections to fill the vacancies left by Pride's Purge. This would explain Cromwell's anger – the Rump MPs would still be there, refusing to give up their seats. Most historians now agree that the bill did provide for a general election, but that the outgoing Rump MPs would judge the suitability of the incoming MPs and exclude any they thought unsuitable.

Cromwell's opponents claimed that Cromwell, like Caesar, wanted supreme power for himself. He didn't want a new Parliament with a fresh mandate, and he was sick and tired of the old one: either way the Rump was doomed.

Three recent interpretations of the facts outlined in Chart 10H are summarised below. Decide which one you think fits in best with the key facts. Then enter your findings in the notes you are making for use in Cromwell's trial at the end of Section 3.

1   The disappearance of the bill isn't particularly important. It is the context of Cromwell's exasperation with the Rump that matters – its endless procrastination, and its failure to 'own' God's cause. (J.C. Davis)
2   Cromwell was driven by feelings of guilt and a desire to regain God's blessing. New elections would have strengthened the political power of civilian republicans who did not share Cromwell's vision of moral and religious reformation. The bill was of no significance to him, and was lost or destroyed. (Barry Coward)
3   The MPs had probably introduced a bill that would have allowed the core of revolutionaries of 1649 to retain their seats. When Cromwell said he wanted a provisional government to take over, they changed their minds and tried to rush through a bill for a general election. Cromwell thought they were trying to pull a fast one and closed them down. When he got home and read the bill he discovered he had been mistaken, but it was too late. Neither he nor the Rump MPs wanted people to know what had happened, so the bill was quietly lost. (Austin Woolrych)

F   The Nominated Assembly: Cromwell's greatest folly?

If Parliament couldn't be safely elected, it would have to be chosen. Two days after expelling the Rump, Cromwell and his officers declared their intention 'to call to the government persons of approved fidelity and honesty'. Over the next fortnight they selected 140 members, including six each for Ireland and Scotland. Cromwell himself avoided taking his seat in the Assembly because he was sensitive to the charge of military intervention in civilian affairs. Cromwell opened the new Assembly with a long, emotional speech in which he reflected on the 'string of providences' which had led to this moment and urged the members to live up to the nations' – and God's – expectations.

■ **Learning trouble spot**

The Barebones Parliament
The Nominated Assembly is also known commonly as the Barebones Parliament, after one of its members, Praise-God Barebones, a Fifth Monarchist. The Fifth Monarchists believed there had been four great monarchies – Babylon, Persia, Greece and Rome and the Papacy – and that the Fifth Monarchy would be the thousand-year reign of King Jesus. Colonel Harrison, a close friend of Cromwell and a Fifth Monarchist, had suggested that England be governed by 70 hand-picked 'Saints' in imitation of the JEWISH SANHEDRIN. Cromwell may have adopted his idea, but gave the group a much broader social and political base. He never referred to the Nominated Assembly as a parliament, seeing it as an interim government only. The notion persisted that the members had been chosen by churches and congregations, when in fact they were chosen by the Council of Officers.

'A pack of weak, senseless fellows'?

Until recently historians tended to accept the image of 'Barebone's Parliament' drawn by its enemies, who portrayed it as a group of religious zealots. Edward Hyde, the Earl of Clarendon, described them as 'a pack of weak, senseless fellows, inferior persons, of no quality or name, known only by their gifts in praying and preaching'. Recent research on the composition of the Nominated Assembly has revealed the following facts about its members.

- At least four-fifths considered themselves members of the gentry.
- They included two peers, four baronets and four knights. Three members went on to become earls, including Anthony Ashley Cooper, later Earl of Shaftesbury, who played a major part in Charles II's reign.
- Eighteen had sat in the Rump Parliament.
- Nearly half would go on to sit in parliaments of the Protectorate.
- Of the 128 members for England and Wales, 117 were Justices of the Peace, 89 of whom had been JPs before the revolution.
- Twenty-eight served as county sheriffs.
- At least 44 had been to university and the Inns of Court.
- Only thirteen were Fifth Monarchists.

DISCUSS

What do you think of Hyde's comments in the light of these facts?

Why did the Nominated Assembly fail?

At first the Assembly seemed likely to fulfil Cromwell's hopes. Its attendance record was exemplary: whereas the Rump had seldom sat for more than twelve hours a week, the Assembly sat six days a week, starting at 8 a.m. The Assembly directly addressed the reforms the Rump had avoided, including poor relief, legal reform, tithes, religion, prisons and corruption. During its five-month existence it passed more than 30 statutes. The Assembly members, now calling themselves a Parliament, obviously intended to avoid the mistakes made by the Rump.

This sense of purpose did not last long. A rift soon opened between moderates and radicals, whose influence was greater than their numbers warranted. In the autumn of 1653, disillusioned moderates began boycotting the Assembly, while radical preachers stirred up expectations of millenarian change that frightened those of moderate opinion. The Nominated Assembly was torn between the radical and the conservative origins of the revolution (see Chart 10I). So was Cromwell, but in the end he felt forced to intervene on the side of moderation.

■ 10I Political divisions in the Nominated Assembly

Issues	Radicals	Moderates
Religion	• No national church • Congregations to support their own ministers • Abolish tithes	• National church leading by example • Toleration for independent congregations • Tithes to be supplemented by the state to iron out regional variations
Law reform	• Fifth Monarchists believed only in those laws found in the Bible, e.g. the law of Moses, the teachings of Christ • Common law seen as non-scriptural • Other radicals saw existing law as the product of the 'Norman yoke', and wanted to replace it with a simple code enforced by elected magistrates • Abolish the Court of Chancery (the court of equity, where the decisions of other courts could be overturned)	• Follow the lead of the Hale Commission, which recommended a range of reforms including: • abolishing imprisonment for debt • making the law more accessible in each county • civil marriages • reform of the Court of Chancery • Preserve common law • Modernise archaic procedures, e.g. open public access to the law by making it cheaper, more easily understood • Make the law more humane, e.g. abolish capital punishment for relatively minor offences

Foreign policy forced Cromwell's hand. For months the Dutch had been trying to negotiate an end to the Anglo-Dutch War. Now the Nominated Assembly, with no experience of foreign policy and no time to give it serious thought, was paralysed by indecision. France, Spain and Portugal were making overtures to the English government, but the Assembly couldn't speak for England as long as Cromwell and the Army refused to wield executive power. The ship of state needed a hand at the tiller.

Events came to a head in early December. For weeks General Lambert had been working on a written constitution that would make Cromwell the chief executive. Cromwell refused to use military force against the nation's representatives for the second time in six months. On 10 December the Assembly narrowly defeated a moderate religious proposal to retain tithes and advowsons (see Chapter 2, page 54). The threat to property triggered a political *coup d'état*: on 12 December the moderates assembled early. With the radicals absent at a prayer meeting, they voted to abdicate power and hand it back to Cromwell. In this way Cromwell was able to accept power through the *coup*, while plausibly denying knowledge of it. Four days later he was installed as Lord Protector under a written constitution called the Instrument of Government.

FOCUS ROUTE: WHO'S WHO?

Make brief notes on Richard Baxter to include in your Who's who? list.

SOURCE 10.14 Cromwell, speaking to his Second Protectorate Parliament, looks back on the Nominated Assembly, 21 April 1657

Truly I will now come and tell you a story of my own weakness and folly . . .

It was thought that men of our own judgement, who had fought in the Wars, and were all of a piece upon that account; it was thought, 'Why surely these men will hit it, and these men will do it to the purpose, whatever can be desired!' And truly we did think, and I did think so, – the more blame to me. And such a Company of Men were chosen; and did proceed to action. And truly this was the naked truth, that the issue was not answerable to the simplicity and honesty of the design.

[If the Assembly had continued any longer] the issue of that Meeting would have been the subversion of your laws and of all the liberties of this nation, the destruction of the ministers of this nation: in a word, the confusion of all things . . .

SOURCE 10.15 Adapted from *Reliquiae Baxterianae*, the autobiography of Richard Baxter, a Presbyterian minister, 1696

The young commonwealth being already headless, you might think that nothing was left to stand between Cromwell and the crown; for a governor there must be, and who should be thought fitter? But there was yet another pageant to be played, which had a double purpose; firstly, to make the need for his government undeniable, and secondly, to make his own soldiers at last fall out of love with democracy. A Parliament must be called, but the ungodly people are not to be trusted with the choice. Therefore the soldiers, as more religious, must be the choosers, and two of each county are chosen by the officers upon the advice of their sectarian friends in the country. This was called, in contempt, The Little Parliament.

Afterwards in the Little Sectarian parliament, it was put to the vote whether all the parish ministers of England should be removed or not. It was accidentally rejected by two votes; and now Cromwell must be their saviour, or they must perish. So it was put to the vote whether the House was incapable of serving the Commonwealth and should go and deliver up their power to Cromwell, from whom they had received it; and they carried it in the affirmative, and away they go, and solemnly resign their power to him. And now, who should rule but Cromwell and his army?

ACTIVITY

Study Sources 10.13, 10.14 and 10.15.

1 What evidence can you find to suggest that Cromwell may have been affected by the Fifth Monarchists' millenarian belief that the Second Coming of Christ was imminent?
2 Why did Cromwell have great expectations that the Nominated Assembly would perform great things?
3 Why did the Assembly fail to live up to Cromwell's expectations?

FOCUS ROUTE

Cromwell's controversies: his installation as Lord Protector
Did Cromwell really hope that the Nominated Assembly would solve England's political problems? Or, as Richard Baxter suggested in Source 10.15, did he simply go through the motions of assembling the Barebones Parliament and allow it to fail in order to justify his seizure of power as Lord Protector?

Look back over Section F on the Nominated Assembly. Then return to the Focus Route on page 200 and record the case for and against Cromwell. Which case do you find more convincing?

G Review: Cromwell and the Commonwealth, 1649–53

The closure of the Nominated Assembly ended the republican experiment that began with Pride's Purge. With hindsight, it seems obvious that the Commonwealth could not have worked: there were too many contradictions built into it from the start, too much tension between the Army and Parliament. We should guard against the temptation to assume that its failure was inevitable, just as we should guard against the temptation to see the Commonwealth as nothing more than an episode before Cromwell took power. Cromwell didn't behave as if he thought the Commonwealth was doomed from the start.

The establishment of the Protectorate is sometimes seen as the beginning of the long road back towards monarchy, the moment when the conservative reaction against the revolution of 1649 set in. This interpretation has been challenged, particularly the idea that the men who closed the Nominated Assembly were conservatives shocked by the radicalism of the 'Saints'. It is more likely that the Assembly was shut down because its chaotic proceedings threatened to bring the cause of radical reform into disrepute. Before we can make a judgement about reactionary politics, we need to look at the Protectorate's record and, in particular, at Cromwell's use of power as Lord Protector. This is the subject of Chapter 11.

The underlying problem was the same one that had existed since 1646. Parliament's victory had been achieved by creating a new kind of state, one in which centralised institutions had usurped (taken over) the traditional easy-going inefficiency of English local government. The New Model Army was sustained by the high taxation that this made possible, and consequently England was able to defeat its enemies in Ireland, in Scotland and on the high seas. But the country yearned for the system to be dismantled, and any regime that owed its existence to the Army's favour was bound to be unpopular. The only justification for such a revolution as England had experienced was that it could usher in a new era of reformation and prosperity, to show that the English Civil War had a meaning and a purpose – that it wasn't simply some ghastly accident. It was now up to Cromwell to show that this was true.

FOCUS ROUTE

Complete the table of Cromwell's controversies you began in the introduction to Section 3 (page 200). You will need this information for the trial of Cromwell that forms the focus of the Section 3 review.

ACTIVITY

Why did the Commonwealth fail?
A number of reasons are suggested in the diagram below.

1 Working back through Chapter 10, find evidence that supports each of the points on the diagram and add it to your own copy of the diagram.
2 Which factors do you think were the most important?

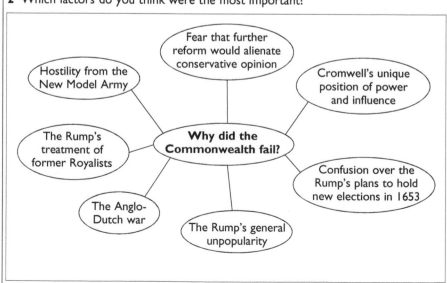

1 In 1649 the Commonwealth had good reason to feel threatened on all sides. It relied on the Army, commanded by Cromwell, to defeat its enemies in Ireland and Scotland, and created a navy to tackle the challenge of the Dutch. Cromwell's prestige was so greatly enhanced that no government could operate without his support.

2 Cromwell embodied the different forces at work in the English Revolution. He was a complex character, torn between his instinctive desire to return to traditional forms of government and his belief that the Civil War had a meaning and a purpose. Above all, this meant godly reformation.

3 The Commonwealth was similarly torn between the desire for stability and the need for change. In time, it became paralysed by its inability to reconcile these different forces.

4 The Rump's failure to deliver godly reformation alienated Cromwell and the Army.

5 By 1654 Cromwell had made enemies of three groups of people, all of whom accused him of betraying the revolution:

• the Levellers, especially his old friend John Lilburne, whom he suppressed in 1649

• republicans such as his old colleague Sir Arthur Haselrig, who accused him of behaving like a military dictator by expelling the Rump

• religious radicals such as his old friend Colonel Harrison, who regarded him as an apostate (someone who has defected from a previously held faith) after the closure of the Nominated Assembly.

6 In December 1653 Cromwell accepted the position of Lord Protector under a written constitution called the Instrument of Government.

Section 3 Review: Oliver Cromwell – Caesar or Cincinnatus?

How different might the history of England have been if one of the millions of bullets fired in the Civil War had hit Cromwell and killed him? His rise to power raises important historical questions. How important is the contribution of the individual to great events? To what extent is a man like Cromwell either the maker or the product of the times in which he lives? Are 'great men' necessarily driven by personal ambition to rise to positions of power?

ACTIVITY

The trial of Oliver Cromwell

This will take the form of a class debate. The charge against Cromwell is that he was driven by personal ambition to take power. Choose two pairs of people. One pair's task is to act as the prosecution, to argue that Cromwell was like Caesar, a ruthless man driven by personal ambition. The other pair is to act as his defence team, arguing that Cromwell was like Cincinnatus, a man who wanted to retire from public life and go home. Ask a member of staff to act as judge and jury; if the speakers have to convince someone from outside the class, they will make a better job of it. Both teams should build their case using their notes on 'Cromwell's controversies'.

The debate should proceed as follows.

1 Starting with the prosecution, the first speaker from each pair should speak, in turn, for no more than ten minutes to present their case. Use PowerPoint to focus attention on each controversy and the main points of your argument.
2 The second speaker from each pair should speak for no more than five minutes to respond to the points made by the opposing pair. They may also introduce new points to support their case.
3 The debate is then thrown open to the class, which may ask questions of both the prosecution and the defence teams. This is open-ended – take as much time as you need.
4 Starting with the prosecution, the first speaker from each pair should speak, in turn, for no more than three minutes to summarise their case.
5 Let the external judge decide which side has won the argument, and explain why.

Evidence of witnesses

You can call witnesses to support your case. Sources 1–4 could be studied by members of the class, who should then present their arguments in their own words. Other class members could use the *Oxford Dictionary of National Biography* and other reference tools to research the following individuals and present their evidence:

For the prosecution	For the defence
Earl of Manchester	Oliver St John
John Lilburne	Henry Ireton
Denzil Holles	Cornet Joyce

SOURCE 1   Richard Baxter, *Reliquiae Baxterianae*, 1696

If I may speak my opinion of Cromwell, I think that, having been a prodigal in his youth, and afterwards changed to a zealous religiousness, he meant honestly in the main course of his life till prosperity and success corrupted him. Hereupon Cromwell's general religious zeal giveth way to the power of that ambition which still increaseth as his successes do increase: Both piety and ambition concurred in his countenancing of all that he thought Godly, of what sect soever; piety pleadeth for them as Godly, and Charity as men; and ambition secretly telleth him what use he might make of them. He meaneth well in all this at the beginning, and thinketh he doth all for the safety of the Godly, and the public good, but not without an eye to himself. When success had broken down all considerable opposition, he was then in the face of his strongest temptations, which conquered him when he had conquered others.

SOURCE 2   Edward Hyde, Earl of Clarendon, *History of the Rebellion and Civil Wars in England*, 1702

Without doubt, no man with more wickedness ever attempted any thing, or brought to pass what he desired more wickedly, more in the face and contempt of religion, and moral honesty; yet wickedness as great as his could never have accomplished those trophies, without the assistance of a great spirit, an admirable circumspection and sagacity, and a most magnanimous resolution. In a word, as he had all the wickedness against which damnation is denounced, and for which hell-fire is prepared, so he had some virtues which have caused the memory of some men in all ages to be celebrated; and he will be looked upon by posterity as a brave bad man.

SOURCE 3   C.H. Firth, *Oliver Cromwell and the Rule of the Puritans in England*, 1900

Cromwell believed in 'dispensations' rather than 'revelations'. Since all things which happened in the world were determined by God's will, the statesman's problem was to discover the hidden purpose which underlay events. With Cromwell, in every political crisis this attempt to interpret the meaning of events was part of the mental process which preceded action. As it was difficult to be sure what that meaning was, he was often slow to make up his mind, preferring to watch events a little longer and to allow them to develop in order to get more light. This slowness was not the result of indecision, but a deliberate suspension of judgement. When his mind was made up there was no hesitation, no looking back; he struck with the same energy in politics as in war.

SOURCE 4   R.S. Paul, *The Lord Protector*, 1955

Cromwell became a 'dictator', but it was not from choice. Events had their own way of pushing him to the fore and ultimately to the head of affairs, and the very circumstances of his rise prevented that popular recognition which would have set the seal to his mission. Nevertheless, although only a person 'mistaken and greatly mistaken' would imagine that he consciously schemed for the position which he came to occupy, when the chance of taking the government presented itself he took it firmly.

Oliver Cromwell – a distant mirror

Cromwell's career was so complex that, over the centuries, many people have used his life to illustrate their views about English history. Not all have been professional historians: Cromwell has long been the subject of popular and oral traditions. Negative or positive views have tended to dominate, but never has there been complete agreement about the meaning of Cromwell's career.

This is the nature of history. In the late nineteenth century, historians committed themselves to the search for objective truth. Before then, it was accepted that history was a form of political philosophy. Even when objectivity became the guiding principle of historical study, it was never possible for historians to detach themselves fully from their own time and approach the past on its own terms. Throughout the twentieth century, historians continued to allow their own experiences and beliefs to influence the way they saw Cromwell. This gives history meaning and relevance. A figure such as Cromwell is like a distant mirror, reflecting our own time.

We are not immune from this process. Until recently the troubles in Northern Ireland made us deplore sectarian violence. How could people kill each other over religious beliefs? The religious conflicts of the seventeenth century appeared hopelessly bigoted and old-fashioned. Then came the terrorist attacks on New York and Washington on 11 September 2001, and the past snapped back into focus. Wasn't the Gunpowder Plot of 1605 similar to 9/11? Suddenly the fears of seventeenth-century English Protestants made more sense: to them, Catholics were the potential 'al-Qa'ida' terrorists of their day. History is like a kaleidoscope: as the wheel of history turns, it reorganises familiar material until we look at it differently. This process has greatly affected the interpretation of Oliver Cromwell over the centuries.

FOCUS ROUTE

You are writing a book about English history. You want to use Cromwell's life to illustrate some key developments. These ideas are listed below.

Divide the class into two groups. At the end of Chapter 11, each group will present evidence drawn from Cromwell's life. One group is going to praise Cromwell for his contribution to these aspects of English history. The other group is going to criticise him for his contribution to these same aspects – either because the aspects themselves were undesirable, or because he worked against their achievement.

• The growth of the British Empire
• England's political stability
• The growth of religious toleration
• The union of England, Scotland and Ireland in the United Kingdom
• The way Parliament changed to make it more representative
• The defence of property rights
• The ability of the English to compromise in the interests of peace
• The survival of the monarchy
• The importance of English sea-power
• The growth of democracy
• English nationalism
• The development of Parliament
• England's traditional reluctance to have a large standing army.

Compare and discuss your findings.

The storm of Drogheda

To illustrate how and why interpretations can change over time, study the example of Drogheda. No single event has produced more criticism of Cromwell than his attack on the Irish fortified town of Drogheda on 10–11 September 1649. In Ireland, the storming of Drogheda is still seen as the story of a massacre of innocent Irish civilians, men, women and children. A massacre certainly took place at Drogheda, but did Cromwell order his army to put the whole town to the sword? Drogheda challenges our ability to look dispassionately upon the past.

Did Cromwell violate the unwritten rules of seventeenth-century siege warfare? Or did he, to the best of his ability, spare the lives of innocent civilians? He was certainly sensitive to the accusation that he had encouraged his army to massacre soldiers and civilians in Irish towns, but even in refuting the accusation he revealed much of his underlying attitude towards Ireland, as Source 1 shows.

SOURCE I Extract from Cromwell's 'Declaration to the Irish Catholic Clergy', December 1649

Good now: give us an instance of one man since my coming into Ireland, not in arms, massacred, destroyed or banished; concerning the massacre or destruction of whom justice hath not been done, or endeavoured to be done. You, unprovoked, put the English to the most unheard of and most barbarous massacre (without respect of sex or age) that ever the sun beheld. You are a part of Antichrist, whose Kingdom the Scriptures so expressly speaks should be laid in blood. We are come to ask an account of the innocent blood that hath been shed; and to endeavour to bring to an account all who, by appearing in arms, seek to justify the same. We come to break the power of a company of lawless Rebels, who having cast off the authority of England, live as enemies to Human Society. We come, by the assistance of God, to hold forth and maintain the lustre and glory of English Liberty in a nation where we have an undoubted right to do it.

■ **Learning trouble spot**

The unwritten rules of seventeenth-century sieges

Sieges played a very large part in seventeenth-century warfare. European wars in the Early Modern period produced several spectacular examples of cities put to the sack – at Magdeberg in 1631, 70,000 civilians were massacred – but in England the massacre of civilians was unusual. Armies generally observed an unwritten code that went something like this: when an army laid siege to a town, the attackers called upon the defenders to surrender. If the town was defensible, the defenders rejected the summons and a siege followed. At some point in the siege, a breach would be made in the walls. The attackers would once again summon the town to surrender. If this summons was rejected, the attacking army might storm the town with no further offer of quarter (mercy) to the defenders.

■ A The storm of Drogheda (Read this chart wih the Activity on page 246.)

SOURCE 12 R. Hutton, *The British Republic, 1649–1660*, 1990, p. 47

But what actually happened? Oliver's instructions were quite specific: to strike terror into other garrisons, he forbade his men 'to spare any that were in arms' within Drogheda. This meant Ormond's soldiers (a lot of whom were English, not Irish) and those of the citizens who were assisting the defence. By the Cromwellians' own account, the latter were quite numerous. But nobody at the time claimed that a single woman or child died, and most of the male population, being unarmed, also survived.

Recent accounts of the Irish campaign

SOURCE 10 Thomas Carlyle, *Oliver Cromwell's Letters and Speeches*, 1849. Carlyle's edited book of Cromwell's letters and speeches was central to the nineteenth-century discovery of Cromwell as a Liberal English hero

Such was the storm of Drogheda. Cromwell, not in a light or loose manner, but in a very solemn and deep one, takes charge for himself, at his own peril, that it is a Judgement of God: and that it did 'save much effusion of blood', we can very readily testify. In fact, it cut through the heart of the Irish War. Wexford Storm followed in the same stern fashion; and there was no other storm or slaughter needed in that country.

Nineteenth-century historians

SOURCE 7 Edward Hyde, Earl of Clarendon, *History of the Rebellion and Civil Wars in England*, 1702

A panic fear possessed the soldiers that they threw down their arms, upon a general offer of quarter; so that the enemy entered the works without resistance, and put every man, governor, officer and soldier to the sword; and the whole army being entered the town they executed all manner of cruelty and put every man that related to the garrison, and all the citizens who were Irish, to the sword.

Memoirs written in the years following 1649, mostly published after the Restoration, when it was fashionable – and politically expedient – to portray Cromwell in the worst possible light

SOURCE 5 The first unofficial account of the battle to reach London, written anonymously by a supposed eyewitness, 14 September 1649

On Wednesday 12th September 1649 the Lord Lieutenant [Cromwell] stormed the garrison of Drogheda where he found much opposition, yet through the glorious power of God (which was wonderfully seen there) they made entry into the town near the Mount by the Church where they found resistance, quarter was offered but it would not be accepted of, so they were forced to fight their way into the town which they did with great resolution and courage and killed of the enemy near three thousand . . . putting all to the sword that were in the streets and in the posture of soldiers. But many that they found in houses and in a quiet and orderly posture they gave quarter to.

News broadsheets published within a couple of months of the storming of Drogheda, some carrying eyewitness accounts of the action

SOURCE 2 Cromwell, writing to the Speaker of the House of Commons

Divers of the Enemy retreated into the Mill-Mount: a place very strong and of difficult access; being exceedingly high, having a good graft, and strongly palisadoed. The Governor, Sir Arthur Ashton, and divers considerable Officers being there, our men getting up to them, were ordered by me to put them all to the sword. And indeed, being in the heat of action, I forbade them to spare any that were in arms in the Town: and, I think, that night they put to the sword about 2,000 men; – divers of the officers and soldiers being fled over the bridge into the other part of the town, where about 100 of them possessed St. Peter's Church-steeple, some the west gate, and others a strong round tower next the gate called St. Sunday's. These being summoned to yield to mercy, refused. Whereupon I ordered the steeple of St. Peter's Church to be fired, when one of them was heard to say in the midst of the flames: 'God damn me, God confound me; I burn, I burn.' I am persuaded that this is a righteous judgement of God upon these barbarous wretches, who have imbrued their hands in so much innocent blood; and that it will tend to prevent the effusion of blood for the future.

Official correspondence from the time of the battle

SOURCE 13 G. Brockie and R. Walsh, *Focus on the Past*, 1990 – a school history textbook used in Ireland

Once the Irish were defeated they were all cut down and killed and no mercy was shown to man, woman or child for twenty-four hours. Not a dozen escaped out of Drogheda, townspeople or soldiers.

SOURCE 14 P. Gaunt, *Oliver Cromwell*, 1996, p. 116

The events at Drogheda have become notorious, divide opinions and arouse intense emotions. It is clear that the order to give no quarter, largely obeyed, came from Cromwell himself . . . and that although the majority of deaths occurred in the heat of battle, some killings continued in a cold, calculated way for a further day or two. It is clear, too, that the scale and nature of the bloodletting were very different from Cromwell's usual practice and from the civil war norm.

SOURCE 11 John Morley, *Oliver Cromwell*, 1900, p. 290

That Cromwell's ruthless severity may have been justified by the strict letter of the military law of the time, is just possible. Though he may have had a technical right to give no quarter where a storm had followed the refusal to surrender, in England this right was only used by him once in the whole course of the war, and in his own defence of the massacre it was not upon military right that he chose to stand. The general question, how far in such a case the end warrants the means, is a question of military and Christian ethics which it is not for us to discuss here, but we may remind the reader that not a few of the most barbarous enormities in human annals have been excused on the same ground. [Cromwell] must have known that of the three thousand men who were butchered at Drogheda not a single victim was likely to have had a part or lot in the Ulster atrocities of 1641.

SOURCE 8 Anthony Wood, in an account published in 1663, describes the stories told by his brother Thomas Wood to his family. Thomas Wood was a soldier in Cromwell's army

He told them that 3,000 at least, besides some women and children were . . . put to the sword. He told them that when they were to make their way up to the lofts and galleries in the church and up to the tower where the enemy had fled, each of the assailants would take up a child and use it as a buckler of defence, when they ascended the steps, to keep themselves from being shot or brained.

SOURCE 9 An anonymous officer in Sir John Clotworthy's regiment

But [the Irish] being overpowered, were all hewed down in their ranks and no quarter given for twenty-four hours to man, woman and child, so that not a dozen escaped out of the town of townspeople or soldiers.

SOURCE 6 Colonel John Hewson, an officer in Cromwell's army and an eyewitness to the battle

The rest fled over the bridge, where they were closely pursued, and most of them slain. Some got into the towers on the wall and some into the steeple, but they, refusing to come down, the steeple was fired; and fifty of them got out at the top of the church, but the enraged soldiers put them all to the sword and thirty of them were burned in the fire, some of them cursing and crying out, 'God damn them' and cursed their souls as they were burning. Those in the towers, being about 200, did yield to the General's mercy, where most of them have their lives and be sent to the Barbadoes. In this slaughter there was by my observation, at least 3,000 dead bodies lay in the fort and the streets . . .

SOURCE 3 The Earl of Ormond, commander of the Confederate/Royalist alliance, describes the battle to Lord Inchiquin shortly afterwards

The cruelties expressed in Drogheda for five days after the town was taken would make as many pictures of inhumanity as are to be found in the BOOK OF MARTYRS *or in the relation of* AMBOYNA.

SOURCE 4 Lord Inchiquin's account of the battle. Inchiquin was a former Parliamentarian who had joined the Royalists after the King's execution

Many men and some officers have made their escape out of Drogheda. All conclude that no quarter was given there with Cromwell's leave but many were privately saved by officers and soldiers; the governor was killed after quarter was given by the officer that first came there, that some of the towers were defended until yesterday, quarter being denied them, and that yesterday morning the towers within were blown up. That [several Confederate officers] were alive in the hands of some of Cromwell's officers twenty-four hours after the business was done, but whether their lives were obtained [taken] at Cromwell's hands or that they are yet living, they cannot tell.

BOOK OF MARTYRS	AMBOYNA
John Foxe's Book of Martyrs, an account of the lives of Protestants who died for their religion.	An infamous massacre of English settlers by the Dutch in the East Indies in 1623.

ACTIVITY

1 Photocopy Chart A, pages 244–45, and cut out the sources so that they can be arranged individually.
2 Arrange the sources into four groups:

• those written during or immediately after the actual campaign
• those written in the later seventeenth century
• those written in the nineteenth century
• those written in the late twentieth century.

3 Now rearrange the sources into two groups:

• those which accuse Cromwell of encouraging/allowing an indiscriminate massacre of unarmed men, women and children
• those which either do not mention such a massacre or deny that one took place.

4 What do you notice about the sources that either deny that an indiscriminate massacre took place or do not mention one?
5 What have you learned from this activity about
a) the storm of Drogheda
b) the nature of history?

Section 4 focuses on the Cromwellian Protectorate and on Cromwell's reputation as Britain's head of state. As you work through Chapter 11, you will be making notes on how successfully he and his Council governed Britain. Talking Points will draw your attention to issues relevant to the larger question of how the decisions made by the Protectorate contributed to the historical debate on Cromwell's character.

How successful was Cromwell's Protectorate?

CHAPTER OVERVIEW

In December 1653, Cromwell was sworn in as Lord Protector of Britain and Ireland. The ceremony contrasted starkly with the investiture of a king: Cromwell wore plain black clothes as befitted a man who had once struggled to maintain himself as a gentleman farmer. For the next five years the British Isles were governed by men who had little or no training in national government, though plenty of experience of civil war. How well did they do?

This chapter focuses on the record of the Protectorate from 1653 to 1658, when Cromwell died. Sources 11.1 and 11.2 are assessments of Cromwell's Protectorate written by modern historians.

SOURCE 11.1   J.C. Davis, *Oliver Cromwell*, 2001

[Charles I] helped to engender a revolutionary situation in which moderate men could only struggle to make an ordered and stable society out of the wreckage. This was Cromwell's tragedy. His greatness is that he did so much more than cling on to the debris. By 1657 he had gone a long way towards finding a stable civilian basis for the regime, a basis not altogether removed from the principles he and others had fought for in the 1640s. But time was running out and the settlement was never to be consolidated. It was a settlement far less radical than those who have aspired to an English Revolution, then and since, would have wished. Nor could it ever possess the hereditary legitimacy of those sympathetic to the fate of the 'martyr' King or sticklers for the untarnished rule of law. But it was admirable none the less.

SOURCE 11.2   B. Coward, 'Your Highness, Cromwell', in *BBC History Magazine*, 2003

How well did Cromwell and the Protectorate Council of State cope? Given their inexperience, the answer must be that they did a fairly good job. [The Protectorate] was a regime that had visionary ideals. The Protectorate was not a stereotypical Saddam Hussein-type military dictatorship, run by men who were determined to keep power only for their own ends. On the contrary, Cromwell and those around him were primarily driven to hold on to power in order to bring about a kind of 'cultural revolution'. They were driven by a passionate desire to purify the lives and thoughts of their fellow countrymen ... Judged by the high aspirations of Oliver Cromwell and others at its heart, the Cromwellian Protectorate was a failure.

> **ACTIVITY**
>
> Study Sources 11.1 and 11.2.
>
> 1 What similarities can you find in these sources in their assessments of the Cromwellian Protectorate?
> 2 What differences of emphasis can you find in these authors?
> 3 What problems can you identify for anyone trying to reach a conclusion about whether the Protectorate was a success or a failure?

This chapter aims to help you to reach your own judgement about the Cromwellian Protectorate. In section A you will consider Cromwell's aims – what was he trying to achieve? From this starting point you will build the criteria against which to measure his success or failure. You need to consider not only what was desirable, but also what was possible in the circumstances. Only then can you expect to reach valid conclusions about the Protectorate's record in power.

At the end of Chapter 11 you must decide whether the Protectorate was a success or a failure.
As you work through the chapter, complete your own copy of the following table.

Policies	Aims and objectives	Success or failure?
Healing and settling	To reconcile former enemies and opponents to the Protectorate	
	To prevent further civil war	
	To establish England's government on a civilian basis	
Religion	To arrive at a workable religious settlement that would protect the liberty of Protestant sects	
	To improve the quality of the parish clergy	
	Godly reformation of manners	
Social and legal reform	To modernise the law	
British policy	To normalise relations with Scotland and Ireland	
Foreign policy	Providing for England's security	
	Promoting trade	
Selling the Protectorate through images	Promoting Cromwell's image as a successful head of state	

■ IIA Timeline of the Cromwellian Protectorate, 1653–58

1653	
December	Instrument of Government
	Cromwell installed as Lord Protector
1654	
January	Oath of Engagement abolished
March	Triers Ordinance
April	Anglo-Dutch War ended
	Ordinance for the union of England and Scotland
August	Ejectors Ordinance
	Chancery Reform Ordinance
September	First Protectorate Parliament
November	George Cony imprisoned for refusing to pay customs duties
December	Western Design expedition sails for the Caribbean
1655	
January	First Protectorate Parliament dissolved
March	Penruddock's rising
May	George Cony's lawyers imprisoned
June	Resignation of Lord Chief Justice Rolle
July	News of the Western Design's defeat reaches London
	Cromwell disturbed by evidence of the withdrawal of God's support
August	Rule of the Major-Generals begins
October	Moral Order instructions issued to the Major-Generals
	Anglo-French defensive treaty signed
	War with Spain
December	Cromwell permits Jews limited toleration
1656	
September	Second Protectorate Parliament
	Over 100 MPs excluded
October	James Nayler's case
1657	
January	Cromwell decides to abandon both the Rule of the Major-Generals and the Instrument of Government
February	Cromwell puts the case for these decisions to a meeting of Army officers and meets with a hostile response
March	Humble Petition and Advice
April	Admiral Blake defeats Spanish fleet at Santa Cruz
May	Cromwell accepts the Humble Petition and Advice
	Cromwell rejects the offer of the Crown
June	Cromwell's 'coronation' as Protector
	First session of the Second Protectorate Parliament ends
1658	
January	Second session of the Second Protectorate Parliament
	Republicans attack the new constitution
February	Second Protectorate Parliament dissolved
June	Battle of the Dunes
	Dunkirk surrendered to England by Spain
September	Death of Oliver Cromwell
	Richard Cromwell installed as Lord Protector

A What were Cromwell's aims?

Healing and settling

One of Cromwell's main aims was what he called 'healing and settling', reconciling former enemies and reconstructing the pre-war institutions of everyday life. The Civil War had torn into the heart of every community, dividing friends and neighbours and disrupting the social and moral order. There existed an enormous backlog of practical issues, personal appeals and financial claims that had to be addressed before the country could return to normal. These problems did not exist in isolation.

The religious settlement was an integral part of this process. Could normality be restored alongside a greater degree of religious liberty? If the regime were to survive, it had to prove that religious toleration was compatible with social and moral order. Cromwell believed that this could be achieved.

Returning to normality was not going to be easy for a regime that had executed the King. Making England respected internationally was one way of doing this. But how could Cromwell maintain a strong international position while appealing to tradition? England's pre-war institutions were too weak to maintain the military power on which his international reputation rested.

> ■ **Learning trouble spot**
>
> **The Royalist problem**
> Reconciling former Royalists to the Protectorate lay at the heart of 'healing and settling'. The Sequestration Ordinance of 1643 enabled Parliament to confiscate the estates of Royalists, who would have to pay a 'composition' fine to redeem their estates. In 1651 the Rump passed an Act of Oblivion intended to let bygones be bygones, but then put up for sale the estates of 780 Royalists to help pay the costs of its military campaigns. Many of these men had surrendered to Parliamentary officers under private assurances for the safety of their property. Resentment at the trashing of these gentlemen's agreements contributed to the Army's loss of patience with the Rump. Cromwell was keen to build bridges with former Royalists and was criticised for instructing judges to show them favour whenever possible.

'Healing and settling' meant resolving hundreds of cases like this one.

- Banaster was a Gloucestershire tenant farmer who owed his landlord, Lord Craven, £150. This was a lot of money, equivalent to maybe £10,000 today.

  - When war broke out in 1642 Banaster supported Parliament. Lord Craven supported the King.

    - Banaster's farm was frequently raided by Royalist cavalry.

      - Banaster gave his all for the Cause. He bought his own weapons, contributed provisions for Gloucester's defence in 1643, organised the defence of his own church, raised a company of foot soldiers and a troop of cavalry for Parliament. By 1646 he was owed £271 back pay, and claimed costs of £628 1s 6d.

        - In 1652 Lord Craven's estate was sequestered (confiscated) by Parliament.

          - In 1653 Parliament demanded the £150 that Banaster owed to Lord Craven.

            - After appealing against the injustice of the demand, in desperation Banaster petitioned Cromwell.

              - In 1655 his case came to Cromwell's notice. An Order in Council remitted the £150 and ordered Parliament to pay Banaster £477 17s 0d.

DISCUSS

What experiences convinced Cromwell that England needed both regular parliaments and a chief executive?

Political stability

Cromwell wanted the political settlement that the Army had offered to Charles I in 1647 – the *Heads of the Proposals*. Power was to be divided between a single person acting as executive and a Parliament that had to face regular elections. Executive authority would be limited by a Council of State, but the executive would also limit Parliament's authority. The settlement as a whole would be approved by Parliament, bridging the gap between the ancient constitution and the new one. Henry Ireton and General Lambert had been the chief architects of the *Heads of the Proposals*, and Lambert was the author of the Instrument of Government. During the first Protectorate Parliament, Cromwell clung to these principles as the 'fundamentals' of the constitution about which there could be no argument.

Godly reformation

The most intangible of Cromwell's aims, and the one he valued the most, was godly reformation. England's troubles would be given meaning and the 'blood and treasure' lost in the civil wars would be redeemed.

Cromwell believed that he and the Army had been entrusted by God with a providential mission. He frequently compared England's troubles with those of the ancient Israelites, whose sufferings marked them out as God's people and prepared them for the Promised Land. This key issue had driven Cromwell to abandon friends and former allies prepared to give up the godly cause in the name of peace.

Godly reformation required a national church settlement that would lead by example rather than by force, with liberty of conscience for Protestant sects. It was the state's responsibility to see that the whole nation was served by a godly ministry, so some means would have to be found to improve and support it.

What made Cromwell different from many of his political allies, and marks him out as a visionary, was his commitment to moral and spiritual reformation. The civil wars had to lead to a better national life, just as his own spiritual troubles had prepared him for a life redeemed by salvation. In practical terms this meant an end to swearing, gambling, prostitution, drunkenness – the sort of behaviour normally punished by parish constables. But Cromwell's vision was not simply one of enforcement: he hoped England's experience of war would transform the hearts and minds of the English people.

■ 11C Cromwell's 'Personal Rule'

The Instrument of Government gave the Lord Protector authority to govern by ordinance until his first Parliament met in September 1654. For eight months Cromwell and his Council had the power to legislate without Parliament.

ISSUES	REFORMS	EXPLANATION
Religion	Triers Ordinance	A central commission was set up to assess all applications for church livings to ensure that all newly appointed ministers were 'men of known integrity and piety'.
	Ejectors Ordinance	County commissions were set up to expel ministers and schoolmasters who were not up to the job.
	Godly reformation	Ordinances banned cock-fighting and horse-racing, outlawed duels, forbade swearing and drunkenness.
Law	Reform of the Court of Chancery	By Charles I's reign Chancery had become the preserve of wealthy litigants. Access to Chancery was made cheaper and easier.
	Making the law more humane	Laws dealing with poor debtors and prisoners were revised. Traitors were no longer disembowelled – just beheaded.
Foreign policy	Ending the Anglo-Dutch War	Necessary if taxation were to be cut.
British policy	Reform of civil and judicial structures	Needed to tie Scotland and Ireland more closely to England.
Security	High Court of Justice created to try treason cases	Needed to distinguish between former and currently active Royalists.
Healing and settling	Dealing with the flood of petitions that poured into the Council	Hundreds of cases like Richard Banaster's were addressed.
	Cutting taxes	Essential if the regime wanted to build popular support.
	Abolishing the Rump's Oath of Engagement	Cromwell thought it did more harm than good to force people to swear allegiance to the government.

DISCUSS

What do the ordinances in Chart 11C tell you about the kind of government Cromwell thought England needed at this time?

THE COURT OF CHANCERY

Chancery was the central court of equity, distinct from the courts of common law, and based on the principle that the *system* of justice should not *get in the way* of justice. Whereas the common law courts operated an increasingly inflexible code of practice based on procedure and precedent, Chancery represented the 'conscience of the king' – the power of the monarch to see that justice was done regardless of the letter of the law. The King claimed the right to set aside the formality of legal procedure and base his judgements on natural law.

FOCUS ROUTE: WHO'S WHO?

Make brief notes on John Lambert to include in your Who's who list.

B The Instrument of Government

General Lambert drew up a constitution that defined the power given to each institution. Parliament, the Council of State and the Lord Protector each acted as a check on the power of the other two.

■ 11D The checks and balances of the Instrument of Government

Council of State	Lord Protector Cromwell	Parliament	Armed forces and other special interests	Church Settlement
Cromwell was empowered to legislate by ordinance from 16 December 1653 to 3 September 1654. Parliament was expected to endorse decisions made in this period.				
• To advise the Lord Protector • No more than 21 members, no less than thirteen • Chooses the Lord Protector's successor after his death	• Chief executive and magistrate in England, Scotland and Ireland • Must call Parliament when England goes to war • May call Parliament whenever necessary • Must sign bills within 20 days or 'give satisfaction' to Parliament; otherwise Bills automatically become law	• Power to make laws, but may not change the Instrument • To meet 3 September 1654 and subsequently every three years • No Parliament to be dissolved within five months • 460 Members, including 30 each for Scotland and Ireland	• Annual provision for an Army of 30,000 men • Constant provision for a navy	• Christianity to be the public profession of the three nations • Provision to be made as soon as possible for the selection and maintenance of diligent clergy • Tithes to be preserved in the meantime • 'That to the Public Profession held forth none shall be compelled . . . but that endeavours be used to win them by sound doctrine and the example of good conversation.' • Liberty of worship for those Protestant sects that do not disturb the peace or abuse their liberty 'to the civil injury of others'.
Majority consent needed when Parliament not in session	• Control of the militia and the navy • Power to make treaties with foreign states	Parliament must give consent when in session	£200,000 per annum to cover costs of law courts and other expenses, paid for from the customs	
Majority consent needed to go to war	Power of war and peace	The vote (franchise) • Property qualification of £200 per annum • Royalists excluded unless they have proven their loyalty • Catholics and Irish rebels excluded • Distribution of constituencies shifted the balance from urban to county representation.		
Examines electoral returns		Elected men to be at least 21 years old and of known integrity		
Selects new members of the Council of State from Parliament's nominees		Nominates new members of the Council of State		

DISCUSS

Was the Instrument of Government a plan for a military dictatorship, or did the checks and balances limit the authority of Cromwell and his Council?

ACTIVITY

1 How and why did the Instrument impose limits on the power of
  a) the Lord Protector
  b) Parliament
  c) the Council of State?
2 In what ways was Cromwell's power as Lord Protector different from that of King Charles I in the 1620s?
3 Why might the Instrument be criticised by the following people:
  a) a tenant farmer with an income of £150 per annum
  b) the Levellers
  c) Republicans?
4 What kind of religious settlement did the Instrument aim for?

C Why did Cromwell's first Parliament end in failure?

■ 11E Peeling the onion: Cromwell's withering political support

Each successive political crisis alienated a new group of people.
By 1654 it was very difficult for Cromwell's regime to work with any kind of parliament.

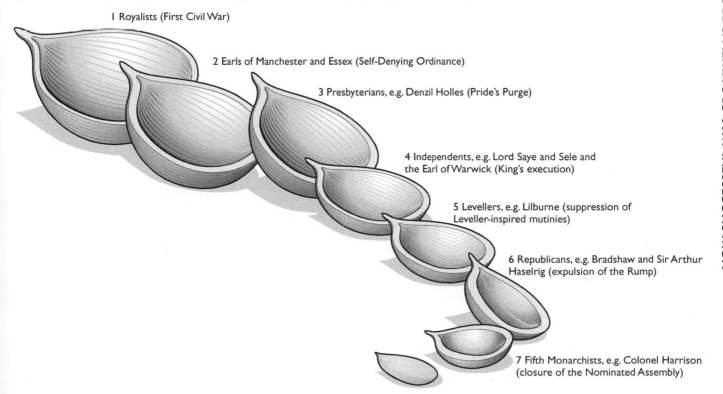

1 Royalists (First Civil War)

2 Earls of Manchester and Essex (Self-Denying Ordinance)

3 Presbyterians, e.g. Denzil Holles (Pride's Purge)

4 Independents, e.g. Lord Saye and Sele and the Earl of Warwick (King's execution)

5 Levellers, e.g. Lilburne (suppression of Leveller-inspired mutinies)

6 Republicans, e.g. Bradshaw and Sir Arthur Haselrig (expulsion of the Rump)

7 Fifth Monarchists, e.g. Colonel Harrison (closure of the Nominated Assembly)

8 Cromwell, the Army and ?

Cromwell's first Parliament failed to live up to his expectations. Within a week his government had come under attack from many MPs who disputed the legality of the new constitution. Led by Sir Arthur Haselrig and John Bradshaw, they attacked Cromwell's right to be Lord Protector. Cromwell patiently defended the legitimacy of the new regime and offered to allow Parliament to suggest changes to some of the Instrument's details – what he called its 'circumstantials'. But there were four 'fundamentals' that were non-negotiable (see Chart 11F).

> **REMINDER**
>
> John Bradshaw had presided over the trial of the King in 1649.

> **FOCUS ROUTE**
>
> Why did Cromwell and his first Parliament fall out? Make notes on the issues, and explain how they reflect the more fundamental political problems that faced the Protectorate – for example, opposition to the Instrument of Government and the regime's lack of political support.

I am prepared to discuss the fine details of the new constitution, but four fundamental principles may not be discussed:
1 Government must be by a single person and a parliament.
2 Parliaments should not make themselves perpetual.
3 There must be liberty of conscience in religion.
4 Control of the Army should be by the Lord Protector as well as Parliament.

All MPs will have to take an Oath of Recognition accepting these principles before being readmitted to Parliament.

Oliver Cromwell

We went to war with the King to defend Parliament's privileges. Now the Army has destroyed the Long Parliament that gave it birth. The Army has power, but no authority. No government established by the Army can be lawful, and none of its laws can ever have the force of law. To speak of 'fundamentals' and 'circumstantials' is to miss the point. The only legal course is to reinstate the Rump immediately and place the Army under its command. The radical sects must be suppressed.

John Bradshaw

Sir Arthur Haselrig

Around 80 MPs refused to take the Oath of Recognition and were excluded from Parliament, but this did not halt the attack on the Instrument. In December, Parliament introduced a 'Government Bill' and began rewriting the Instrument line by line. The MPs demanded the power to make constitutional amendments and to choose the Lord Protector's successor. Parliament, not the Council, should give its consent before the Protector took the nation to war. In an echo from the 1620s, Parliament also demanded the sovereign right to raise taxation, threatening the Army's existence. By the end of the year, Cromwell had had enough. On 22 January 1655 he dissolved the Parliament, which had failed to pass a single Act.

SOURCE 11.3 Cromwell speaking to the first Protectorate Parliament, 12 September 1654. The extract has been simplified to make it easier to read

I shall enumerate my witnesses as well as I can. When I had agreed to accept the government some important people accompanied me to Westminster Hall to take my oath. There was an explicit consent of interested persons, and an implicit consent of many. I had the approbation of the officers of the army in the three nations and of the great City of London. The Judges declared that they could not administer justice until they had received commissions from me; and they did receive commissions from me, and by virtue of those commissions they have acted. All the people in England are my witnesses, and many in Ireland and Scotland. All the sheriffs in England are my witnesses. Yea, the returns of the elections on behalf of the inhabitants in the counties, cities, and boroughs, all are my witnesses. And I shall now make you my last witnesses, and ask you whether you came not hither by my writs?

ACTIVITY

Study Source 11.3 and Chart 11F.

1 Explain in your own words Cromwell's argument that his government is legitimate.
2 What counter-argument could be used against Cromwell's view?

Early in 1655, things were not going well for Cromwell. In March came Penruddock's rising, a Royalist rebellion in Wiltshire which, although easily suppressed, showed that the Royalists were still plotting the overthrow of the Protectorate. In July, news of a foreign policy disaster reached London. The Western Design was a naval expedition to the Caribbean (see page 258), but it was beaten off. Its bid to secure a major base from which to challenge Spain's domination of the West Indies ended in failure.

Alarmed both by the threat to the Protectorate and by God's apparent forsaking of the cause, Cromwell turned to the Army. England and Wales were divided into eleven military districts, each governed by a Major-General (see Chart 11G). Security was to be strengthened by local militias, paid for by a new 'Decimation Tax' on Royalists' estates. Cromwell hoped that the Army could be scaled down, which would allow him to cut taxes. The Major-Generals would continue godly reformation and improve the efficiency of local government at minimal cost.

The problem was that these aims were incompatible. The Decimation Tax made healing and settling more difficult. Military rule was unlikely to appeal to civilian magistrates. The Major-Generals were generally of lower social standing than the Justices of the Peace, whose power they usurped. To promote godly reformation, the Army would have to work with leaders of religious sects, who were regarded as dangerous radicals by conservative country gentlemen.

The Army's rule was never coherent enough to form a military dictatorship. The Major-Generals were inconsistent in the way they applied their orders. Lambert and Fleetwood were too preoccupied with national politics, and there were differences of emphasis and application elsewhere. The Army enforced laws against drunkenness, profanity and blasphemy. Alehouses were regulated more strictly; theatres, brothels and gaming houses were closed; and bear-baiting, cock-fighting and horse-racing were banned. The Major-Generals tried to support the work of local Justices of the Peace, enforcing the Poor Law, regulating weights and measures and helping the EJECTORS remove unlicensed clergy. Typically, Cromwell trusted his generals to interpret their instructions according to local needs. He fell back on the Army to provide proactive government in the absence of Parliament.

The rule of the Major-Generals was not popular. There was widespread resentment of military interference in civilian administration, and only the godly minority approved of the reformation of manners by force. The Decimation Tax failed to curb the costs of government: by 1656 expenditure was outrunning income by £230,000 per annum, so military rule became another burden on the Exchequer. When the Spanish War (see page 258) forced Cromwell to recall Parliament in the summer of 1656, the nation passed judgement on the Major-Generals' rule. Despite their assurances, the Parliament that opened in September 1656 contained few candidates promoted by the Army.

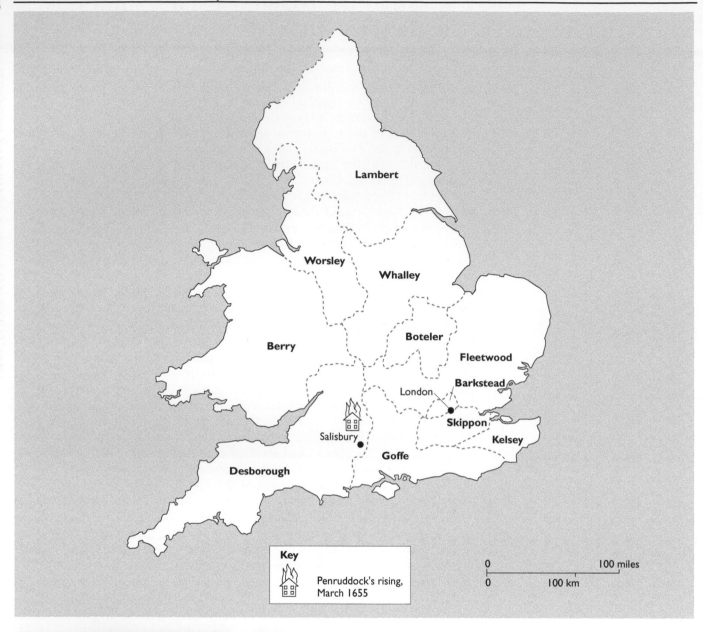

Key

Penruddock's rising, March 1655

0   100 miles
0   100 km

ACTIVITY

In Source 11.4, how did Cromwell justify military rule?

FOCUS ROUTE: WHO'S WHO?

Make brief notes on George Cony to include in your Who's who? list.

DISCUSS

1 Compare Cony's case to the Five Knights' case of 1627 (pages 22–23). What similarities can you find between them? What does this tell you about the trend of government under the Protectorate?

2 Does the rule of the Major-Generals stand comparison with twentieth-century dictatorships?

SOURCE 11.4 Cromwell, speaking to his second Parliament on 17 September 1656, justifies the rule of the Major-Generals

If this were to be done again, I would do it! And truly England doth yet receive one day more of lengthening out its tranquillity by that occasion and action. It hath been more effectual towards the discountenancing of vice and settling religion, than anything done these fifty years. But if nothing should be done but what is according to law, the throat of a nation may be cut, till we send for some to make a law.

THE TRIAL OF GEORGE CONY

Cony was a silk merchant who refused to pay customs on imports. He was imprisoned in November 1654 and put on trial. His lawyers argued that customs raised by the Protector and Council were illegal, because only Parliament could raise taxes. Cromwell and the Council made an example of Cony's lawyers by imprisoning them for challenging the Protectorate. Lord Chief Justice Rolle resigned when he was punished for allowing Cony to challenge the legality of the tax.

E   How successful was Cromwell's foreign policy?

FOCUS ROUTE

English foreign policy under Cromwell was more successful than at any time since the reign of Elizabeth I; that is the common view. How far can this view be sustained? Complete your own copy of the following table to show the successes and failures of Cromwell's foreign policy. Then add your findings to the Focus Route on page 248.

Date	Event	How successful?
1654 April	Peace with the United Provinces	How did this help the revival of trade? Why did peace with the Dutch appeal to English Protestants?
1654–55	Western Design to capture Hispaniola (now Haiti) from Spain	Why did the Protectorate launch the Western Design? What did it achieve? How did it affect Cromwell personally?
1655 May October	Support for Protestants in Piedmont Defensive alliance with France War with Spain	What effect did the Piedmontese massacre have on English foreign policy? Was the war with Spain motivated more by religion or trade?
1657 April	Anti-Spanish alliance with France Battle of Santa Cruz – English naval victory over Spain	What did the Protectorate gain by the war with Spain?
1658 June	Battle of the Dunes Dunkirk captured from Spain	

ACTIVITY

1   After studying Chart 11H, consider the following aims of Cromwell's foreign policy. Alongside each one, mark Cromwell's success on a scale of 1 to 5, with 1 being the least successful and 5 the most successful.

   - To defend England against the threat of foreign invasion
   - To regulate and promote profitable trade
   - To support the Protestant cause in Europe
   - To deny comfort to the Stuart cause
   - To bolster England's international prestige

2   Compare English foreign policy in the 1650s with that in the 1620s. How successful was Cromwell compared to Charles I?

3   How do you explain the successes of Cromwell's foreign policy?

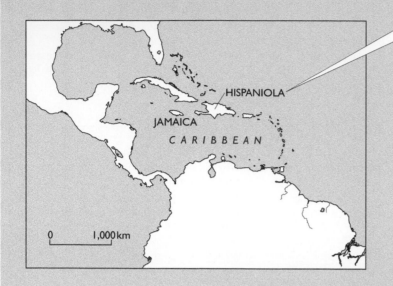

Key

━●●●● Trade agreements

The Western Design

As soon as the Anglo-Dutch War was over, Cromwell and the Council launched an unprovoked war against Spain's Caribbean empire. The Western Design aimed at capturing the Spanish island of Hispaniola. The motives for the expedition appear not to have been very well thought through. It was a blatantly populist move, pandering to traditional English Puritan prejudices against Spain. The historian Ronald Hutton has argued that the expedition sprang from the Protectorate's inability to pay off the 160 warships that were suddenly unemployed after peace broke out with the Dutch. This was the kind of war that Parliament wanted Charles I to fight in 1625, a war that would pay for itself. It was a fantasy.

The expedition was a failure. The English were driven off from Hispaniola and took Jamaica instead, which in 1655 had no real value. When news of the disaster reached London, it drove Cromwell into a crisis of confidence. For the first time in his life, Cromwell's God had refused to 'own' the Protector's cause. What had he and the nation done to lose God's support? A national Day of Fasting and Humiliation was called to help regain God's blessing.

War with Spain

The Western Design escalated into war with Spain in Europe. This was essentially a naval war. Admiral Blake achieved a spectacular success against the Spanish treasure fleet in 1657, but failed to capture the silver bullion. Spain severed trading links with England and launched a privateering war against English trade. The war cost the Protectorate about £1 million per year, forcing Cromwell to recall Parliament. In 1658 a brigade of the New Model Army was sent to fight alongside the French against the Spanish Netherlands. The Spanish were defeated in the Battle of the Dunes. France rewarded England by giving it the port of Dunkirk – but did England need it? Dunkirk was not very useful for trade, it cost a lot to maintain, and England couldn't afford further European campaigns.

To the south, in 1657, Admiral Blake destroyed a Spanish treasure fleet off the Canary Islands, crippling Spain's war effort against Portugal and France.

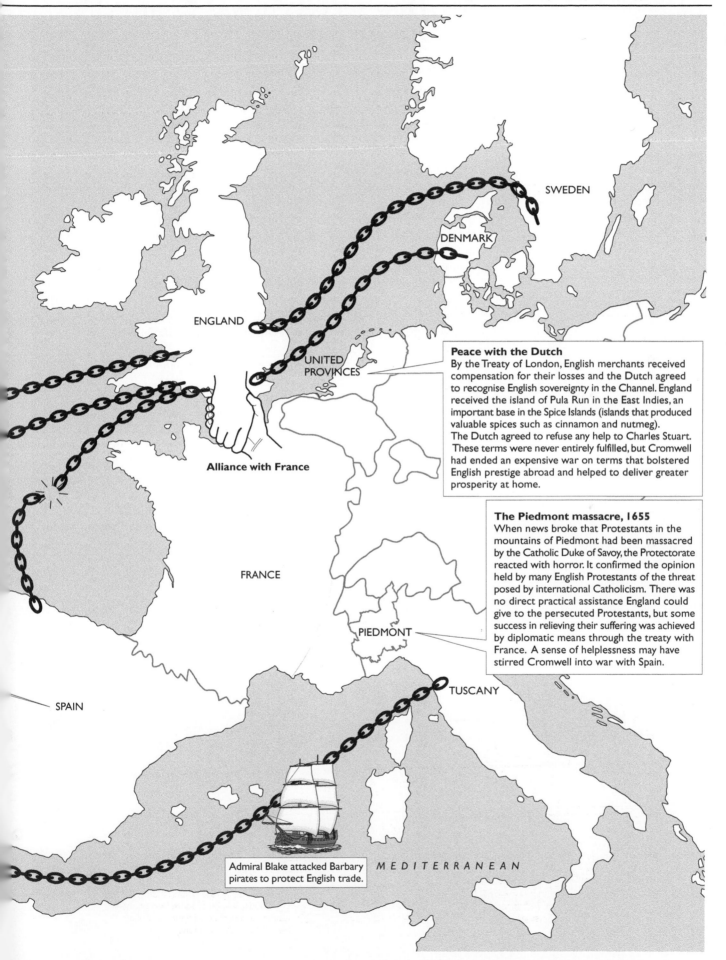

SWEDEN

DENMARK

ENGLAND

UNITED
PROVINCES

Peace with the Dutch
By the Treaty of London, English merchants received
compensation for their losses and the Dutch agreed
to recognise English sovereignty in the Channel. England
received the island of Pula Run in the East Indies, an
important base in the Spice Islands (islands that produced
valuable spices such as cinnamon and nutmeg).
The Dutch agreed to refuse any help to Charles Stuart.
These terms were never entirely fulfilled, but Cromwell
had ended an expensive war on terms that bolstered
English prestige abroad and helped to deliver greater
prosperity at home.

Alliance with France

The Piedmont massacre, 1655
When news broke that Protestants in the
mountains of Piedmont had been massacred
by the Catholic Duke of Savoy, the Protectorate
reacted with horror. It confirmed the opinion
held by many English Protestants of the threat
posed by international Catholicism. There was
no direct practical assistance England could
give to the persecuted Protestants, but some
success in relieving their suffering was achieved
by diplomatic means through the treaty with
France. A sense of helplessness may have
stirred Cromwell into war with Spain.

FRANCE

PIEDMONT

TUSCANY

SPAIN

Admiral Blake attacked Barbary
pirates to protect English trade.

MEDITERRANEAN

F How successful was Cromwell's British policy?

The Protectorate in Ireland

Cromwell's policy towards Ireland changed over time. In 1651 there was talk of Ireland being like a ball of clay, ready to be moulded to suit England's needs. There was even speculation that Ireland might set the agenda for the spiritual and moral reformation of England. These ideas were soon replaced by a far less ambitious policy aimed at restoring Ireland to civilian rule under a Protestant ascendancy.

After Ireton's death in 1651, Cromwell's new son-in-law, Charles Fleetwood, was appointed Lord Deputy of Ireland. Fleetwood supervised a military occupation by an army that shared his vision that Ireland could be reborn through sectarian religion and English colonisation. But the radicalism of the occupying army conflicted both with the older English Protestants in Ireland, many of whom were former Royalists, and with the Presbyterian Scots in Ulster.

In 1654 Cromwell sent his younger son Henry to Ireland to investigate the growing friction between the Army and the rest of the country. Henry's arrival led to friction between himself and Fleetwood. Fleetwood returned to England in 1655, and Henry Cromwell governed Ireland from 1655 until Cromwell's death in 1658.

Henry Cromwell aimed at healing and settling Ireland by encouraging reconciliation between English Protestants (Royalists and Parliamentarians), old English Catholics and the Protectorate. The native Irish Catholics were the losers, as land was transferred from their hands to create a common bond of interest between the English. The Anglican Church of Ireland was reinstated to restore good relations with the old Protestant communities, with a committee acting as Triers and Ejectors (see page 251) to improve the clergy. The poverty of the Church was addressed by restoring tithes, but many problems remained.

Once Ireland was secure, the Protectorate accepted the impossibility of stamping out the Catholic faith. No serious attempt was made to convert Catholics, whose existence was virtually ignored. Parliament passed an Oath of

> **FOCUS ROUTE: WHO'S WHO?**
>
> Make brief notes on Charles Fleetwood to include in your Who's who? list.

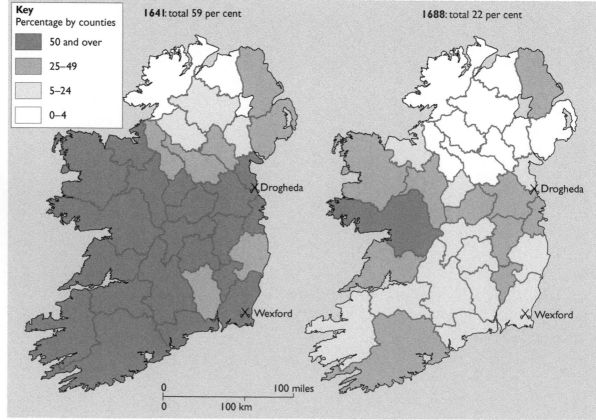

SOURCE 11.5 Land owned by Catholics in 1641 and 1688

(Irish casualties at Drogheda and Wexford were dwarfed by the numbers of Irish Catholics transported to the West Indies in the following decades)

Key
Percentage by counties

- 50 and over
- 25–49
- 5–24
- 0–4

1641: total 59 per cent

1688: total 22 per cent

Drogheda

Wexford

Drogheda

Wexford

0   100 miles
0   100 km

Abjuration to force all Catholics to renounce the Pope's authority in Ireland, but Henry Cromwell did not enforce it. Priests were officially expelled from Ireland, but those who were caught were transported to the West Indies, not executed. Over the next 30 years the transfer of land into Protestant hands continued. This unfolding catastrophe fixed the gaze of later Irish nationalists on Cromwell's military campaign as the origin of their problems.

SOURCE 11.6 Ireland – the maths (1651–58)

	Irish assessments	English subsidies
Commonwealth, 1651–54	£30,000 per month	£22,000 per month
Protectorate, 1654	£10,000 per month	
Protectorate, 1657	£9,000 per month	£8,000 per month

By 1658 the cost of maintaining the Army in Ireland was significantly greater than the Army's income from Ireland and England combined. The soldiers' pay was nine months in arrears, and a considerable debt had accrued.

SOURCE 11.7 Scotland – the maths in 1659

Total cost of governing Scotland	£307,271
Total revenue from Scottish sources	£143,652
Financial burden of Scotland on England	£163,619

ACTIVITY

1 Compare the treatment of Scotland and Ireland under Cromwell. How do you account for the differences in approach?

2 How far did Cromwellian rule in Ireland and Scotland live up to the worst fears of the people living in those countries?

3 How successful do you think Cromwell's government was in terms of
   a) England's vital interests
   b) the interests of the people living in Ireland and Scotland?

FOCUS ROUTE: WHO'S WHO?

Make brief notes on General George Monck to include in your Who's who? list.

The Protectorate and Scotland

The English civil wars were disastrous for Scotland. The country lost its national independence and around ten per cent of the adult male population was killed. After 1651 the Rump appointed a commission led by Generals Lambert and Monck to govern Scotland, and imposed a monthly assessment of £13,500 to pay for the English army of occupation – a heavy burden for a country impoverished by war. A rebellion in the Highlands in 1653 clarified the problem faced by the English government: an army had to be maintained to meet any possible Royalist threat, but the costs of that army made such a threat more real. The only way out was to make England help pay for it, which made the settlement of England more difficult.

Cromwell's aim was to reconcile Scotland to defeat by showing its people the benefits of political union with England. Monck's Highland campaign of 1654 was followed by an Ordinance of Pardon and Grace. Local chiefs and lords were given the power to police the settlement in their own areas. A new Scottish Council gave Scottish civilians a place in government alongside English soldiers and administrators. The Protectorate backed away from trying to force the pace of change in administration and civil law. Responsibility for law enforcement was restored to Scottish magistrates, as was the authority of local municipalities. Crucially, no attempt was made to undermine the Presbyterianism of the Scottish church.

George Monck (1608–70)
George Monck was a professional soldier whose life reads like a potted history of the whole civil war period. When he was sixteen yeas old, in 1624, he joined the army to escape being prosecuted for beating up the sheriff of Devonshire, who had arrested his father for debt. He took part in both of Buckingham's ill-fated expeditions, to Cadiz and the Ile de Ré, in the 1620s. In the 1630s he fought as a volunteer for the Dutch against the Spanish in the Thirty Years' War. He returned to England in 1640 and fought in Charles I's army in the Second Bishops' War. In 1641 he fought for the King in Ireland against the Irish Confederacy. During the First Civil War he served in the King's army. He was taken prisoner in 1644 and spent the rest of the war in the Tower of London.

In 1646 he declared his loyalty to Parliament and took the Covenant. In 1647 he became Parliament's commander in Ulster, fighting both the Irish Catholics and Royalists. In 1650 he joined Cromwell's army in the Scottish campaign, commanding the English infantry at the Battle of Dunbar. When Cromwell marched south in 1651 to intercept Charles II's army at Worcester, Monck was appointed Commander-in-Chief in Scotland, where he fought a campaign in the Highlands to quell a Royalist uprising.

In 1652 Monck joined Admiral Blake as a General-at-Sea in the Anglo-Dutch War, and the following year took command of the English fleet. He returned to Scotland in 1654, where he commanded the English army until 1660. He played a decisive role in the restoration of Charles II in 1660 and with James Duke of York and Prince Rupert, went on to become one of the King's best admirals.

How progressive was Cromwell's government?

Progress is a concept that wouldn't have appealed to Cromwell. Our modern idea of progress was born in the eighteenth century from two historical developments: the Enlightenment, which stressed reason over religion; and the industrial revolution, which focused on the material improvement of mankind rather than its spiritual healing. Cromwell was too wedded to the idea of the ancient constitution and spiritual values to have found much comfort in the eighteenth century. Nevertheless, it is valid to ask whether England's brief experience of Cromwellian government advanced any of the changes that were to make England a more 'modern' country.

Relaxing the laws against Jews

When Cromwell stressed his commitment to liberty of conscience, it wasn't because he believed in the absolute right of everyone to worship publicly in the religion of their own choice. Catholics were excluded from his idea of toleration. The ultimate aim of liberty of conscience was to enable Protestants to work towards unity in faith. The Holy Spirit, working on the free consciences of men, would bring them together in love and understanding. This was very different from the expansion of churches made possible by the Enlightenment, which downgraded religion from a public to a private matter and so eventually led to Catholic emancipation.

In 1655 Cromwell granted the Jewish community the right to live in England free from persecution. England's Jews had been expelled in the thirteenth century, but a small Jewish community survived in London. Anti-Semitism was common in Elizabethan England. To extend liberty of conscience to the Jews was therefore an act of considerable bravery and an important step towards a more tolerant society, though Cromwell probably hoped that many could be converted to Christianity. Cromwell's motives were not entirely pure. When war broke out with Spain in 1655, the Jewish community offered to use its commercial contacts with Spain for gathering information for the war effort. Europe's Jews had a long-standing antipathy towards Spain, which had expelled them in the 1490s.

Developing the nation-state

In the 1650s Cromwell faced the dilemma of which way to move England – 'forwards' towards the military-fiscal state (see box) or 'backwards' towards a weaker central government and the tradition of unpaid local office-holders. It wasn't an easy choice. Healing and settling involved going 'backwards' to the status quo before the war. But godly reformation involved going 'forwards' because it depended on the Army's support.

Cromwell didn't necessarily perceive his choices in this way. He was more interested in building consensual networks that would be prepared to work with his government to achieve stability, security and reform. He placed more value on people than on institutions (see Chart 11I). Nevertheless, he had to react to the pressures these dilemmas exerted on his government.

DISCUSS

Why is Cromwell's decision to end the official persecution of Jews regarded as an important decision?

THE MILITARY-FISCAL STATE

Parliament's victory in the Civil War could have placed England on the path to becoming a more efficient, centralised, powerful nation. Historians call this 'statebuilding', and the kind of nation that emerges from statebuilding they call the 'military-fiscal state'. Such a state is able to maintain a larger army and navy because it can assess and tax the actual wealth of its people more successfully. Statebuilding is inevitably unpopular, because it seeks to alter the relationship between the individual and central government. The point of doing it is to make the nation more powerful and more competitive with neighbouring states, which may themselves be engaged in a similar process. In the 1650s, for example, France was replacing Spain as the most powerful nation in Europe.

Cromwell placed more value on consensual networks than on rigid forms of government or religion. His own personal networks underwent major changes between 1640 and 1658

SOURCE 11.8   Cromwell speaking to the Second Protectorate Parliament, 13 April 1657

I am a man standing in the place I am in; which place I undertook not so much out of the hope of doing any good, as out of a desire to prevent mischief and evil, which I did see was imminent in the nation. I am ready to serve not as a King, but as a constable if you like! For truly I have, as before God, thought it often that I could not tell what my business was, nor what I was in the place I stood in, save comparing myself to a good constable set to keep the peace of the parish. And truly this hath been my content and satisfaction in the troubles that I have undergone, that yet you have peace.

H Why did Cromwell reject the offer of the crown in 1657?

In April 1657, Parliament offered to make Oliver Cromwell King of England. By accepting the offer, Cromwell could have ended the long constitutional crisis that stretched back to 1640, since the offer of the crown came with a new constitution that would establish a limited monarchy similar to that envisaged in the Nineteen Propositions of 1642. At first Cromwell welcomed Parliament's proposals, but the offer of the crown threw him into a quandary. After five weeks he turned it down, thereby losing the best chance of making the changes of the 1650s permanent. Why did Cromwell decide not to accept it?

Why did Parliament offer Cromwell the crown?

In September 1656, Cromwell recalled Parliament to pay for the war with Spain. He was not enthusiastic: his first Parliament had not gone well, and by 1656 the regime faced a serious financial deficit as expenditure was outrunning income by £230,000 per year. The Major-Generals failed to deliver a compliant (obedient) Parliament. The Council of State excluded about 100 MPs, and others stayed away in protest. Cromwell seems to have played no part in these exclusions, not wanting to interfere blatantly with the political process.

Cromwell's second Parliament was initially more successful than his first. The war with Spain was popular and the remaining MPs had no stomach for an argument with the Lord Protector. Parliament got down to business with such speed that after two months Cromwell commended it for making 'many good laws'.

The case of James Nayler

In 1656 Nayler re-enacted Christ's entry into Jerusalem by riding into Bristol on a donkey. Some local people were persuaded that he was Jesus and spread branches on the ground in front of him. He was arrested by the local magistrates and sent to London for trial.

Nayler was a Quaker and a follower of George Fox, who taught that the spirit of Christ is present in every person. Quakers rejected the need for ordained ministers and encouraged each worshipper to follow his or her own conscience. Some Quakers refused to obey civil authorities and disrupted church services. The Quakers were widely regarded as one of the more dangerous religious sects in the 1650s.

The MPs decided to make an example of Nayler and try his case before Parliament. Since the Lords had been abolished, the Commons would act as both jury and judge. One speaker after another warned Parliament that Nayler's blasphemy was a consequence of too much toleration. His punishment (see Source 11.9) was similar to that of Prynne, Burton and Bastwick in 1637 (see Chapter 3).

The case of James Nayler was a turning point in Cromwell's relations with Parliament. It revealed a weakness in the Instrument of Government: without the House of Lords, the Commons' judicial power was unchecked. Appalled by Parliament's cruelty towards Nayler, Cromwell became convinced that the Instrument had to be modified. Only this time it would be Parliament, not the Army, that wrote the new constitution.

SOURCE 11.9 The punishment of James Nayler

James Nailor Quaker set 2 howers on the Pillory at Westminster whiped by the Hangman to the old Exchainge London: Som dayes after, Stood too howers more on the Pillory at the Exchainge, and there had his Tongue Bored through with a hot Iron, & Stigmatized in the Forehead with the Letter:B: Decem[r]. 17: anno Dom. 1656.

In January 1657, Nayler was whipped through the streets from Westminster to the City, where he was put in the pillory. A hole was bored through his tongue with a hot iron and his forehead was branded with a B (for blasphemer). He was taken back to the scene of his crime at Bristol and forced to ride through the streets facing backwards on a horse. He was then whipped again before returning to London to face perpetual imprisonment

By the end of 1656, the main issue facing Cromwell was whether his regime could be shifted from a military to a civilian basis. The officers continued to support the Instrument of Government. But the Army's unpopularity drew Cromwell towards the advice of lawyers anxious to return to civilian rule under a constitution written and approved by Parliament. Cromwell was visibly ageing and his illnesses, combined with the threat of assassination, made a decision about the future urgent. In January he accepted Parliament's rejection of the Major-Generals' Decimation Bill, which would have provided additional funds for the Army. By doing this he signalled that the rule of the Major-Generals was over.

On 23 February 1657, an MP called for sweeping changes to the Instrument of Government. It provoked a confrontation between Cromwell and his own generals. On 27 February he met with nearly 100 officers. After angrily blaming the Army for many of the constitutional crises of the 1650s, he argued that it was time to 'lay aside arbitrary proceedings so unacceptable to the nation' and build the government on solid foundations. On 25 March Parliament voted to offer Cromwell the kingship by a majority of two to one. Six days later the new constitution – the Humble Petition and Advice – was presented to him on the understanding that he had to accept or reject the whole package of reforms. It included the offer of the crown.

The Humble Petition and Advice

The Humble Petition and Advice was different from the Instrument of Government in several vital ways. Apart from offering Cromwell the crown, it provided for the return of the House of Lords as a chamber nominated by Cromwell to balance the power of the Commons. Parliament would gain the power to nominate the great officers of state. Parliament would have to approve all taxation, and would cut the size of the Army to reduce the tax burden.

Current thinking about the Humble Petition is inclined to criticise it both for its vagueness and for its creating a Parliament that Cromwell's successor couldn't handle. But Cromwell didn't expect it to die so quickly, and was probably prepared to accept its defects in order to secure the settlement which had long eluded him – a constitution originating from Parliament and granting him legitimate authority.

■ 11J Cromwell's military and civilian advisers – a house divided

General John Lambert
General John Desborough
General Charles Fleetwood
Bulstrode Whitelocke
Lord Broghill
Edward Montagu
Viscount Fauconberg

Officers defended the Instrument of Government:
- guaranteed financial support for the Army
- gave the Council power to appoint Cromwell's successor
- advanced the cause of godly reformation.

Civilians supported the Humble Petition and Advice:
- Cromwell to become King and nominate his own successor
- House of Lords to be replaced by a nominated chamber
- financial settlement to reduce the size of the armed forces
- Parliament to approve the great officers of state
- Parliament to approve all taxation.

Why did Cromwell reject the offer of the crown?

On 6 May Cromwell seemed ready to accept the title of King. The Army did its best to dissuade him; Lambert, Fleetwood and Desborough all threatened to resign. In a more sinister threat, Colonel Pride delivered a petition against monarchy from the regiments in and around London. Yet there were other considerations, possibly more important to Cromwell's decision. As king, Cromwell might be unable to fulfil his quest for godly reformation. It is possible, too, that he feared the sin of pride. If he became King, how could he plausibly deny that ambition had been his true motive? Nor had he forgotten the string of providences which had led to the abolition of the monarchy. For several weeks he agonised over his decision. At the same time he wore down Parliament's insistence that the package was non-negotiable. When it was clear that he could accept the Humble Petition without accepting the crown, he gave his final answer. The offer was rejected.

Cromwell then acted as if he had accepted it. He was invested as Lord Protector in a new ceremony at Whitehall, wearing an ermine-lined robe in the presence of ambassadors. After taking the oath of office, he was presented with a gold sceptre and the sword of state. Henceforth he was addressed as Your Highness and lived at Whitehall rather than Hampton Court. To all intents and purposes he was King, except that he wasn't.

SOURCE 11.10 William Bradford, an old soldier, urges Cromwell to reject the offer of the crown, 4 March 1657

I am of that number, my Lord, that still loves you, and greatly desires to do so, I having gone along with you from Edgehill to Dunbar. The experiences that you have had of the power of God at these two Places, and betwixt them, methinks, should often make you shrink, and be at a stand in, this thwarting, threatened change.

SOURCE 11.11 Cromwell explains why he has decided to reject the offer of the crown, 13 April 1657

Truly the providence of God has laid this title aside providentially. God has seemed providentially not only to strike at the [Stuart] family but at the name [of King]. God hath not only dealt so with the persons and the family, but he hath blasted the title. I would not seek to set up that that providence hath destroyed and laid in the dust, and I would not build JERICHO again.

1 How was Cromwell seen by his contemporaries?

How did Cromwell appear to his contemporaries? Was his regime successful in presenting an image of the Lord Protector as a viable alternative to a king? In trying to answer this question, there are three aspects of his image that need to be taken into account:

- What did Cromwell actually look like?
- How did the Protectorate want Cromwell's image to be understood?
- How did his enemies portray him?

What did Cromwell look like?

This might seem to be an easy question to answer. Cromwell famously instructed Sir Peter Lely to paint him as he really was, and portraits by other artists confirm certain aspects of his physical appearance – his large nose, receding hairline and the famous warts. Even here there are problems. Several copies of Lely's portrait survive, some possibly by Lely himself and others by his 'school'. These may have been used to publicise Cromwell's preferred self-image as an ordinary Englishman called by Providence to serve his country. Cromwell wanted to emphasise his humility to reinforce the republican virtues of the Interregnum – to be seen as a Cincinnatus, not as a Caesar.

DISCUSS

How significant is Cromwell's rejection of the crown in understanding his motives and aspirations?

ACTIVITY

Construct a spider diagram with the following title: Why did Cromwell reject the offer of the crown? Place on it any possible explanations you can find in this section, together with any relevant evidence taken from source material.

JERICHO
The town destroyed by Joshua and God, described in the Old Testament.

Cromwell's appearance changed considerably during the last ten years of his life – the only period for which portraits survive. He aged quickly after the Irish campaign. In searching for the true likeness of Cromwell, this must be taken into account.

ACTIVITY

Here are four portraits of Cromwell (Sources 11.12–11.15).

1 Match the portraits with descriptions **A–D** given below.
2 Compare these portraits with that by Robert Walker on page 206. Which one of the images do you think Cromwell himself might have preferred, and why?

Descriptions
A A portrait by Edward Mascall, 1657, the year before Cromwell's death
B A portrait by Sir Peter Lely, 1654. Cromwell is supposed to have told Lely to 'use all your skill to paint my picture truly like me, and not flatter me at all; but remark all these roughnesses, pimples, warts, and everything as you see me, otherwise I will never pay a farthing for it.'
C An unfinished miniature by Samuel Cooper
D A portrait by Robert Walker, 1649
You can check your answers on page 291.

SOURCE 11.12

SOURCE 11.13

SOURCE 11.14

SOURCE 11.15

How did the Protectorate want Cromwell's image to be understood?

We have seen how Cromwell was torn between the radical desire for godly reformation and the conservative desire to win support from the traditional country gentry. Did official images of the Lord Protector reflect this clash of interests? Did Cromwell's public image develop a distinctive republican style or was the symbolism of the Protectorate based on that of the monarchy? When the public looked at images of Cromwell, did they know what he stood for? Study Sources 11.16–11.19 and answer the questions on page 270.

SOURCE 11.16 William Faithorne, 'The Emblems of England's Distractions', 1658

SOURCE 11.17 Portrait of Cromwell as Lord Protector by Thomas Wyck, based on a portrait of Charles I by Van Dyck (see inset)

DISCUSS

During the Cold War the motto of America's Strategic Air Command, which carried nuclear weapons, was 'Peace is Our Profession'. What do you think of Cromwell's motto (see Source 11.18)?

SOURCE 11.18 A half-crown of 1656. The motto on the reverse means 'Peace is sought by war'

SOURCE 11.19 Cromwell in 1650

OLIVARIVS CROMVELL EXERCITVVM ANGLIÆ
TENENS ET CVBERNATOR HIBERNIÆ OXO

Cernimus hic omni Caput admirabile Mundo;
Quod Reges, Populi, Barbaries; stupent.
Regibus Hic Fraex; Populis Pater; Hostis, inultam
Barbariem, verá Relligione, domat.

F. Maugi ærudit

REIPVBLICÆ DVX GENERALIS. LOCVM-
NIENSIS ACADEMIÆ CANCELLARIVS

Nullius Ille timet quàm Summi Numinis arma
Non timet; at Pacem Cuilibet ense parat.
Quis dubitat? Sacro hoc si pergat Flamine Victor,
Quin subitò Meretrix de Babylone cadet.

ACTIVITY

1 Study Source 11.16 on page 268. Explain the significance of the following images:

   • Noah's Ark being guided to safety on a mountain top
   • the three crowns on Cromwell's sword
   • Abraham preparing to slay his son
   • the dove of peace over Cromwell's head
   • symbols of industry and prosperity in the foreground
   • the symbols of error being trampled underfoot
   • the twin pillars either side of Cromwell.

2 Study Source 11.17 on page 269. In what ways is Wyck's portrait of Cromwell
   a) similar to   **b)** different from
   the portrait of Charles I by Van Dyck?

3 Study Source 11.18 on page 269. What image of Cromwell is the coin intended
   to convey?

4 Now look at all of Sources 11.16–11.19. Which, if any, of the following
   statements is best supported by the evidence presented in these sources?

   a) The Protectorate wanted Cromwell's image to reflect the republican virtues
   of simplicity, honesty and godliness.

   b) The Protectorate wanted Cromwell's image to be associated symbolically
   with the monarchy.

   c) The Protectorate made no real effort to project an 'official' view of Cromwell.

   If none of these statements satisfies you, make up your own statement about the
   way Cromwell's image was used by the Protectorate.

How was Cromwell portrayed by his enemies?

The Protectorate made no serious attempt to prevent people from publishing critical views and images of Cromwell. Unlike a modern dictatorship, there was no rigid censorship of the press. In pamphlets, cartoons, newspapers and popular ballads, a wide range of critical images circulated. Cromwell was portrayed as a man of low social origins: an ambitious hypocrite who abandoned both friends and principles in his pursuit of power. Study Sources 11.20–11.23 and answer the questions that follow on page 272.

SOURCE 11.20 'The Royall Oake of Brittayne', by an unknown artist, *c.*1651

SOURCE 11.21 'A Coffin for King Charles: a Crown for Cromwell: a Pit for the People' – a popular ballad of the 1650s

Cromwell on the throne:
So, so, the deed is done, the Royal head is sever'd.
As I meant when I first begun, and strongly have endeavour'd.
Now Charles the first is tumbled down, the second I don't fear.
I grasp the sceptre, wear the crown, nor for Jehovah care.

King Charles in his coffin:
Think'st thou base slave, tho' in my grave, like other men I lie?
My sparkling fame and Royal name can, as thou wishest, die?
Know, caitiff, in my son I live
(the Black Prince call'd by some).
And he shall ample vengeance give on those that did me doom.

The people in the pit:
Suppress'd, depress'd, involved in woes, Great Charles, thy people be.
Basely deceiv'd with specious shows by those that murdered thee.
We are enslav'd to tyrants' hests, who have our freedom won:
Our fainting hope now only rests on thy succeeding son.

SOURCE 11.22 A Royalist woodcut showing Cromwell in league with the Devil

SOURCE 11.23
A Dutch cartoon of Cromwell, c.1649

ACTIVITY

1 Study Source 11.20 on page 271.
   a) What is happening in the picture?
   b) Explain the significance of the books hanging from the limbs of the royal oak:

   • the Bible
   • Magna Carta
   • Statutes
   • The *Eikon Basilike*
   • Law reports

   c) What is Cromwell saying and what is its significance?

2 Study Source 11.22. This is a picture of Cromwell with his Council. What had the following people done to warrant their inclusion in the drawing?

   • John Bradshaw
   • Colonel Harrison.

3 Study all of Sources 11.20–11.23. How effective do you think images and ballads like these were in undermining popular loyalty to the Protectorate?

Is there any evidence that Cromwell saw himself as a failure by the time of his death? If so, does this prove that Cromwell was a failure?

J Did Cromwell die a disillusioned man?

When Cromwell dissolved Parliament in February 1658, he sounded like a man who had given up. In his final speech he warned that Charles Stuart was ready to invade England, waiting only for dissension in the Army to cause chaos. In what sounded like a farewell to Parliament, he ended on a note of defiance: 'Let God judge between you and me.'

Why did Cromwell dissolve his second Parliament?

The second session of Cromwell's second Parliament lasted less than three weeks. The revival of opposition came from several sources. The hundred or so MPs who had been excluded in 1656 were allowed to take their seats. They included many Presbyterians and republicans, including Sir Arthur Haselrig and Sir Henry Vane, who immediately launched an attack on the new constitution. Cromwell might have had more support in the Commons had it not been for the need to nominate members for the Upper House. Many of his old Independent allies turned down his invitations, so the reconstituted House of Lords had to be filled with loyal MPs. When elements in the Army threatened to support the attacks on the Humble Petition and Advice, Cromwell hurried to Westminster and dissolved Parliament.

SOURCE 11.24 Cromwell speaking at his dissolution of Parliament, 4 February 1658

I would have been glad, as to my own conscience and spirit, to have been living under a woodside to have kept a flock of sheep, rather than to have undertaken such a place as this was. But undertaking it upon such terms as I did I did look that you, that did offer it unto me, should have made it good. But upon such terms really I took it, and I am failed in these terms.

The final seven months

During the last months of Cromwell's life there was plenty to be depressed about. His relationship with the Army never fully recovered from the arguments over the Humble Petition and Advice (see page 265). In July 1657 Lambert was forced to resign for refusing to take an oath of loyalty to Cromwell under the new constitution. On 11 February 1658 Cromwell dismissed six more officers for publicly criticising him. The regime was in a deep financial crisis, making it more and more dependent on loans from the City of London. It would be wrong, however, to assume that Cromwell's spirit was broken. Victory at the Battle of the Dunes on 4 June suggested that the nation had regained God's favour, and Cromwell's government continued to function effectively, even if there were no major new initiatives. There was even thought of summoning another Parliament.

With his own health faltering, Cromwell had to contend with the death of his son-in-law Robert Rich, followed by the painful death from cancer of his own daughter Elizabeth Claypole in August. A month later, on 3 September, Cromwell himself died. His effigy lay in state for two months before being buried with full ceremony. The Protectorate passed smoothly to his nominated successor, his son Richard Cromwell.

Return to the Focus Route at the beginning of this chapter (page 248). You should now have reached a judgement about Cromwell's performance in each of the categories listed there. If not, go back now and complete the table. Make sure that you have included reasons for reaching the conclusions you have reached.

K Review: how successful was Cromwell's Protectorate?

Cromwell and his Council governed Britain for five years. How well did they do? You need to consider:

a) whether Cromwell achieved the objectives he set for himself
b) whether Cromwell governed well according to more objective criteria.

The problems faced by Cromwell in this period were complicated. We need to consider what had to be achieved in each area of policy for it to be successful. It is difficult to reach a simple conclusion that Cromwell was a 'success' or a 'failure'.

ACTIVITY

Select one of the following essay titles:

a) How successfully did the Protectorate govern Britain between 1654 and 1658?

b) Examine the view that the conflicts between Oliver Cromwell and the Parliaments of the Protectorate were largely of his own making.

c) Why did the Instrument of Government not fulfil Cromwell's hopes?

KEY POINTS FROM CHAPTER 11

How successful was Cromwell's Protectorate?

1 Cromwell became Lord Protector through the Instrument of Government, a constitution drawn up by General Lambert and other Army officers.

2 During his first eight months as Lord Protector, Cromwell governed by issuing ordinances. He expected his first Parliament to endorse these decisions and develop the reforms they initiated.

3 Cromwell's first Parliament ended in failure when it attacked the Instrument of Government and questioned Cromwell's right to be Lord Protector.

4 For the next eighteen months Cromwell ruled through the Army, using the Major-Generals to maintain order and implement social reforms associated with godly reformation.

5 In the meantime, the Protectorate's foreign policy was remarkably successful, with the notable exception of the Western Design. This was made possible by high levels of taxation.

6 In both Ireland and Scotland, the Protectorate followed up the Commonwealth's victories (which were Cromwell's victories) with measures aimed at maintaining peace and security. This was achieved, but at a high cost to English taxpayers.

7 Cromwell's government was remarkably tolerant. In many cases where the government passed harsh, punitive laws, they were never rigidly enforced.

8 Cromwell showed little interest in developing the fiscal and bureaucratic machinery central to state building. He was more interested in developing consensual networks.

9 By 1654, however, Cromwell had already lost many of his former friends, relations and political allies. He had to try to construct new ones from within the Army and among civilian advisers.

10 In 1656 Cromwell called a new Parliament. Nayler's case convinced him that the Instrument of Government wasn't working, so when Parliament wrote a new constitution he was tempted to accept it. However, in the Humble Petition and Advice, Parliament offered him the crown.

11 The offer of the crown split the new network of soldiers and civilians around which Cromwell was trying to build a consensus. He rejected the crown, but the Humble Petition was modified to allow him to accept it.

12 The second session of Cromwell's second Parliament ended in failure when the attempt to readmit MPs excluded in 1656 backfired. Cromwell dissolved Parliament after just three weeks. No further parliaments were called in the final eight months of his life.

Further information about Oliver Cromwell is available on the Cromwell Association website at www.olivercromwell.org

Section 4 Review: Oliver Cromwell – a distant mirror

Cromwell's career was not one-dimensional, but multifaceted. He shows us a different face depending on the angle from which we view him

In Section 3 we focused on Cromwell's rise to power. In Section 4 we have looked at what he did with power once it was in his hands. The Protectorate can be regarded as either a success or failure, depending on your view of the evidence. But your assessment of Cromwell cannot stop there. You need to consider how history has judged him. Why has his reputation changed over the centuries?

■ A Timeline 1660–2001

Note that this is a simplified model – in reality the interpretations are always more complex.

Late seventeenth century	A period of reaction against the civil wars. After the Restoration, Cromwell is vilified as a monster, an ambitious regicide who abandons his friends and allies in his quest for power. He is even accused of being in league with the Devil.	
Early eighteenth century		As memories of the civil war fade, several primary sources are published for the first time, including Clarendon's *History of the Rebellion and Civil Wars in England* (1702) and Ludlow's *Memoirs* (1698). These are highly critical of Cromwell, but grudgingly accept that he possessed great talents. England is at war with France.
Late eighteenth/ early nineteenth century	Dominated by the French Revolution and the wars against Napoleon. In England it is a period of conservative reaction opposed to reform. Cromwell is criticised for executing the King and for enthusiasm for reform. Such criticism is tempered by admiration for his martial talents and, like Napoleon, for bringing order out of chaos.	
Mid-nineteenth century		An age of industrialisation, liberalism and the rise of the middle class. Many changes are taking place, such as the abolition of slavery and the reform of Parliament. Greater religious toleration is shown by Catholic emancipation and the growth of Noncomformity. A huge revival of interest in Cromwell takes place, with an emphasis on his personal qualities. Cromwell becomes an English hero.
Early twentieth century	Dominated by imperialism, the threat of war, the growth of democracy and the rise of socialist parties. Admiration for Cromwell, who has become a cult figure, is fuelled by Whig historians focused on the growth of Parliament and limited monarchy. The civil wars are seen as a Puritan revolution, and Cromwell as the greatest of all Puritans.	
1930s		Dominated by the rise of fascism in Europe. Comparisons are made between Cromwell and the dictators Hitler, Mussolini and Stalin. Nazis express admiration for Cromwell's willingness to use force against Parliament in the interests of order.
1950s – mid-1970s	The era of the Cold War. Academic history is dominated, though not entirely, by Marxist history. Cromwell tends to be seen as a product of his social origins, and is criticised for putting the interests of the propertied classes above political reform.	
1970s–1990s		This period sees the end of the Cold War and the fall of communism. Marxist history collapses under the weight of cumulative research. More emphasis is placed on local history and relations between England, Scotland and Ireland. Cromwellian studies focus more and more on religious issues.
1990–2001	Since the fall of communism the world has become a more complicated and unpredictable place, in which successful countries such as the USA contrast sharply with 'failed' states such as Afghanistan. Historians focus on the international context of England's problems, with political crises generated by attempts to remedy the structural weaknesses of the English state. Recent years have seen the emergence of a new consensus that the seventeenth century has to be understood in its own terms.	

Historians' views

SOURCE 1

No sovereign ever carried to the throne so large a portion of the best qualities of the middling orders, so strong a sympathy with the feelings and interests of his people. He was sometimes driven to arbitrary measures; but he had a high, stout, honest, English heart. Hence it was that he allowed so large a share of political liberty to his subjects, and that, even when an opposition dangerous to his power and to his person almost compelled him to govern by the sword, he was still anxious to leave a germ from which, at a more favourable season, free institutions might spring.

SOURCE 2

A conservative by social instinct and early political training, he was inspired to spiritual radicalism by his role as God's instrument of victory in the civil war, by his intimacy with his troops, and by his informal but weighty responsibilities as patron of the religious sects. What resulted was (to simplify) a kind of ideological schizophrenia, setting him on an almost predictable course of political self-destruction. Whenever the social order seemed in peril, whenever the spectre of anarchy was raised, he would expound the virtues of harmony and property and set about repairing the damage; but when he had done so, and when inevitably the cause then strayed once more from the paths of righteousness and reform, he would inveigh against the soullessness of his more temperate colleagues, and destroy the goodwill he had so scrupulously fostered. Endlessly patient in building political unity, Cromwell was sudden and terrible in its destruction.

SOURCE 3

Without doubt, no man with more wickedness ever attempted any thing, or brought to pass what he desired more wickedly, more in the face and contempt of religion and moral honesty; yet wickedness as great as his could never have accomplished those trophies without the assistance of a great spirit, an admirable circumspection and sagacity, and a most magnanimous resolution.

SOURCE 4

With a noble sorrow, with a noble patience, he longs towards the mark of the prize of the high calling. He, I think, has chosen the better part. The world and its wild tumults, – if they will but let him alone! Yet he too will venture, will do and suffer for God's cause, if the call come. His eldest son Oliver, now a stout young man of twenty. 'Thou too, Boy Oliver, thou art fit to swing a sword. If there ever was a battle worth fighting, and to be called God's battle, it is this; thou too wilt come!' How a staid, most pacific, solid Farmer of three-and-forty decides on girding himself with warlike iron, and fighting, he and his, against principalities and powers, let readers who have formed any notion of this man conceive themselves.

SOURCE 5

It is no mere accident that the past dozen years have seen an extraordinary number of books and articles about Cromwell in German. It is no mere accident that for perhaps the first time there have appeared such contributions in Russian. It is no mere accident that comparisons have been made between Cromwell, Hitler and Mussolini. In the same fashion that Napoleon's rise to power helped the people of the continent to understand Cromwell better, so the rise of an Austrian house-painter to the headship of the German Reich, of a newspaper editor-agitator to the leadership of Italy, and of a Georgian bandit to the domination of Russia, have modified our concept of Cromwell's achievement, and perhaps our concept of his place in history.

SOURCE 6

What he did ... being for his own singular advancement ... is unpardonable, and leaves him a person to be truly admired for nothing but apostasy and ambition, and exceeding TIBERIUS in dissimulation [lies].

TIBERIUS
A Roman emperor and tyrant.

SOURCE 7

When men of rank sacrifice all ideas of dignity to an ambition without a distinct object, and work with low instruments and for low ends, the whole composition becomes low and base. Does not something like this now appear in France? Other revolutions have been conducted by persons who sanctified their ambition by advancing the dignity of the people whose peace they troubled. They had long views. They aimed at the rule, not at the destruction, of their country. They were men of great civil and great military talents, and if the terror, the ornament of their age. Men like Cromwell were not so much like men usurping power, as asserting their natural place in society. Their rising was to illuminate and beautify the world. The hand that, like a destroying angel, smote the country, communicated to it the force and energy under which it suffered. I do not say (God forbid), I do not say that the virtues of such men were to be taken as a balance to their crimes: but they were some corrective to their effects. Such was our Cromwell.

SOURCE 8

Like statebuilding, restoration too had a history before 1660. We may chart the progress of the attempt to restore what the troubles had destroyed throughout the interregnum. Though in relation to the church and monarchy Cromwell 'would not build Jericho again', he was in other respects a spokesman for this impulse. It was consequently within the context of 'healing and settling' that constitutional restoration made as much progress as it did between 1649 and 1659 ... Thus it was not only in fiscal and administrative terms that the agenda of restoration was partly established by the interregnum.

SOURCE 9

When the decision had been taken to send an army to Ireland, the occasion was seized to weed out the Leveller-influenced regiments. There was a mutiny in London, and Robert Lockyer, who had fought all through the civil war, was shot as ringleader. Parliament declared mutiny in the Army to be treason. The revolt was suppressed after a lightning night attack by Cromwell on the rebels at Burford, not without suggestions of treachery on his part. Three leaders were shot after the surrender and a fourth, William Thompson, was caught and shot three days later. The Leveller mutiny was over. Fairfax and Cromwell returned to Oxford, where they were given honorary degrees by that formerly royalist university, and to London where they were feasted by the City. Property had been saved.

Is the search for truth a waste of time?

You might get the impression from this activity that Oliver Cromwell is a figment of our imaginations. Towards the end of the nineteenth century a profession of history emerged, dedicated to the search for objective truth. But if every age has redrawn Cromwell in its own image, is the search for truth pointless? Have historical relativism and 'political correctness' turned history into a mere parlour game, a kind of intellectual one-upmanship with no resolution or end product?

My personal opinion is that the study of Cromwell and the whole civil war period is more vibrant and interesting than ever before. It is also more demanding, because historians have realised that they have to understand Cromwell and his contemporaries on their terms, and in their language, not ours. Modern society equips us very badly for this challenge. Oliver Cromwell would not have wanted to live in our secular, multicultural society. He believed the English were God's chosen people, so it is difficult for us to make the imaginative effort needed to understand the seventeenth-century world; difficult, but worthwhile. It is intrinsically interesting; and for our multicultural, secular society to work, we need to be capable of making this kind of effort.

Most of the interpretations seen in the activity above will not stand up to modern scrutiny, so progress is being made. The *real* Cromwell is out there somewhere, and although we may never find him, we can at least begin to speak of him in ways that he would have understood. The pursuit of objective truth is the engine that drives this process forward.

ACTIVITY

Choose one of the following essays.

a) How, and why, have historians differed in their assessments of the character and achievements of Oliver Cromwell?

b) 'Every age has its bias, and historians consciously or unconsciously reflect this bias.' Discuss this comment with reference to the historiography of Oliver Cromwell.

Epilogue

What was the significance of the civil war period?

The Restoration of the King

In 1651 Charles Stuart was a fugitive. After fleeing from the battle of Worcester, dressed as a servant he made his way south through the west of England to Bridport in Dorset. On the journey he had many close calls. At Bridport he stopped at an inn, where he found the yard full of Cromwell's soldiers, who were searching for him. With great courage Charles blundered into the yard, leading his horses through the soldiers to the stable.

At that moment Charles's prospects could not have been bleaker. He proceeded to Shoreham and found a boat that took him to France. For the next nine years, Charles lived in exile and could only watch helplessly the establishment of Cromwell's Protectorate.

FOCUS ROUTE: WHO'S WHO?

Make brief notes on Samuel Pepys to include in your Who's who? list.

SOURCE 1   The diary of Samuel Pepys, entry for 23 May 1660

All the afternoon the King walked here and there, up and down (quite contrary to what I thought him to have been), very active and stirring. Upon the quarter-deck he fell into discourse of his escape from Worcester, where it made me ready to weep to hear the stories that he told of his difficulties that he had passed through, as his travelling four days and three nights on foot, every step up to his knees in dirt, with nothing but a green coat and a pair of country breeches on, and a pair of country shoes that made him so sore all over his feet that he could scarce stir. Yet he was forced to run away from a miller and other company that took them for rogues. His sitting at table at one place, where the master of the house, that had not seen him in eight years, did know him but kept it private; when at the same table there was one that had been of his own regiment at Worcester could not know him, but made him drink the king's health and said that the King was at least four fingers higher than he. At another place, he was by some servants of the house made to drink, that they might know that he was not a Roundhead, which they swore he was.

In 1651 Charles Stuart was public enemy No. 1

SOURCE 2 Portrait of King Charles II in coronation robes by Wright, 1660

ACTIVITY

What was restored by the Restoration? In the interests of peace it was necessary for Charles II and Parliament to reach a compromise in 1660. Complete your own copy of this table with details drawn from the summary of the Restoration given on page 281.

Issue	Things that were restored to the pre-war status quo	Things that were permanently changed by the Civil Wars
The constitution		
Religion		
Landed property		
Finance		
The Army		

DISCUSS

How did the Restoration settlement compare with the *Heads of the Proposals* of 1647?

RELIGIOUS NONCONFORMITY PUNISHED – THE 'CLARENDON CODE'

- Corporation Act 1661: Excluded members of religious sects from public office. Members of town corporations had to take Holy Communion according to the rites of the Church of England, renounce the Solemn League and Covenant, and swear loyalty to the King.
- Licensing Act 1662: Censored theological publications.
- Five Mile Act 1665: Prohibited DISSENTER clergymen from coming within five miles of corporate towns (towns with a royal charter). Aimed to deprive sectarian clergy of contact with congregations and schools.
- Conventicle Act 1664: Imposed heavy penalties for attending non-Anglican church services.
- Quaker Act 1662: Imprisoned leading Quakers.

CONSTITUTIONAL SETTLEMENT

- Triennial Act 1641 repealed.
- Triennial Act 1664: Stipulated that Parliament should meet every three years, but created no mechanism for forcing the King to comply.
- Legislation signed by Charles I in 1641 otherwise left unchanged:
  – no prerogative courts
  – no knighthood fines, Ship Money or forest fines.
- Some of the Protectorate's legislation adopted:
  – Navigation Acts of 1650 and 1651
  – Act of 1656 abolishing feudal tenures ended the crown's rights to PURVEYANCE and WARDSHIP
  – all the rest of the legislation passed between 1642 and 1660 declared null and void.
- Act of Indemnity and Oblivion 1660: All but about 50 individuals were pardoned.
- Army and Navy placed in the King's hands by the Militia Act.
- The King kept the power to appoint his ministers.

Cromwell's head

In 1660 Charles Stuart returned in triumph to England and was crowned King in Westminster Abbey.

Oliver Cromwell's body, with those of Ireton and Bradshaw, was exhumed and hanged from a gibbet at Tyburn. His head was stuck on a pike at Westminster, where it stood for many years. Ten regicides were publicly executed.

Over the next two years a series of Acts restored the crown and wiped away almost all the laws passed since the summer of 1641. England was turning its back on Cromwell, the English Revolution and the Civil War.

THE CHURCH OF ENGLAND RESTORED

- Bishops returned to their dioceses.
- Church lands sold during the civil wars returned.
- The *Book of Common Prayer* restored.
- Act of Uniformity 1662: Forced all clergy to swear to use the Anglican liturgy. All clergy not ordained by a bishop to surrender their benefices. Some 2000 clergy – nearly one-fifth of the Church – were forced to resign.

FINANCIAL SETTLEMENT

- Parliament collected a further eleven months' worth of assessments and raised a Poll Tax to pay off the Army.
- Parliament granted the King customs and excise duties worth £800,000 per year.
- The King was expected to raise a further £100,000 per year from crown lands.
- Dunkirk was sold to France for £400,000.
- These measures left the crown with a deficit estimated at £120,000 per year.

THE LAND SETTLEMENT

- Charles II promised to leave the settlement of the problem in Parliament's hands.
- Royalists whose estates had been sequestered and sold by Parliament were able to get them back through the courts.
- Royalists who had sold land to pay Decimation Taxes or fines or to raise forces for the King had little chance of receiving compensation.

HISTORY REWRITTEN

In 1660 the names of some of the Commonwealth's ships were changed.

Naseby	= Royal Charles
Richard (Cromwell)	= James (Duke of York)
Speaker	= Mary (Charles's sister)
Dunbar	= Henry (Charles's brother)
Winsly	= Happy Return
Lambert	= Henrietta (Maria)

DISSENTERS AND NONCONFORMISTS

People who refused to conform to the Anglican form of worship.

PURVEYANCE AND WARDSHIP

Two medieval royal privileges. Purveyance was the right of the Crown to buy provisions for the royal household at a lower-than-market price. Wardship was the Crown's right to manage estates inherited by minors until they came of age. Both were very unpopular. (See also Chart 2F, page 49.)

SOURCE 3 Edward Hyde, Earl of Clarendon, speaking at the opening of Parliament, 10 May 1661, reflects on the Interregnum

You have made, Mr. Speaker, a very lively description of the extravagency of that confusion which this poor nation groaned under, when they would throw off a government they had lived and prospered under so many ages to model a new one for themselves, which they knew no more how to do, than the naked Indians know how to dress themselves in the French fashion; when all ages, sexes and degrees, all professions and trades, would become reformers . . . and abject men, who could neither write nor read, would make laws for the government of the most heroic and the most learned nation in the world . . .

■ B Two theories of the Restoration

THEORY I – THE RESTORATION WAS INEVITABLE

Once Cromwell was dead, no one could reconcile the contradictions within the Protectorate. Cromwell was the buckle that held together the Army, the religious sects, the City of London and the civilian supporters of the Republic. His death condemned the regime to self-destruction. England had been slowly returning towards monarchy ever since 1649, and by 1658 Cromwell was King in all but name.

> **Step 1: Defending the House of Lords, 1649**
> This shows that Cromwell didn't want the revolution to challenge the fundamental social structure.

+
> **Step 2: Suppressing the Levellers, 1649**
> This put an end to further radical social and political change.

+
> **Step 3: Expelling the Rump, 1653**
> Cromwell reached a conclusion that Charles I had reached in 1642 – the long Parliament was out of control and had to be stopped.

+
> **Step 4: The Instrument of Government, 1653**
> England needed a chief executive, so Cromwell became Lord Protector.

+
> **Step 5: The Humble Petition and Advice, 1657**
> Parliament offered to make Cromwell King of England. He turned the offer down, but was reinvested as Lord Protector in a highly regal ceremony. A second chamber was restored to replace the House of Lords.

=
> **Step 6: The return of the King**

SOURCE 4   The return of the King

THEORY 2 – THE RESTORATION WAS NOT INEVITABLE

The Republic faced a difficult situation when Oliver Cromwell died, but not an impossible one. The Royalists were disorganised and weak. When the Army and Parliament failed to establish stable government, the threat of another civil war drove the City of London to demand the return of the King. Public opinion supported this because of the growing fear of religious radicals, especially the Quakers.

Phase 1: Richard Cromwell fails as Lord Protector, September 1658–April 1659

Richard's failure was not inevitable – he succeeded his father without opposition, and when Parliament met in December 1658 it agreed to his control of the armed forces. Richard was brought down by the refusal of both the Army Council and republican MPs to support the Third Protectorate Parliament.

- Republicans such as Haselrig, Ludlow and Vane worked against Parliament. They wanted to return to the Commonwealth (to restore the Rump).
- Generals such as Fleetwood and Desborough on the Army Council worked against Parliament. They wanted to return to the Instrument of Government.
- Failure of Army colonels to support Richard Cromwell against the Army Council.

Phase 3: Military rule fails, October 1659–January 1660

Military rule had little chance of success, as it was more or less naked military dictatorship. General Lambert returned to the Army Council, probably with the aim of reviving the Instrument of Government and making himself Lord Protector. But Lambert's ambition to succeed Cromwell provoked hostility within the Army itself.

- The City of London resented military rule and sectarian influence. Serious riots broke out and, for the first time, troops were assaulted in the streets.
- Haselrig and the Commonwealthmen demanded the return of the Rump.
- General Monck, commanding the Army in Scotland, condemned the military coup of October 1659.

FOCUS ROUTE: WHO'S WHO?

Make brief notes on Richard Cromwell to include in your Who's who? list.

Phase 2: The Rump fails, May–October 1659

In May 1659 the Instrument of Government was abandoned and the Rump was determined to show that the Army took its orders from Parliament. Sir Arthur Haselrig, the leading Republican, picked a fight with the Army Council over the commissioning of officers, and threatened to replace the New Model Army with a militia that would have to swear an oath to the Commonwealth. The Army wasn't ready to hand over power to Parliament, so it put an end to the Rump.

Phase 4: General Monck intervenes, January 1660

Monck led his Army south over the border into England. Like Charles I's army in 1639, Lambert's army in the north fell apart as men deserted through lack of pay and unwillingness to fight Monck.

Phase 5: The Rump fails again, February 1660

Monck restored the Rump to give it another try. Haselrig insisted on showing the Army who was boss. Lambert was imprisoned and half the officers were purged. Haselrig, who owed this last chance to Monck, then made the mistake of treating Monck as he had treated the rest of the Army by trying to remove him. Monck responded by insisting that the whole of the old Long Parliament should be restored. It was time to undo Pride's Purge and pick up the broken thread of the ancient constitution.

Phase 6: The Declaration of Breda, April 1660

If Charles Stuart had been as stubborn as his father, he might never have returned to England as King. Edward Hyde persuaded Charles to issue a declaration offering religious liberty and settlement of the land problem subject to the will of Parliament. He offered a general pardon (regicides excepted) and arrears of pay to the soldiers in Monck's army – a stroke of genius, since it encouraged other troops to desert. The constitutional royalists had won at last.

Phase 7: The return of the King, May 1660

After the Declaration of Breda, the Restoration was inevitable. The Long Parliament finally dissolved itself, and writs for a new parliament were issued. Royalists were elected unopposed to the Convention Parliament, which voted for Restoration.

DISCUSS

Was there something about England – its concept of law, social structure, perhaps its 'corporate identity' – that made the republican experiment of the 1650s unlikely to succeed in the long run?

ACTIVITY

Hindsight – help or hindrance?

Your view of the inevitability or otherwise of the Restoration ultimately depends on your perspective. Viewed with hindsight, the Restoration – or something like it – appears unavoidable. Can you imagine England still being a republic 100 years after 1649? Yet the closer you focus on the events that led to Charles II's return, the more problematical this interpretation becomes. So is hindsight a help or a hindrance to historical understanding?

1 a) Choose an important political event that is currently in the news and whose outcome is uncertain – a war, a civil conflict, a forthcoming election or something similar.

   b) Why is it difficult to predict the outcome? Draw a spider diagram showing different possible outcomes based on your current knowledge of the events taking place.

2 Is the analogy with the 1650s helpful or not?

Did the Great Rebellion have any lasting consequences?

Historians have argued almost as much about the consequences of the Great Rebellion as they have about its causes. The two questions are clearly related. Your view of what happened as a result of this 'event' depends on what you think the 'event' was. Before reaching conclusions about the links between causes, consequences and terminology, you need to consider some of the possible consequences of the Great Rebellion.

■ C The constitutional revolution

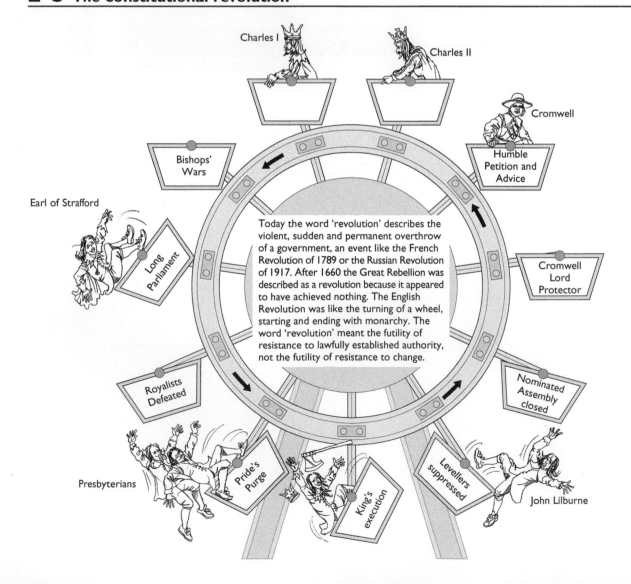

Today the word 'revolution' describes the violent, sudden and permanent overthrow of a government, an event like the French Revolution of 1789 or the Russian Revolution of 1917. After 1660 the Great Rebellion was described as a revolution because it appeared to have achieved nothing. The English Revolution was like the turning of a wheel, starting and ending with monarchy. The word 'revolution' meant the futility of resistance to lawfully established authority, not the futility of resistance to change.

FOCUS ROUTE

Did the Great Rebellion have any lasting consequences? Look at the evidence on these pages and answer the following questions.

1 Which of these developments might be traced back to the Great Rebellion? Why?

2 Which of these developments cannot be traced back to the Great Rebellion? Why not?

3 What other developments might be traced back to the Great Rebellion? Look at Chart A on page 108 for ideas.

The decline of religion

SOURCE 5   David Hume, an eighteenth-century political philosopher, describing England in 1742

Most people, in this island, have divested themselves of [got rid of] all superstitious reverence to names and authority: The clergy have lost much of their credit: Their pretensions and doctrines have been ridiculed; and even religion can scarcely support itself in the world. The mere name of king commands little respect; and to talk of a king as God's vice-regent on earth, or to give him any of those magnificent titles, which formerly dazzled mankind, would be to excite laughter in everyone.

By the middle of the eighteenth century, England was well on the way to becoming a secular society. Nonconformity was common, and even the most radical of seventeenth-century sects – the Quakers – had become socially respectable. There were many reasons for the decline of religion: the growth of a national life through commerce and industry; the growth of towns and cities; the scientific revolution; the development of clubs and societies; the expansion of universities, and the entire intellectual and social milieu of the times.

Did the civil wars contribute to this change? In the 1660s the Clarendon Code (see Chart A on page 281) restored a High Anglican Church and tried to drive the sects to the margins of English life. But the sects survived this persecution because by 1660 they were too strongly established to be rooted out. England's 'wars of religion' had a sobering effect and lowered expectations that religion could solve the nation's problems. Puritanism was dead as a national cause, and people became more sceptical of religious enthusiasm. This paved the way for greater religious toleration, but for reasons that would have shocked Oliver Cromwell.

Building the United Kingdom

The temporary union of the 1650s was dismantled in the 1660s. Scotland was later united with England by the Act of Union 1707, followed by Ireland in 1801. Did the civil wars contribute to the permanent union of the three kingdoms? The Acts of 1707 and 1801 were the product of political decisions taken at those times, but it could be argued that the Great Rebellion established a precedent and shifted the balance of power permanently in England's favour. Only in recent years has devolution (the creation of a Scottish parliament and a Welsh assembly) seen some weakening of England's domination of the British political system.

The growth of democracy

Did England's experience of political radicalism contribute to the extension of the franchise? Here the answer must be 'No'. The Levellers were suppressed by Parliament soon after the King's execution. The Restoration aimed at placing political power firmly in the hands of the landed classes. Parliament didn't begin the process of giving the common people the vote until the Great Reform Act of 1832. If anything, the civil wars delayed the growth of democracy because democracy had become associated with political radicalism.

SOURCE 6 In the Palace of Westminster a series of paintings asserts the Whig view that the Civil War played a crucial part in the rise of Parliament. In this picture, the Speaker (William Lenthall) is shown refusing to tell the King the whereabouts of the Five Members

POPISH PLOT

This refers to a wave of anti-Catholic hysteria unleashed by the false allegations of one Titus Oates. He claimed that he had overheard Catholics plotting the assassination of King Charles II in 1678.

EXCLUSION CRISIS

This was a political crisis between 1679 and 1681 brought on by attempts to exclude the Catholic Duke of York, the future James II, from the English throne. The crisis played an important role in the formation of political parties in England, the 'Whigs' being for exclusion and the 'Tories' being against it.

Some people believe that the Civil War played a crucial role in the rise of Parliament. Representative government was strengthened by the defeat of Charles I. Charles II governed cautiously because he had greater respect for Parliament than his father had. His brother James II, a Catholic who ignored the constitutional lessons of the Civil War, reigned for less than four years before he was overthrown in the Glorious Revolution of 1688 (it was glorious because almost no one died).

The main problem with this view is that in 1660 the monarchy was restored without any specific conditions, apart from the surviving legislation of 1641. The various crises of Charles II's reign – the Popish Plot, the Exclusion Crisis – were played out against the recent memories of the Civil War, but they also had their own context and logic. Not until 1688 would the constitutional problems facing seventeenth-century England be resolved.

What would have happened to Parliament if it had failed to confront the King in 1640? The Civil War might not have extended Parliament's legal authority, but it may have defended its existing authority against a king who misunderstood – or wilfully overlooked – the nature of England's common law.

The development of political theory

The revolutionaries of 1649 tried hard to justify the execution of Charles I. They called him a tyrant, accused him of breaking his coronation oath, and produced examples of Old Testament kings who were overthrown with God's approval. Their arguments looked back towards the medieval and biblical past. They didn't break new ground.

In 1688 King James II was overthrown in a *coup d'état* known as the Glorious Revolution. The following year, John Locke published his *Two Treatises on Civil Government*. In these he argued that a social contract existed between a king and his subjects. As with a legal contract between two businessmen, if the King failed to keep his side of the bargain the people were released from their obligation to obey his commands.

SOURCE 7 The frontispiece of Thomas Hobbes's *Leviathan* shows the King as the physical embodiment of the rights of his subjects. According to Hobbes, the people have formed a social contract by subjecting themselves to the sovereign. By doing this, they protect themselves from each other

LEVIATHAN
Or
THE MATTER, FORME and POWER of A COMMON-WEALTH ECCLESIASTICALL and CIVIL.

By THOMAS HOBBES *of* MALMESBVRY.

London
Printed for Andrew Crooke
1651

ACTIVITY

Study Source 7.

1 How does the image of the King reflect Hobbes's view of a social contract?

2 Suggest possible explanations for the pictures that are shown on either side of the title (a castle, a crown, a cannon, etc.).

3 A leviathan is a whale. In the Bible, Job chapter 41 is sub-titled 'Of God's great power in the leviathan'. Why do you think Hobbes called his treatise 'Leviathan'?

This 'social contract' had nothing to do with religion: it was based on philosophical principles, especially the idea of *utility* or usefulness. Locke was hugely influential in forming the modern world. In 1776 the American, Thomas Jefferson, used Locke's ideas to justify the American Revolution. His ideas were taken up by Thomas Paine to justify the French Revolution in 1789, which in turn inspired many of the revolutions of the nineteenth century. But John Locke was not the first person to put forward the idea of a social contract.

The first Englishman to do this was Thomas Hobbes, a philosopher from Malmesbury in Wiltshire, who fled to Europe when the Civil War broke out. Hobbes didn't believe in the Divine Right of Kings. He argued that civil war was the greatest evil that could befall a nation. It was therefore every subject's duty to obey the King, even if they thought he was a tyrant. The people had formed a social contract, surrendering their freedom to the King for their own self-preservation. In other words, people should obey the King not because it was *right*, but because it *made sense*.

ACTIVITY

What's in a name?

What should the events of 1640–60 be called? 'The Great Rebellion' was the name commonly used for the English Civil War in the later seventeenth century. It preserved the memory of how events had spiralled out of control. It was a 'rebellion' because people had forgotten their prime duty of obedience, but it was also 'great' because many of those who forgot to obey were themselves the natural rulers of the kingdom. Below are some names that have been used to describe the period as a whole. On the left-hand side are some views as to why these events happened – their causes. On the right-hand side are some views of their consequences. The causes and consequences appear in no particular order.

Causes

Motivated by envy, fear and extremism, the leaders of Parliament took advantage of the King's momentary weakness to seize power for themselves.

Driven by the fear of absolutism, the godly attempted to complete the process of reformation started in the mid-sixteenth century.

The civil wars were caused by the King's unsuccessful attempts to bring order and unity to the territories he ruled.

Economic and social development transformed the aspirations of Parliament, leading to a violent challenge to the old political order.

Names

The Puritan Revolution

The English Revolution
(The word 'revolution' is being used here in the modern sense.)

The Great Rebellion

The Wars of the Three Kingdoms

Consequences

Parliament's success permanently altered the balance of power between it and the Crown, paving the way for England's commercial expansion and, in the next century, the industrial revolution.

The enduring legacy of the civil wars was England's supremacy over Scotland and Ireland.

The inevitable outcome – the Restoration of the King – was a warning to anyone who might consider challenging the natural political and social order.

The failure of Cromwell's drive for godly reformation represents the end of the Puritans as a powerful political force.

1　Match the names with the causes and consequences that go with them.
2　Choose the name that you think best describes the events of this period. Write it down on a piece of paper.
3　In no more than three sentences, explain why you prefer this name over the others.
4　Read out your answers and discuss why you have chosen them.

Conclusion

The English Civil War represents a false start on the road towards the military-fiscal state (see page 262). Charles I's experience of the 1620s persuaded him that the relationship between central and local government had to change if England were to compete with its continental neighbours. This meant squeezing out the discretion in local government, which he held responsible for the failures of royal policy. Since Elizabethan times, the nation had been allowed to stagnate by the Crown's failure to develop closer control of local government by the Privy Council. In the 1630s Charles I attempted to impose uniformity by developing greater accountability at all levels of secular and religious government. This reflected his patriarchal view of monarchy – the King was putting his house in order.

The context in which this happened was potentially explosive. Religious wars in Europe were reaching a climax. In Britain, the Reformation's legacy was religious chaos, with diversity across the British archipelago and, in England, wide regional variations in religious practice. Royal policy provoked fears for ancient liberties at a time when Parliament was asserting its fiscal and legal powers. A different king might have taken Parliament into partnership in the drive for greater efficiency, but religious differences made this impossible. Archbishop Laud placed the Church at the service of the King's efforts to squeeze the discretion out of local and parish government, arousing suspicions of a hidden (Catholic) agenda behind the Personal Rule. If the King succeeded in creating a 'Thorough' government, whose interests would it serve?

The descent into civil war took everyone by surprise. It was a result of instability within the three kingdoms, combined with growing unease at the way that Parliament's attack on the Personal Rule turned into an assault on royal prerogative and the King's honour. The Irish Rebellion propelled the crisis towards military confrontation. In the ensuing scramble to seize control of the militia, civil war broke out throughout the kingdom.

Parliament won the Civil War because it put in place the essential elements of a military-fiscal state. Parliament's war combined two elements which had aroused opposition to the King in the 1630s – the defence of traditional rights and liberties, and the determination to ensure that any revolution in government served the Protestant faith. These two elements were incompatible, because ancient rights and liberties had to give way if the military-fiscal state were to be sustained. When Parliament won the war the two elements split apart, with Presbyterians trying to return to the ancient constitution while the Army fought to maintain militant Protestantism.

After 1646 Charles I's refusal to negotiate in good faith caused havoc. The King skilfully exploited the differences between the Army and Parliament, the Army and the Scots and, within the Army, between the rank and file and the officers. Ironically, Charles came to be seen as the champion of the ancient constitution, but his attempt to build a coalition between the Royalists, the Scots and the parliamentary Presbyterians backfired when Parliament and the Army came together again to defeat the old enemy in the Second Civil War. As the war ended, however, Parliament acted as if the King had won it by revoking the Vote of No Addresses. The revolution that followed – Pride's Purge, the King's execution, the abolition of the House of Lords – removed all the constitutional brakes on militant Protestantism.

A rebellion that had begun in defence of the ancient constitution had inadvertently destroyed it. Civil War had turned into revolution. The question now facing England was whether it would retain the central government machinery created in the 1640s and all that went with it (godly reformation, high taxation, military strength, successful foreign policy) or dismantle it and return to the ancient constitution – low taxation, military weakness, the Church of England. Cromwell was torn between the two. He cherished the traditions of civilian government, but would not abandon his men or the cause of further reformation. The result was a remarkably progressive, reforming regime lost in a constitutional cul-de-sac. Cromwell's personal authority held off the day of reckoning and gave England a demonstration of the alternative uses of political power. But in the background lay a relentless budget deficit and the fact that, given a free choice, the electorate would vote for a return to cheap, inefficient government.

Cromwell's death threatened to plunge the nation into further civil war. Faced with this possibility, the City of London withdrew its support from the Army, backing the ancient constitution and the King that went with it. The civil wars ended as they had started, with an invasion from Scotland. The 1660s saw the rejection of the turmoil of the 1650s, as England sought safety in tradition. With tradition came weakness, and in the 1660s England found itself back where it had been in the 1620s, unable to support a viable independent foreign policy.

In the 1690s England once again began laying the foundations of sustainable military power. This time it was done differently, avoiding the unpopularity of county committees and crippling assessments by creating a national debt through the newly formed Bank of England. The 'Great Rebellion' had left behind a legacy no future government could ignore: abhorrence of civil war, suspicion of standing armies, confirmation of Anglicanism, but also the knowledge that any reforming regime had to take the nation into its confidence. And it is just possible that, by standing up to Charles I, Parliament had preserved the rule of law.

Answers to activities

p. 87
Charles I trustworthiness survey
Check your answers against the following grid. Add up the numbers in the weighting column to find your score.

Question	Answer	Weighting	Question	Answer	Weighting
I	a	3	6	a	3
	b	2		b	2
	c	4		c	4
	d	I		d	I
	e	5		e	5
2	a	I	7	a	5
	b	2		b	4
	c	3		c	2
	d	4		d	3
	e	5		e	I
3	a	2	8	a	I
	b	5		b	2
	c	I		c	5
	d	4		d	4
	e	3		e	3
4	a	I	9	a	5
	b	2		b	3
	c	3		c	I
	d	4		d	4
	e	5		e	2
5	a	4	I0	a	4
	b	5		b	3
	c	2		c	I
	d	3		d	2
	e	I		e	5

Your score:

10–18: The King is not to be trusted. Further safeguards must be put into place to protect Parliament against what he might do in the future. You will give Pym your full support.

19–26: The King is not very trustworthy. Like a wounded lion, he is still dangerous. We need to be vigilant, but most of Parliament's work has now been done. You will support Pym's attempt to keep the King isolated in the near future.

27–34: It is unclear what the King will do next. We need to be cautious, but Parliament should now make some gesture to show that it is grateful for his co-operation and wants him to succeed.

35–42: The King is quite trustworthy. He has been taught a lesson and is anxious to work with Parliament to solve the kingdom's problems. We need to take him into Parliament's confidence and work together.

43–50: The King is very trustworthy. He has shown himself willing to change the way he rules. It is time for Parliament to back off and show Charles that it supports him. You will oppose any further attempts by Pym to take away the King's authority.

pp. 195–96

Source	Summary
1	e)
2	b)
3	d)
4	a)
5	c)

p. 267

Source	Description
11.12	B
11.13	C
11.14	A
11.15	D

pp. 277–78

Sources used in Activity	Position on timeline
1 Lord Macaulay, *Critical and Historical Essays*, 1903	Early twentieth century
2 B. Worden, *The Rump Parliament, 1648–1653*, 1974	1950s–mid-1970s
3 Edward Hyde, Earl of Clarendon, *History of the Rebellion and Civil Wars in England*, 1702	Early eighteenth century
4 T. Carlyle, *Oliver Cromwell's Letters and Speeches*, 1849	Mid-nineteenth century
5 W.C. Abbott, *The Writings and Speeches of Oliver Cromwell*, 1937–1947	1930s
6 Slingsby Bethel, *The World's Mistake in Oliver Cromwell*, 1668	Late seventeenth century
7 Edmund Burke, *Reflections on the Revolution in France*, 1790	Late eighteenth/early nineteenth century
8 J. Scott, *England's Troubles*, 2000, p. 404	1990–2001
9 C. Hill, *God's Englishman*, 1970, p. 105	1970s–1990s

Teacher's notes

Managing the role play in Chapter 6

1 It is important that all the players should remain in the classroom throughout the simulation, so that they can all listen to the discussions and benefit from the insights gained from them.

2 Depending on the number of students in the class, they can either double up on role cards or one of the tenant farmers, yeomen and/or gentlemen can be dropped from the simulation.

3 The event cards are presented to the village council either by the teacher/referee, the Royalist army player or the Parliamentary army player. To show who is in charge of the various event cards, a baton or some other symbol of authority can be passed among these three.

4 Event 2: when Tewkesbury was presented with this problem, the town chose the third option.

5 Event 6: the Battle of Ripple Field offers an opportunity for added realism – for example by playing a recording of battle sound effects.

6 Players representing the Royalist and Parliamentary armies could dress up in period costume to add a further element of authenticity. However, weapons are banned from the classroom.

7 One corner of the classroom can be designated to represent a gaol, into which the council or the army players can throw individuals.

8 When the game is over, the teacher needs to hold a plenary session to draw out the following issues raised:

   a) The Civil War drove a wedge into local communities for various reasons:

   - People were forced to choose sides.
   - The demands of both armies compelled individuals to protect their own interests. Sometimes the only way to do this was to inform on their neighbours.
   - The war provided an opportunity for local people to settle old scores – arguments between rival families, personal rivalries, etc.

   b) In 1642 the people of Deerhurst chose to support Parliament to defend their 'liberty', by which is meant their ancient freedom to regulate their own affairs and to use their discretion when enforcing the law.

   c) In order to win the war, Parliament was forced to centralise power at the expense of local liberties. This is shown in the creation of county committees, higher taxation, the confiscation of property and the imposition of stiffer penalties.

   d) The experience of Deerhurst may have been unusual in that the area changed hands so often, but the effects on local government were much the same throughout the country.

   e) The future was therefore full of difficulties. What problems would the country face? These include the following:

   - What Cromwell later called the 'healing and settling' of the Commonwealth. Can the people ever forgive and forget?
   - By 1646 the roles played by Parliament and the King in the 1630s seemed to have been reversed. Parliament was beginning to appear as the 'innovator' – the threat to traditional liberties – while the King was beginning to appear as the defender of the old constitution.
   - Parliament took a major step in the direction of 'statebuilding' – in other words towards the creation of a centralised military-fiscal state (see Chapter 11). Would Parliament now deconstruct this power and return to the status quo ante?

Bibliography and selected reading

Alexander, H. G., *Religion in England 1558–1662*, University of London Press Ltd., 1968

Ashton, R., *The English Civil War: Conservatism and Revolution 1603–1649*, Weidenfeld and Nicolson, 1978

Aylmer, G. E., *Rebellion or Revolution? England from Civil War to Restoration*, Oxford University Press, 1986

Barnard, T., *The English Republic 1649–1660*, Longman, 1982

Bennett, M., *The English Civil War*, Longman, 1995

Braddick, M. J., 'The Rise of the Fiscal State', in Coward B. (ed.), *A Companion to Stuart Britain*, Blackwell Publishers Ltd., 2003

Bradley-Birt, F. B., *Tewkesbury: The Story of Abbey, Town and Neighbourhood*, Phillips & Probert Ltd., 1931

Carlton, C., *Going to the Wars: The Experience of the British Civil Wars, 1638–1651*, Routledge & Kegan Paul, 1992

Carlyle, T., *Oliver Cromwell's Letters and Speeches*, Chapman and Hall Ltd., 1893

Coward, B., *Oliver Cromwell*, Longman, 1991

Coward, B., *The Stuart Age: England 1603–1714*, Longman, 1980

Coward, B., *The Cromwellian Protectorate*, Manchester University Press, 2002

Coward, B. and Durston, C., *The English Revolution*, John Murray, 1997

Davis, J. C., *Oliver Cromwell*, Arnold, 2001

Downing, T. and Millman, M., *Civil War*, Collins and Brown, 1991

Firth, C., *Cromwell's Army*, Methuen & Co. Ltd., 1902

Gardiner, S.R. (ed.), *The Constitutional Documents of the Puritan Revolution 1625–1660*, Oxford University Press, 1958

Goldie, M., 'The Unacknowledged Republic: Officeholding in Early Modern England', in Harris, T. (ed.), *The Politics of the Excluded*, Basingstoke, Palgrave Macmillan, 2001

Haythornthwaite, P. J., *The English Civil War 1642–1651: An Illustrated Military History*, Blandford Books Ltd., 1983

Hexter, J.H., *Reappraisals in History*, Longmans, 1961

Hexter, J.H., *The Reign of King Pym*, Harvard University Press, 1941

Hill, C., *God's Englishman: Oliver Cromwell and the English Revolution*, Weidenfeld and Nicolson, 1970

Hill, C., *The World Turned Upside Down*, Maurice Temple Smith Ltd., 1972

Hill, C., *The Century of Revolution 1603–1714*, Thomas Nelson & Sons Ltd., 1961

Hill, C. and Dell, E. (eds.), *The Good Old Cause: The English Revolution of 1640–1660*, Frank Cass Publishers, 1969

Hirst, D., Authority and Conflict: England 1603–1658, Hodder Arnold, 1986

Hughes, A., 'Religion 1640–1660', in Coward, B (ed.), *A Companion to Stuart Britain*, Blackwell Publishers Ltd., 2003

Hughes, A., *The Causes of the English Civil War*, Palgrave Macmillan, 1991

Hutchinson, L., *Memoirs of the Life of Colonel Hutchinson*, Phoenix Press, 2000

Hutton, R., *The British Republic 1649–1660*, Palgrave Macmillan, 1990

Hutton, R., *The Royalist War Effort, 1642–1646*, Longman, 1982

Hyde, E., Earl of Clarendon, *The History of the Rebellion and Civil Wars in England Begun in the Year 1641*, Oxford University Press, 1958

Jessup, F.W., *Background to the English Civil War*, Pergamon Press, 1966

Kenyon, J.P., *The Stuart Constitution*, Cambridge University Press, 1986

Kishlansky, M., *A Monarchy Transformed: Britain 1603–1714*, Allen Lane, The Penguin Press, 1996

Lockyer, R., *The Early Stuarts: A Political History of England, 1603–1642*, Longman, 1989

Ludlow, E., *Edmund Ludlow and the English Civil War*, Heinemann, 1994

Morrill, J., *The Revolt of the Provinces: Conservatives and Radicals in the English Civil War 1630–1650*, Longman, 1976

Morrill, J., *The Nature of the English Revolution*, Longman, 1993

Morrill, J. ed., *Oliver Cromwell and the English Revolution*, Pearson Education Ltd., 1990

Reilly, T., *Cromwell: An Honourable Enemy*, Brandon, 1999

Roots, I., *The Great Rebellion 1642–1660*, B. T. Batsford Ltd., 1966

Roots, I., *Speeches of Oliver Cromwell*, J. M. Dent & Sons Ltd., 1989

Russell, C. J., *The Fall of the British Monarchies, 1637–1642*, Oxford University Press, 1991

Russell, C. J., *The Causes of the English Civil War*, Oxford University Press, 1990

Scott, J., *England's Troubles: Seventeenth-Century English Political Instability in European Context*, Cambridge University Press, 2000

Sharpe, K., *The Personal Rule of Charles I*, Yale University Press, 1992

Smith, D. L., *Oliver Cromwell: Politics and Religion in the English Revolution, 1640–1658*, Cambridge University Press, 1991

Stone, L., *The Causes of the English Revolution 1529–1642*, Routledge & Kegan Paul, 1972

Turtle, J., *In the Time of that Unhappie War: Gloucestershire in the Civil War*, Gloucestershire County Record Office, 1993

Wilson, C., *England's Apprenticeship, 1603–1763*, Longman, 1965

Woodhouse, A. S. P. (ed.), *Puritanism and Liberty, being the Army Debates (1647–1649)*, J. M. Dent & Sons Ltd., 1938

Woolrych, A., *Britain in Revolution 1625–1660*, Oxford University Press, 2002

Worden, B., *The Rump Parliament*, Cambridge University Press, 1974

Worden, B., *Roundhead Reputations: The English Civil Wars and the Passions of Posterity*, Allen Lane, The Penguin Press, 2001

Wroughton, J., *An Unhappy Civil War: The Experiences of Ordinary People in Gloucestershire, Somerset and Wiltshire, 1642–1646*, Lansdown Press, 1999

Text acknowledgements

p.17 source 1.5 *History of the Rebellion and Civil Wars in England Begun in the Year 1641* by Edward Hyde, Oxford University Press, 1958; **p.20** source 1.7 *The Causes of the English Civil War* by Conrad Russell, Oxford University Press, 1990, p.185; **p.57** source 3.1 *The History of the Rebellion and Civil Wars in England Begun in the Year 1641* by Edward Hyde, Oxford University Press, 1958; **p.62** chart 3C from statistics in *The Personal Rule of Charles I* by Kevin Sharpe, Yale University Press, 1992, p.583; **p.71** source 3.11 *The Fall of the British Monarchies, 1637–1642* by Conrad Russell, Oxford University Press, 1991, p.83; **p.72** *The Fall of the British Monarchies, 1637–1642* by Conrad Russell, Oxford University Press, 1991, p.86; **p.73** source 3.13 *History of the Rebellion and Civil Wars in England Begun in the Year 1641* by Edward Hyde, Oxford University Press, 1958; **p.125** source 6.2 *Memoirs of the Life of Colonel Hutchinson* by Lucy Hutchinson, Phoenix Press, 2000; **p.137** source 6.7 *The English Revolution* by Barry Coward and Chris Durston, John Murray, 1997, pp.74 and 77; **p.171** chart 8B with thanks to Mr D. Wise for the contribution of these models; **p.173** chart 8C based on David L. Smith 'The Impact on Government' in *The Impact of the English Civil Wars*, by John Morrill (ed.), Collins and Brown, 1991; **p.196** source 1 from Michael J. Braddick, 'The Rise of the Fiscal State', in *A Companion to Stuart Britain* by Barry Coward (ed.), Blackwell Publishers Ltd., 2003, pp.69 and 79; source 2 *The Rump Parliament* by Blair Worden, Cambridge University Press, 1974, p.40; source 3 *The English Civil War: Conservatism and Revolution 1603–1649* by Robert Ashton, Weidenfeld and Nicolson, 1978, p.349; source 4 *The Good Old Cause: The English Revolution of 1640–1660* second edition by Christopher Hill and Edmund Dell (eds.), Frank Cass Publishers, 1969, p.27; source 5 *The Nature of the English Revolution* by John Morrill, Longman, 1993, p.394; **p.207** source 9.9 *History of the Rebellion and Civil Wars in England Begun in the Year 1641* by Edward Hyde, Oxford University Press, 1958; **p.215** source 9.25 *History of the Rebellion and Civil Wars in England Begun in the Year 1641* by Edward Hyde, Oxford University Press, 1958; **p.241** source 2 *History of the Rebellion and Civil Wars in England Begun in the Year 1641* by Edward Hyde, Oxford University Press, 1958; source 3 *Oliver Cromwell and the Rule of the Puritans in England* by C. H. Firth, Oxford University Press, 1900; source 4 *The Lord Protector* by R. S. Paul, Lutterworth Press, 1955; **pp244–245** chart A adapted from *Cromwell: An Honourable Enemy, The Untold Story of the Cromwellian Invasion of Ireland* by T. Reilly, Brandon, 1999, source 7 *History of the Rebellion and Civil Wars in England Begun in the Year 1641* by Edward Hyde, Oxford University Press, 1958; source 10 *Oliver Cromwell's Letters and Speeches* by Thomas Carlyle, Chapman and Hall Ltd., 1893; source 11 *Oliver Cromwell* by John Morley, Macmillan, 1900, p.290; source 12 *The British Republic, 1649–1660* by R. Hutton, Palgrave Macmillan, 1990, p.47; source 13 *Focus on the Past* by G. Brockie and R. Walsh, Gill and Macmillan Ltd., 1990; source 14 *Oliver Cromwell* by P. Gaunt, Blackwell Publishers, 1996, p.116; **p247** source 11.1 *Oliver Cromwell* by J. C. Davis, Arnold, 2001; source 11.2 B. Coward, 'Your Highness, Cromwell', in *BBC History Magazine*, 2003; **p.277** source 1 *Critical and Historical Essays* by Lord Macaulay, Methuen & Co., 1903, source 2 *The Rump Parliament, 1648–1653* by B. Worden, Cambridge University Press, 1974, source 3 *History of the Rebellion and Civil Wars in England Begun in the Year 1641* by Edward Hyde, Oxford University Press, 1958, source 4 *Oliver Cromwell's Letters and Speeches* by T. Carlyle, Chapman and Hall Ltd., 1893, source 5 *The Writings and Speeches of Oliver Cromwell* by W. C. Abbott (ed.), Oxford University Press, 1937–47, source 8 *England's Troubles: Seventeenth-Century English Political Instability in European Context* by J. Scott, Cambridge University Press, 2000, p.404, source 9 *God's Englishman: Oliver Cromwell and the English Revolution* by C. Hill, Weidenfeld and Nicolson, 1970, p.105.

Index